LVX
OMNIVM
CIVIVM
MDCCCLII
MDCCC
LXXVIII

We Are Called Human

WE ARE CALLED HUMAN

The Poetry of Richard Hugo

Michael S. Allen

The University of Arkansas Press
Fayetteville
1982

The University of Arkansas Press, Fayetteville, Arkansas 72701
Library of Congress Catalog Card Number 81–69840
Printed and bound in the United States of America

CIP information can be found on p. 159.

Chapter 6, "'License for Defeat': The Turning Point," originally appeared in *Contemporary Poetry* in slightly different form.

Chapter 7, "'Only the Eternal Nothing of Space': A Westerner's West," originally appeared in *Western American Literature* in a different form.

Excerpts from Michael S. Allen, "'Because Poems Are People': An Interview with Richard Hugo," are reprinted with the permission of the editors of *The Ohio Review*.

Excerpt from "In a Dark Time" copyright © 1960 by Beatrice Roethke, as Administratrix of the Estate of Theodore Roethke, from the book *The Collected Poems of Theodore Roethke*. Reprinted by permission of Doubleday & Company, Inc., and Faber & Faber, Ltd.

Lines from *The Cantos of Ezra Pound* by Ezra Pound copyright 1948 by Ezra Pound. Reprinted by permission of New Directions Publishing Corporation and Faber & Faber, Ltd.

Extracts from *Migrants, Sharecroppers and Mountaineers: Volume II of Children in Crisis* by Robert Coles are reprinted with the permission of the publisher, Little, Brown and Company.

Extracts from "Stray Thoughts on Roethke and Teaching," "Writing Off the Subject," "The Triggering Town," "Ci Vediamo," and "Statements of Faith" from *The Triggering Town: Lectures and Essays on Poetry and Writing*, by Richard Hugo, reprinted with the permission of W. W. Norton & Company, Inc. Copyright © 1979 by W. W. Norton & Company, Inc.

Excerpts from *The Lady in Kicking Horse Reservoir, What Thou Lovest Well Remains American, 31 Letters and 13 Dreams, White Center,* and *The Right Madness on Skye,* by Richard Hugo, reprinted with the permission of W. W. Norton & Company, Inc. Copyright © 1973, 1975, 1977, 1980, and 1980, respectively, by W. W. Norton & Company, Inc.

All excerpts from the poetry of Richard Hugo have been reprinted with the permission of the author.

For Dick and my parents

We don't take
others by the hand and say: we are called people. The power to make
us better is limited even in the democratic sea. Discovery of cancer,
a broken back, our inability to pass our final exam—I guess the rain
is finally getting me down. What matter? I plan to spend my life
dependent on moon and tide and the tide is coming, creeping over the
rocks, washing the remains of crippled fish back deep to the source,
renewing the driftwood supply and the promise of all night fires on the
beach, stars and dreams of girls, and that's as rich as I'll ever get.
We are called human. Ciao. Dick.

—"Letter to Wagoner from Port Townsend"

Preface

This book began some ten years ago when a friend, Bob Kaven, a student at Iowa Writers Workshop, handed me a manuscript of poetry. The author, Kaven's teacher, had suddenly left Iowa City and was driving back to Montana. Kaven said I would like the book. We had been talking about W. S. Merwin and Galway Kinnell, whose *Book of Nightmares* seemed appropriate reading for someone like me, an objector to the war, working out my alternate service in a Chicago hospital. As much as I liked Merwin and Kinnell, the manuscript of *The Lady in Kicking Horse Reservoir* impressed me with a music that stayed with me, as if it were part of a landscape that I had been living in most of my life.

When Kaven later sent me a copy of the printed book, that landscape had become clearer, and I soon began my research on Richard Hugo. All writing is a form of self-discovery (Hugo would say "self-acceptance"), and this book is no different. A member of the Vietnam generation, I was fascinated by the violence and the control that inform so many lines of Hugo's poetry, and I was particularly drawn to the book about his war experiences, *Good Luck in Cracked Italian*. Having parents and grandparents who throughout my childhood had recalled the Depression with a ferocity of memory I could not grasp, I felt my way to an understanding of poems like "Duwamish" and "The Way a Ghost Dissolves."

As I discovered, or accepted, parts of myself, I also discovered what stance I wanted this critical study to take. Divorcing the poetry entirely from the poet seemed to make for a technological sterility in the criticism. Likewise, purifying the critic of his or her personal history and context leads to a scholarly aridity that can only distance the poetry from the reader. Furthermore, merely making the poetry an occasion for a critical performance that weaves a multiplicity of vague perceptions as easily as the weaving of smoke in a closed room renders poetry a vacuum, makes the poet's life irrelevant and disposable, and leaves the community of readers out in the cold.

We all have our histories; all of us come from some identifiable matrix of culture and class that marks us with differing needs, desires, and tastes. Those differences shape our language and what Hugo would call our "stance." To ignore that background in the poet or the critic is to ignore an essential perspective on the poems and on the act of reading that criticism fundamentally is. Criticism has equal obligations to the context of the poet's history and to the context of artistic evaluation. This type of criticism is only fitting for American literature, speckled as it is with regional, racial, ethnic, and even sexual allegiances, and it is necessary for a culture sometimes obsessed with conformity. It is, moreover, especially fitting when considering Hugo's poetry, a body of work built up through connections to important trout streams and bars, towns and friends—without which, one feels, the living of a human life could not be done.

As with Hugo's poems, so with this book; it could not have lived without some essential, fundamental connections: to Dick Hugo, who has been supportive, generous, and kind; to Bob Kaven, who said I could do it and survive; to Jim Justus, my adviser at Indiana University, who knows very well how to fly fish a graduate student's mind; to Roger Mitchell, also at Indiana, who knows the limits of Marx, Pound, and my syntax; to Craig Werner, who knows more about Hugo than I because he knows the West; to a farmstead awash with cornfields outside Gosport, Indiana, where much of this was written; to Miller Williams, who knows patience and courtesy as only the best of the South do; to north Mississippi, where I learned most vividly what it means to be poor; to my wife Susan, who knows me and yet somehow still stays around.

M. S. A.
September 1981
Indianapolis, Indiana

Contents

Part I
From the Poetics of Sound to the Poetics of Need

1

"By Right of Obsessive Musical Deed": Roethke and *A Run of Jacks*

In the fall of 1947 Richard Hugo sat in a classroom in Seattle, and Theodore Roethke walked in to teach the class. Like other students of Roethke, such as William Stafford, James Wright, and David Wagoner, Hugo learned much from the man John Berryman called "the Garden Master." Roethke the poet was an accomplished craftsman, urging his students to learn from poets who had "good ears" for the music in poetry, requiring exercises in forms and readings in the art of Wyatt, John Davies, Herrick, Yeats, Hopkins, and Auden to understand that music. Roethke the man, taking risks in order to write, teaching with a gruff manner and a sometimes brutal honesty, was a personality that could not be ignored; he attracted the imaginations of young poets, then and now.

Influence from such a powerful personality can be stifling to a poet's own development. Hugo points out that several of Roethke's students—Wagoner, for one[1]—had trouble developing their own voices after writing under Roethke. The "anxiety of influence," however, does not seem particularly operative in Hugo's growth. Although he "wasn't particularly attracted to" Roethke's poetry, Hugo readily admits a perhaps more important attraction to Roethke's personality: Roethke was "an outrageous man who would take outrageous stances and create something beautiful out of them. And since I was an outrageous person too, that gave me a faith that you could be a pretty ridiculous person and still do something worthwhile or beautiful."[2] It was this personal, psychological influence—not some strong misreading of an elder poet's work—that helped Hugo to feel that, by taking similar chances with his writing, by adopting those stances that would unlock the psychological doors to poetry, he could become a poet.

The words *risk* and *emotional honesty* appear prominently whenever Hugo praises Roethke[3] and they can be used to describe Hugo's poetry as well. Roethke came to the University of Washington in the first flush of achievement after writing those long, intensely psychological, and risky poems that were to appear in *The Lost Son and Other Poems* (1948) and that would secure his place in modern American poetry. More than "the dreary text-creepers, the constipated agrarians and the other enemies of life,"[4] Roethke took emotional and psychological chances to discover the hidden aspects of his life, to make his poetry an essentially psychological act, a transference of psychic energy. He was a man writing and often living on the edge of consciousness and sanity:

> I know the purity of pure despair
> My shadow pinned against a sweating wall.
> That place among the rocks—is it a cave
> Or winding path? The edge is what I have.[5]

The word *edge* recurs in Hugo's writing, but, as Frederick Garber has pointed out, the important word for Hugo is *marginal*[6]—the word Hugo has reserved for his in-progress autobiography, *West Marginal Way*. The difference between the two words is far-reaching. Where Roethke's "edge" is clear-cut, dramatic, theatrical with suggestions of precipice, Hugo's "marginal" is more inclusive and contains a significant pun: it is that unclear area on either side of a boundary, but it can also refer to those marginal farms of the rural poor, whose poverty has never left the underside of America's glitter, fine cars, Hollywood, and the vast holdings of agribusinessmen. Whereas Roethke on the "edge" is working out the interior landscape of the human psyche, Hugo in the "margin" works out those emotions rising from social conditions: failure, defeat, poverty, and want. Because of his experiences of emotional dispossession and early deprivation in Depression, Hugo highly values that emotional bond that keeps poor people together even as their anger and destructive impulses tend to alienate them from each other. His "margin" is fundamentally inclusive; he is not about to take his reader to an esoteric edge, consciously or unconsciously.

The difference between *edge* and *margin* as watchwords for Roethke and Hugo also corresponds to the slightly different traditions behind each poet. Roethke stands in a direct line to Yeats, Hopkins, and several major figures in romantic poetry: Wordsworth, Blake, Keats, and John Clare. Hugo shares most of these connections, especially those to Wordsworth and Yeats. Although Roethke's obsession with sound is also an integral part of Hugo's poetics, Roethke's attention to sound is more traditional, extending to his love of Davies's Elizabethan poem *Orchestra* and of older, closed poetic forms that Roethke brought stunningly to life in "The Waking" (villanelle) and "In a Dark Time" (heroic sestet). Roethke's intense perceptions and intuitions led him to risk much in writing *The Lost Son,* in which he reveals the psychological chaos just below the firm order of the stratified, exclusive, and very "normal" society of post war, cold-war America. Much has changed since then, however, and Hugo's poetry reflects a realism that parallels the changes in American society and that suggests a different tradition from that of Roethke's psychological theater.

The high romanticism of Wordsworth, Blake, and Keats that plays so great a part in Roethke's work is largely missing from Hugo's. Not necessarily the Wordsworth of the "Intimations Ode" or of the ascent up Mount Snowden in *The Prelude,* book XIV, Hugo's Wordsworth is the author of the "Preface" to *Lyrical Ballads,* of "Michael," "Tintern Abbey," and "Resolution and Independence"—that Wordsworth who reestablished poetry on the basis of experience (instead of classical mythology), on the rhythms of common speech (instead of poetic diction), and on having (instead of a fixed upper-class readership) an important place in the creation of a moral sensibility, a better society. Reading the whole of Hugo's work, one is impressed not only by the natural beauty of his native Washington and adopted Montana but also by the social landscape of those regions: the angers, failures, and needs of the people in towns like Port Townsend, Seattle, Tahola, and Philipsburg. Therein lies the emotional energy of Hugo's poetry.

For, unlike Roethke, Hugo is a regional poet: he has a particular landscape that he haunts and is haunted by. This important aspect of his work connects his poetry with the Lake District of Wordsworth, the Ireland of Yeats, the Tilbury Town of Robinson, the New England of Frost, the Chicago and Midwest of Sandburg and Masters. Hugo's landscape is first noticeable as the streams and rivers of the Pacific Northwest and the expanse of land that is the Big Sky country of Montana. Looking closer at the map, however, one notices a marginal region: the border of the United States with Canada; the continental divide; a dominant white culture and those reservations of Indians whose land it once was. Closer, one sees a geography of opposites: mountains and plains, semiarid deserts and lush rain forests. Hugo needs this region of conflicts and its rich crosscurrents of history, guilt, suffering, work, and honest boredom, as much as Roethke needed his interior landscape, the drama of the unconscious.

Both Roethke's interior landscape of the edge and Hugo's more social landscape of the margin are unlocked by the poetics of sound. Wordsworth knew "the power of sound" to excite the imagination, and in his teaching Roethke stressed that "repetition in words and phrases and in ideas is the very essence of poetry," claiming that "the recurrence of stress and unstress" was related to the rhythms of nature.[7] To Hugo, Roethke's—and any good poet's—love of sound was obsessive: "Good poets have obsessive ears. They love certain sounds and not others. So they read aloud what they love, responding to their own obsessive needs in the poetry of others."[8] Roethke's "fierce love of kinds of verbal music" fits well with Hugo's preestablished "arbitrary rule."

> When I was a young poet I set an arbitrary rule that when I made a sound I felt was strong, a sound I liked especially, I'd make a similar sound three to eight syllables later. Of course it would often be a slant rhyme. Why three to eight? Don't ask. You have to be silly to write poems at all.[9]

Thus, Roethke's teaching strengthened impulses that Hugo already felt toward sound and toward taking risks and outrageous stances. The interior landscape of Roethke's poetry was not the area for Hugo's direct attention—not until the dreams of *31 Letters and 13 Dreams* (1977)—but the approach to poetry by sound was a shared attitude, part of a poetics that Hugo would later put to his students in this way: "So you are after those words you can own and ways of putting them in phrases and lines that are yours by right of obsessive musical deed . . . . Your obsessions lead you to your vocabulary. Your way of writing locates, even creates, your inner life."[10]

That inner life, however, is not the stuff for symbols or the longing for metaphysics, as with Roethke at his most glorious. In Hugo, the poetics of sound—that long tradition that connects Roethke to the Renaissance villanelle and to Davies—is secondary to a "poetics of need" that has grown out of that psychologically risky experiment that Roethke undertook in writing *The Lost Son*. As the edge in Roethke's poetry often waxes numinous with the supernatural, it is fitting to compare a vision of paradise from a Hugo poem, "The House on 15th S. W.," from *What Thou Lovest Well Remains American* (1975); it is a vision based firmly on human emotional needs.

> North surely was soft. North was death
> and women and the women soft. The tongue
> there was American and kind. Acres of women
> would applaud me as I danced, and acres
> of graves would dance when sun announced
> another cloud was dead.[11]

Repetitions—the mark of obsession—lead the stanza: "North . . . soft. North . . . soft." "Women" is repeated three times in two lines, and the letter *o* is used fourteen times in six lines. With such repetition of key words and sounds, and with the added consonance of "North . . . death," the lyric sings itself into the reader's attention; as the current of sound rises, the reader wants to know what is behind such obsession. The key lies in the pain reflected in the following long sentence, bitten into phrases by regret.

> No grating screams
> to meals or gratuitous beatings,
> no crying, raging fists against closed doors,
> twisted years I knew were coming at me,
> hours alone in bars with honest mirrors,
> being fun with strangers, being liked
> so much the chance of jail was weak
> from laughter and my certainty of failure
> mined by a tyrant for its pale perverted ore. (p. 8)

Whatever the beauty of "North surely was soft" and the paradise of women and the kindness one finds there, the poem finds its feet back on the ground of pain: "screams," "beatings," "fists," "twisted years." Beneath the longing for the imagined paradise is the obsessive realism of early psychological scars, the image of a man at odds with himself, deeply divided, terribly conscious of how anger and failure translate into images in the context of American society: "fists against closed doors," "hours alone in bars," "being liked / so much the chance of jail was weak," and the final, forceful image of work (here, the poet himself writing) highly clotted with assonance, consonance, and rhyme—"m*i*ned b*y* a t*yr*ant f*or* i*t*s *p*ale *pert*ed *ore*." That last word is a near-rhyme to "failure," appropriately accentuating the brevity of the soft paradise in anything—even in lines of poetry.

When Hugo has allowed himself an interior landscape like that of Roethke, it has been, more often than not, underwater. In some ways fishing is to Hugo what his father Otto's greenhouse was to Roethke. Here is part of "Trout," the first poem in Hugo's first book, *A Run of Jacks* (1961):

> Quick and yet he moves like silt.
> I envy dreams that see his curving
> silver in the weeds. When stiff as snags
> he blends with certain stones.
> When evening pulls the ceiling tight
> across his back he leaps for bugs.
>
> I wedged hard water to validate his skin—
> call it chrome, say red is on
> his side like apples in a fog, gold
> gills. Swirls always looked one way
> until he carved the water into many
> kinds of current with his nerve-edged nose.[12]

The first stanza quickly places the reader in a web of matched sounds: *i* sounds repeat three times in the first line, and the *t*'s break the line at caesura and end. The second line adds long *e* sounds to the assonance mix: "dreams . . . see . . . curving." By the end of the first stanza the *e* sound has pulled the reader into the poem as tightly as the evening is pulled across the trout's back when it leaps.

As the sound of the poem grabs our attention and hooks it deeply, we begin to feel an intimacy, an involvement with the poet's point of view that goes beyond a normal suspension of disbelief. The intimacy is in the music of the words, in the minute closeness of the imagery ("he moves like silt," "curving / silver in the weeds," "stiff as snags"), and in the poet's presence in the lines: "I envy dreams that see his curving"; "And I have stared at steelhead teeth / to know him." We begin to sense that the trout is almost as important as the poet himself. When we see the trout as closely as Hugo has, we have also seen something of Hugo.

"Trout" is an introduction to the first obsession in Hugo's poetic career: trout fishing in the streams and rivers of the Pacific Northwest. Lush in its imagery as in its sound, the poem is beautifully descriptive: "red is on / his side like apples in a fog." Remarkable in its diction as in its rhythm, the poem displays an important voice, a small colloquial intrusion—"call it chrome, say red is on / his side"—that arises from the intimate position the poet takes with the reader (and with the trout). This conversational tone leads eventually in Hugo's development to poems that are full of gestures of speech, addresses, and monologues and comes to provide the basis for the letters in *31 Letters and 13 Dreams*. That Hugo has written letters in poetry is a significant indication of his desire for intimacy as well as of the social basis of his entire work.

His obsession with fishing does not necessarily make Hugo a reincarnation of John Donne's friend, Isaak Walton. The fishing poems—and the many others that contain allusions to the world of water—are about more than fishing. Besides the artful struggle—the work of patience and quickness that fills poems such as "Bass," "Underwater Autumn," and "At the Stilli's Mouth"—there is the imaginative world beneath the water's surface. In "Skykomish River Running" Hugo gives voice to a credo that moves fishing beyond art and sport and into a statement about the imagination.

> I will cultivate the trout, teach their fins
> to wave in water like the legs of girls
> tormented black in pools. I will swim
> a week to be a witness to the spawning,
> be a trout, eat the eggs of salmon—
> anything to live until the trout and rain
> are running in the river in my ear.
>
> The river Sky is running in my hair.
> I am floating past the troutless pools,
> learning water is the easy way to go. (p. 40)

More than once in Hugo's poetry these girls appear, curving as if trout. Sometimes they swim in the light shining through a glass of beer. Always they are in water, in some other world that can be seen but that cannot be grasped. In this early credo Hugo says that he will "be a trout," that he will do anything to live in that world on the other side of the water's surface, that world of heightened feeling. Behind the love of trout, of girls like trout, of fishing, is the "river in my ear," the "river Sky"—a great play on the name—"running through my hair." That river is poetry itself, the power of sound, the imagination's current. Through the imagination's opening in the poem, the poet feels the water around him and in him, as if he were a fish. Although far from the "troutless pools" of his life, the imagination opens as a place that is essentially closeness itself: close to skin, to ear, to hair. In this richer world things fit together snugly as vowels in assonance or as sounds in consonance; they have the beauty of agile girls, of agile shifts in a poem's rhythm, that satisfying undercurrent of emotional support that any good poem gives a reader. Things fit together, and the water flows around the poet: all these aspects of Hugo's imagination point again to his desire to include, to make a margin of acceptance where the diffuse can come together in a chaotic, cruel world. Even in a poem ostensibly about fishing, Hugo finds the energy that unifies and brings together disparate elements, overcoming isolation with intimacy.

In "Trout" and in "Skykomish River Running" we can see Hugo's debt to Roethke and the differences between them. To Hugo's attention to sound, his consciousness of rhythm, and his willingness to risk emotional honesty within the poem's framework—to take a chance on sentiment—is added a richness of natural imagery that parallels Roethke's lush vision of nature in the "Greenhouse" poems. But there the similarities stop. The vitality and exuberance of growth—the "vegetal radicalism" that Kenneth Burke pointed out[13]—eventually led Roethke toward those meditative and metaphysical journeys of *The Far Field* (1964). Hugo's natural imagery, however, never leads to symbols, nor does his search lead to a near-mysticism that turns away from society. Rather, the natural beauty and terror in the trout streams are at the heart of the economy and social order of the Pacific Northwest. The paradise of beautiful trout is attractive not just because it is more pleasing than the harsh realities above the water's surface; it is attractive also because it is so near. The river is the "marginal way" of two worlds: just below the water's surface is a world of the imagination as tantalizing as anything in Samuel Taylor Coleridge's "Kubla Khan," but closer; just above the surface are the poverty, cold wind, and loss of human society. The beauty of the imaginative world lies in its intimacy; the coldness of our given world lies in the isolation that comes from poverty of the flesh or of the spirit. Hugo's marginal way must include both worlds.

In "Duwamish" Hugo shows the other side of the marginal way, where cold wind blows over the water through a world that does not fit together and is at odds with itself: violent, poor, and full of need. As the Duwamish is identified more with this world, it is significant that Hugo's first mention of the river places it outside the specialness of the Pacific Northwest in a more industrialized part of the country. That cold world is midwestern.

> Midwestern in its heat, the river's
> curves are slow and sick. Water knocks
> at mills and concrete plants, and crud
> compounds the gray. On the out-tide
> water, half salt water from the sea,
> rambles by a barrel of molded nails,
> gray lumber piles, moss on ovens
> in the brickyard no one owns.
> Boys are snapping tom cod spines
> and jeering at the Greek who bribes
> the river with his sailing coins. (p. 58)

Although the vision isn't beautiful, it is full of a strength at odds with itself, especially in its rhythm. Besides being hard sounds, "Water knocks," "and crud," and "On the out-tide" enjamb the lines; there is a constant rhythmic crosscurrent until the smooth end of the stanza. Faithful to the things of this world, full of junk and refuse, the Duwamish, like Hugo, is bound on both sides: half salt water from the ocean of the imagination, half jetsam from the world of man, and at odds with that human society where so much is lost and so much is thrown away.

Behind the waste appear various shades of cruelty: boys snap cod spines and jeer at a Greek fisherman; Indians in a tavern, themselves marked by cruelty, "ignore the river" because its name is Indian. Random emotions, random cruelty, the cheap thrills of boys and men despoil the river and its gifts. But the river is not heroic; it also is cruel. Because of it, the sun is dull, "obscured" on bright days: "And what should flare . . . is muted." Boys nail porgies to the pile because of the sameness, the boredom, the dullness that is an essential part of Hugo's vision of the marginal way: "There is late November / only, and the color of a slow winter."

Hugo expands this surface to cover both banks, all the houses, and all the efforts of the men and women in those houses near the river. The result is a stanza obsessed with cold, full of that low moan in the wind.

> On the short days, looking for a word,
> knowing the smoke from the small houses
> turns me colder than wind from
> the cold river, knowing this poverty
> is not the lack of money but of friends,
> I come here to be cold. Not silver cold
> like ice, for ice has glitter. Gray
> cold like the river. Cold like 4 P.M.
> on Sunday. Cold like a decaying porgy. (p. 58)

The cold runs deep; repetitions of the *o* sound through nine lines sink the cold deeper. The poverty has gone beyond economics to loneliness. But the statement that "this poverty / is not a lack of money but of friends" only underscores the economics and strengthens the feeling that our inner emotional weakness is tied to outward economic weakness. This poverty leaves a psychological scar, makes boys cruel, and thrives in a society where friends are kept with money and mistrust is prevalent. If it were just a lack of money—so the poem implies—the poverty would be like ice and melt. But the emotional state of poverty is weakness, the lack of something to do; it is that boredom that hangs at the edge of "glitter," of an American society always doing something new.

By keeping to the river, moreover, Hugo finds that the Duwamish is a place where normal words fail as the poverty of spirit rises. Whether they are boys' jeers, Greek threats, or Slavic chants, the words fail, and the failure of these languages underscores another social perception: the majority of American society is made up of people who are, spiritually, still poor immigrants. The words that last, the words that the Duwamish finally gives, are Indian and simple: "Love is Indian for water, and madness / means, to Redmen, I am going home."

These two lines encompass the main substance of most of Hugo's work in *A Run of Jacks* and in his second book, *Death of the Kapowsin Tavern* (1965). The lines reveal a sensibility more complex and delicate than might first appear. Already evident is the idea that "Love is Indian for water"; for Hugo, love must be something as close and full of wonderful possibilities as is that world beneath the water's surface. But now Hugo shows us that the word for that world is Indian, and we remember the Indian who ignores the river and sits with his beer in the bar. His silence is as out of reach as the world of water; his words are not spoken but felt, showing the world at a tilt, where madness equals going home. The white word *cold* is spoken, almost chanted; it is a word full of poverty and hurt.

Love and *water* are Indian ideas not because of some obscure religious or poetic text from the Quinalt or Nez Percé, but because they are to Hugo, a white man, uncommon. The houses on either side of the Duwamish are "normal" American; it is only by concentrating on the feelings that he has invested in that landscape that Hugo sees the deeper landscape, the one that comes up from the river as if it were an Indian dream. Love and home are old things. They have no glitter and may seem as dull as the rest of the dull. But no other words survive.

"Duwamish" is as important as any poem that Hugo has ever written. The two metaphors of love-and-water and madness-and-home strike deep chords that resonate throughout his career. The interplay of meanings in these clusters attests to their psychological depth: love is as close as water and can as quickly go away; madness may be a simple act of going off alone, and home is not a place of smooth sanity. The cold that forms the context for these key words is the poverty, the easy cruelty, and the faculty for ignoring social problems that American soceity has developed to an art.

In the working out of his poetics, in being led by the sounds of words and the Roethkean obsession with nature, natural sounds, and rhythms, Hugo is able, finally, to say the Indian words of that deeper language that leads to psychic and emotional survival in a harsh world. The poverty and cruelty along the banks, the cold wind, and the haunting presence of Indians become, along with the recurrent paradisal vision beneath the water's surface, the major obsessions of Hugo's poetry. What we see emerging in his first book, contrary to Roethke's development toward mysticism, is a primarily social vision that brings with it an essentially social sensibility attuned to the crosscurrents of emotion that make up American society, its cruelties and freedoms, its love and madness, its glitter, and its need for going home. That social sensibility is Hugo's poetics of need, and it lies at the heart of his investigations and images of towns, as in "Duwamish"—as in "the Hugo town."

2

"Until the Town You Came from Dies Inside": The Shape of the Hugo Town

Towns have always bothered Richard Hugo. Looking at the whole of his work, one sees just how important the image of the town is to his poetry and to understanding his poetics of need. Much of his poetry concerns towns in the Pacific Northwest, in Montana, and even in Italy and on the Isle of Skye. But not until his sixth book of poetry, *White Center* (1980), was Hugo able to entitle a poem and a book after his hometown, a working-class suburb of Seattle. White Center can be seen in the background of "Duwamish" in Hugo's first book, *A Run of Jacks* (1961), but writing about towns at all, much less his hometown, has been an evolving development that we can now see as central to his poetry and to the place his poetry has in American literature. In his second book, *Death of the Kapowsin Tavern* (1965), Hugo entitled the section containing portraits of Northwest towns "Limited Access," but the towns kept defining Hugo's poetry. In *Good Luck in Cracked Italian* (1969), the important towns are Spinazzola and Maratea; in *What Thou Lovest Well Remains American* (1975), images from an unnamed White Center dominate the first two sections of the book; in *31 Letters and 13 Dreams* (1977), towns such as Big Fork, Butte, and Pony provide the occasions for the letters that Hugo writes to friends and fellow poets, connecting a vast landscape of human needs; in his latest book, *The Right Madness on Skye* (1980), Uig, though Scottish, is very much the same town that lies in the background of "Duwamish," with its images of dispossession and peasant tenacity in the face of economic and physical hardships. In all, Hugo's poetic career revolves around the development of something of a type—the Hugo town—and in that development lies Hugo's importance in contemporary American poetry.

The image of the Hugo town first takes on its clear current of feeling in his fourth book, *The Lady in Kicking Horse Reservoir* (1973). While the landscape of that book is Montana and not Washington, towns like Dixon, Silver Star, Milltown, Hot Springs, Ovando, and Philipsburg have streets, bars, shacks, and an underlying sense of rage that haunts the earlier towns, such as Port Townsend and Tahola, and those that come later, such as White Center, Fairfield, and Uig. In that fourth book Hugo gives us, as always, an image of the town seen from its underside, a town no self-respecting chamber of commerce would ever advertise, a town populated by drunks, angry boys, lonely travelers in bars, miners and their failed lives, workers who mistreat their wives—all people who have hurt each other and who need desperately those few things in life that keep them going. The undersides of towns are not new to American literature: Edwin Arlington Robinson's "Tilbury Town," Sherwood Anderson's *Winesburg, Ohio,* Edgar Lee Masters's *Spoon River Anthology,* Sinclair Lewis's *Main Street,* and William Faulkner's stories of Yoknapatawpha County are all different regional aspects of the same American problem of people living together in their self-made culture with various degrees of failure in their sense of community. Roy Harvey Pearce discusses Tilbury Town's relation to the greater tradition of American literature in this way:

> It is a village world, to be sure, but a village world whose sense of community has been destroyed. Most of its inhabitants are failures: sometimes resigned to their failure, sometimes unresignedly crushed by it. . . . Even the relative successes like Flammonde cannot communicate. Still, whatever their degrees of failure or success, they are persons meaningful to us. For they signify something important in the nature of the modern psyche—even if it is only as they are made to recall, in their inability to communicate directly, a condition and a time when such a thing as self-reliance (in any of its various forms) was a radical possibility for all men. In them, Robinson pushes to an outer limit a sense of the exhaustion, perhaps even the bankruptcy, of the simple, separate person. Tilbury Town is the underworld of Walden and Paumanok.[1]

Creating "the underworld of Walden and Paumanok" was partially a revolt against romanticism, partially an appraisal, through realist eyes and with modernist intentions, of the complacency and narrowness of the small town. After its early ascendancy in American culture, the small town came to be shown as hollow, its sense of community lost, its sense of purpose questioned, its people become—in the outlook of Anderson, Robinson, and others — bankrupt and grotesque. Regional coloring aside, the insights of Anderson, Faulkner, Lewis, Robinson, and others challenged accepted stereotypes and achieved permanent places in American literature. But America has changed. The decline of the town to bankruptcy has been a fact of sociology for some time and may even be outmoded as many small towns expand in the shifting strata of the American population. Apart from sociologists, few writers have continued to explore the small town as a source for literature and fewer of those have been poets. William Carlos Williams's *Paterson* and Hart Crane's *The Bridge* turned toward more culturally complex images of the city, and, when addressing the problem of community in American terms, other poets have also relied on urban settings—as with Gwendolyn Brooks's Bronzeville, the San Francisco Beats, and sometimes the New York School. Increasingly with the modernists, American poetry became technically oriented and personally obsessed. The brilliance of Roethke, Lowell, Plath, and Berryman rises in each case from an isolated intensity of craft. We may extrapolate from Henry Pussycat to contemporary American society, but that extrapolation is our inference, not Henry's overt comment.

Enter Hugo, who reverses the modernist perspective on the small town in the first effort since the time of Robinson and Sandburg to present an extensive image of American community. Taking the bankruptcy of the single, separate person as a given, Hugo shows us an image of the town based in that underworld of Walden and Paumanok, a world of bars and failure and fears, in which the most important success is the rare achievement of human connection, the creation of some dim sense of human community. There is, moreover, much in the Hugo town that seems oddly connected to Robinson's Tilbury Town. Like Robinson, Hugo shows psychological and social conditions as interrelated. Those odd individuals—Berwick Finzer, Miniver Cheevy, and Richard Cory—come to psychological disaster in great part because they live in a deteriorating society and are unable to make the necessary connections to a changing world. In Hugo's town the speaker inhabits a deteriorated society of fixed isolation; the world of change lies elsewhere, impinging on the town like a 4:00 P.M. freight train or a sudden northern wind. Once a seat of smugness, Hugo's town is already depressed, likely a collection of buildings and people dominated by failure, often encased in the ache of poverty. The failure of the town and of its people is cause for a struggle of self-acceptance and for acceptance of the odd, the old, the people tucked away at the margin of society. The bankruptcy is not just of the individual or of the town but of society as a whole.

The failure and bankruptcy that inhabit Hugo's towns are not, however, cause for overt social or political comment. Hugo needs only local history and geography: the silver boom, the silver-bill repeal, the failed mines, farms ravaged by winter or by bad droughts. The West is dotted by desertion—the people have moved away, leaving the town ghostly, cut off, and isolated. The division and fragmentation in the body politic, Hugo implies, are the cause for sickness in the soul. The overcoming of social fragmentation rests not in some political or social program but in what sense each individual can make, town by town, of what human connection means, of what human intimacy is. The sharing of feelings in Hugo's town comes hard and happens only in special places, but happen it must: the individual's feelings of bankruptcy and isolation cannot be borne alone; some attempt must be made to re-create a sense of community.

An early town poem from *Death of the Kapowsin Tavern,* "Port Townsend," begins to reveal the architecture of failure that is basic to the structure of the Hugo town. That architecture comes to include some specific, special places—bars, jails, baseball diamonds—but primarily the town is a place where dreams fail to materialize in a landscape of division and opposition.

> Arriving here is feeling some old love—
> half a memory—a silly dream of how
> a war would end, a world would settle down
> with time for hair to gray before you die.
> The other half of memory is sight.
> The cliffs will hold another thousand years.
> The town is rotting every Sunday night.[2]

Always present in the Hugo town are the poor who live in failure with their dreams; here, the dreams are the residue of post–World

War II patriotism. Against those dreams is that other half of memory, which is based on fact: the cliffs, where the rich live and will live for another thousand years, are far above the squalid rotting town, shrouded by a cloud as "the pulp mill shoots bad odor at the sun." Hugo's social comment inheres in his landscape in "Port Townsend" and in other town poems governed by the architecture of opposition: rich and poor, cliffs and squalor. The prototype of Hugo's town poems from *A Run of Jacks,* "Duwamish," is not ostensibly about a town but shares a similar structure of opposites. In that poem, however, the opposites are town and river, where wealth belongs to the river (fish, lumber for the mills) while the banks hold the particular poverty of the Hugo town, a coldness not just from "lack of money but of friends," as "the smoke from the small homes / turns me colder than wind from / the cold river." In "Duwamish" also appears the violence that is as much a part of the lives of the poor as the smoke from the pulp mill in "Port Townsend": boys snap tom cod spines, jeer at a Greek fisherman, and even the water "knocks / at mills and concrete plants."[3]

The same consciousness of division, loss, and violence informs the towns of *The Lady in Kicking Horse Reservoir* (1973). In "Helena, Where Homes Go Mad," Hugo adds the historical awareness of how many western towns were settled in boom times, only to have the times change. The rowdy past is over; the "cries of gold or men about to hang" have faded and now "gold is where you find it in the groin." A town born crazy in a rush for gold is still crazy in a rush for children.

> Nowhere gold. Nowhere men strung up.
> Another child delivered, peace,
> the roaring bars and what was love
> is cut away year after year
> or played out vulgar like some game
> the bored make up when laws are firm.[4]

The opposition of gold and groin points out equal debasements of human effort. By *Lady* the Hugo town has become a place where historical and social facts are matched by penetrating psychological insight. Violence of whatever form—economic, social, or sexual—becomes an expression of the town's instability and the society's insanity.

Hugo begins *Lady* with a look at the violence and craziness of a whole state that spreads out "thick as a fist or blunt instrument." In "A Map of Montana in Italy" he plays tour guide to his West.

> The two biggest towns are dull deposits
> of men getting along, making money, driving
> to church every Sunday, censoring movies and books.
> The two most interesting towns, Helena, Butte,
> have the good sense to fail. There's too much
> schoolboy in bars—I'm tougher than you—
> and too much talk about money. (p. 3)

The contrast between the two biggest towns and the two that are the "most interesting" is between stability and rage: Billings and Great Falls are prosperous, religious, censorious; Helena and Butte "have the good sense to fail" but still need that barroom western image, "I'm tougher than you." Much as when they were first settled, Hugo's towns are made up of people who move on "to the west / where ocean currents keep winter in check," trying to find something vaguely better, not as brutal in its weather, and, as the image of the frozen children implies, not as brutal in its inhumanity.

The underside of Walden and Paumanok, then, has become more than the genteel decline evident in, say, "Miniver Cheevy." Opposing the self-confidence of Thoreau and the unquenchable optimism of Whitman, the underside of Hugo's American town is marked by fear, need, and neglect, where even the failed romantic notions of the past have given way to the hardness of historical, economic, and physical facts. Built up near veins of ore and rivers of good fishing, Hugo's towns are dominated by vast, unseen, and highly changeable economic and geographical forces. The towns did not grow as much from the ideals of American independence and optimism as from American acquisitiveness and exploitation. In Whitman's town activity brings plenty, energy is unbounded, and doors open as every individual breathes deeply. In Hugo's town failure is constant, boredom unremitting, and important possessions and human connections irretrievably lost.

This sense of loss informs the poverty, the anger, and the need of the Hugo town and connects it to some hazy, distant dispossession. In "Cataldo Mission," where "more's bad . . . than just the sky," a "haze" rises from the landscape and opens a vision of the

West, showing how "two centuries of immigrants in tears / seem natural as rain" (p. 43). "Cataldo Mission" expresses the failure of immigrant hopes, a failure as much a part of the landscape around the Hugo town as the weather. As the immigrants were dislocated from their homeland, so, on reaching the West, they are dispossessed of their vague dreams and hopes of the Promised Land. Hugo once said, "Disconnection in itself is wrong,"[5] and his sense of disconnection informs his vision of the West and western towns. If "Cataldo Mission" shows the immigrants' disconnection from their hopes in a new land, "Cleggan" presents the original dispossession.

> Ireland is free. The young leave every year
> for England and the bad jobs there. Pretty girls
> stay virgin and the old men brag of nothing.
> It's something to go on when life's as empty
> as the sea of anything but life, swimming
> way down aimless, most of it uncaught. (p. 53)

In Ireland, Port Townsend, or Montana, the poor leave to find bad jobs with a dim feeling that the full life they could have had is out of reach, whether on cliffs above them or "swimming . . . uncaught" below them. The stanza reads like a variation on a theme of Yeats: "Parnell came down the road, he said to a cheering man: / 'Ireland shall get her freedom and you still break stone.'"[6] The difference between the two poems is that, as in all of Hugo's work, "Cleggan" is told from the peasant's point of view, without recourse to politics, broader historical perspectives, or studied mythology.

The original disconnection, the act of dispossession that haunted any generation of immigrants to America, becomes a dominant theme in Hugo's latest book, *The Right Madness on Skye*. What is true for "Cleggan" is true for "The Clearances," a poem about that dispossession of highland peasants (crofters) to make way for the better economics of more sheep and less people. In this more recent poem, however, the scope of Hugo's presentation is larger, as the dispossession becomes not just Scottish or Irish but human.

> Want an equation? O.K. The lovelier the land
> the worse the dispossession. I know that's not right.
> Blacks weep when put out of a shack.
> Puerto Ricans to see the slum torn down.

We've all lost something or we're too young to lie,
to say we hear crofters sobbing
every high tide, every ferry that sails
Uig for Lewis, that vague shape out there in haze.
We don't hear them sob. We don't know that they did.
And that form in haze might be nothing,
not a destination, no real promise of home.[7]

Again, the haze we have seen in "Cataldo Mission." We have no sure knowledge of how the crofters felt as they left; theirs and all immigrants' emotions are shrouded in the haze that is not only history but also the neglect of anyone poor, disconnected, lost. But as in other Hugo poems, the fact of that dispossession is presented clearly and haunts the speaker and ourselves as readers. That dispossession enters into the landscape and the architecture of the Hugo town: all that remains of home is a promise, a dream.

To recall those dreams one must go to the one place in the Hugo town where that sense of life "swimming way down aimless" can be caught: the bar. The center of the Hugo town, the bar provides the background for several poems in *The Lady in Kicking Horse Reservoir* and provides the subject of a few others. "The Only Bar in Dixon" shows us how the dreams of the dispossessed reach from place to place to find "some other home."

This is home because some people
go to Perma and come back
from Perma saying Perma
is no fun. To revive, you take 382
to Hot Springs, your life savings
ready for a choice of bars, your hotel
glamorous with neon on the hill. (p. 72)

Much less raucous than the stereotyped western saloon, Hugo's bars are for memory and dream, albeit colored by alcoholic repetition and slurred speech. In some ways, the bars in Hugo's poems are closer to Robinson's "Claverly's" (*The Town Down the River,* 1910)[8] than to the barroom brawls of B westerns. In "To Die in Milltown," the speaker is able to see that the train that divides the town—"one half, grocery store and mill, / the other, gin and bitter loss"—becomes a figure for death and loss.

To die in Milltown, die at 6 P.M.
The fast train west rattles your bourbon warm.
The latest joke is on the early drunk:

sing one more chorus and the nun you love
will dance here out of habit. (p. 13)

The drunken pun about the dancing nun—a desperate joke —exemplifies the lengths people in the bar will go to to get around the divisions and disconnections outside the bar. "To live / stay put," the speaker says, calling bourbon the only way to cheat the train, to cheat death. Those drinks in Milltown are "full of sun," full of space and dreams of aging eagles climbing up the river canyon "on their own." Only in the bar, that closed-in space, can the town's disconnection and need lose their power and that haze the poor live in become momentarily an opening for them to breathe.

A bar in Philipsburg provides the backdrop for the most anthologized Hugo poem, "Degrees of Gray in Philipsburg." More than any other poem, "Philipsburg" presents the tension and anxiety that inhere in the Hugo town and shows how minimal human feelings survive in the face of dispossession.

You might come here Sunday on a whim.
Say your life broke down. The last good kiss
you had was years ago. You walk these streets
laid out by the insane, past hotels
that didn't last, bars that did, the tortured try
of local drivers to accelerate their lives.
Only churches are kept up. The jail
turned 70 this year. The only prisoner
is always in, not knowing what he's done.

The principal supporting business now
is rage. Hatred of the various grays
the mountain sends, hatred of the mill,
The Silver Bill repeal, the best liked girls
who leave each year for Butte. One good
restaurant and bars can't wipe the boredom out.
The 1907 boom, eight going silver mines,
a dance floor built on springs—
all memory resolves itself in gaze,
in panoramic green you know the cattle eat
or two stacks high above the town,
two dead kilns, the huge mill in collapse
for fifty years that won't fall finally down.

Isn't this your life? That ancient kiss
still burning out your eyes? Isn't this defeat
so accurate, the church bell simply seems
a pure announcement: ring and no one comes?

> Don't empty houses ring? Are magnesium
> and scorn sufficient to support a town,
> not just Philipsburg, but towns
> of towering blondes, good jazz and booze
> the world will never let you have
> until the town you came from dies inside?
>
> Say no to yourself. The old man, twenty
> when the jail was built, still laughs
> although his lips collapse. Someday soon,
> he says, I'll go to sleep and not wake up.
> You tell him no. You're talking to yourself.
> The car that brought you here still runs.
> The money you buy lunch with,
> no matter where it's mined, is silver
> and the girl who serves you food
> is slender and her red hair lights the wall. (pp. 78–79)

"Philipsburg" is a map to isolation: the streets are "laid out by the insane," go past churches "kept up" from duty, and lead to failure. At the center of the town, as if it were the goal of the poem's map, is a jail. Certainly the jail provides the emotional center of the poem: isolation surrounded by a town where rage is "the principal supporting business," where history and pollution drive "the best liked girls" to Butte, where the failed mill and "two dead kilns" (an important pun) stand over the town somewhat like those rich Victorian houses in "Port Townsend." All this surrounds the jail, where the only prisoner is a stranger to the town and to himself, "not knowing what he's done." A map to the bankruptcy of the isolated, self-reliant self, the town also represents a human life, a life in which feeling has been lost from defeat "so accurate" that the church bell gains a new purity: "ring and no one comes." Defeat, the poem implies, is a condition hard to leave, hard to let go. As the town, so the man is a living defeat, an imprisoned life that, unless some great change occurs, will never reach other towns of "towering blondes, good jazz and booze."

Clearly the Hugo town not only surrounds the speaker but is also part of his psychology. Divided, scornful, remembering ancient losses and deprivations, the speaker can easily identify with the man in the jail. The town is no longer the scene of decline, the place of narrow minds or hardship or nostalgia; it has become the image of isolation and division, qualities that stand as negatives to those classic American ideals of independence and self-reliance on which the American small town was built. In a way not unlike Wordsworth's idea of the mind "fitted" to nature, Hugo shows how interior psychology is "fitted" to exterior social conditions. Made up of four increasingly tense questions, the third stanza implies that there must be something other than this imprisonment, if the speaker is to be free and human. The town inside the self must die. When it does, the political and social failures of the town—and of the speaker's life—can also die, and something new in the man and the town, a new intimacy, can begin.

Interior isolation dissolves not through some romance of booze, jazz, and women, but by attending to the realistic facts of the bar in Philipsburg. The old man in the last stanza, alive before the jail was built, sparks the fire that leads to escape from this emotional prison. A grim, neglected presence, the old man jokes about his age, and his lips collapse as he speaks. As stubborn and standing as the old mill "that won't fall finally down," he survives and laughs even in his defeat. When the speaker says no a second time, we realize that the poem has neared ritual in working out some psychic cure: the second no is "to yourself" and implies that the speaker also will not accept defeat. The rejection made, a new energy awakens the poem: his car still runs; his money is good silver; and, what is more, the first woman to ease this tightfisted male scene enters the poem, "slender and her red hair lights the wall."

In the midst of division, rage, and loss, one realistic human connection is made to an old man, and soon that romance of women, jazz, and booze, though still far off, no longer seems unattainable. Freud would have called it reawakened libido. Jung would have pointed to the way the old man figures, in this poem by a man, to rekindle psychic energy and release the magic of the encircling prison. Whatever the psychological rendering, the imagery is clear. Inside the walls of the town, the prison house where boredom and rage dominate, there is a flame, a fire, an energy. The waitress may be only a waitress, but the chance she offers for human intimacy, for an end to isolation, failure, and rage, is like a flame against the wall.

As the Hugo town was born in opposition and dispossession, Hugo begins his reclamation of community in the American town with "Degrees of Gray in Philipsburg." The walls of the American town may have become a prison house of isolation and boredom, but "Philipsburg" offers an emotional escape from those harsh facts. Moreover, while the architecture of the Hugo town allows only a little room for community inside the bar, there is one other place where Hugo finds community possible: the ball park. "Missoula Softball Tournament" is, therefore, an important poem to be included in *Lady* because it points out the fragility of community in the American town (it is discussed in more detail in Chapter 7). The poem implies that community survives only on the margin of that town, protected by the rules of the game from the realities of "routine, like mornings / like the week" (p. 70). Alongside the baseball poems (there are now several) stand the letter poems from *31 Letters and 13 Dreams:* each letter is written from a different town, with its detritus of everyday life, to a friend far distant. Again, only in a protected arena is Hugo able to make real an expression of human community, to overcome the distances that separate individuals in our society.

Following *The Lady in Kicking Horse Reservoir,* Hugo entitled his next book *What Thou Lovest Well Remains American* (1975), a significant alteration of a line from Pound's Pisan Cantos ("What thou lovest well remains, the rest is dross"). In the title poem we are again taken into the Hugo town. This time, though still unnamed, it is clearly Hugo's hometown, White Center. Failure still informs his neighborhood, with its Jensens and Grubskis and the lots that Hugo needs to remember "empty and fern." He blames the neighborhood for his failures, but as in "Philipsburg" the poem moves from feelings of defeat to finding some blessing hidden in that defeat.

> You loved them well and they remain, still with nothing
> to do, no money and no will. Loved them, and the gray
> that was their disease you carry for extra food
> in case you're stranded in some odd empty town
> and need hungry lovers for friends, and need feel
> you are welcome in the secret club they have formed.[9]

Out of need—a word repeated twice in the penultimate line—out of the "gray that was their disease," comes that energy that recognizes other needs, the hungry lovers in some empty town like, perhaps, Philipsburg. That energy is a food and can lead to welcome despite the secret club that keeps up social isolation and fragmentation. There is no specific mention in the poem of American society, of the conditions of those towns in the Northwest and Montana and across the continent that are failed booms, failed mills, or country markets—no such concepts would help to clarify the current of feeling in Hugo's poetry as he explores the energy of need arising out of dispossession and loss. But the title of the poem implies much. The Hugo town is very much an American town where, despite the enclosures of rage and isolation, the elemental social connections of human community can still be found.

3

"The Self as Given Is Inadequate and Will Not Do": *The Triggering Town* and the Poetics of Need

In much of contemporary culture, including contemporary poetry and poetics, it has become difficult to separate the valuable from the flash and glossy, the "hype." We have a culture, it seems, that breeds on the new, that devalues small increments of discovery, and that ruins, through the leveling factor of mass consumption, any attempt at revolution. Sometimes what seems new is merely a rehash of earlier insight—witness Charles Olson's "Projectivist" manifesto, a replay of Pound but without Pound's dazzle and insight. Sometimes what seems a thoroughly traditional restatement of the poetics of sound and meter, tied to ancient and respected names such as Wyatt, Davies, Blake, and Wordsworth, has embedded in it a significant though small step toward fundamental change. Such is the case with Roethke's poetics, which Roethke himself never published in anything like a manifesto. And sometimes what appears to be restatement, developing out of an identifiable matrix of thought, is passed over, nearly unnoticed, because no new ground seems broken, no shibboleths smashed. Such is the case with Richard Hugo's poetics, his collection of lectures and essays on writing entitled *The Triggering Town* (1979).

Although the book was awaited by many poets and readers who had seen chapters from it published in *American Poetry Review* and *The Atlantic*, *The Triggering Town* risks anonymity because, instead of waving banners, Hugo merely takes the same current of poetic thought that Roethke worked in and moves it one significant step further. Even though one essay is entitled "*Stray* Thoughts on Roethke and Teaching" (italics added), there is much in the tone of the book that reminds one of Roethke's essays and lectures, which have been collected by Ralph Mills, Jr., in *On the Poet and His Craft* (1965). Like Roethke, Hugo takes the concerns for poetic technique, the indebtedness to the romantic traditions of lyric and landscape, and then moves the understanding of poetry beyond the aspects of tradition and imaginative wholeness and places it in the messier roots of psychology: according to Hugo, poetry is "psychogenic."[1]

Of course, Hugo does not emblazon the word on a banner; indeed, he says he could be argued out of believing such a claim. But the bulk of his book belies this disclaimer. What Hugo is saying is hardly literary-critical orthodoxy; he must know that calling poetry psychogenic will raise either grave scholarly doubts, replete with phantoms of Freud's Dora and Skinner's box, or grave silence. (The latter seems to have happened.) For if poetry is psychogenic, then are not poets pathological and are not the claims of puritans and philistines thereby justified? Isn't poetry just the outpouring of sick emotion, not to be taken seriously? Hugo, for all his bulk (and he is, as was Roethke, a bear of a man), is graceful as he surrenders nothing of the poetic tradition while saying the literary treason that Roethke only hinted at and that Yeats dared express only through the hazy vocabulary of gyres and theosophy. Hugo is able to speak this treason because even as he admits the psychogenic nature of poetry, he lays as firm a claim to the social necessity (not merely usefulness) of poetry as has come along since Sidney. He makes this claim with the same talent for complexity that underlies his poetry: he links awareness of the social condition with awareness of the psychological (and, therefore, the psychogenic).

Poetry, for Hugo, does not just uplift or bring sweetness and light; it is not simply the repository of culture and a medium for myth, footnote, and the extraordinary idea. The poet, moreover, is not just related to society in some vague commonality, as in Wordsworth's "man speaking to men," nor in some equally vague exaltation, as in Eliot's "tradition and the individual talent." Hugo recognizes that because they write, poets are not like other people; he also recognizes that there is not much tradition left in a rapidly changing technological society. Even though the poet's place in society has become random and unclear—becoming everything from culture star to syllable counter—and even though poetry has become increasingly tied to the academy, a matter of scholarship and anxious studies of influence, Hugo knows that the process of writing poetry has become more important to more people than ever before in our history. Why? Hugo suggests that poetry is neither a romantic curse nor a symptom of probable suicide; he maintains that the writing of poetry is a stabilizing, integrating, balancing force in a technological culture so adept at metamorphosis that all known quantities and qualities are in perpetual threat of loss. People engage in the writing of poetry because they need to survive as human beings. Those psychological aspects of poetry that Roethke worked toward in *The Lost Son* have become, for Hugo, a poetics of need that supersedes the more traditional poetics of sound.

Hugo's poetics does not follow the nearly obligatory itch for the new in contemporary poetry. There is no call for new metrics or breath units or new frontiers in imagery or sensibility—there isn't much in the way of a call for anything, except number-two pencils (not ink), a hard-covered notebook with green-lined pages (easy on the eyes), and no semicolons. Writing for Hugo approaches the delicacy of the Japanese tea ceremony (see "Nuts and Bolts," pp. 37–40). He has no quarrel about form but sticks to blank verse and internal rhyme.[2] What is more important than all of this is not the substance of the poem—its subject or even its technique—but those feelings in the poet that engendered the poem, that caused the writing process to begin. That is where mystery makes her house and that is the door that Hugo knocks on, albeit quietly. He takes as his standpoint a common enough assumption in a decade of group therapies and self-centered introspection, a standpoint that has been important since Keats's "negative capability": *How you feel about yourself* is probably the most important feeling you have" (p. 67). The statement comes early in "Statements of Faith" and immediately marks that essay as one of the two most central to Hugo's thought; the other is the title essay, "The Triggering Town."

"How you feel about yourself" may have become a cliché in popular psychology, but that does not make the idea any less valid or any less supported by the wealth of humanistic psychology since Freud. Hugo's use of the idea, however, is related to the romantic concept of poetry as being "the overflow of emotion" or emotion set free. He does not ask us to see the emotion without noticing what emotion is set free from; in fact, he demands that we see both the emotion and the conditions from which it arises. Confessional poets such as Plath, Berryman, and Lowell may have ransacked warehouses of neuroses and psychoses to write the true word, but they spent little time discovering what goes on inside the poet when private wounds open. Hugo's awareness of things psychological—like that of the confessionals—has grown more from his own struggle with psychological problems than from anything else, and his poetics reflects this experiential basis. There is nothing systematic; insights and terms have risen intuitively, and there are overlaps and gaps among essays like "The Triggering Town," "Writing Off the Subject," "Assumptions," and "Statements of Faith." But these insights lead us further into the mysterious process of writing than we have been led before: we write by way of feeling—as Roethke wrote in "The Waking," "We think by feeling. What is there to know?"

Hugo has admitted that there are poets who do not write from feeling, but these are "the very very clever, a limited number of people" who believe that "music has to conform to the truth." However, for people like Hugo and the rest of us—"who are kind of dummies"—poetry happens when "truth has to conform to music."[3] This idea is basic to his way of writing and to his egalitarian conception of who can write poetry: "If you believe the truth has to conform to music, then you're saying that all of us could conceivably write a poem and that there is a good reason for creative writing classes." The final clause in that sentence seems humorously added, but in fact Hugo's interest in creative-writing classes (witness "In Defense of Creative Writing Classes") indicates the orientation of his ideas on writing toward the society at large. Like Roethke, Hugo shares little of the disdain some poets have held for amateur student writers. Also like Roethke, he believes not only in the power of the poem but also in the power of writing, of working with words, as an essential part of developing identity in contemporary society. Moreover, that seemingly high-sounding aesthetic statement, "truth has to conform to music," is as broadly oriented as is his offhand remark about writing classes—it is an essentially simple but deep insight into how the mind functions.

Hugo puts it this way: "You see, everybody's mind likes to get rigid, to get set." As poems are, poem making is an arrest to our normal perception. The recognition of that natural tendency toward order is present in Hugo's work as it is in the essays on poetry that make up Wallace Stevens's *The Necessary Angel,* and the contrast between the two collections is illuminating. Whereas some twenty years ago Stevens could write with the breadth and sometimes even the categories of Coleridge ("the subject matter of poetry is . . . the life that is lived in the scene that it composes"),[4] Hugo now writes with all the directness of a guide, a mechanic—someone who knows that the knowledge he possesses may be the result of learning, but who also knows that such learning has now become essential to survival. When Stevens says, in a vein close to the essence of Hugo's own often tense poetry, "[the mind] is a violence from within that protects us from a violence without,"[5] he is looking at the poem of the mind as a means of salvation from a dangerous world. But when Hugo speaks of how the mind can be changed, how the writing of the poem makes an exchange of worlds, he is looking at the act of writing as a means to save the mind. "It's a matter of transferring the rigidity of the mind from substance to the structure of the poem. You see, everybody's mind likes to get rigid, to get set. It does no good to scream at people, 'Don't be so rigid. Be fluid.' That isn't going to help anybody."[6]

From his attention to the process of writing, Hugo calls for a transference of attention among writers, especially amateurs, from substance to structure—not in the way of ancient prosodies and forms, but as a means to let the mind find its deeper concerns, not those the student thinks he or she ought to have. This transference of rigidity from substance (what the poem is about) to structure (how the words are chosen) underlies Hugo's own use of internal rhyme and controlled meter. Technical solutions solve mental rigidities and problems: using "*immaculate* within, say, seven syllables after I use the word *chocolate*" increases the chances "to say things you never expected to say," to find the poem instead of forcing it from however noble a preconceived idea. If Hugo's "transferring of rigidity" ended with the structure of words as music, his account of the writing process would be nothing more than a restatement of Stevens and Roethke. But there is more. The mind "likes to get rigid" in other ways, and other transfers of energy need to be made before the poem can take shape.

The most necessary transfer lies behind Hugo's development of his concept of *stance*. No other single word has meant so much to Hugo's poetry, and no word is so far-reaching in comparison with earlier poetic theories. *Stance* "has to do with how strong a person's urge is to reject the self and to create another self in its place."[7] The meaning of the poem must be held suspended as the mind attends to the structure of the words, but the meaning or identity of the poet must also be held suspended as the mind creates a new self, a stance, an altering of consciousness so that the poem might be written. This process is related fundamentally to the question "how do you feel about yourself." The technical transference of rigidity from substance to structure of the words may lead to discoveries "about things that were hidden," but that is a limited prospect leading to "a dozen, fifteen, maybe twenty poems in your whole life." The impulse to write is stronger than a reliance on any technique: "in the majority of poems you find yourself creating a way of feeling about things and believing in that for the duration of the poem."[8]

To create that stance is to reject the self as known. Hugo sees this process as central to many important poetic theories since the romantics: "Behind several theories of what happens to a poet during the writing of a poem—Eliot's escape from personality, Keats's idea of informing and filling another body, Yeats's notion of the mask, Auden's concept of the poet becoming someone else for the duration of the poem, Valery's idea of a self superior to the self—lies the implied assumption that the self as given is inadequate and will not do" (p. 67). Feelings of inadequacy are not, however, confined to poets nor are they behind the writing of all poetry; but they are an important part of poetry and are often present in one way or another. Hugo notices Auden's idea that "fear of failure is the nemesis of American writers" and how, late in life, Roethke sought his companions among the wealthy because "he wanted proof that the self he was starting to accept was truly of worth. In his mind, only the rich and 'well chosen' could verify this" (p. 72).

The stance, then—like the use of structure to release the mind—grows out of the necessity of alleviating the mind's rigidity, in this case, the poet's constant feelings about himself or herself: "certain feelings can lead to certain stances in the poem. If the feelings are strong enough the stances may be overstances, or poses. This might result from extreme feelings of shame and degradation (Roethke) or intense self-hatred (Dylan Thomas)" (p. 69). It is essential to remember the importance of praise throughout Roethke's work and the importance of that powerful, sensual indulgence in Thomas's poetry. The stance, meant to overcome the mind's rigidity, accentuates characteristics opposite those that the poet feels describe himself. In Hugo's case, the stance is tough and masculine, seen as a shadowy outline of the speaker, revealed in the tone and tension of these lines:

> You might come here Sunday on a whim.
> Say your life broke down. The last good kiss
> you had was years ago.[9]
>
> Not my hands but green across you now.
> Green tons hold you down, and ten bass curve
> teasing in your hair.[10]

Whether the speaker reminds us of "a broken down Gary Cooper"[11] or of Raymond Chandler, the stance behind the poems—the image of a tough guy, cowboy, or detective—fulfills all the requirements of conventional masculinity in American culture.

An early poem, "Duwamish," pinpoints the first acceptance of this stance. Hugo walks beside the river, which was the scene of his loneliness as a boy.

> On the short days, looking for a word,
> knowing the smoke from the small houses
> turns me colder than wind from
> the cold river, knowing this poverty
> is not the lack of money but of friends,
> I come here to be cold.[12]

The gray of Philipsburg, the weight and cold of the water in Kicking Horse Reservoir, the tone of Cooper or Chandler all have their roots here, where poverty "is not the lack of money but of friends." The tough stance grows out of such emotional impoverishment as a means of survival in a world where emotional connections are few and distrust is plentiful. Remembering his writing of "Duwamish," Hugo has said, "when I imagined myself along that river, I found I wrote in direct, hard language. I believe now that unconsciously I felt that for the duration of the poem, I was as tough as I'd wanted to be in real life."[13]

Hugo did not know his father, and the question of what it meant to be a man was central to every feeling he had about himself while he was growing up. It is not surprising, then, that the stance he finds to generate poems takes on the coloring of a Cooper or a Gregory Peck when the locale of the poem is a Montana town; nor is it surprising that the stance of a Chandler or a Humphrey Bogart arises in a poem about a woman who hurt him. These images, along with their many copies, have been part of American culture since the 1930s, that crucial period in Hugo's life, and have entered into the culture as emblems of masculinity, shared by millions through the most influential art form in our culture, film. The value of such a stance in these poems is, therefore, twofold. It works from powerful internal psychological sources while using characteristics of types widespread in popular taste. The private pain, channeled through an assumed stance recognizable to many, obtains a wider appeal without sacrificing the psychological validity that has been the mark of confessional poetry.

But, although his concerns, like those of W. D. Snodgrass, Plath, and Berryman, are psychological, Hugo is in no sense a confessional poet. An important difference between Hugo and the confessionals lies in the stability that Hugo gains from using a stance that has the simplified lines of popular taste and stereotype. Along with allowing him to work from the simple to the complex, the stance gives Hugo a form of acceptance and stability before the writing of the poem. Because his stance has wide connections to the film-influenced dreams of many people, Hugo gains a stability that allows him to say things a more tentative sense of self would not allow him to say. Among the confessionals, Berryman's Henry fulfills a similar function, the main difference being that Henry and Berryman do not change much in their relationship to each other during the extent of *The Dream Songs*. Closer to Hugo's idea of stance is Yeats's concept of the mask, where the poet expresses characteristics in his poems that are opposite to those of his personal life. But where Yeats saw the differences between the man and the mask narrowing as he wrote poem after poem, Hugo sees a different dynamic: after a while, the stance can be discarded, and the poet can become "more naked" and express himself more directly in his work. The best example of Hugo walking out of the stance can be seen in "The Lady in Kicking Horse Reservoir," where his more than usual toughness fades away before the poem ends:

> the first stanza is very nasty and vengeful and the speaker's very hard. He says, "Lie there lily still," and "I hope each spring / to find you tangled in those pads . . . stars in dead reflection off your teeth"—really a vicious, gleeful kind of "Boy, am I glad you're dead, you rascal, you!" kind of thing. Then of course, and as often happens in my poems, I get closer to what I really am, deeper in the poem; a couple of stanzas later I'm saying, "Sorry. Sorry. Sorry" and I become the soft slob that I really am at heart.[14]

One senses, however, the psychological importance of that tough stance to the whole of Hugo's work. Even after that important book, *Good Luck in Cracked Italian* (1969)—where, as Hugo says, "Humphrey Bogart begins to soften up and becomes Leslie Howard . . . and I never did quite go back"[15]—the tough stance continues to be felt. It still begins many poems in *The Lady in Kicking Horse Reservoir:* "On this map white. A state thick as a fist" ("A Map of Montana in Italy," p. 3); "Eighty-nine was bad. At least a hundred/children died, the ones with money planted / in this far spot from the town" ("Graves at Elkhorn," p. 9); "Cries of gold or men about to hang / trail off where the brewery failed" ("Helena, Where Homes Go Mad," p. 18). In *What Thou Lovest Well Remains American* the stance continues: "Cruelty and rain could be expected" ("The House on 15th S.W.," p. 8); "Burn this shot. The gray is what it is" ("A Snapshot of 15th S.W.," p. 10). But in *What Thou Lovest,* the tough stance is tied to poems about Hugo's past: "15th S.W." was the address of his grandparents' home in White Center.

Stability is one of the reasons Hugo takes a stance: a stability in generating poems and a stability in the precarious intensity of psychological expression. There is a corollary concept to Hugo's concept of the stance, another means of generating poems and providing stability for the opening of the subconscious. This concept, "the triggering town," helps us to see the overall unity of Hugo's insights into the process of writing poetry. Hugo has written so many poems about towns that "the Hugo town" is an important part of his poetry, an image directed toward the loss of a sense of community in our lives. Apart from this critical position in his poetry, the town is also fundamental to Hugo's poetic theory. Like the stance, its chief function is prior to the poem, as the poet's consciousness alters in the shaping of a town, the choosing of a specific locale for the poem. In "The Triggering Town" Hugo describes this shaping process as "a stable set of knowns that the poem needs to anchor on" (p. 12).

The dynamic of the triggering town, as that of the stance, shifts the rigidity of the mind from a preconceived, personal reference to a reference that is known but is slightly strange and unfamiliar, a place that can be seen as opposite to the personal framework of the poet's world. "With the strange town, you can assume all knowns are stable and you owe the details nothing emotionally" (p. 12). As with the stance, here a poet does not find a stable base for writing unless he or she shifts from something assumed known to something assumed strange. Hugo explains the shift in ways that help us to understand both concepts.

> The relationship is based on fragments of information that are fixed —and if you need knowns that the town does not provide, no trivial concerns such as loyalty to truth, a nagging consideration had you stayed home, stand in the way of your introducing them as needed by the poem. It is easy to turn the gas station attendant into a drunk. Back home it would have been difficult because he had a drinking problem. (p. 12)

The examples of the drunk and the attendant with a "drinking problem" highlight the dimensions of the concept. What we know most about, what we are closest to, what our minds are fixed to write about are all part of our conceptions of self and world that rely on large quantities of knowledge that make the mind rigid. It takes a lot of sense impressions, decisions, thought, and sheer technological awareness to live in America. This knowledge is intricately tied up in our feelings about ourselves, our attitudes toward others, and our understanding of the world. But in its sheer complexity and in its rationality this knowledge cannot help us to write a poem. A poem is basically emotional; it is truth that "conforms to music." To write a poem, what is known well must be suspended: "I think it's easier to do a poem on a place you don't know very much about because you can add, whereas if you know the place really well you have to subtract in order to get the poem written. . . . addition was always easier than subtraction."[16]

When they write, all poets select, but it is by the addition of those selections that a poet makes his or her world. If we imagine a world, a "stable set of knowns" not subject to the complexities of knowledge in our world, then "the imagination can take off from them and if necessary can return." As the strange town "triggers" the imagination, the set of knowns about that town "gives a body of emotion behind the poem" (p. 13). "The more stable the base" of the poem, the more secure the poet is in the general outline of the town or stance, and "the freer you are to fly from it in the poem." But with the town as with the stance, a pattern of indirection emerges as the means to achieve what the poet started out to do at the beginning of the writing process: "If the poem turns out good, the town will have become your hometown no matter what name it carries. It will accommodate those intimate hunks of self that could live only in your hometown" (pp. 17–18). The town, like the stance, is an expression of self, a creation of a world much as the stance is the creation of a momentary self. The two concepts are necessary complements.

What lies behind both concepts is another scheme of indirection, a knowledge of self that is psychological in its depth even if it has not been determined by analysis or framed in psychological terms. The writing of a poem is a way not only of creating a self and a world; it is a way of seeing oneself, of learning about those "intimate hunks of self that could live only in your hometown." As a process, writing is a psychological function: "an act of imagination is an act of self-acceptance" (p. 71). Hugo follows that last statement with an axiom, "All art is failure," and we see once again how his insights into the writing process are cut from the whole cloth of his work and his life.

Hugo links his ideas about poets having feelings of worthlessness—feelings that "the self as given is inadequate and will not do"—to what he calls "the accelerated loss of knowns." The poem is a necessary act of self-acceptance in a world where intimate knowledge of even one place, one town, or one person has become harder with the advances of technology and the complexities of a pluralistic society. We are tired of hearing how American life is hectic, how things change daily, how the expansion of media and information has been revolutionary in the past decades. We are tired of hearing such truisms perhaps because they remind us of the psychological stress that all this change causes. The self experiences "the accelerated loss of all things that can serve as visual checkpoints and sources of stability" (p. 73). From this perspective we can see the psychological importance of stance and the town in the process of beginning to write. The self is inadequate for many poets because it is under great stress; the stance provides a means of simplifying our response to those demands. Similarly the town provides a simplified and therefore stable set of knowns—a simpler, though not necessarily nostalgic, world—in which the self can be momentarily more secure. In this framework that other side of the self, where the imagination holds its shadows, can be brought into the open, made part of the self as stance, and find expression in a world momentarily made sure.

This need for expression and the auxiliary needs of identity and stability are at the base of Hugo's psychological theory of poetry. The writing of the poem is an opening of possibilities, a way of gaining intimacy with that pool of the unconscious that stays with us day and night. That gain of intimacy is the taking of emotional possession of a part of one's life; it leads to an energy that the reader can share. With a stable base to the writing of the poem, the mind can give itself freely to the relativity of values in the unconscious. As Hugo says, "the imagination's a cynic": "it can accommodate the most disparate elements with no regard for relative values. And it does this by assuming all things have equal value, which is a way of saying nothing has any value, which is cynicism" (p. 15).

In saying "the imagination's a cynic," Hugo is placing the imagination, that area of mind where subconscious contents first become evident, opposite the stance and the stable set of knowns that lie at the base of the writing process. As a poet lets go of his preconceived self-knowledge and knowledge of the world to locate himself and his world more specifically, he gains a freedom from the complexities of personal and social values in much the same way that he has gained freedom from the advances of technological society (and freedom from that sense of loss, of "sources of stability," that haunts such advances). Although it sounds alarming to have "no regard for relative values" and to assume that "all things have equal value," we must remember the strong conservative impulse—the need for identity, stability, and expression—that lies behind the writing process. We should also remember that ever since the discoveries of Freud and Jung we have known that each imagination, each subconscious, is a primitive place where values are suspended in the light of emotional need.

Emotional need is the foundation of Hugo's concept of poetry. We can see his early writing as impelled by a need to write not just *of* but *out of* and *away from* a deep emotional impoverishment. His attention to that need has led him to insights that mark the furthest advance in our understanding of the way that human emotion comes to be poetic expression. In attending to the dynamics of emotional need, Hugo has placed the writing of poetry in a wider social context than it has had for years—wider perhaps than it has ever had. The writing of poetry is not only the province of scholars and trained members of a literary tradition; it is a process that can be learned and that has great value as it places the writer in touch with his or her feelings, giving the poet insights into "that body of emotion" behind the words. Moreover, if Hugo's poetry is considered, the writing of poetry becomes a means of strengthening those necessary conservative impulses for identity, stability, authentic expression, and community in a technological society that advances further into a future haunted by loss.

Part II
The Poetry of Need, the Poetry of Dream

4

"A Town Where Children Get Hurt Early": The Early Poems

Rejected. Humiliated. Degraded. Again and again when speaking in interviews, autobiographical essays, and poems, Richard Hugo brings these words into the discussion of his life. Besides offering, as Roethke had, a psychological theory for writing from obsession, Hugo also talks freely about the psychological problems in his past, covering the bleak areas of his life with an evenhandedness free from self-pity or posturing, admitting the power of emotional forces that we are sometimes born with and sometimes learn to submit to too easily. His talking about such matters in interviews and essays provides a basis for understanding the importance of those poems scattered throughout his work that refer to loss and degradation. Poems like "Between the Bridges," "Neighbor," "The Way a Ghost Dissolves," "No Bells to Believe," "Duwamish," and others from *A Run of Jacks* (1961) contain a presence of hurt that cannot be missed. They stand as a tacit admission of the importance, for survival in this world, of integrating and making whole a sense of self.

Hugo's problems are always tied to specific forces—economic, regional, historical, personal—that make the grist for the mill of his poetic obsessions. Hugo is very much *the* American Depression poet, coming to prominence forty years after that great economic shock haunted his childhood and that of a whole generation of Americans. The Depression shaped his consciousness of need, leaving a background from which he struggled to escape.

> Poets in my generation, a lot of us, grew up in poor, often degrading circumstances. For example, both James Wright and David Wagoner saw their fathers enslaved to lousy factory jobs. When we were kids, making a living, even finding a job, was tough. We have had to struggle with memories of a working class past and acceptance of a middle class present . . . . The Depression, threats of poverty and dispossession

> loyalty to defeated people we still love and desire not to be like them, and then a feeling of having violated our lives by wanting to be different—oh, very complicated matters.[1]

Poverty haunts him, with its unglamorous ache; it infests the town he carries with him, wherever he goes, as in this poignant opening to one of the best of his "letter poems," "Letter to Levertov from Butte":

> Dear Denise: Long way from, long time since Boulder.
> I hope you and Mitch are doing OK. I get rumors.
> You're in Moscow, Montreal. Whatever place I hear
> it's always one of glamor. I'm not anywhere glamorous.
> I'm in a town where children get hurt early. Degraded
> by drab homes. Beaten by drunken parents, by other
> children.[2]

This town may be Butte, Montana, but the town that Hugo carries with him is Seattle, more specifically, Hugo's working-class neighborhood just outside Seattle, White Center. He carries that town with him since what he sees, in any town, is an organization of human society that allows the hurts of poverty to ruin people's lives.

Next to White Center, when Hugo was growing up, were two other working-class neighborhoods, Riverside and Youngstown, where Hugo had most of his early friends. There, near the Duwamish River, the boys saw every day "the castle, the hill, West Seattle, where we would go to high school."

> What a middle class paradise. The streets were paved, the homes elegant, the girls well groomed and simply by virtue of living in West Seattle, far more beautiful and desirable than the girls in our home district. Gentility and confidence reigned on that hill. West Seattle was not a district. It was an ideal, to be accepted there meant one had become a better person. West Seattle was too far to be seen from White Center, but to the children of Youngstown and Riverside, it towered over the sources of felt debasement: the filthy, loud belching steel mill, the oily slow river, the immigrants hanging on to their odd ways, Indians drunk in the unswept taverns, the commercial fishermen, tugboat workers and mill workers with their coarse manners. In many minds White Center was no better. When people from White Center applied for work in the 20's and 30's, they seldom mentioned White Center, either in the interview or on the application form. The smart ones said they lived in West Seattle; White Center had the reputation of being just outside the boundary of the civilized world.[3]

That last sentence's smooth sarcasm hardly covers the hurt of the previous sentences, the brute facts of poverty, unemployment, and the utter necessity of work. What hurts is the eternal presence of the ideal: the social acceptance and economic confidence that are just out of reach. The ideal could be had with money. Attaining the ideal meant being beautiful and safe, secure in the knowledge of power, and being able to understand and control social and economic realities. Money was the key to power, beauty, and love. Without money, faces were not calm, want was real, and love was something spurred by need.

Beneath the lack of money—the dispossession from society and the things of this world—lay another dispossession: Richard Hugo was born Richard Hogan, the son of a father who deserted his teenaged wife, Hugo's mother; she, in turn, left her infant son to be brought up by her parents. When she later married a man named Hugo, young Richard decided that that would be his surname.[4] Thus a double dispossession lies behind Hugo's early poems. In some ways his first two books, *A Run of Jacks* and *Death of the Kapowsin Tavern* (1965), are haunted by the intertwining of those two emotional scars: his personal tragedy is seen in economic terms, and economic degradation is seen as intensely personal. A poem from Hugo's second book, "Houses Lie, Believe the Lying Sea," indicates the depth at which those two scars join.

> Rooms are sick for light. That male doll
> fractured in the corner means
> the rage of children went remote
> in sea light and the humming flies.
>
> The well still works. Pump, and water
> coughs out brown. Did a father weep
> and shout at weeping children: we are poor?
> And when they moved without a buyer,
> did the mother turn Chinese with shame?
> An empty house can teach a rat despair.[5]

Although the poem ends with an outright rejection of the old house, its presence is still strong: homes don't really die the way houses do. With his first wife, Barbara, Hugo used to "house-haunt" places like that in the poem, finding places in which to imagine failed homes. The reality of the house is only a metaphor for the greater emotional burdens inside the poet, for those charged images that the house evokes: the father crying to his children, the mother shamed, the children enraged. If a poem is, as Stevens said, "the cry of the occasion," then that cry is from places deeper than the present occasion and must be heard.

As often happens in Hugo's poetry, the sea, that world of water that he imagines as the only beautiful and constant thing in his life, redeems the scene. "Sea light" calms the children's rage. The image connecting house and sea, the well, first appears in the poem as a hopeful sign beginning the second stanza, but then there follows a stark change: "Pump, and water / coughs out brown." The water, given human properties in "coughs," leads the poet to the other water in the house: the tears of the weeping father and children. The deft shift of images has a simplicity that avoids sentimentality without letting go of that powerful feeling of failure.

Hugo's experience in the abandoned house stands as a paradigm for those other images, scattered through so many poems, of shacks, tenements, peeling slats, and rooms that don't feel right. In such poems as "Hideout," "Between the Bridges," "No Bells to Believe," and "Kapowsin," the houses or buildings stand, sometimes barely, as aspects of failure highlighted by the power and beauty of the natural landscape, often the sea. Critically, an opposition between the poverty of Hugo's neighborhood and the wealth of West Seattle may be implied in such contrasts between ruined buildings and rich natural imagery, but the image of the sea is used in a more complex way. The sea beyond the poor houses is rich, inaccessible, and powerful, and its power is as inaccessible to money as it is to poverty. The poor, in their feeling for their lives and surroundings, do have some claim on the power of the sea; they are tied to it economically and even literally, as they live along the banks of the river that leads to it.

Not merely metaphor, the sea is a tangible presence that demands the attention of all workers in Riverside and Youngstown, fishermen or mill workers. Whatever their fathers do, the boys of those neighborhoods fish and learn that men have fights in taverns by the river. This is the ethic that Hugo, left mainly alone by his grandparents, adopted as a means to survive. An unquestioned power in his life, the sea becomes part of the psychological landscape of his poetry.

Very much a part of the experience of poverty, the almost palpable sensation of being tied to a landscape or seascape that provides jobs, work, and a way to survive has been studied by psychiatrist Robert Coles in his monumental work, *Children of Crisis*.

> More often than not, mountaineers and tenant farmers and migrants can be found living near that water, near creeks and not far from lakes and quite close to the waters of any number of rivers. The mountain settlements are squeezed into a valley a river has carved out, or pressed close to a creek whose banks actually provide a clearing, a way down, a road out of the wilderness; or settlements are crammed near a lake, where a hungry migrant or tenant farmer can search for fish, which is one thing that costs nothing. "We never lose sight of water, and we never lose sight of the sky, and we never lose sight of the land, that's how we live," I was told by a tenant farmer who lives in what history books variously call the Black Belt, the Black Prairie, the Cotton Belt.[6]

In a psychological study as notable for its honesty and humanity as for its clinical adeptness, Coles masterfully presents the feelings, the emotional landscape, of the poorest rural workers in America. He is at his most persuasive when he admits how much he learned about human feeling while talking to, visiting, and revisiting poor families. The emotional landscape that Coles describes is not unlike that of Hugo's poems. Although their experiences are far more devastating than those Hugo experienced as a boy, migrant children have emotional lives that come close to that sense of hurt that we find in Hugo's poetry.

> As for their emotions, they are, to my eye, an increasingly sad group of children. They have their fun, their outbursts of games and jokes and teasing and taunting and laughing; but they are for too long stretches of time downcast and tired and bored and indifferent and to themselves unkind. They feel worthless, blamed, frowned upon, spoken ill of. Life itself, the world around them, even their own parents, everything that is, seems to brand them, stigmatize them, view them with disfavor, and in a million ways call them to account—lace into them, pick on them, tell them off, dress them down. The only answer to such a fate is sex, when it becomes possible, drink, when it is available, and always the old, familiar answers—travel, work, rest when that can be had, and occasionally during the year a moment in church where forgiveness can be asked, where the promise of salvation can be heard, where some wild, screaming, frantic, angry, frightened, nervous, half-mad cry for help can be put into words and songs and really given the body's expression.[7]

There are obvious connections between the emotional lives that Coles has described and the life that Hugo has spoken of in his poetry and prose: the same hurt, sense of worthlessness, boredom, need, and momentary release from the necessity of work. Though his life, even during the Depression, was not characterized by the utter desolation of the migrants' lives, Hugo can claim the feelings of the very poor as his own partly through the heightening effect of the personal desertions in his life. With his greater sense of self and easier economic life, he gains strength to look at his and others' poverty and to feel his way to a language that adequately expresses that pain.

For Hugo the pain goes deeper than the poverty that engenders it. The psychological dislocation that arises from a childhood desertion can create the same sense of degradation and unworthiness that underlay the surrounding experience of poverty in his neighborhood. The two worlds, outside the house and inside the home, are connected by that same spoiled water of failure and humiliation. The psychological hurt complements the economic need; the constant burden of work is like the constant search for a sense of self-worth; the anger toward money and prestige parallels the deep internal anger arising from being betrayed and deserted. We can take the parallels further and say that the Great Depression was a social and economic desertion—given the hierarchy of America's social structure—and was as palpably traumatic in economic terms as a parent's rejection would be to a child's emotional well-being.

As the migrant children do, Hugo must learn to work with what he has. His being reared by his grandparents shaped his sense of self and his relation to the society around him. It also left him with a developed sensitivity to the fragility of life for the old and with the greater sense of boredom for a boy brought up among tired and defeated people.

> My grandparents raised five children and had known little other than a life of hard work. They must have been worn when my teen-age mother left me with them. They were well into their fifties by then and I was less than two. I was to grow up with far more freedom than most boys, but with little guidance or attention.[8]

It is easy to picture Hugo living at home with his grandparents, respectful but itching to get out. He wandered, went to Riverside, played in deserted mills, collected pop-bottle caps, and fished the

Duwamish with other boys in the area. When he returned home, it was with a clear sense of economic necessities and emotional need.

> I was pleased when my grandparents asked me to go to White Center for a pint of ice cream. I loved ice cream and I felt I was contributing something, being part of the family. I ran out the back door, across the hard dirt walk between two plots of garden and through the woods on the dirt path to 16th, then the block and a half south to Bill Gagnon's drugstore in the White Center business district. We had no refrigerator and to make sure the ice cream was solid when I handed it to grandmother, I ran back as fast as I could. She divided the ice cream into three equal pieces and we would sit in the kitchen and eat without speaking under the bare light bulb at the end of the cord hanging from the ceiling.[9]

Hugo's autobiographical essays strike us, at times, with the emotional completeness of a poem, as this paragraph does. When Hugo mentions his grandparents his manner is quite different from his description of the world outside the house. Once outside, physical details leap into the prose: directions are precise to Gagnon's store; he enjoys the freedom of movement. Once back in the house, the prose is slower and more sensitive to the levels of feeling, to the slight shifts in the silence that surrounds the family's internal relations. The two parts of the experience are held together by need: because they had no refrigerator, Hugo runs the ice cream home.

The presence of the old—whether people, objects, or even ideas—is widespread in Hugo's poetry. At times the land itself is old, something our contemporary culture is losing sight of, like a road along the interstate highway. Certainly houses are old, as in "Houses Lie, Believe the Lying Sea." What is old needs attention, affection, understanding, and help. The old have as fragile and precarious an existence as does a young boy; in Hugo's poetry this attention to the old is not the expression of some predisposed ethic but a necessary part of the poet's coming to know himself.

> Our problem is the value of the old,
> the value of the cruel. A sadist thinks
> a bruise is just a rose. Pyromaniacs
> would bruise this town to cinder
> had they not gone big-time in the east. Out west
> the oldest thing is neon. Here, antiques
> warn us to be tolerant of dust.[10]

Hugo's sensitivity to the old is tied to an awareness of the abuses of power: "the value of the old" is a problem linked with "the value of the cruel." In this poem, placed in Indiana at a safe distance from Seattle, Hugo can have moments of fun with the problem, can show the mixed feeling of "on that plate, a rose survives the cracks" and "Let's run and love the old and know tomorrow / whatever trails our running leaves in air / a tiny crone will price and call antique." But the poem ends on a more ominous note: an antique doughboy levels his bayonet "level as your frown / when salesmen come . . . their baskets heavy / with those bullets armies wouldn't buy." Behind the play of fragility and the small cruelties of age is something as powerful and as cruel as a pyromaniac and as economically unethical as a salesman trying to foist bad goods on unsuspecting customers.

"The value of the old" is an extension of Hugo's youthful sensitivity to his grandparents. Early in his poetic career he dealt with the important presence of his grandmother in "The Way a Ghost Dissolves." With her life bounded by hard work, need, faith, and age, she is seen by Hugo as a ghost. The imagery of the poem, though placed outdoors, reinforces an interior, "close" feeling by playing with those boundaries.

> Where she lived the close remained the best.
> The nearest music and the static cloud,
> sun and dirt were all she understood . . . .
>
> Up at dawn, the earth provided food
> if worked and watered, planted green
> with rye grass every fall. Or driven wild
> by snakes that kept the carrots clean,
> she butchered snakes and carrots with a hoe.
> Her screams were sea birds in the wind,
> her chopping—nothing like it now.[11]

The ghosts dissolves in an essentially passive acceptance of whatever comes. Behind the work is the earth's reaction, "provided," as if all of the woman's activity is circumscribed by that agrarian patience that has often given more to the land than it has gained in return. Hugo claims the life of this ghost as his own future.

> I will garden on the double run,
> my rhythm obvious in ringing rakes,
> and trust in fate to keep me poor and kind

and work until my heart is short;
then go out slowly with a feeble grin,
my fingers flexing but my eyes gone gray
from cramps and lack of oxygen.

The verbs outline the life set forth in the whole poem: "garden," "trust," "work," "go out," "gone." Early in his career Hugo sees his life locked in the same heartless working routine his grandparents had survived.

"The Way a Ghost Dissolves" is a touching and frightening poem: frightening in that such a life will be lived again, contained by a force so strong that a man can see his life set before him, closed in the same way that age closes the lives of us all. Such an emotional condition is nearly barren, even ghostly. Indeed the last image of the poem is simple suffocation. Surely there is some other life to imagine, something else for a young man to do.

There is: in the neighborhood outside the house where boys played themselves to toughness, jeering at Greek fishermen, hiding in abandoned mills, and finding fights. Many men have known this world while growing up, and Hugo's description of it, again, has about it the wholeness of a poem.

> The first time I saw Bill Gavin was at Youngstown where he lived. I was thirteen at the time, playing end on a neighborhood football team from Highland Park. Since many of the players were older, some of them sixteen and seventeen, I was mostly getting out of the way, though I was a good place kicker and kicked off and tried the extra point. After the game a fight started. One of our players, Willard Purvis, started punching one of their players, Bill Gavin, in the face. Purvis threw his best shots, roundhouse lefts and rights. He must have hit Gavin six times as hard as he could right in the chops and all Gavin did was stand there and glower. Purvis might as well have been slugging ingots in the steel mill nearby. When he realized the futility of his fists he started to turn white and retreat. Gavin had ended the fight simply by glowering. What a man, I thought. Within a year he was spending evenings in White Center, one of the toughs I admired. I thought him super masculine and in high school, where he was in an English class with me, three or four grades older than the rest of us and soon to flunk out for good, his weakness as a student didn't mar the heroic image I'd made of him. Not one bit.
>
> Twenty years later, when I imagined myself along that river (the Duwamish), I found I wrote in direct, hard language. I believe now that unconsciously I felt that for the duration of the poem, I was as tough as I'd wanted to be in real life.[12]

Such an image of masculine toughness makes a deep impression. One remembers an earlier Hugo statement: "When we were kids, making a living, even finding a job, was tough." For a boy who feels the effects of poverty and rejection, such an image can become the vehicle for several unspoken feelings: in a world where survival is a constant question, being tough can mean being someone who cannot be destroyed, who is not hurt deeply by the dangers that happen daily; someone who can go on, tap some power beyond that of normal beaten-down reality, and win. This tough, self-reliant masculinity grows to be a central image in Hugo's poetry: the archetypal western loner, so self-reliant, American, and tough that his emotional life feels gray like a jail, as in "Degrees of Gray in Philipsburg."

But there is a dimension to masculine toughness that gains clarity when the image of Bill Gavin is compared to the guiding image of "The Way a Ghost Dissolves." A young boy must survive not only the tough world of poverty but also the passive acceptance of such a defeated life. What Hugo in his poetry has in common with Purvis and Gavin is their anger, their instinct to fight in whatever way they can to protect what self-worth they have. That anger is a defense is now a psychological truism, but it is defense at the bottom line and therefore an emotional state that the poor know well.

"Neighbor" offers a masculine parallel to "The Way a Ghost Dissolves" and shows anger turned on itself in the image of a drunk lying flat in the garden that Hugo's grandmother worked devotedly.

> The drunk who lives across the street from us
> fell in our garden, on the beet patch
> yesterday. So polite. Pardon me,
> he said. He had to be helped up and held
> steered home and put to bed, declaring
> we got to have another drink and smile. (p. 57)

It's funny, this parody of socially accepted manners, and Hugo makes the fun gentle and polite. As in any number of comic sketches, the drunk wants only to be liked and is so compliant that he has to be "helped and held." But this compliance masks—as Karen Horney pointed out in her famous study, *Our Inner Con-*

flicts[13]—a lot of anger, a hatred so severe that a man may kill himself emotionally by bending over to deny its existence.

Getting drunk is a way to survive the hurt of poverty and the sense of worthlessness that develops into self-hatred. As Hugo imagines the scene, he identifies with the drunk, helps him, knows his habits and the shack where he lives. Later Hugo came to realize that "Neighbor" had been "no idle curiosity, no chance subject for a poem. I felt I might very well end up that way, and to this day the idea isn't unattractive."[14] Such a statement demonstrates the depths of Hugo's sense of defeat and indicates the depth of struggle he has had with alcoholism. In this poem, resignation, defeat, and need combine to unlock a further area of the landscape of the imagination.

> I try to guess what's in that dim warm mind.
> Does he think about horizoned firs
> black against the light, thirty years
> ago, and the good girl—what's her name—
> believing, or think about the dog
> he beat to death that day in Carbonado? (p. 57)

The drunk's vista is a stark, expansive horizon of firs that contracts first to the girl whose name escapes him and then to the dog that does not escape the brutal anger, which is expressed well in the *b* and *d* sounds of the last line. The anger is just beneath the polite and comic surface; as it emerges we feel how well Hugo has unlocked this inner landscape, to bring the reader that mixture of disdain and sympathy evident in the final stanza.

> I hear he's dead, and wait now on my porch.
> He must be in his shack. The wagon's
> due to come and take him where they take
> late alcoholics, probably called Farm's End.
> I plan my frown, certain he'll be carried out
> bleeding from the corners of his grin. (p. 57)

Most of the language is almost casual, but there is an underlying care: the wagon is "due to come," and the unseen officials will take the neighbor "where they take / late alcoholics"—the assonance and word choice are gentle, in fact, polite. They add a heavy irony to the casual prose of "probably called Farm's End," and we remember the drunk at the beginning of the poem, face down in the beets. The frown the poet assumes is protective, a social mask meant to insulate him from the bloody image certain to come into view as the drunk is carried out.

The way "Neighbor" carefully traces the connections of inner landscape and social failure shows us how deeply Hugo is aware of the pity and anger that are the emotional condition of the poor. Like the poor in Coles's book, Hugo's drunk feels a resignation and a loss of self-esteem that make him keep his place and be polite. And, as Coles described it, beneath the resignation is rage, directed more often toward self than toward society. The imaginative power of that rage is unlocked in Hugo's poetry. Anger seems to be a force welling from the unconscious, taking landscapes or figures of loss and poverty and making them felt presences, momentarily made whole as that anger raises them up to full height and then allows them to collapse. A major source of Hugo's poetry, that deep rage beneath the surface pity and politeness of the poor is both let loose and channeled in the language of the poems. The drunk does not control his rage; he is controlled and killed by it. The poet, in making the patterns of sound and images that are the poem, controls his own anger by triggering the release of that emotional energy that can kill. It is an imaginative act that asks for and evokes a fundamental sympathy on the part of the reader as the unlocking of the inner landscape becomes an occasion for the sharing of emotional health.

With Hugo's first two books we find a statement and an exploration of the interior landscape of poverty. In *A Run of Jacks* that statement is clear; the emotional scars of poverty are evident. In *Death of the Kapowsin Tavern* the statement takes on larger dimensions and assumes a regional outline that identifies the Pacific Northwest with the landscape of poverty and anger. There are moments, of course, when the burden of past hurt lifts and the sheer natural energy and beauty of the regional landscape are an illumination. But not all discoveries are beautiful and not all illuminations carry with them the confidence that the world is beautiful and right. There are drunks in taverns, rivers full of crud, and shacks where boys leave home early and never want to go back. The energy in Hugo's poetry owes much of its richness to that hurt that carries the weight of pain from the experience of poverty.

5

"Where Sea Breaks Inland": Toward a Geography of Feeling

If Richard Hugo's poetry has become known as regional, it is due to so many poems in *Death of the Kapowsin Tavern* that refer specifically to the Pacific Northwest. The title of the first section of the book—"Duwamish, Skagit, Hoh"—sounds, to someone born and raised east of the Mississippi, less like the names of three rivers than some strange incantation. Other fine poems, built solidly up from the ground of Northwest towns such as Port Townsend, Fort Casey, and Coupeville, seem to place the poetry so forthrightly under the heading "regional" that it may seem the rankest amateurism for a critic to question that classification. But such a question is necessary, since a reader of Hugo's poetry is impressed repeatedly by how Hugo uses his region to make not only a geography of names and regional associations but also a geography of those essential human feelings that hold society together and make a sense of community.

Moreover, Hugo seems to have come to his geography of names and regional references by feeling his way, by making tenuous connections to the area surrounding himself, not knowing exactly whether to approve or disapprove of what he sees. One would think it easy to be a regional poet about the Northwest, considering its magnificent landscapes, streams and rivers, mountains and wilderness. Perhaps Hugo's consistently strong imagery of that natural beauty encourages the regional identification, but labeling his poetry as regional is a mistake. Even when Hugo's poetry is thoroughly embossed with rich images of the Northwest, it is less the natural landscape toward which the poem's emotional energy points than toward the people—scattered, lonely, in conflict, and often struggling to survive.

Herein lies the reason Hugo's poetry demands another look at the word *regional;* for if there is a geography that lies at the center of his poetry, it is a primitive map of that area between people in which human feelings create those slight but essential bonds of community. The regional geography of the Northwest supports this geography of feeling that develops throughout *Death of the Kapowsin Tavern.* From the river poems of "Duwamish, Skagit, Hoh," to the last, title poem of the book, the progression is from unpopulated landscape toward town. In *A Run of Jacks* those hurts from human society that Hugo had felt as a boy led him away from home, toward the Duwamish and the world of imagination beneath the water's surface. In *Death of the Kapowsin Tavern* rivers lead Hugo back to that society, slowly and painstakingly, first to solitary figures on the landscape, then to important persons in his life, and then to towns.

If Hugo's turning toward human community is slow, and if the "death" of the Kapowsin tavern provides an occasion to regret the failure and loss of community, these are signs that reflect his deliberate, tenuous search for safe footing in the psychological landscape that forms human community. To Hugo it is all slippery territory, both the regional geography of rivers and rain forests and the interior geography of human feelings. He faces both geographies with an equal regard for those physical and economic forces that powerfully shaped how people learned to live in the Northwest and how they still live. Frederick Garber, Hugo's chief critic, has noted that the poet's consciousness is "still elemental and conservative, bound deeply into the enduring forms of confrontation."[1]

Confrontation is an essential part of both the physical geography of the Northwest and the geography of feeling that must have shaped Hugo's awareness of himself in a working-class neighborhood in Seattle. Whereas in the physical landscape the forces of water and earth meet to create the rain forest, rich soil, and streams, in Hugo's home neighborhoods of White Center and Riverside economic and social forces met to create needs for money, acceptance, stability, and approval. These are important emotional forces in a single human life and in the makeup of those feelings that shape a neighborhood's sense of community. Shared needs can cause the sharing of resources and sympathy; unshared needs can cause fear, suspicion, competition, and a sense of worthlessness that deadens the color of any joy. We find similar guarded, minimal, possessive connections when we read Hugo's account of himself as a regionalist.

> I am a regionalist and don't care for writers who are not, though of course there are several ways of defining region. I find it hard to write unless I have a sense of where the speaker is, and I have a hard time appreciating writing if I sense the author has no clear idea of where things in his work are happening. Most places that trigger poems for me are places where little or nothing is happening. They become stage sets where I can imagine the drama of the poem. When I write a poem, I lay emotional claim to the setting . . . .
>
> When I say I'm a regionalist I'm being very exact and admit to those qualities in myself that depreciators of regionalism find objectionable. I am small minded, limited to the local, immediate minded, gossipy and given to stagnancy. When I'm writing I have no trust in change or progress. As soon as I stop writing I'm in favor of wholesale social changes, equality, justice, elimination of poverty, etc. . . .
>
> In my experience, neither Yeats nor Williams had it right, though I speak for myself. The place triggers the mind to create the place.[2]

Hugo's definition of his regionalism is itself a confrontation: he imagines what "depreciators of regionalism find objectionable," and he admits wholeheartedly to being so limited. It is a fiercely independent, personal idea, this regionalism: "I lay emotional claim to the setting." There is nothing mythic involved, as in Yeats, or any claim for the reality of the thing perceived, as in Williams; there is only Hugo's emotional claim to the place—a claim, in fact, to no place at all, for "the place triggers the mind to create the place."

Essential to Hugo's regionalism is its basis in emotional reality, in the alogical workings of the human psyche that guide all perceptions of any place to those images that satisfy psychic needs. Such a definition of regionalism is a cut deeper than most because it includes the psychological nature of writing and the complexities of emotion. In criticism it has been customary to speak of how a regional writer creates a world view for all humanity by using the confines of a specific locale to create a mythic place—Robinson's Tilbury Town and Faulkner's Yoknapatawpha are good examples. Without disregarding the strong insights into human nature that Robinson and Faulkner develop in their created worlds, we can say that the development of Hugo's regionalism takes a decidedly different tack and thus lies just outside the convenient literary terms. His Northwest is not so much a place as a condition; rather than developing a world within the confines of a locale, Hugo uses each landscape or town to record those elemental needs and dreams and passions that make up the failure of human community. We are not given either a Flammonde or a Snopes to represent human values and their failure. What we find is a man looking for a place, within the failures of society, to survive. In this light Hugo's region is a place of confrontation, a place too close to the necessities of survival to foster the mythic or representative characters that other regional writers have developed.

It may well be that this aspect of Hugo's regionalism is, after all, part of a myth: in American literature the West has always been that margin between civilization and wilderness where survival is always at stake. The difference in Hugo's poetry is one of emphasis. What is threatened is not physical or personal survival but the survival of human feeling itself in the collapse of human community. By not projecting his psychological insights into mythic, larger-than-life figures, Hugo tacitly admits that all myth is psychological and that the problems of human community are based in that not completely understood structure of the human heart.

The first poem in *Death of the Kapowsin Tavern,* "Introduction to the Hoh," shows us a place that triggers Hugo's mind; far away from towns and other men, it is never far from the memory of human presence.

> Nearly all the rivers color like the sky
> and bend in other places after extra pour.
> This blueness is high ice. Cartographers
> are smiling at the curves that will recur.
> . . . .
> Think of stark abundance, a famous run of jacks
> the vanished tribe at the mouth once bragged about.
> Think of hungry Mays, the nets reversed
> to snag whatever rot the river washes out.[3]

This place not only triggers lush description—"blueness is high ice," "the milk flow / high enough to run the smaller aspen down"—but also wakes the memory of human presence, of "stark abundance," and of famine. As the Indians who once lived there depended on the abundant rush of salmon and knew the force of "hungry Mays," so the poet also knows this dependency of the imagination and human emotion on both the beauty and the terror in the landscape. On the confrontation between abundance and famine, lush imagery and pain, rests the poem: the rhythm of these opposites is human as well as natural. The underlying balance of these confrontations makes up Hugo's region, whether his attention is drawn toward wilderness or town. If there is a predilection in some of the early poems for wilderness over town, the implication is that in the town the balance is lost, human feelings fail, and the direction of the poet's attention turns back toward balance, as in the following lines from "Duwamish No. 2":

> When the world hurts, I come back alone
> along the river, certain the salt
> of vague eyes makes me ready for the sea.
> And the river says: you're not unique—
> learn now there is one direction only—
> north, and though terror to believe—
> quickly found by river and never love. (p. 6)

Love is a word Hugo uses somewhat elusively and ambiguously. In this poem love lies within the town, and the river's voice is almost parental as it denies human love in favor of its own inevitable, natural direction of energy: north, toward the sea. We are shown the power and varying beauty of the river: "Mudhens, cormorants and teals" in the reeds along its banks; the river's tides and birds that "insist the wind / will find the sea." Other images dominate, however, when there is no water: we learn that "wrens have claws," and we are shown men "oiling / guns beside ripped cows." With its world complete, balancing itself with tides, the river is a force that nurtures and supports—as if love, but the river is not love. Love is human and should, like a river, carry and support; but too often human love fails and pollutes: "Home. The word is dirty. Home is where / the dirty river dies" ("From the Rainforest Down," p. 3).

Along the river sit the houses of that human community where "love" and "home" are dirty, where they fail. In "Bad Vision at the Skagit," when Hugo sees those houses and remembers the "bending backs and sweat" and wages ("weak / as yesterday's manure") of

Mexicans and Serbs, he says: "I should see injustice, / not slow water and the beating birds / that never move a foot against the sun" (p. 7). Again the contrast is between love—here in a political context—and the enduring processes of nature; again Hugo chooses what can endure. The slow water, the wind, the sun —these are forces that men, like the birds, cannot move against but must move with.

This enduring world of natural forces creates minimal emotional and physical support for the man inside "the shack / the wind paints white" in the poem "Hideout." Inside his hideout against human society, the man may or may not be the poet; he is, however, an alienated man whose shack is a place where dreams from the sea, the river, and the human world are all one dream, and human enterprise is little more than a child's game:

> What odd games children play.
> One shouts himself into a president.
> Another pins the villain salmon
> into the air with spears. (p. 10)

The greater, enduring dreams are those the elemental forces of nature bring.

> Morning brings a new wind and a new
> white coat of weather for the shack.
> The salmon moved upstream last night
> and no bird cuts the river, looking
> for a smelt. Ships sail off to Naples
> and the bent face bobbing in the wake
> was counted in another cloud gone north. (p. 13)

In a longer poem, "Duwamish Head," love and the river meet in an ode to the failure of love. It is a complex poem, full of the contrarieties of human emotion and effort and the pollution that such effort leaves in human lives and in the river. The refrain, "River, I have loved, loved badly on your bank," sounds vaguely Elizabethan in rhythm; it points clearly, however, to Hugo's involvement in the failures of personal and collective feeling that have brought hurt and pollution.

> To know is to be alien to rivers.
> This river helped me play an easy role—
> to be alone, to drink, to fail.

The world goes on with money. A tough cat
dove here from a shingle mill on meat
that glittered as it swam. The mill is gone.
The cat is ground. If I say love
was here, along the river, show me bones
of cod, scales and blood, faces in the clouds
so thick they jam the sky with laughter. (p. 13)

Throughout "Duwamish Head" the failures of human love are so much detritus in the unchanging natural and economic forces. With the physical landscape marred repeatedly by human activity and crisis, the reader almost feels the "inhumanism" of Robinson Jeffers's great poems emerging. But unlike Jeffers, who sees humanity as a blemish, a brief disease in the biological and geological history of the landscape, Hugo keeps his poetry away from intellectual or mythic extensions. Rather than the feeling that humanity despoils what it touches because of its uncontrolled passions, Hugo shows us how human failings move in much the same way as the river feeling its way to the sea. Hugo speaks of his own passion in terms of the river: "My fins are hands"; "in the shack I licked her knees in"; "her arms and eyes had power like the river / and she imitated salmon with a naked roll." The river and the power of human emotion are much the same, whether in sexual embrace or in the rhythm of a life with its vagaries, impulses, and routine.

When I see a stream, I like to say, exactly.
Where else could it run? Trace it back to ice.
Try to find a photo of your cradle.
Rivers jump their beds and don't look back
regretting they have lost such lovely rides. (p. 12)

The one emotional reality that Hugo never loses sight of in his poetry is the way in which human passions and emotions are no one thing. Love causes as much pain as pleasure; and, in its extensions as sympathy, trust, and community, love is seen as a double-edged sword. A human community is often held together not only by mutual cooperation but also by love of those fantasies and small romances that have no reality, that pervert human sympathies into prejudice and hatred. From the second section of *Death of the Kapowsin Tavern,* this other side of love comes clear in two poems: "Tahola" and "Road Ends at Tahola."

In "Tahola" Hugo sees not only the ocean, a river, and a town but also the play of whispers, prejudice, the meeting of white and Indian cultures, and those economic facts that tie human emotion to need. Moreover, imbedded in the specific emotional fabric of the poem is the long history of Indian defeats and white exploitation of Indian culture. The poem takes these facts and, following emotional currents as well as the geographic landscape, it arrives at a feeling deeper than expected.

> Where sea breaks inland, claiming the Quinalt
> in a half saltwater lake, canoes turn gray
> waiting for the runs. The store makes money
> but the two cafes, not open, rot in spray.
> Baskets you can buy are rumored Cherokee.
> . . . .
> When whites drive off and the money's gone
> a hundred mongrels bark. Indians
> should mend the tribal nets in moonlight
> not drink more and hum a white man's tune
> they heard upstream. What about the words?
> Something about war, translated by the sea
> and wind into a song a doll sang
> long ago, riding a crude wave in. (p. 16)

As the "sea breaks inland, claiming the Quinalt" Indians, it acts as if it were human feeling coming onto shore or into town to claim the human associations there. The sea, as the poet's imagination, begins to change—as if with spray—the visible appearances in the landscape for those subtler dynamics of relationship that are the interior landscape. Canoes may wait, as they have always in Northwest Indian tribes, for the run of salmon, but here they wait for white fishermen. Although the store makes money, the closed cafés and the backhanded compliment ("The best house / was never envied for its tile") all show the town to be a place clouded economically as well as physically and emotionally. The physical, economic, and emotional nets are interrelated: a quaint fishing village is more than simply a place where a white man can escape the pressures of white society.

The poem brings together white fantasies and Indian realities as the two cultures meet in the simple act of arranging a fishing trip. The whites now harvest the salmon, taking Quinalt guides and giving them bourbon to "pry stories" that will feed their white dreams in this clouded territory. The fantasy that Indians "should mend the tribal nets in moonlight" is sentimental and unreal. The rumors about Cherokee baskets and the purchased fantasies brought by whites spread to cloud the Indians' emotional lives as they "drink more and hum a white man's tune / they heard upstream." As in "Bad Vision at the Skagit," there is no overt political comment, no abstraction into consciously decided political opinion. The poem is not at all argumentative; its power rests completely in its description of the landscape. The sea, that home of the river, translates the drunken songs of Indians and whites into a dimly evocative music; it also takes a doll and translates it into a dimly archetypal image: "a song a doll sang / long ago, riding a crude wave in." The sympathies that could create a sense of community in the place the poem embodies —those sympathies become crude as the waves that bring the dream image to shore. Perhaps the suggestion is that only by such emotional claim, as the sea makes on the shore, can the bringer of songs—the poet—reestablish those sympathies that have decayed. Only the dream image has the power to unite temporarily the two cultures; only at that depth of unconsciousness is there a sharing of human feeling.

Both river and sea provide occasions for comments on the imbalances in human feeling and community. As the river provides an opposition or opposite direction to the failings of human love, so the sea, opposed to the visible landscape, provides something that cannot be completely understood: the dream image of the doll. The sea is a place beyond reach, a place that can bring to human understanding only a sense of where and how opposites meet. In "Road Ends at Tahola" the presence of the sea underlies both the romantic urge for "somewhere *mare nostro*" and the shame and danger two lovers face in themselves and their world while on the beach.

> My nostrils tell me: somewhere *mare nostro.*
> Here the wolf-fish hides his lumpy face in shame.
> Pines lean east and groan. Odors of a booze
> that's contraband, are smuggled in by storms.
> Our booze is legal Irish and our eyes
> develop felons in the endless spray.
> *Mare nostro* somewhere, and eternity's
> a law, not a felony like here.
> . . . .
> I can't say *mare nostro.* Groaning pines
> won't harm you, leaning east on galaxies.

I know I'm stone. My voice is ugly.
A kelp bed is a rotten place to hide.
Listen. Hear the booming. See the gleam,
the stars that once were fish and died.
We kiss between the fire and the ocean.
In the morning we will start another stare
across the gray. Nowhere *mare nostro.*
Don't claim it and the sea belongs to you. (p. 26)

The sea is as dangerous and booming as it is beautiful. It is never just the lovers' sea; it is also something foreign, bringing in contraband, a felon, a derelict—foreign in its beauty as it brings in the phosphorus of dead fish on its waves: "See the gleam, / the stars that once were fish and died." As the sea is alien, it moves with that same energy of shame and anger that the speaker feels in the third stanza as he remembers a scene from a film by Ingmar Bergman. In the scene the clown and his naked woman, both terribly vulnerable, survive; what Hugo imagines immediately afterward is the shame of the ugly wolf-fish, reduced so low that he is beneath scorn.[4] The sea is so powerful and all-encompassing that "Whatever gave us pride . . . dies."

Shame, anger, alienation—those opposites of love, of "somewhere *mare nostro*"—come welling out of the sea, making it impossible to claim it as a single emotional landscape. In fact, by the fourth stanza the speaker sinks to the level of the wolf-fish: "My voice is ugly. / A kelp bed is a rotten place to hide." And yet with all this booming and anger comes the work of hope, the minimal courage in the final lines: "In the morning we will start another stare / across the gray. Nowhere *mare nostro.* / Don't claim it and the sea belongs to you." There are few lines of poetry so "Hugo" as this last. No matter if the kiss releases the lovers to give up their ideal *mare nostro* or if the giving up of the ideal enables the kiss; the emotional claim, withdrawn, in fact becomes more secure. By giving up to the sea, to its presence and passions, instead of abstracting it to an ideal, a fantasy, the fantastic becomes an emotional reality: the sea that "belongs to you" has become *mare nostro,* "our sea."

If the river provides the direction away from the failures of human love, the sea provides a place where the fundamentals of love can begin and can be claimed. A vast image, the sea suggests the permanence of feeling, a place where human emotions and conflicts can come together. Both river and sea are fundamentally images of distance: there is mystery in them. There is a similar mystery in wind, as Hugo notices in "Plunking the Skagit": "It's mystery, not wind, the men / endure." The overcoming of distance, the recognizing of distant landmarks or waves or outcroppings of stone (as in "Cape Nothing") or towns or histories or failed homes—these dynamics of recognition rest at the heart of Hugo's use of physical landscape and make up the geography of feeling. As the patterns of imagery and emotion work themselves out in each poem, they work toward a human presence that must be seen just in back of the landscape, that must be felt and crawled toward dimly in the reading of the poem.

In the background of each landscape is the town, as if the poem were something like a medieval painting with the spires of a church just visible over the trees. Like the early landscape artists, Dürer or Brueghel, Hugo feels his way toward the town; it is for him, as for them, essentially a religious or emotional idea. In medieval and Renaissance paintings, the town, dominated by the cathedral spire, represented an iconography that went back to Augustine's *City of God*. In Hugo's poems the iconography is not as profound but just as essential: the town represents the presence of human community that could work, that could satisfy emotional needs.

The huntsmen in Brueghel's *Winter Scene* head toward a town below them that is small and distant, although just at the base of the hill. In Hugo's poems that town may be a shack, a sign, something a friend or lover has said; it may be a bar, a tavern that has been destroyed, or it may be graves or other signs of human loss. Whatever fragment of human community stumbles into Hugo's lush natural landscape, its presence leans the poem away from the physical landscape and toward that fragmentary community behind the poem. The signs in his poems, then, are just as mysterious and as sacred as the town was symbolic to the early landscape painters. Presumably the medieval iconography of the town was an emotionally charged symbol. In Hugo's poems we are not able to claim that logical and constant meaning a symbol would present; we are only able to feel the presence of the same power that an image of human sympathy and community still has in the imagination.

Sometimes the power of that image lies in its negation. In the middle of these regional poems of *Death of the Kapowsin Tavern,* Hugo has placed a poem that seems to have nothing to do with the Northwest: "Mission to Linz," one of the finest poems written about World War II (Hugo's service as a bombardier stationed in Italy is discussed in Chapter 6), and perhaps one of the finest poems written about flying. In that poem the wind and its extended distances of atmosphere from human community become hauntingly enticing.

> It must seem weird, incommunicable
> the desire for ozone
> cold and the unremembered terrible.
> . . . .
> Nothing is heard in the north,
> and the northern temperatures grow cold with the height.
> There is the stark crack of voice
> taking oxygen checks and the sharp static answers.
> You are beyond birds, a season called summer.
> There are places away from the world where the air is always winter.
> Nothing is heard in the north. (p. 29)

The poetry is graceful, its rhythm of line extending to the breathtaking and then withdrawing to refrain. The poem never leaves this grace; it is never caught in the thick of conflicting emotions, allegiances, or syntax—those marks of style so consistent throughout most of Hugo's work, especially in his second book. The poem's vision is marked by detachment, by an eerie feeling of dislocation, of being in a place where nothing is heard as everything becomes sight: "Now you / who, so high, can only see / the puff like a penny dropped in dust / at your toe on a country road" (p. 30). As a hymn to flight and machine, the poem has no equal. But for all its grace and cool terror, there is a yearning in this thin air for the ground, for those thick confusions of feeling there.

> The engines sing you to the home of men,
> the earth, and think of it; its brownness,
> its solidity, its greenness. You can build
> warm rooms on its hills, love on it,
> and if you die on it you remain
> long enough to be lied about, buried in it. (p. 32)

When the poem turns toward earth, its phrases turn toward each other, and the syntax gains some complexity as the lines lose some of the eerie grace of the earlier parts of the poem. When it touches down to earth—as if poem were airplane—it touches three times quickly: brownness, solidity, greenness. And then there are things to be done: "You can build . . . "

Again, it is the human community waiting in the distance that makes the landscape of the poem point toward the mystery of human feelings. The wind and distance of "Mission to Linz" will become governing images in some important poems of Hugo's fourth book, *The Lady in Kicking Horse Reservoir* (1973). Here, however, the poem adds another dimension to the geography of feeling in Hugo's regional poems. Unseen and powerful, with changeable direction and grace, the wind, the sky, and the distances inherent in those images provide another area of space alongside the enduring direction of rivers and the felt but unknowable sea. All these charged images supply the mainstays of Hugo's elemental vision, a vision in which the energies of the natural landscape can be seen to parallel the powerful, unseen, and changeable energies of the human psyche. The other remaining area of Hugo's geography is that place beside the sea or the river, beneath the sky, where the natural and psychological come together with the political and the economic: the town.

The final section of *Death of the Kapowsin Tavern* is entitled "Limited Access," as if to imply that access to understanding the makeup of human community is limited and tenuous. The poems are mostly about towns or places such as Port Townsend, Coupeville, and Fort Casey, or about people like "Eileen," "a Northern Woman," or "The Squatter on Company Land." Both types of poems concern the vulnerable, the failures, those about to be destroyed by the new and the successful. The overall effect of this group of poems is scattered: the town is not yet completely outlined, is not yet a charged or guiding image like the sea or the river—and it will not become so until *The Lady in Kicking Horse Reservoir*.

Fittingly, as if the town is just coming into full view, two of the poems in the last section of *Death of the Kapowsin Tavern* are about roads: "The Blond Road" and "What the Brand New Freeway Won't Go By." The first of these gives us some indication of the connection, as in "Mission to Linz," between distance, road, and wind and how traveling a road provides a powerful metaphor for transformation. The blond road is a river that "dips and climbs but never bends"; it divides the landscape between "miles of high grass" and "the sea reflecting tone of a wild day." With this elemental confrontation, the road is no way out, cannot be cheated, cannot release its grim fields and birds that are "always stone." Unlike the river that bends and finds direction as an easy way that lies before it, the blond road goes straight, divides everything, and turns brown and dull with the work of sun and wind. The two lovers in the poem feel the wind and "claw each other orange"; it is as if the road—unbending, thought-centered human direction—provides the occasion for all the loss.

If "The Blond Road" shows us a too-straight human swath cut through the wilderness, "What the Brand New Freeway Won't Go By" shows the hardships of unbending human logic in the city: in an "ugly brick hotel," a second-floor roomer, "in underwear, unshaven, fries a meal":

> To live here you should be a friend of rain,
> and fifty with a bad job on the freights,
> knowing the freeway soon will siphon
> this remaining world away
> and you die unseen among your photos—
> swimmers laughing but the day remembered cold. (p. 37)

The image of the hotel and the roomer with his bad job grows from a deep anger at the way progress, that unflinching direction of urban renewal, can "siphon / the remaining world away." The next stanza suggests suicide: "Rooms have gas. The place was in the papers. / Police have issued statements about cancer / and the case is closed"—all with that calm indifference of power that ignores the emotional realities of the poor and their neighborhoods. A similar anger at complacent, single-minded political power arises in "Pike Place Market" as that famous Seattle landmark—a place where "it is assumed all things have value" (p. 52)—was threatened with urban renewal. The complexities of human feelings are at the heart of the human community; as "Brand New Freeway" ends, the intolerance of single-minded, unbending progress metamorphoses into a newer political code: "we are older too—live here— / we'll never treat you badly again." It cannot be believed: the anger resonant in the poem is too deep; the road, the freeway of human progress, is too straight.

The poor, the old, the people who do not fit easily into the structures of the political and economic community—Hugo sees these people first in any town, and this is where he begins his map. "The Squatter on Company Land," another outcast like the roomer in "Brand New Freeway," is not, however, seen with the same kind of sympathy. An employee of the company, the speaker thinks of "our land" and begins to explain the eviction away:

> We had to get him off, the dirty elf—
> wild hair and always screaming at his wife
> and due to own our land in two more years—
> a mud flat point along the river
> where we planned our hammer shop.
> Him, his thousand rabbits, the lone goat
> tied to his bed, his menial wife: all out. (p. 49)

Again the poor—here, the literally dispossessed—are the central concern of the poem, an important one for the way it brings the dispossessed and the respectable together. Although he worked for the Boeing Company, Hugo is not the speaker; rather, it is his boss, a man Hugo designates as "C," a thoroughgoing company man:

> As C. talked, a picture started to form. The squatter, evidently insane, frightened, even terrified at the idea of moving. The woman, totally dependent, probably masochistic, maybe subnormal. What also fascinated me was C. I could sense his complicated feelings. He was troubled by the man even after all these years because the man was so irredeemably outside any values my boss assumed normal. He was regretful because he had been assigned to the eviction and so was partly responsible for throwing those sad people out. And secretly, even to himself secretly, he admired, almost envied, the man because the man was not civilized, and I suppose basically no one wants to be civilized. In his own way, C. was civilized and at what price.[5]

The man in the shack in "Hideout" is as wild in his dreams as the squatter is wild in his appearance. The two poems stand as complements, but the second is far more complicated as it seeks to present not a figure for the imagination but the conflicts of feeling, economics, lack of sympathy, and a secret envy, all of which play a part in what we call progress. In "Graves at Coupeville" Hugo says, "Men are islands," fragments within themselves, as in the case of "C." Hugo's poetry maps out a region where those visible islands connect in an unseen geography: out of isolation can come a complicated sympathy; out of desolation and loss can arise a form of love.

That urge in Hugo's poems to preserve, to keep the landscape, whether rural or urban, as it is, points to the great value our unplanned, undirected human creations have. In a sense, human communities cannot be planned; they grow out of the reactions and connections made from the stuff of human feelings, however limited, prejudiced, or destructive those connections or reactions might be. Those connections of human feeling are as natural as wilderness landscape, Hugo seems to say, and when, in the title poem of the book, a place where such connections lived and flourished has been destroyed, the loss is deep.

> I can't ridge it back again from char.
> Not one board left. Only as a cat explores
> and shattered glass smoked black and strung
> about from the explosion I believe
> in the reports. The white school up for sale
> for years, most homes abandoned to the rocks
> of passing boys—the fire, helped by wind
> that blew the neon out six years before,
> simply ended lots of ending.
> . . . .
> Nothing dies as slowly as a scene.
> The dusty jukebox cracking through
> the cackle of a beered-up crone—
> wagered wine—sudden need to dance—
> these remain in the black debris.
> Although I know in time the lake will send
> wind black enough to blow it all away. (p. 55)

The poem is an elegy for a bar. Although not exactly in the same tradition as "Lycidas," the elegiac mode is just as powerful, considering how often in American society the connections of human sympathy have failed. The tavern at Lake Kapowsin, some forty miles from Seattle where Hugo and his first wife went each May to fish, was a place where they "ate hamburgers and drank beer late into the night, playing old tunes on the jukebox and chatting with the locals."[6] It was a place, then, where elemental human feelings of sympathy survived for Hugo. By careful examination of the debris he lets the reader feel the value of each board. It is a fitting conclusion to a book that slowly, painstakingly, points out how the natural landscape leads to the human, and how human community, so fragile in the face of natural forces, is even more fragile, ephemeral, and easily lost.

The ultimate region of Hugo's poetry, then, is contained not in the Northwest rain forest or on the ocean shore, but in the town, in the image of human community. The progression is inevitable, as trout streams lead eventually to navigable rivers. The squatter, the hideout, the people in that good tavern with their beer and the old tunes on the jukebox—each wants to hold on to and cannot have a place of enduring connection, a place to feel most whole and alive. Rather than some dream of wildness, for Hugo that place must be found—indeed, it must be made out of—a town that he remembers: where children get hurt early or are left too much alone; where human needs are unmet and depend too often on a lack of money; where the impulses of emotion are hard to control; but where, after all, human connections are essential to survival. In that town, boys were taught to be tough and to die by various ritual ways: by drink, violence, overwork, or alone. Toughness inheres in that town, even as lush natural beauty surrounds it. In understanding the limits of toughness, Hugo touches the turning point of his poetry and of his life.

6

"License for Defeat": The Turning Point

The most important single poem in Richard Hugo's career may be an often overlooked poem from his third book, *Good Luck in Cracked Italian* (1969): "Spinazzola: *Quella Cantina Là.*" If he had not written "Spinazzola," Hugo might never have written "Degrees of Gray in Philipsburg" and might not have become known as a poet who figures in language that current of tension, that dull explosive anger that runs through the way most American men have conventionally seen themselves and that appears over and over in poems such as "Ovando," "Silver Star," "Invasion North," "Cattails," and "The Milltown Union Bar." Hugo's West is a place obsessed with violence; his own wrestling with the everlasting moral question of violence, which Robert Warshow saw as the essence of the film western,[1] began in a field of grass in Italy during World War II when Hugo was a bombardier—scared, lost, bored, and haunted by violence and fear.

Like many youngsters during the thirties, Hugo grew up bored and poor. He spent as much time as he could in the dark of George Shrigley's White Center Theatre, watching tough male characters—Ken Maynard's athletic cowboys, James Cagney's explosive gangsters, Humphrey Bogart's Rick, and Clark Gable's Rhett —create an image of American men as capable, unflinching, unidealistic, surviving, and alone. The image coincided with Hugo's experience of what it meant to be a man. He knew what it meant to survive—most of the poor do—and the tough image corresponded to his experiences growing up in his grandparents' house, where feelings were seldom expressed and physical touching was infrequent. Hugo did not have much physical affection when he was young; in one essay he states that he had never seen a man kiss a woman until he saw it in a movie.[2]

When Hugo went to war, therefore, he carried with him what many Americans carried: a clear-cut image of masculine toughness and the expectation that he should measure up. The difference for Hugo was the depth of his attachment to that image and the depth of his fear that he might fail. But the image was not the truth: the soldiers were more often boys, not men, and their boys' feelings were out of place in that image of toughness they had seen on the screen. The idea was to be a Bogart, or at least to be as self-composed, competent, and unflappable as a Herbert Marshall.[3] Hugo wanted to be like such men, but his experience of war led him to turn his attention away from such images and toward the strengths he could find in himself, strengths he began to recognize in a field of grass outside Spinazzola, a town he had reached by mistake one day while on leave. What occurred in that field during the war led Hugo back to Italy in 1963, where, in writing the poems of his third book, the tough masculine stance of such earlier poems as "Duwamish" and "Duwamish Head" began to fade as Hugo found in himself the more enduring toughness of the human heart.

Good Luck in Cracked Italian shows us both the beginning of a softening in the voice of Hugo's poems and the event in his life that led to this change. The waste of war and the impoverishment of a war-torn country prepare us to see that the power of feelings is stronger, ultimately more capable of sustaining survival, than toughness. The strong man in Hugo's third book is the man who feels, who knows the value of sympathy, of shared experiences and emotional ties with people whose lives are no better or worse than his own. For Hugo, Italy is a place "where all doors open in"[4] to a world where the only common language is human feeling. In such a place a man gains strength from his ability to face defeats not as desolation but as occasions where feelings can be shared.

In the first section of *Good Luck in Cracked Italian,* Hugo's attention is drawn to the violence throughout history that has become part of the Italian landscape. In a small poem about a small painting, "S. Miniato: One by Aretino," that landscape becomes a Hugo landscape. The poem focuses on the masculine toughness that is the book's central concern. The painting compares two male images, a saint "retrieving the hoe" so that "Farms will prosper now" and a hunter:

> to the right
> a hunter chases two deer, whatever they were—
> hounds after hare—up a bare hill
> that breaks at the apex, spilling what's male,
> animal, hunger or hate from the world.
> Other males persist. One beats his ass
> in the ass with a stick. Another, not here
> but in the chapel next door, dabs at his eyes
> while Latin locks him down tight.
> A peasant hacks at stone he must rent
> and must hack until rain turns it to soil. (p. 19)

The roles are either powerful or powerless: from the powerful spiritual forces of the saint and the physical force of the hunter to the internal violence of the man in the chapel locked "down tight" and of the peasant locked to the stone he must farm. One man, however, and "most male of all," is a fisherman who has little to do with these other men. He is "focused mad as a lover on trout" and "is central" in the painting (and in the poem); he offers the only clear-sighted male image in the poem.

> His adamant eye and red robe mean
> the fisherman knows retrieving a tool
> is no miracle, not when the lake
> has no depth and your halo is gold. (p. 20)

The foundation of the masculine tenderness that develops in Hugo's third book is expressed not through saints or hunters but through the interior power of a fisherman concentrating "mad as a lover" and paying no attention to the glory and strength of men in the world. Hugo's identification of the hunter with "spilling what's male" seems to identify "male" with "animal, hunger or hate," until we see the fisherman as "most male of all." While the hunter's energy is spilled as he finds food, the fisherman's is concentrated along lines that fit easily into natural surroundings: "the pole and dark trout / curling through green really matter." The implication is that the other side of the hunter's violence is an internal energy, a madness called love that concentrates and controls energy, instead of spilling it, in order to survive.

"S. Miniato: One by Aretino," though seemingly an inconsequential set piece, has deep connections to Hugo's concern for what is masculine in *Good Luck in Cracked Italian.* It indicates the importance of the fisherman image in Hugo's understanding of himself; in the context of this book of poems generated by memories of war, the poem shows the greater permanence of the private strength of feeling. The hunter, indulging in violence, is more properly phallic than masculine. That one aspect of masculine sensibility, though not the whole of masculine feeling, is at the heart of the experience of war: survival in the context of waste, physical power in the shadow of death. What tenderness Mailer's Gallagher or Croft in *The Naked and the Dead* can muster, however, is not as deep as that in Hugo's personae in *Good Luck in Cracked Italian.* Mailer's men survive, but Hugo's survive with a strength of compassion that is remarkably innocent as they return to the scene of waste to see if the place still exists, to make the experience finished at last and whole. This sense of the emotional defeat that war causes in every part of society it touches—in the victors as well as in the defeated and the occupied—enables Hugo to look at the waste of war straightforwardly, without political comment, religious appeal, intellectual abstraction, or moral intent. His response is to point to the simple emotional fact that is everywhere present in his book, as in these lines from "G.I. Graves in Tuscany": war is loss, no matter which side wins.

> The loss is so damn gross. I remember
> a washtub of salad in basic, blacktop acres
> of men waiting to march, passing three hours
> of bombers, en route to Vienna, and bombing
> and passing two hours of planes, coming back.
> Numbers are vulgar. If I stayed
> I'd count the men in years of probable loss. (p. 29)

The sardonic insurance adjustor's eye in the last line of the stanza is dark humor indeed. The loss is large, democratic, and as mechanized as basic training or the fleets of bombers passing each other to and from Vienna. Everything is numbers and process. Success in World War II came through an American machine that won battles with an energy that seemed ceaseless: "Coming from a country where we never fail, / grow old or die, but simply move unnoticed / to the next cold town." Hugo does not deny or dispute this image of America; it existed powerfully in him as a boy and as a soldier and still exists in him today. Ever since his earliest poems, however, he has been aware of the underside of American life, a side that is neither powerful nor ceaseless. In "A View from Cortona" he is aware of how that side of life remained with G.I.s.

> Remember? No view? Long nights at home.
> Nothing to do. Radio down so the old
> could sleep. Staring at walls and trying
> to write. Brown sugar on bread
> and your life that might go on forever. (p. 31)

Only twice in the poem are the lines unbroken by quick shifts of thought, by tense speech. For decades the American idea of a man has included control of any emotional expressiveness: a man keeps his feelings to himself and does his job. But such holding tight is an emotional defeat, an abandonment of emotional needs, and that personal defeat is the complement of the images of physical defeat and waste in war. Such knowledge was the insight Hugo gained in Italy and reinforced when he returned there in 1963. Perhaps that knowledge came because he was in the heart of a condition of anger—a war—and instinctively he recoiled from that angry part of his earliest experiences; perhaps it was brought about simply by the warmth of Italian peasants such as the Vitolo family of Maratea.

What Hugo begins to find in Italy is the way out of sadness: the strength of emotion that peasants anywhere in the world find to keep themselves steady in the face of impoverishment and need. In contrast to the silent and bored people he remembers from White Center are the Italian peasants who show him how to cry. In "Maratea Porto: Saying Goodbye to the Vitolos," Hugo makes clear the difference between his life as an American soldier and his present life.

> Should I say my people? I turned stone
> against them long ago. The soupy pictures
> of Christ, the crosses drugstores sell.
> Cruelty that often goes with stone
> makes men virginal or wrong. (p. 62)

Though Italian, the people Hugo "turned stone against" while a soldier bear no little resemblance to those earlier Americans from White Center with other sentimentalities and cruelties in their lives. Whatever their location, they are "defeated people" and are therefore special to Hugo. By sharing their feelings he has found the other side of that condition of stone, that American, masculine, tough silence where feelings are constrained.

> I forgot my people long ago, reduced them
> to some words and wrote their stones away.
> Sea slants off their tears with light
> no one should forget. I'm still American.
> See, afraid to cry. How awkwardly I lean
> to kiss them and how suddenly I say
> good luck in cracked Italian as I turn my face. (p. 62)

The ending of this poem, which provides the title for the book, shows a face turned from stone to human feeling. The tears are as much Italian as they are American: they are human and freely given.

Throughout *Good Luck in Cracked Italian,* the poems present an energy that opens tough silence to feeling. This turning is presented in its full context in "Spinazzola: *Quella Cantina Là,"* in a spontaneous moment when the structures of a world at war fall away as the poet becomes reliant on interior strengths rather than on exterior force or power. A field of grass outside Spinazzola is where World War II stopped for Hugo.

> A field of wind gave license for defeat.
> I can't explain. The grass bent. The wind
> seemed full of men but without hate or fame.
> I was farther than that farm where the road
> slants off to nowhere, and the field I'm sure
> is in this wine or that man's voice. The man
> and this canteen were also here
> twenty years ago and just as old. (p. 43)

The two strains of the book—Italy defeated and surviving and Hugo the Bogart-tough victor with an emotional defeat inside himself—come together in a field of wind: an image at once turbulent with possible terror from the air war and full of the tenacity of natural processes, self-regeneration, and renewal. Although he says "I can't explain," the image speaks for him: the heavy wind, "full of men but without hate or fame," defeats the field of grass much as Hugo's bombers brought defeat to other places on the ground. But the wind itself is also defeated, not by some counterforce, but by "license" from the natural processes of life—as natural as men drinking in a cantina, as natural and old as something the poet calls "home."

It is not a specific home, not White Center or childhood nostalgia or obsession; on that account the poem is clear. The field leads Hugo off the road that "slants to nowhere" and toward "this wine or that man's voice," the cantina and the old man who runs it. An old man in a bar, then—as in "Degrees of Gray in Philipsburg"—provides the impetus for a moment of self-regeneration, a coming home to one's own self, to a world one accepts because one also accepts one's self. This was the world that Hugo had wanted to destroy as a bombardier and as a young boy who wanted to be tough.

> Hate for me was dirt until I woke up
> five miles over Villach in a smoke
> that shook my tongue. Here, by accident,
> the wrong truck, I came back to the world.
> This canteen is house-old. (p. 43)

To reach a sense of home in the middle of a war requires a bit of indirection. For a soldier to forget the war, he must be a little less a soldier; he must make a mistake that shows he is only human. Hugo's mistake was taking a wrong turn while hitchhiking to Cerignola to see a friend. Taking rides on various trucks from one town to the next, he got into one loudly rumbling ammunition truck and yelled "Cerignola" to the driver; he thought he heard "Cerignola" in return, but the driver took him to Spinazzola, miles off course.[5] This breakdown of communication in an ammunition truck carried some special irony for Hugo: his missed direction as a hitchhiker parallels his experiences as a bombardier. He was, in his own words, one of the "world's worst," one day even missing the entire Brenner Pass, thirteen miles wide.[6] Missed targets during the war were not, therefore, unusual for Hugo. But this time the missed target landed him in a field of grass that became for him the greatest target during his years as a soldier.

> After I'd walked for well over an hour, I sat down to rest by a field of grass. I was tired, dreamy, the way we got without enough sleep, and I watched the wind move uphill across it, wave after wave. The music and motion hypnotized me. The longer the grass moved, the more passive I became. Had I walked this road when I was a child? Something seemed familiar. I didn't care about getting back to the base now. I didn't care about the war. I was not part of it anymore. Trucks went by and I didn't even turn to watch them, let alone thumb a ride. Let them go. I would sit here forever and watch the grass bend in the wind and the war would

> end without me and I would not go home, ever. Years later in psychoanalysis I would recount this and the doctor would explain it as a moment of surrender, when my system could no longer take the fear and the pressure and I gave up. If that's how to lose a war, we were wrong to have ever won one.[7]

The field of wind is where the war ends with an acceptance of what is given, whether victory or failure, mistake or pain. In the poem there is a crucial identification of things natural as wealthy, supportive, and honest, and of things man-made—including that signal word for Hugo, *home*—as cheap, absurd, and lonely.

> Olive leaves were silver I could spend.
> Say wind I can't explain. That field is vital
> and the Adriatic warm. Don't our real friends
> tell us when we fail? Don't honest fields
> reveal us in their winds? Planes and men
> once tumbled but the war went on absurd.
> I can't explain the wine. This crude bench
> and rough table and that flaking plaster—
> most of all the long nights make this home. (pp. 43–44)

There is a crucial slant rhyme in the repetitions of "wind" and "wine"; if the wind defeats grass—and by extension the airborne bombers defeat human beings, including Hugo—then the wine not only provides an occasion for placing the memory ("the field is east / toward the Adriatic from my wine") but also acts to make memory alive and vital, not repressed or forgotten. The memory is brought back in all its terrible impact, demanding that it be made a part of the peaceful present: "the man / will serve me wine until a bomber fleet / lost twenty years ago comes droning home."

Despite the repeated phrase "I can't explain," the poem is a clear effort to make sense of the war and its losses, to bring the horrors of war and the blessings of a peaceful cantina together in some sense of wholeness. Hugo renders this wholeness by juxtaposing the fierce and ghostly destruction of war as wind next to the durable, old, neglected, and—for the early Hugo—the repressive energies of earthbound life at peace. It must be remembered that Hugo went to war primarily to leave White Center. Combining these two opposites is the image of clouds; dangers to the pilot, they are gifts to those at peace.

> Clouds are definite types. High one, cirrus.
> Cumulus, big fluffy kind, and if with rain,

also nimbus. Don't fly into them.
I can't explain. Somewhere in a gray ball
wind is killing. I forget the stratus
high and thin. I forget my field
of wind. . . .

I'll find the field. I'll go feeble down
the road strung gray like spoiled wine
in the sky. A sky too clear of cloud
is fatal. Trust the nimbus. Trust dark clouds
to rain. I can't explain the sun. The man
will serve me wine until a bomber fleet
lost twenty years comes droning home.

I can't explain. Outside, on the road
that leaves the town reluctantly,
way out the road's a field of wind. (p. 44)

Whatever appears beautiful, powerful, dominant—whether clouds or wind or sun—has, somewhere inside it, "killing." What appears feeble, old, spoiled, going nowhere ("The road strung gray"), or dark and terrible like nimbus clouds gives rain, gives the missing home. The opposites have been at war through the whole poem and are hardly resolved into a neat synthesis or hierarchy. Such a work of the intellect is precisely what is defeated by the power of the experience in the field of grass, by the suggestiveness of the image. In its suggestiveness, however, lies the acceptance of the war, the internal war of opposites, the field of wind and its "license for defeat" that brings a crucial awakening to what it means to live, to feel as a human being.

The final section of *Good Luck in Cracked Italian* begins with a parallel to "Spinazzola: *Quella Cantina Là*"—"South Italy, Remote and Stone." The poem takes a complex of feelings—wonder, regret, loss, and an eerie sense of victory from cherishing one's defeats—and shows how it is deeply tied to the way a poor man feels about himself and his ability to love. Beginning with "The enemy's not poverty. It's wind," the poem has, as have many of Hugo's poems, a clear evocation of the angry love of despair that is so integral a part of being poor.

Your hoe and wind
have fought this stone forever and lost.

. . . Your hands
are not abandoned, and the harsh length

of each day forces you to love whatever is—
a screaming wife, a child who has stared
from birth. (p. 73)

As in "Spinazzola," wind is enemy. The figure in the background of "South Italy" is also a war, although this one is for simple economic survival. This poem helps to clarify the earlier poem; indeed, Hugo's entire wrestling with what it means to be masculine is rendered in a peculiar sexual fantasy.

Even your tongue is hard. Syllables whip
and demons, always deposited cruel
in the prettiest unmarried girl,
must be whipped by the priest into air
where bells can drive them to rivers. Or she
will be sent out forever, alone on the roads
with her madness, no chance to be saved
by a prince or kind ox. And so on, a test
of your love. Only the ugly survive. (p. 73)

The poem suggests, with that peculiar logic of peasant folktales, that in the austere poverty of southern Italy, the poor lose their beauty early in order to survive. The only way to survive that "test / of your love" that poverty gives is through the death of pleasure.

The fantasy also has deeper connections in Hugo's life and in his poetic career. We have reached a level of the imagination that may be the center of Hugo's poetic career, in impulse if not in theme. Whether in his early poems or in the Montana poems of *The Lady in Kicking Horse Reservoir*, crucial to Hugo's imagination are images of the old, the neglected, the desolate, and the self-destructive—those unglamorous and ugly images that test one's attention, sympathy, and love. Such tests of emotion are important to Hugo, rooted as they are in that original sense of deprivation brought on by the neglect he felt as a child. After the war, Hugo came home from thirty-five bomber missions, "drinking heavily to ward off vivid anxiety dreams that came any night I went to bed sober. I had never had a woman."[8] The external war over, an interior war, his feeling of sexual inadequacy, still had to be won. He went to the University of Washington on the G. I. Bill, studied under Roethke and began that slow, interior drama that the writing of poems has meant for all our best poets. The fantasy of the whipped girl provides a clue to his coming to terms with those fears. Whipped by the priest for unseen demons, the pretty girl is an image of those pleasures denied the peasant with his hoe and Hugo with his bombs—denied by the masculine impulse for rules and glory, whether spiritual or physical. At the height of such measures of strength and devotion—such tests "of your love"—is the effort to see what it is like to survive. In a sense that effort is what war is all about and what the economic war called poverty involves in a person's psychological makeup. Survival, in both cases, is all there is. Any surviving human feeling says, "only the ugly survive."

But, in Hugo, there is more than survival, more than that ultimate masculine test in the manner of a Hemingway or a Mailer. Simply put, as in "Spinazzola," there are human feelings that are at least as important as physical survival, that are as natural and spontaneous as a man in a cantina or a field of grass that needs rain. Put in the greater context of Hugo's life, there are sexual feelings that are not absorbed by an obsession with inadequacy, inferiority, or doubt. It is in those feelings—not "a test / of your love"—that Hugo finds what is "most male of all."

The field of grass that "gave license for defeat" became for Hugo an important place in his coming to maturity. He felt drawn back to it, and, once back in Italy, the trip to Spinazzola became as important as anything he did while he was there. Perhaps he did not realize it when he was a twenty-year-old bombardier, but that field opened a door into his psyche that brought him to a new strength of feeling, an acceptance of himself. It might have been an unthinkably hard process without this unconscious turning away from the tough, masculine image of Bogart to the calm, supportive field of grass where no war could be felt and no sense of degrading home could touch him. In a field of grass the world became clear, if just for a moment, before the "world of denial and self-possession"[9] became dominant again.

7

"Only the Eternal Nothing of Space": A Westerner's West

Any understanding of Richard Hugo's West must begin back in the 1890s when three easterners invented the West that has played such an important part in American culture in this century. The West of Frederic Remington, Theodore Roosevelt, and Owen Wister grew out of the expansive energies of easterners who made, consciously or unconsciously, a myth of American toughness overcoming the vast potentialities of the West's natural resources. Wister wanted his novel, *The Virginian* (1902), to become a national fable, uniting North and South, East and West; what he created was a male hero who would have few feelings, few human connections, and few needs; who would do his job in the wilderness successfully and make that wilderness accessible to eastern expansion. Since Wister, the popular understanding of the West as a region has always been tied to that male hero: the tough man and the vast landscape are as inseparable as cowboy and horse. Perhaps, as G. Edward White maintains,[1] Wister merely gave voice to an expression of popular temperament; whatever the root of the myth, its making bears Wister's name. His Virginian has given us generations of men who have feared feelings, who have been quick to fear aliens of whatever color and to deny their need for human contact for fear of being less than masculine; who have valued the physical above the emotional, the big above the necessary, the tough above the humane.

It is, therefore, a short jump from the laconic toughness of Wister's Virginian to that of the several incarnations of John Wayne, and it is only fitting that, having explored his own confrontations with the limits of male toughness in *Good Luck in Cracked Italian,* Hugo should turn to the American landscape so identified with those tough, emotionless, cowboy figures who inspired American fighting men during World War II. For Hugo, taking an initially similar tough-guy stance and living in a similar landscape as the Virginian, has given us, in *The Lady in Kicking Horse Reservoir* (1973), a poetry that works against this pervasive myth of the West and the western hero. Unlike Wister, Remington, and Roosevelt, Hugo is a born westerner who owes nothing to eastern expansion or to that eastern establishment from which the three makers of the West came: nothing, perhaps, except his childhood poverty during the Depression. Where Wister and his friends found beautiful solitude and toughness, Hugo takes that same landscape and expresses the need for human community, for the necessary presence of human feelings to keep a man sane and whole. He has seen the remains of those expansionist energies that Roosevelt and Wister applauded, and, as in "Helena, Where Homes Go Mad," he has seen them as hardly heroic.

> Cries of gold or men about to hang
> trail off where the brewery failed
> on West Main. Greedy fingernails
> ripped the ground up inch by inch
> down the gulch until the hope of gold
> ran out and men began to pimp.
> Gold is where you find it in the groin.[2]

If Hugo had seen that early Wyoming settlement of Medicine Bow, from which the Virginian rides off into the mountains, he would have made far more of the bottles and tin cans outside the saloons. That trash was part of the human presence, indicative of the needs and dreams of the people who lived there. For Hugo, the West is a dream that does not belong to those who would—and do—exploit its land; the dreams of the West are those failed hopes of the poor and the greedy and the wishful who went there to find a better life. To Hugo, the American dream is not the unlimited possibilities of expansion but the ache of need. His landscape, vast and rugged, is a place where a man's possibilities are limited by that ruggedness and by its associated weathers and winds that beat against human enterprise and make those connections between people that much more important.

In Montana, then, Hugo's West is born, big and "thick as a fist / or blunt instrument" where "long roads weave and curve / red veins of rage" ("A Map of Montana in Italy," p. 3). There is less a romance of landscape than an education in the realities of space, a sensitivity to the effects that wind and weather can have on human lives and settlements, as in "Camas Prairie School":

> The schoolbell rings and dies before
> the first clang can reach the nearest farm.
> With land this open, wind is blowing
> where there is no wind. The gym's so ugly
> victory leaves you empty as defeat,
> and following whatever game
> you will remember lost, you run fast
> slow miles home through grain
> knowing you'll arrive too late
> to eat or find the lights on. (p. 68)

In such a place, humanity barely survives. "With land this open, wind is blowing / where there is no wind": the line could have been part of a novel by Wright Morris or Larry McMurtry, so central is it to the contemporary experience of the West, so separated from the myth of the West and western expansion. What is open is not always free; there are things unseen in the widest vista. Those shifting capacities of wind, from breeze to dust storm, become a governing metaphor in Hugo's poetry, and lead—as in *Ceremony in Lone Tree* or *The Last Picture Show*—to the past and what is left of it in the interiors of buildings and the memories of human lives that have survived. "What endures," Hugo says in "Ghosts at Garnet," "is what we have neglected, / tins that fed them, rusting now in piles" (p. 65). What Wister neglected in his push for a western myth is, in fact, what has endured: those human lives and remnants, those human connections among the poor and the greedy who moved west out of need.

The physical and emotional needs of a man characterize Hugo's western hero. The speakers in his poems do not have the qualities that Robert Warshow, in "The Westerner," sees as being typical of the many western film heroes who owed their existence to *The Virginian:* Hugo's speakers are not gentlemen or men of leisure, free to roam because they possess a wealth of inner or external resources.[3] Hugo's people are the dispossessed; they wander not for adventure but for some better life that lies, all too often, as in "Ovando," only at the bottom of a drink.

> Dust that clouded your last drunken dream

thickens in this degrading wind.
Sage uproots and rolls and ducks streak over
every day, reconnaissance, one inch
out of range. If you need meat, resort
to money, never charm. (p. 59)

Ovando is just one of the many Montana towns that dot Hugo's western landscape. The towns are often haunted by the ghosts of film or Zane Grey westerns: "The weak ghost / of a horse demands false fronts, lean poles / to tie your wife to, automatic love / you and the town hate to make to clouds" (p. 59). The West of bars and tough guys does survive in poems such as "The Only Bar in Dixon," "The Milltown Union Bar," "Dixon," and "Phoning from Sweathouse Creek." The bar is the center of the Hugo town; it is the place where those unattainable dreams meet the all-too-evident reality, where love and violence meet and regulars and strangers can share an intimacy isolated from a society that recognizes success and power more than it recognizes human need. "To Die in Milltown" displays the day of the town, the life of a man, and the region surrounding the town—all from the viewpoint of the bar.[4] Divisions, disconnections, and separations in the lives of the town and the man shift easily as though aided by bourbon.

To live,
stay put. The Blackfoot, any river
has a million years to lend, and weather's
always wild to look at down the Hellgate—
solid gray forever trailing off white rain.
Our drinks are full of sun. These aging eagles
climb the river on their own. (pp. 13–14)

There is no satisfactory way out: the only way seems to be by train—the same train that divides the town both physically and spiritually. As the town surrounds the isolated man with divisions, he turns away from the losses that make up society to a dream that makes things whole; the same process informs Hugo's most widely quoted poem, "Degrees of Gray in Philipsburg" (see Chapter 2).

Philipsburg, Ovando, Milltown—those failed towns are proof enough that the western expansion celebrated by Wister and Roosevelt was not all gold. Outside the walls of the bar, the jail, beyond the town festering in its boredom and isolation, lies the landscape that drew those white settlers. Rather than seeing the landscape as potential wealth and actual beauty, Hugo sees the dust and wind as much as the trout streams. And if that wind—that "degrading wind" from "Ovando"—has worn down the opportunities for America's expansion into the West, there is good reason. According to Hugo, that wind is finally not what we commonly call "American"—not, that is, white American. It is Indian, and the converging sympathies and sorrows from that other side of the history of American expansion find an eloquent place in the poem "Bear Paw."

> The wind is 95. It still pours from the east
> like armies and it drains each day of hope.
> From any point on the surrounding rim,
> below, the teepees burn. The wind is
> infantile and cruel. It cries "give in" "give in"
> and Looking Glass is dying on the hill.
> Pale grass shudders. Cattails beg and bow. (p. 76)

As the poem opens, the wind is white, a metaphor for the armies of the Fifth Infantry that pursued Chiefs Joseph, Yellow Hand, and Looking Glass of the Nez Percé northward as the tribes tried to reach Canada in September 1877. Hugo, in 1972, is standing at the site near the Bear Paw Mountains where Chief Joseph, seeing that his people were dying of cold and starvation, surrendered. The Indians had followed their hopes as much as the wind, but the winter storms came sooner than usual; they thought the wind had led them to Canada, but they were still in Montana. As Hugo recalls the history, he studies the names on plaques and graves but notices how the wind now "takes all you learn away to reservation graves."

Turning from history, its data and detachment, Hugo demands in the third stanza an acceptance of the suffering: "close enough to struggle, to take blood / on your hands." As if such acceptance were like the "lull in wind" that the Indians felt before their defeat, things change: the wind is now not "senile," and Looking Glass, long dead, "will not die." What appears as an acceptance of historical fact has been overturned. There is something more than history; there is the wind, the weather itself. What is needed is not just history but prayer, not facts learned but surrender experienced, an action taken in the heart that overcomes the isolations and divisions. The last lines of the poem are unmistakably spoken by a white man who compares his surrender of the spirit to the surrender of Joseph and his tribe nearly a hundred years earlier. What this white man surrenders to is not an army with superior weapons and fresh troops but the wind itself, that spirit so thoroughly part of Indian religion, a "lone surviving god" that has filled the Hugo landscape with both defeat and the possibilities of change, a new vision.

In his surrender, Hugo recognizes the necessity of a culture that has more than victories, historical facts, and cars that make clouds of dust. In the heart of "Bear Paw" one line is resonant with both Joseph's experience and Hugo's: "only the eternal nothing of space." Not eternal possibilities or opportunities or adventure—there are no metaphoric extensions possible from defeat and dispossession, no place for human heroism and independence, no matter how tough. The nothing of space, that "lull in wind," is as fine and calm a response to manifest destiny and to the appetite of American expansion as there could be. There is no newer frontier and no new tough hero to exploit it; there is only human need and the importance of human connection—something Chief Joseph knew as he surrendered. Hugo's landscape has developed into that of a man who knows the harsher realities of space, wind, and weather that drive people not toward new schemes for wealth but toward each other for warmth.

As if *The Lady in Kicking Horse Reservoir* were preparation, Hugo's next book, *What Thou Lovest Well Remains American* (1975), shows a lessening of the images of prison towns (Philipsburg, Hot Springs, Dixon) and of the image of the harsh wind as metaphor of defeat. Instead, Hugo concentrates on presenting images of individual human beings and their struggles to keep a hold on life, on each other, on the sympathies of the poet, and, by extension, on the reader's. Hugo would like his readers to feel the lonely awkwardness of "The Swimmer at Lake Edward," the toughness of a madman's truth in "Reconsidering the Madman," and how it must feel to work for the Trio Fruit Company in Missoula. In the first part of this fifth book, many poems arise from that area of Hugo's first home, Seattle: "Saying Goodbye to Mrs. Noraine," "The House on 15th S.W.," "Again, Kapowsin," and "Remember Graham" ("If we spend our life remembering what we love / to be sure who we are, Graham endures like ivy").

A nostalgic return, "Remember Graham" presents a town unlike earlier Hugo towns; this town is not a bleak enclosure but a collection of people: "the poisoner" with nine dogs to his credit; "the bigot who ran the bar"; "the author of books / about peach trees." The town is Hugo's own, complete with violence, and there is in the background a sadness that is "a replay in the throat / of some old deeper grief we'd rather forget." But in Graham the violence and sadness do not stand like thick walls. The poem ends with a flourish as a landscape opens, indeed wells up, from the trees inside the town.

> And things are the same. Poplars sway like early girls
> in dream and sun flushes the swallows
> who ride thermals wisely into the world
> of black dazzle and take their place with stars.[5]

The town opens to the larger landscape, even gives itself to the wind, and as it does, those disconnected isolated lives of people—not the least of which is the poet's—seem to open also.

Hugo's imagination may be drawn to exploring images of failed towns, isolated people, and communities imprisoned in walls of boredom and rage simply because the experience of human community is so deeply valuable to him. In *The Lady in Kicking Horse Reservoir* he allows himself only a few poems that satisfy this ache for community; "Missoula Softball Tournament" is perhaps the best example. General readers love it and the more scholarly—if they let themselves—need not be disappointed. The problem with "Tournament," however, is the same problem with any poem at this moment in American culture: how to imagine any complete community with all the differences, antagonisms, and pluralism of American life. In "Tournament" women seem the injured party; the poem can be seen as too reliant on an image of women as only housewives and mothers: "the beautiful wives in the stands, basic, used, / screeching runners home, infants unattended in the dust" (p. 69). Hugo is aware of his own male chauvinism (Adrienne Rich once called him "more honest" than most male poets), and he once thought the poem was "crude."[6] However, for Missoula, Montana, and for that poem, he later found those images of women to be entirely realistic.

The problem of how to present community, however, stands central to Hugo's writing as his poetry has moved from those images from the Old West myth—the hardened hero, the isolated town, the harsh wind—to images from the lives of people who live somewhere besides the saloon or open range. Perhaps the central problem of this change within the Hugo town involves Hugo's desire to separate the brutality associated with the expansion and exploitation that shaped the first western myth from the need that still remains in the human beings left behind by that myth. Perhaps what survives the surrender of that western myth is a neglected intimacy between people. The overall effect, in any case, is the displacement of the western myth by the image of a society struggling to work, as images of workers and lonely travelers, of outcasts and the poor, of Indians and the neglected fill the pages of *The Lady in Kicking Horse Reservoir* and other books. Hugo's West is built on the image of a society just beginning to be aware of itself as a collection of people, not simply walls and tough guys and the wind on the horizon.

Hugo's sixth book, *31 Letters and 13 Dreams* (1977), is overwhelmingly autobiographical, but there also he turns to the image of the West and to the important presence people have in the vast distances of western space. Moments of poetic uplift in the general prose of the letters make definite claims for the people, if not for the land or the toughness, of the West. The tough guy is older and wiser, more the John Wayne of *The Shootist* (1976) than of *The Searchers* (1956): "We are older than our scars. We have outlasted / our wars and it turns out we're not as bad as we thought" ("Letter to Logan from Milltown," pp. 38–39).[7] Hugo recognizes the presence of Wayne as an emblem of the Old West mythos in "Letter to Gale from Ovando": "It looks anytime like Sunday with John Wayne in church, / leaving me helpless, waiting for the villains to ride in" (p. 41). In contrast with the earlier poem "Ovando," he stops now in Ovando "to feel a part of the west, the brutal part we wave goodbye to / gladly and the honest part we hate to lose, those right days / when we helped each other and were uniformly poor" (p. 41).

Hugo fears that both parts of the West—the tough and brutal, with its accompanying isolation and expanse, and the honest and open, with its acceptance of human cruelty and need—will fade with the changes that an expanding technological society will bring. He would like to see the honest part remain; it is an image of the West less myth than fact, based as it is, not on Wister's novel or on Remington's paintings or on Roosevelt's rhetoric, but (as in "Letter to Goldbarth from Big Fork") in the memory of a particular historic time in America's past when the expansion of America's territory and of its economy abruptly halted for a while—the thirties:

> the forlorn towns
> just hanging on take me back to the thirties where most poems
> come from, the warm meaningful gestures we make, the warm ways
> we search each other for help in a bewildering world,
> a world so terrifyingly big we settle for small
> ones we can control. (p. 59)

Those warm gestures hold society together. Those expressions of warmth, of the common and essential connections of feeling, which can only be called social, have not often been part of American poetry. What we often read is political or private poetry that verges on commenting on American society. Pablo Neruda could make exemplary poetry that expands outward toward society simply by writing about a gift of socks, but America does not have the social cohesion (natural or forced) of Chile: American society is just too vast, too full of potential, unseen, hidden surfaces in its extensive landscape. Perhaps therein lies the enduring gift of the myth of the West: as a western hero once learned how to read that vast expanse of land for its potential values and dangers, so now a very western poet offers to make the western landscape a metaphor for American society. Despite our complexities and sometimes unseen differences, warm gestures between people, even across wide spaces, can overcome the isolation, boredom, and loss of community that were the image of that earlier West.

8

"Isn't It Wrong, the Way the Mind Moves Back": Overcoming Regression in *What Thou Lovest Well Remains American*

Like *The Lady in Kicking Horse Reservoir* (1973), *What Thou Lovest Well Remains American* (1975) contains several themes that are constant in Richard Hugo's mature poetry. There are towns like Philipsburg, such as Keokuk, Dumar, and Drummond, where neighborhoods, factories, and "stores are balanced / on the edge of failure and they never fail."[1] There are landscapes where lonely individuals feel the weight of wind, of the wild western past dissipated into shades of gray in such poems as "Reconsidering the Madman," "Cattails," and "Ghost in a Field of Mint." But most of the poems in this fifth book return to Hugo's past, to the sense of failure that he learned in his neighborhood of White Center. It is in this personal context that the major themes of *The Lady in Kicking Horse Reservoir* now come to rest. In that personal context the intense isolation of the Hugo town relaxes, and the harsh, embittered landscapes become less wide and alien. Those odd strangers, moreover—the hermits, squatters, and lonely tenement dwellers that have been with Hugo since *A Run of Jacks*—are not shut out or shut within themselves with such finality but can be "welcomed in the secret club" that society has formed.

As *The Lady in Kicking Horse Reservoir* sets up isolation as a principle concern of his poetry, Hugo's fifth book presents images where that isolation becomes transformed into a moment of intimacy. There are, to be sure, grim poems, as tightfisted and white-knuckled as any Hugo has written, such as "The House on 15th S.W." where "Cruelty and rain could be expected" and "The Swimmer at Lake Edward." But in both these poems, the isolation that exists through most of the stanzas dissolves as the final image turns our attention toward children. In "House," the speaker is left "neutral," imagining light "soft and full, not harsh and dim remembered," as he envisions "children . . . normal, clean, not at all / the soiled freaks I had counted on." The swimmer, "crude as a loon on land," is another of Hugo's isolated characters whose tongue "drove girls away" as he "sat in taverns hours / and the fat piled up." Failure follows failure with black humor as the swimmer waddles home and "makes friends" with the wall and the chair and argues with a recorded voice: "He dialed Time / to hear a voice, and when the voice said 4 A.M., / he said, no, that couldn't be the time." But when in water and no longer the failure he is on land, the swimmer is seen, dimly felt, and understood.

> The first warm day, he dove from the sky
> into the lake we named for the king. We stood
> on the shore and marveled at his wake.
> When we applauded, he flashed away,
> his dorsal fin the only point in the glare.
> What was his name? We took home the salad
> left over but forgot one blanket, a thermos
> and the baby's favorite toy. (p. 43)

As in most of the poems in this crucial book, something changes toward the end of the poem; in this case, the poem itself changes as its omniscient narrator's voice becomes part of a family. The isolation of the main character and the complementary isolation of the speaker, so distant from the swimmer even though he knows so much—even how he "sang alone / in his mind"—give way without warning as description of an isolated *he* gives way to a communal *we*. When that *we* applauds, the swimmer flashes away, and there is one more missed meeting, one more lonely situation. But the people on the beach are so impressed by his grace that their civilized, normal picnic becomes disrupted; they leave behind basic necessities that might not have much material value but that are personally important: a blanket, a Thermos, and even "the baby's favorite toy." It is as if the family, recognizing the swimmer's urge for survival, also dimly understands that the failures of life create beauty that disrupts civilized smoothness.

These two poems, then, outline the principal concern in Hugo's fifth book: the overcoming of the isolation that he had presented so unmistakably in poems like "Hot Springs," "Dixon," "Ovando," and "Degrees of Gray in Philipsburg" in *The Lady in Kicking Horse Reservoir*. Hugo's approach in *What Thou Lovest Well Remains American* organizes this dissolution of isolation in two metaphors that stand in subtitles of the first two sections of the book—"A Snapshot of the Auxiliary" and "Strangers." As he works out the metaphors of snapshots and strangers, Hugo builds to a crucial poem, one that is pivotal in his life, "The Freaks at Spurgin Road Field," which contains a statement of the theme central to the whole book: "Isn't it wrong, the way the mind moves back." The first two sections present the psychological harms in Hugo's past and the social harms present in society; he sees both harms as ways "the mind moves back." The third section—"Lectures, Soliloquies, Pontifications"—sounds like a falling off, and it is, but it contains a series of fantasies that culminate in a poem that is simultaneously artificial and very personal: "The Art of Poetry." This last poem in the book, thick with images and oblique in its references to Hugo's past, stands as a complement to "The Freaks at Spurgin Road Field" as it looks not to "the way the mind moves back" but to the way "twice a moment tides come in." The art of poetry is precisely that movement of imaginative tides that change the outline of what we know of ourselves; unlike the tides of ocean, the tides of poetry can move twice a moment, with each line of poetry.

The whole of *What Thou Lovest Well Remains American* works out a theme that has been as central to Hugo, if not as evident, as his working themes of poverty, alienation, and the landscapes of the lush Northwest and bleak Montana. That theme—if it can be said to have literary perspective at all—is the working out of, and the working against, regression, that psychological dynamic that yearns for what is past and builds, nostalgically, a glow around events gone by, and that ultimately creates visions of "the good ole days," the Golden Age, and unfallen Eden. Even though Hugo had neither "good ole days" nor a Tom Sawyer childhood, but only an adolescence of fear following a childhood of dispossession and a freedom born of neglect, he still shares the human need for hallowing something of one's past, bad as it was. Even popular culture in America reflects the psychological fact that people cling to their identifying origins, often by embossing deprivation, as was the case with that television glorification of poverty called "The

Waltons." Against this all-too-human erring into easy "clouds of glory," which must be traced to William Wordsworth—although he did not at first have anything like that in mind—Hugo, in *What Thou Lovest Well Remains American,* takes a phrase from Pound's Pisan Canto LXXXI—"What thou lovest well remains, / the rest is dross"—and alters it significantly. In his alteration, Hugo turns our attention toward the enduring problems and essence of what it means to be American and, oddly, to be spiritually related to Pound. However, Hugo ends where Pound began: "make it new."

The alchemy of this change, this making of the new out of a reverence for the old, this cherishing of things American by using a phrase from an expatriate poet, is a fascinating process that takes us to the heart of Hugo's work and life. In Hugo's poetry the overcoming of regression is part of a refusal to follow a common intellectual perspective that derides things American, things common, things emotional. If his analysis of "the way the mind moves back" is not easy to outline, it is due to the fact that Hugo, unlike overly intellectual poets and critics of his generation, refuses to analyze human emotion or American society from any other standpoint than one that admits its basis in the vagaries of emotion, in sympathy, and in a feeling for the necessity of community over and above the quickness and precision of the individual, often alienated, intellectual mind.

Hugo is not alone in this latter-day reaction to modern poetry of the intellectual perspective that characterizes such poets as Eliot, Ransom, and Pound. James Wright, Robert Bly, and Philip Levine share Hugo's urge for presenting images and themes that can reach to the heart of American experience and not just to the academy. They do not, however, display as constant an awareness of the mundane in American society, which can be shared and—from the implications of Hugo's poetry—must be shared. The characters of Hugo's poems—farmers or hermits or workers or the infirm or the drunk—are not alienated because of some inexplicable machinery in society, as are Kafka's characters, or because of some dark corner in their souls, as in the works of Camus. Such solitaries are intellectual in nature; Hugo's are not. His speakers and characters are conscious of "a lake the odd can own" ("Turtle Lake," p. 30), of stores "balanced on the edge of failure," and of how "a dancehall burned and burned a hundred degradations" ("Why I Think of

Dumar Sadly," p. 14). They are conscious of remembering "dandelions adult years / had taught me to ignore. . . . Their greens are excellent in salad" ("Saying Goodbye to Mrs. Noraine," pp. 5–6). Most important, despite—or perhaps because of—his connection to the West and to the figure of the lone cowboy on his horse, Hugo is conscious of that fundamental of American society, the car: "My Buick hit a note too high / for dogs at 85" ("Turtle Lake"); or, "Again, my car, not old this time, not burning oil, / dives down the hill I've hoarded twenty years, to Graham" ("Remember Graham," p. 12). At times, this consciousness provides the substance of the poem, as in "Late Summer, Drummond."

> With mean traps bypassed, no more fines to pay,
> we're free to love the movement east, east bound trees,
> traffic on the freeway. Speed law: safe and sane.
> Real speed: blinding. Real chance to make it: none.
> Our best chance: love the leaf flash spreading white
> above the napping cows. The town drunk knows
> the world blurs, drunk or sober, and the world moves on
> out of reach against the wind or with. (p. 31)

In Hugo's work, "the town drunk knows" because his interior world is as blurred as that exterior American world of speed and as that essence of America, the "chance to make it," with all its associations of sex, success, and survival.

It is fitting, then, that "Strangers," the second section of *What Thou Lovest Well,* begins with a frankly autobiographical poem, "Goodbye, Iowa," which was written about his being on the road after his breakdown and subsequent resignation of his teaching post at the University of Iowa in 1971.

> Once more you've degraded yourself on the road.
> The freeway turned you back in on yourself
> and you found nothing, not even a good false name.
> The waitress mocked you and you paid your bill
> sweating in her glare. You tried to tell her
> how many lovers you've had. Only a croak came out.
> Your hand shook when she put hot coins in it.
> Your face was hot and you ran face down to the car. (p. 27)

Speed is a blur and the speed of the freeway turns "you back in on yourself," just as the town drunk, to find "nothing, not even a good false name." The situation—"you've degraded yourself on the road"—gives us the outlines of that emotional impoverishment that runs much deeper than mere intellectual alienation from society. This impoverishment is an inescapable part of a society where the road, roadside restaurants and bars, rapid meetings and casual relationships are so prevalent that in Hugo's hands they provide the basis for a common, even an oddly communal, experience of what it means to be American.

Most of the "Strangers" section expresses this commonness of emotional impoverishment. "Turtle Lake" is the place "the odd can own" after their "homes have burned down / back where wind turned hungry friends away." The warehouse of "Ode to the Trio Fruit Company of Missoula" is where "the sickening odors / of some former fruit order us to cross the days off / on the calendar and wait, two life term prisoners" (p. 33). In that poem two lines trace that interior process that builds up equally on the freeway or in the drunk's mind: "we should fly the stale air of our tiny cells, / poking the corners light ignores." That interior world, isolated from common human sympathy, is host to terrifying or lovely sexual fantasies, such as the fearsome one in "Invasion North" or its more humane opposite in "Cattails." In "Invasion North," the speaker is inside an "igloo fortress" armed against squadrons of women, "armor gleaming on their breasts" (p. 38). The women win: "Those women / in military nylon had beaten us. I cried." The speaker alone survives. He doesn't surrender; by radio he stays in touch with the conquering women and has "developed a terrible arsenal / in case I'm taken and I've stockpiled berries, / roots and dry meat, enough to last fifty years." The women, not imagined lovely, offer him "the captain's skeleton, have promised amnesty / if I come in." "Invasion North" is as honest an expression of male fear as has been written. This fantasy and others, such as "Living Alone," "The Swimmer at Lake Edward," and "Reading at the Old Federal Courts Building, St. Paul," attest to Hugo's honesty about sexual feelings and point to that psychological dimension of his life that has caused him the greatest pain.

"Announcement" takes on the liberal stance of men giving women "their rights" with a fine, sarcastic hand:

> Tomorrow morning at four, the women will be herded
> into the public square to hear their rights read aloud.

> I'm pleased to sign this new law. No longer
> will women be obliged to kneel and be flayed
> by our southern farmers. This law says, farmers
> must curb their mean instincts. (p. 54)

Although the poem's principal satiric object is any political pronouncement, Hugo's honesty about the masculine voice that informs most American political statements makes the satire cut both ways.[2] It is often impossible, in his poetry, to separate what is generally male from what is individually Hugo, and the problems, obsessions, and regressions that his poetry reveals are also often shared by many men.

The second section of Hugo's book is entitled "Strangers" because that word suggests American society with its emotional distances created by physical speed and its successes creating failures—the odd, the old, and the poor. The beauty of the final sexual fantasy of "Cattails" is poignant, arising as it does from the same distance, strangeness, and essential violence that underscore "Invasion North." In "Cattails," a man dreams of dying a gangster death "in cattails / and cold water, my body riddled, face down / in the reeds, hounds and siren howling red." As in "Announcement" so in "Cattails": everything in the Hugo town is shown to be related to that fundamental male terror, the fear of women. As in gangster films, where portrayals by Edward G. Robinson or James Cagney highlight the violence of American society, so here that violence is seen as an abiding fantasy, a part of what it means to be male and American:

> It's what I'd planned. The barbershop alone
> at the edge of Gray Girl swamp. The town beyond
> drowsing that battering raw afternoon,
> the radio in the patrol car playing westerns,
> the only cop on duty dreaming girls. (p. 39)

The naming of "Gray Girl swamp" is crucial, reminding us vaguely of another important poem, "The Lady in Kicking Horse Reservoir." The two poems are closely related, and their differences point to how that feeling of isolation in so many of Hugo's poems is resolved in *What Thou Lovest Well Remains American.* In "Cattails," as in "The Lady in Kicking Horse Reservoir," the dramatic situation and the space of the poem are made masculine: a barbershop, harsh wind, westerns on the radio, a cop dreaming about girls. As the speaker enters that space, the shadows of Bogart and Cagney deepen: "When I walked in, first customer, the barber / muttered 'Murder' and put his paper down. / I hinted and hinted how sinister I am." A boy's tough dream, the poem shows a man who makes society stop, who attracts attention and either plans or controls everything: the forceful wind, the way women whisper over him, the clouds, even the foreign names on his credit cards. But no one knows him; they only know his potential deeds, the threat that he poses for others. The poem leaves this tough male fantasy and finds its complement in a more pleasurable, and socially acceptable, masculine dream.

> When my hair was cut, I walked along the bank
> of Gray Girl swamp and watched the cattails rage.
> When I drove out, my radio picked up the same lament
> the cop had on. I tuned in on his dream.
> They came to me, those flashing, amber girls,
> came smiling in that wind, came teasing laughter
> from my seed like I'd done nothing wrong. (p. 39)

The poem ends in the same masculine space that began it: cattails raging in the harsh wind. Through the radio in his car, the speaker reaches the only semblance of community he gains in the poem: another dream, though less brutal. Those "flashing, amber girls" have been in and out of Hugo's poems since *A Run of Jacks,* where they appear as trout in "Skykomish River Running":

> I will cultivate the trout, teach their fins
> to wave in water like the legs of girls
> tormented black in pools. (p. 40)

or again, where they suggest that sexual insecurity is tied to social and economic facts:

> Once I changed my name to race the rich
> on those expensive lakes where girls are gold
> from living and their legs and bellies brown
> with threats of garden love.[3]

"Cattails" shows us what the lovely, narcissistic dream springs from: not from a sense of free pleasure and enjoyment, but from a sense of release from guilt: "like I'd done nothing wrong." The only possible "wrong" thing the speaker could have done in the poem is his wanting to be tough and die like a gangster. The implication is that sexual pleasures are tied to such a tough stance and are rewarded only when one is tough enough to die that way. The irony of such a fantasy, however, is obvious: maintaining such a stance only undercuts sexual enjoyment; the speaker is too isolated by his toughness ever to find those girls. In dreaming himself sinister, he in fact has done something wrong.

What he has done is "degraded [himself] on the road" ("Goodbye, Iowa") and refused intimacy and love to keep a love for that tough, gray atmosphere of the freeway, its space and speed. "Goodbye, Iowa" puts the elements of distance, isolation, sex, and self-hatred together in their proper constellation of emotional forces.

> Miles you hated her. Then you remembered what
> the doctor said: really a hatred of self. Where
> in flashes of past, the gravestone
> you looked for years and never found, was there
> a dignified time? Only when alone,
> those solitary times with sky gray as a freeway. (p. 27)

Those miles of distance are a hatred of a woman and, perhaps, of all women. In "Goodbye, Iowa" Hugo understands the miles, the hatred, as being hatred of self. This understanding is reached only by the experience of a breakdown. Though successful, accepted, and popular as a teacher of writing at Iowa, Hugo had begun drinking heavily and dwelling on his failure to measure up to what he thought he should be.

> But that "success" clashed with my dwelling on a painful past. I played over and over scenes where I was degraded or humiliated by women. That's a neurotic business and according to the doctor people who do it do it because they unconsciously believe that if they play some painful scene in the past over and over, one day they will play it and the pain will be gone and they will have won a victory over the hurt. But of course, they never win. Nor did I. Finally, I started dating women I liked very much, getting drunk and having some conversation that would insure their hatred. . . . I'm the last person to deliberately alienate others, least of all women I admire and respect, yet that's what I was doing.[4]

The psychic wound that produced such a crisis is deep, connected to Hugo's sense of worthlessness and inadequacy in adolescence and probably to his having been left at age two by his mother to be brought up by his grandparents. Sex and the intimacy of a family were confusing and terrifying to him. He describes how he felt when an adolescent friend showed him how to kiss a girl:

> I had never seen a man kiss a woman before except in the movies, and I'm not putting anyone on when I say that I really thought people kissed only in films. I can never remember being kissed as a child nor did I ever see any show of affection between my grandparents. I walked out, my face flushed with shame, through the dark living room where one of the older boys yelled some insult at me, and finally after years of groping, into the fresh air outside, free and alone. I walked the mile home, degraded and in anguish, and as I cried my tears created a secondary glow around the streetlights. I wanted to be like Ralph Lewin, like Betty Moore's brother, like anybody else. At home, my grandparents were already asleep, but I sat alone, as I did so many times in that still house, and stared into the solitary void I was certain would be my life.[5]

With such an introduction into sexuality, the sexual identity of a boy and later of a man turns to proofs, to tests, to an undercurrent of doubt that undermines power and potency and seems to need some action or violence to clear the air. None, of course, came. The pattern repeated, especially after Hugo's close relationship with his first wife, Barbara, ended after fourteen years. That first marriage and its failure were, as Hugo recalls, "necessary for both of us" and as much a part of their similar pasts as of their relationship: "We helped each other to survive and each made it possible for the other to go on. We'd both had a bad shake from life and we respected each other's pain. I blame myself for the breakup of the marriage though she was the one who had the courage to separate."[6]

After his marriage had ended, but before his eventual crack-up in Iowa, Hugo had another relationship that ended badly and with much pain. It provided the impetus for "The Lady in Kicking Horse Reservoir," a poem that stands at the center of Hugo's fear of women and his lifelong fight against regression. The poem is extraordinary in its working out of male fears and in its attainment of masculine tenderness. What begins with deep bitterness—

> Not my hands but green across you now.
> Green tons hold you down, and ten bass curve
> teasing in your hair. . . .
> I hope each spring
> to find you tangled in those pads
> pulled not quite loose by the spillway pour,
> stars in dead reflection off your teeth—

turns beautiful by degrees of the lovely and the grotesque to this oddly enchanting vision of the "lady," released from her bondage in reservoir vegetation, bringing water to crops, freedom to the speaker, and sexual dances to fish (the Dolly Vardon) and whales:

> The spillway's open and you spill out
> into weather, lover down the bright canal
> and mother, irrigating crops
> dead Indians forgot to plant.
> I'm sailing west with arrows to dissolving foam
> where waves strand naked Dollys.
> Their eyes are white as oriental mountains
> and their tongues are teasing oil from whales.[7]

Not a statement about women at all, the release of the "lady" is a statement about Hugo as a man. The poem enacts what amounts to a giving up of loss, of the past that had given him the words *defeated* and *degraded* as emblems of himself. To release the power of those emblems, of that loss, something darkly feminine must also be released. It is as though, in order to be a man, Hugo must let go of that image of a woman over whom he has control.

Having correspondences to other darkly feminine figures in literature, as in Shakespeare or Keats, the "lady" has been present from the first in Hugo's work. As early as *A Run of Jacks* we find a stanza that presents a similar figure of a woman, but in earth.

> There is a woman rots and laughs down there.
> In the earth her bones are long and soft
> as whips in air. In a dream a whip
> is coiling in the wormy water
> where I dive to set my face on fire
> from the flint and granite chips that hang
> unmoved by wind, in any diver's air.[8]

The dynamics of the release ring true enough for Hugo's life, although they play havoc with the possibility of any easy understanding of the poem. Before the lady can be let out of that reservoir of guilt and anger that has been his emotional life, Hugo must confront and overcome himself and that figure of a defeated boy that he has held with him all his life. This symbolic episode takes shape in the terms of Hugo's childhood as the fifth stanza returns to a working-class neighborhood and the ethic of the tough male:

> One boy slapped the other. Hard.
> The slapped boy talked until his dignity
> dissolved, screamed a single "stop"

> and went down sobbing in the company pond.
> I swam for him all night. My only suit
> got wet and factory hands went home.
> No one cared the coward disappeared.
> Morning then: cold music I had never heard. (p. 58)

It isn't enough to say, as Hugo does in the fourth stanza, "Sorry. Sorry. Sorry"; that is "no way to float her up." The only way to set the release of a powerful emotion—an archetypal possession, Jung would say—is to circumvent it, to transfer the emotional weight or psychic energy from one part of the self to another. Here the figure of the woman can be released only when that hurt boy, who still lives within the speaker, is put with the woman in the bottom of the lake. Hugo has described this pivotal stanza in this way:

> One thing that's key to that poem is that there's a stanza in it where two boys have a fight. That was actually a dream I had during the time when I was trying to recover from the broken heart this woman left me with. Because there was a real woman in "Kicking Horse Reservoir"—only she wasn't in the reservoir—and she broke my heart. And I had a dream about the two boys fighting and I think that I put that down almost as the dream happened. There was the factory; people came to watch these two boys have a fight and I think that they're two sides of the self having the fight. One is the regressive, self-pitying side, who is the boy who loses the fight, and the other is the survivor. And once the self-pitying side is defeated and sinks in the pond—and "No one cared the coward disappeared"—then the survivor is free to release the woman from the reservoir. Of course she's still dead, but she's now serving a function: she's gotten into the irrigation ditches and she's irrigating and propagating life and so forth. That was the key stanza, the most difficult to understand; but the point was that one could survive one's regressive tendencies—to feel sorry for oneself, to beg, to whine and complain, to have had one's heart broken.[9]

For much of his life Hugo has fought, in imaginative landscapes, situations, and characters, a battle that has all those psychological proportions that many forms of psychoanalysis and therapy discern: the retreat from experience to patterns, the playing back of loss, the sense of guilt and degradation that hangs on a human sensibility nurtured by an early coldness and dispossession, by an early lack of love. It has been a long struggle and—if we can use the term at all in a day when the media make or break presidents, sports figures, and superstars—it has been heroic. No other male poet has traced his sense of masculine identity and sexuality so thoroughly in an effort to see and overcome the forces of regression in his life. Although we cannot say for every man that regression is itself a reliance on sexual roles and stereotypes, the implications of Hugo's poetry are clear. The tough, aggressive stance of "Not my hands but green across you now," and hundreds of other Hugo lines, is itself regressive, tied to past loss; the true survivor, the tougher man, is seen submerging his weak, regressive half, which is tied to sexual and other failures, and gaining independence. He emerges from the fight whole and capable of swimming all night for that other, lost half; he is, in other words, capable of caring instead of being locked inside himself and inside a struggle. Such wholeness, then, can turn from the past and find a hope that is vague but merciful: "the far blue of your bones in May / may be nourished by the snow" (p. 58). The whole man is able to release those feelings that he had locked with the lady in the reservoir.

This overcoming of regression, marked by an important, knotty poem, stands behind the special grace of *What Thou Lovest Well Remains American*. The past is no longer a loss carried into the present but is placed inside marked boundaries, framed as snapshots that can be seen, studied, and then put away. As with the poems of the "Strangers" section, the poems in the first section, "A Snapshot of the Auxiliary," point out failure and disconnection in society, specifically in the neighborhoods and houses of his life. When he wrote earlier poems, such as "Duwamish" or "Hideout," Hugo had imagined himself as someone else, someone tougher, to distance himself from pain. In the Montana of *The Lady in Kicking Horse Reservoir,* writing about different places that held similar pains, he was able to be more direct. Now, in his fifth book, Hugo is able to return to the memories of his earlier life; an initial regression has led to openness and honesty, and those places that reminded him of pain have become limited, their associations contained.

As with "Strangers," the "Snapshot" section shows that these failures have limits. The sarcasm of the title poem, a thinly veiled anger toward that kind of religious upbringing that inhibits life ("My eyes were like this photo. Old"), is fragmentary.

> Many of them have gone the way wind recommends
> or, if you're religious, God. Mrs. Noraine,
> thank the wind, is alive. The church

> is brick now, not the drab board frame
> you see in the background. Once I was alone
> in there and the bells, the bells started to ring.
> They terrified me home. This next one in the album
> is our annual picnic. We are all having fun. (p. 3)

We can take that last line as one more sarcastic shot, or we can take it at face value. Inside the church is terror, but outside it fun is possible. Mrs. Noraine, after all, is kind, and some hymns, "the ones they founded jazz on," are good.

The entire section contains such a mix. The terror of "The House on 15th S.W." is matched by the warm center of "Saying Goodbye to Mrs. Noraine," and the elegy of "Again, Kapowsin" is matched by the idyll of "Remember Graham." Several of the poems — among them "Places and Ways to Live," the title poem "What Thou Lovest Well Remains American," and most clearly, "A Snapshot of 15th S.W."—refer specifically to Hugo's childhood home.

> Burn this shot. That gray is what it is.
> Gray gravel in the street and gray hearts
> tired of trying love. Your house:
> that ominous gray shade alone on the right,
> pear tree bent in what must have been wind
> and gray boy playing. The wind had a way
> of saying The Lord Is My Shepherd high
> in electric wires. That blur could be
> a bitter wren or a girl named Mary Jane
> running away from a prehistoric father. (p. 10)

The gray he grew up with became the hallmark of Hugo's most famous poem, "Degrees of Gray in Philipsburg," having its roots here, in a small house in White Center outside Seattle. No other stanza so simply expresses the boredom and neglect Hugo felt when growing up, tracing those degrees of gray that surround him to the appearance of a "prehistoric father" like the one he never knew as a boy. The snapshot reveals the depth of gray as Hugo shows how such grayness grows around a boy's life:

> The longer the gray heart took to teach
> the heavier the thicket, the crazier
> the plains and small towns. Lovers
> forever foreign. . . . When women crawled like dogs in the mean
> beating sun, your gray blood warmed. (p. 10)

The boredom evokes from a boy's imagination "exotic poison," "cruel men / from another planet," and the greater terror of women seen not as persons or even as pleasurable objects but as a species of animal. The only passion grayness evokes is sadistic. And yet the poem does not end with such terror; the harshness of the gray dissolves as the snapshot metaphor again emerges.

> Don't burn it. The gray is what it was.
> Clouds are piling white above the sea
> like phrases you believe. Echo of swallow.
> Rings from a swallow tick widening
> over the river and salmon refusing to mourn.
> Deep back, out of camera range
> the sun pulses on fields you still might run to,
> wind a girl's hand on your ear. (p. 11)

What went wrong in the past is confined by the snapshot, just as the gray of that past was in itself a confinement. In "A Snapshot of 15th S.W." a swallow touches the river to show rings widening, a way out of confinement. Similar swallows in "Remember Graham" "ride thermals wisely into the world / of black dazzle and take their place with the stars" (p. 12). The birds give themselves to that ever present Hugo wind, which is both close to the body and strong enough to carry it. Born in gray isolation, Hugo's poetry reaches a wholeness that goes beyond the tough stance and the angry towns of his earlier work. He is no longer "dispossessed, forced to wander / a world the color of salt with no young music in it" ("Places and Ways to Live," p. 22). In "A Good Day for Seeing Your Limitations" the limits Hugo sees do not confine him but his dispossession:

> where a home
> burned down and men from neighboring farms
> pitched in to build a new one free.
> They said "Don't worry," and the dispossessed
> stopped worrying and danced to ringing mauls. (p. 7)

It is in this light at the end of dispossession—that powerful word in Hugo's vocabulary—that we should see the poem that stands almost at the literal center of *What Thou Lovest Well Remains American,* "The Freaks at Spurgin Road Field."

> The dim boy claps because the others clap.
> The polite word, handicapped, is muttered in the stands.
> Isn't it wrong, the way the mind moves back.

One whole day I sit, contrite, dirt, L.A.
Union Station, '46, sweating through last night.
The dim boy claps because the others clap.

Score, 5 to 3. Pitcher fading badly in the heat.
Isn't it wrong to be or not to be spastic?
Isn't it wrong, the way the mind moves back.

I'm laughing at a neighbor girl beaten to scream
by a savage father and I'm ashamed to look.
The dim boy claps because the others clap.

The score is always close, the rally always short.
I've left more wreckage than a quake.
Isn't it wrong, the way the mind moves back.

The afflicted never cheer in unison.
Isn't it wrong, the way the mind moves back
to stammering pastures where the picnic should have worked.
The dim boy claps because the others clap. (p. 46)

For Hugo, as for many American men, growing up meant growing up with baseball. Considering himself a failure in most respects, as a boy he felt that he could "do something about it on the ball field": "I promised myself no one would ever fool me again on a change of pace, and I kept my promise. I developed a technique of hitting late, of starting my swing at the last possible moment."[10] The technique was adopted out of vulnerability; Hugo's desire to play ball was a desire for acceptance "so overwhelming in high school that out in the field or at bat I was dizzy with tension and fear of falling in front of the students."[11] Years later, then, it is remarkable that the sight of young people—"some of them seemed retarded, others afflicted with physical and neurological problems"[12]— should evoke from Hugo this fine poem. Hugo seems conscious that the word *freak* is a socially loaded term, suggestive of the way society pulls back from anyone who is physically, intellectually, or emotionally handicapped. A freely structured villanelle, the poem stands at the center of Hugo's feeling for how our society fails and how we fail individually. The two lines that alternate in the villanelle structure—"The dim boy claps because the others clap" and "Isn't it wrong, the way the mind moves back"—are social and psychological statements, respectively. To gain acceptance, to appear normal, the dim boy claps.

His intellectual and psychological condition is a social statement supported by the way that the crowd's mind moves back to the safety of a "polite" word: *handicapped.* "Isn't it wrong, the way the mind moves back" first implies that it is wrong to move away from the stranger, the "freak." But as Hugo uses the line in the poem, it also becomes a psychological statement as his mind regresses and moves back toward his past.

The images that correspond to the repeated lines tie the social and psychological threads together: Hugo sweating through a drunk in Los Angeles in 1946, the baseball game, how the crowd's attention is attracted from the pitcher to "Isn't it wrong to be or not be spastic?" The baseball game, like the one in "Missoula Softball Tournament," becomes a place where Hugo's struggle for self-acceptance becomes entwined with his presentation of fissures in the social fabric. His laughter at "a neighbor girl beaten to scream" is disconcerting, embarrassing, but all too common an occurrence in conditions of poverty. The wrongness of the way the mind moves back is that regression that keeps alive old failures and accepts the wreckage of lives as final in the confinement of personal and societal conditions. The mind moves back from self-acceptance into that dim, gray world where we rely on others to tell us whom to like, how to act, and when to clap. Such regression to roles and conformity, to self-doubt, and ultimately to self-degradation is, to someone who had lived it, wrong.

In this meeting of the social and the psychological Hugo's poetry gains a greater context, and his use of a line from Pound comes into high relief. "The Freaks at Spurgin Road Field" presents the harm of regression in the most American of terms: at a baseball game with the fans muttering about freaks and with the poet himself remembering how baseball played a part in his growing up and overcoming of defeats. The America of *What Thou Lovest Well Remains American* is a place conscious of defeat, of loss, and of the need for human feeling and community. Those elements are at the heart of the snapshots and the poems about strangers. It is an America still not formed, still fragmented into isolated individuals who live dreams and nightmares and move back from each other, but it remains, with its Buicks and speed traps and Lutherans and baseball games, American. Pound's Canto LXXXI, from which Hugo takes the title of his book, is also a portrait of a mind moving back. The movement of Pound's mind, however, is an elegy for things past, a wish that the beauty of European culture, destroyed by world wars, were still alive.

> What thou lovest well remains,
>   the rest is dross
> What thou lov'st well shall not be reft from thee
> What thou lov'st well is thy true heritage
> Whose world, or mine or theirs
>   or is it of none?[13]

According to critic George Dekker, Pound is concerned in the Pisan Cantos with things that exist "only in the mind, and there only because he had studied them with affection and taken careful mental note of them."[14] Unlike Hugo, Pound remembers events, people, creations that are, in the words of Canto LXXXI, "scaled invention or true artistry," which were cultural achievements: "But to have done instead of not doing / this is not vanity . . . To have gathered from the air a live tradition / or from a fine old eye the unconquered flame / This is not vanity." Nor was it vain for Pound to be the interlocutor of such achievements; again Pound, as Dekker has said, "*is* only in so far as the things and men he loves define his being. They do not exist because of him."[15] How utterly opposite all this is to Hugo! When he remembers, Hugo places his experiences in the context not of cultural achievements, those high points of civilization, but of common people like those fans who watched the baseball game at Spurgin Road Field: "It was pleasant saying hello to a lot of nice people, most of whom ask little from life or from others."[16]

Whether they mutter "handicapped" or not, whether the social fabric holds or frays, the people of Hugo's "true heritage" do not define him but share with him the failings of a society based on self-doubt, where people impelled by dreams of speed, success, and acceptance have left so little room for human feelings—and which makes those feelings more valuable. It is in the minimal, essential elements of community that Hugo is defined, not wanting to keep alive or "play again / and again Mrs. Jensen pale at her window" ("What Thou Lovest Well Remains American") but knowing that we must, as Americans, "spend our life remembering what we love, to be sure who we are" ("Remember Graham"). What Pound remembers and what Hugo remembers from the thirties are as far apart as Pisa and White Center. As Pound's Pisan Cantos are memorials, Hugo's *What Thou Lovest Well Remains American* is a memorial to growth from past degradation and regression, a way out of failure.

Seen in that light, Hugo's poetry reveals its impetus as psychological, implying strongly that our culture's problems can never be significantly improved by homage to the "unconquered flame" of a "live tradition." Rather than the traditions of a culture, Hugo knows that the harder but more important task is understanding and curtailing those aggressions and regressions that move the mind back from human community. Therefore, in this volume the classic statement of Hugo's role as a poet comes in a poem reminiscent of "Degrees of Gray in Philipsburg" and of Pound's confinement in St. Elizabeth's hospital. "Reading at the Old Federal Courts Building, St. Paul" shows the poet as an angry man, isolated from community:

> What had I done wrong? The judge was marble.
> The young girl witness laughed at all those years
> I'd serve in isolation. The pillars smiled.
> In my cell, I sobbed vengeance on their world. (p. 32)

But the role does not last; the second stanza begins "That was years back, understand," and we are immediately taken into the confidence of a speaker who begins to overcome his isolation. He understands himself as "cowardly / and born infirm" and begins to understand his rage, his "licensed anger," and so writes poems.

> The renovation's clearly underway. Today
> girls ask me how I started writing. I read
> the poems I wrote in jail. Warm applause.
> . . . The girl who laughed,
> first trial, is teaching high school and she
> didn't know me when she said she loved my poems,
> was using them in class to demonstrate how
> worlds are put together, one fragment at a time. (p. 32)

With cool irony the anger is controlled, and out of infirmity and cowardice a victory is won. Like Pound, whose poetry demonstrates "how / worlds are put together, one fragment at a time," Hugo uses anger and sarcasm, but to different ends. He has little use for the failures of culture or for the economics of "usura"; Hugo's world is just not that concerned with tradition or abstraction.[17] But the experience of jail, of isolation, of overcoming failure to find human community, of putting worlds together in poetry—these are things minimal enough, essential to our understanding of perhaps not Western civilization but of what it means to be an American and male.

What Thou Lovest Well Remains American ends with a poem that seems to counter most of the poems in the book, but that also displays an opposition to "the way the mind moves back." "The Art of Poetry," one of Hugo's more consciously poetic poems, is not placed in Montana or Seattle or even in the human communities of baseball or jail. Addressed to "Sad Raymond" —who can be a name for the poet, the muse, or any man who dreams—the poem ranges far and wide: to Syria, Asia Minor, Norway, and Borneo. But these flights embellish a map of poetry's sources and directions. Starting with "the man in the moon was better not a man," the poem locates the sources of poetry in dissatisfaction: "Think, sad Raymond, how you glare across / the sea, hating the invisible near east / and your wife's hysteria" (p. 70). The succeeding stanzas begin with psychological directives, such as "Envy your homemade heroes when the tide is low" and "Think once how good you dreamed," and every eleven-line stanza ends with some variation on "Better the moon you need. Better not a man. / Sad Raymond, twice a day the tide comes in" (p. 70).

It seems a highly structured poem; full of the distance of artifice, the center of the poem contains the essence of that all-too-intimate rage that Hugo has had to handle most of his life.

> And think,
> sad Raymond, of the wrong way maturation came.
> Wanting only those women you despised, imitating
> the voice of every man you envied. The slow walk
> home alone. Pause at door. The screaming kitchen.
> And every day this window, loathing the real horizon.
> That's what you are. Better the man you are.
> Sad Raymond, twice a day the tide comes in. (pp. 70–71)

What seems artificially poetic—the moon, the tide, the man in the moon—emerges in the poem as elements that were as much a part of Hugo's childhood as the anger: "the screaming kitchen" and "your raging playfield." Those tides were present along the

Duwamish River where he used to fish and play in abandoned mills. That ocean that the moon controls, that touches Asia Minor, Norway, and Borneo, was a horizon familiar to a boy with time on his hands. The man in the moon becomes, in the final stanza, another part of Hugo, perhaps similar to that self that emerged from the dream fight in "The Lady in Kicking Horse Reservoir": "Those days you walk the beach / looking for that man who's pure in his despair." But in the last few lines of the poem, as with many others in this book, the longing, despair, and anger stop:

> He's never there. A real man walks the moon
> and you can't see him. The moon is cavalier.
> Better to search your sadness for the man.
> Sad Raymond, twice a moment tides come in. (p. 71)

The change in that final line from "twice a day [or night]" to "twice a moment" underlines the importance of "cavalier." The moon, the tides, the Near East, even Sad Raymond's name ("What if you were Fred"), are not what they might seem. The man the speaker searches for is not outside himself but is in his "sadness," in the anger that impelled the search. The "art" of poetry is interior, and "twice a moment" its tides roll, so changeable that they offer new readings of the past, the present, and new possibilities that run counter to the regression of "the way the mind moves back." The movement of those tides is the movement of self-acceptance in the poet, paralleling Hugo's statement, "an act of the imagination is an act of self-acceptance."[18] If there is, in *What Thou Lovest Well Remains American,* a fundamental statement that is at once crassly American and at the same time true, it concerns how the individual can shape and control his past failures and make something lasting and valuable.

The regressions of fixed roles and patterns are broken by this openness to "twice a moment," which is the foundation of poetry. As Hugo says to his wife, Ripley (to whom the book is dedicated), "We quit that road of sad homes long ago" ("Listen, Ripley," p. 57). The usefulness of poetry is not its memorializing of things beautiful but past, as in Pound's Pisan Cantos, but in its power to help the self gain at least a momentary strength to shape the psyche and transcend the poverty, the anger, "the wrong way maturation came" in this all-too-American life.

9

"The Strangest of Tongues, the Human": The Quest for Wholeness

It is no secret that contemporary American society breeds psychological stress and the resulting instability—especially among creative personalities. Names like Roethke and Plath, Berryman and Lowell, rapidly spring to mind when we consider post–World War II poets for whom psychological stress was a constant companion. Richard Hugo's *31 Letters and 13 Dreams* offers a similar portrait, but with an essential difference. Perhaps no American poet since Whitman has created a work in which the psychological quest for self-integration has been achieved in such a thoroughly social dimension. As Whitman made "Song of Myself" a poetry of all these states—embracing all about him in an expanding tide of catalogs—so Hugo has discovered a similar strength of self in a bipolar outreach of letters to friends and of dreams from his haunted psyche. The psychological quest for wholeness and the social discovery of personal connections in a fragmented society combine to make *31 Letters and 13 Dreams* a hallmark in contemporary poetry, best understood from the twin perspectives of psychological quest and social discovery.

31/13 began out of need. Hugo, an emerging poet teaching at the Iowa Writers Workshop in 1971, found himself drunk more often than not, alienated by his own actions from colleagues and from the women he dated, and haunted by images of western toughness and long-standing personal wounds: his father's abandonment of his mother and by his mother's abandonment of himself; the lingering aftershock of the collapse of his fourteen-year marriage six years before; and his nagging sense of worthlessness, a psychological by-product of those early abandonments and of his early poverty in White Center during the Depression. These facts he could not escape. They provide the psychological outline of a man for whom the added stress of acceptance and success became too much to bear. In the spring of 1971 the drinking, the alienation, isolation, and the fears of worthlessness all reached a climax, a "crack-up" as he put it, and after long-distance calls to friends like Carolyn Kizer and a short, desperate talk with Marvin Bell, director of the workshop, Hugo got into his car, left Iowa in midsemester, and drove nonstop back to Missoula, his home, and then to Seattle, where his history began, to seek therapeutic treatment for his alcoholism.

The facts of his crack-up appear in the first poems of *31/13*, three letter poems to Kizer, Bell, and Madeline DeFrees. Although the psychohistory underlying those facts appears in other letters by suggestion and implication, the nature of Hugo's psychological wounds is primarily left to the dream poems. True to the psychological condition that engendered the book, the letters and dreams reflect the deep divisions between self and society and within the self. The letters present facts, landscapes, and realistic details that hover around an image and a theme that seem to grow out of the detritus of everyday experience into a poetic epiphany. Each dream follows several letters and concentrates on an image or surreal landscape that embodies the psychological wound or, later in the book, reveals a hopeful, talismanic image as a way out of the chaos. At the time he wrote them, Hugo certainly did not apprehend this underlying organization—indeed, we are indebted to poet Ruth Whitman for finding the poems' arrangement—but his poetic imagination created the bipolar structure, presenting a picture of the process that Hugo unconsciously followed in reintegrating his concept of self.

31/13 is a book about healing ourselves and our society. This dimension becomes apparent as soon as one notices the relation of the letters to the dreams. The facts of Hugo's crack-up, presented in those letters to Kizer, Bell, and DeFrees, circle around and refer to the primary psychological scar of Hugo's flight from Iowa, the alienation displayed in "In Your Fugitive Dream." Anyone familiar with Hugo's earlier poetry, especially *The Lady in Kicking Horse Reservoir,* will notice the centrality of the town image in this dream poem. Appearing later in "In Your Small Dream" and "In Your Blue Dream," the strong presence of the town image locates *31/13* as an essential Hugo work and the poem "Fugitive Dream" as an emblem of a long-standing obsession in his poetry. Here, however, Philipsburg is no longer a town in a poem; it is a condition of the psyche, and that tough, isolated drifter in Hugo's most famous poem has become a fugitive, afraid to stop anywhere.

The parallelism of realist letters and psychologically oriented dreams continues throughout the book. Hugo's experiences in World War II—his flying thirty-five missions as a bombardier in Italy and his watching the Nisei, the Japanese-Americans, being shipped away to concentration camps—appear in letters to Charles Simic and William Matthews. They are followed by "In Your War Dream," where the haunted imagination says "you must fly your 35 missions again" and the dream landscape shifts from the bombardier's map to a place back home, as the isolated poet must "keep watch on Stark Yellow Lake." The racial reference is true to America's racist condition and shows how deeply the social wounds intertwine with personal scars in the psyche. When Hugo leaves his isolation and breaks into the cabin to be among the lovers there, he finds instead mothers baking bread—mothers who ship him back to the war, to fly his thirty-five missions again.

By this point in the book, we find that the dreams reflect social problems in American life as well as inner psychological trauma. The American image of tough, self-reliant, and isolated masculinity stands at the center of "In Your Bad Dream" and "In Your Young Dream." The constant, almost mechanical, and gearlike urgings for success through competition locate "In Your Racing Dream" among cyclists racing. The sexual fires of American culture set the ocean aflame in "In Your Hot Dream" while the social isolation of the poet defines "In Your Small Dream," where the town becomes a jail. Similarly, "In Your Blue Dream" unleashes a posse of women who hound the dreamer out of town, pointing derisively at him as he bleaches in the desert. "Blue Dream" begins to show the interrelatedness of the psychological scars; "In Your Wild Dream" continues this coalescence as several essentially American wounds—fear of women, fear for survival, fear of social isolation—create a complex of surreal surprises rising out of the one activity that Hugo has always trusted: fishing. But all this corruption—the dead fish that turns to vicious dog, the poetic town (Athens) that the fish leads into the poem, and the Arabs of that town—disappears: simple fishing returns; the dream becomes just a dream, not a nightmare. With the poet we reach an important psychic plateau, an image of freedom: "birds above you keep flying away."

"Wild Dream" follows three remarkably warm letters: the letter to Gary Snyder is a charming dream; the letter to Denise Scanlon a recounting of the values of "degrees of gray"; the third letter, to James Wright, is a romance of clouds and trout, that same primal poetic scene from *A Run of Jacks* that "Wild Dream" recapitulates. All three letters are essentially personal, connecting Hugo not only with friends but also with experiences important to his life: poetry, his early dispossession, and fishing. Following "Wild Dream," the connections are more social: the letter to John Haislip concerns the social isolation of the old; the letter to Edward Mayo points to the way that cheap publicity in the poetry business devalues the "long hard road" that poetry is; finally, the most important social letter in the book, "Letter to Levertov from Butte," recounts the sheer terror of that early poverty embedded in Hugo's life and in American society.

With "Letter to Levertov" the social connections of the letters reach a climax; the following dream, "In Your Dream on the Eve of Success," creates the psychological climax. After it, the dreams are no longer haunted: "In Your Big Dream" reveals a new Parnassus, the poet climbing above the birds to an atmosphere he calls home; "In Your Dream after Falling in Love" opens the prison doors around the psyche as that epitome of grace and charm, Fred Astaire, dances out and all prisons are abolished; "In Your Good Dream" shows the good Hugo town—jails open, people walking arm-in-arm—bathed in the glow at the end of a western movie. Surely it is unreal; surely it is a deep dream in American society, easily evoking wholeness, peace, and calm.

"Letter to Levertov from Butte" and "In Your Dream on the Eve of Success" provide the intersection of the social and the psychological, the heart of the matter in *31/13*. The realism of "Levertov" —the enduring poverty of the American underclass—is set off by the dream that is most American: success. For someone born in the lower class—as Hugo was—success becomes a distant, tantalizing dream. Defer that dream too long and its imminent arrival can endanger the entire self-image of a man who has felt neglected, isolated, and used to living at the tougher edge of rage. For Hugo, such a change in self-image threatens to destroy the poetic abilities that have grown up entwined around the poetic mask engendered by that psychology. In order to no longer see himself as poor, as a survivor of the empty mills down by the Duwamish River, Hugo had to learn to see himself as a success and to find a way to loosen the intertwining of poetic craft and mask, to reassess himself, and to keep "the value of the old, the value of the cruel."[1] He had to establish something entirely different in his poetic mask and style—something less reliant on tension, isolation, confrontation, and loss. He had to, in other words, make a newer poetry as he made a new man, overcoming the past and recognizing the grace of poetry apart from tension. All these factors combine in *31/13,* especially in the poem "On the Eve of Success."

Besides its pivotal position between nightmares and good dreams, "On the Eve of Success" is set apart by four other differences from the other dream poems: first, rather than landscape, this dream's setting is interior, perhaps indicating the interior of the self; second, rather than the shifting chaos of a divided consciousness, this dream is calm; third, rather than a fluid dream present with sudden changes in time, this dream has a clear sense of time past separated from numinous present and of life separated from dream; and, fourth, rather than faceless, nameless stick figures who pop in and out, this dream gives us two identifiable characters on whom the poem is built.

One of those characters—a warm, gregarious lout who in life tends bar and in the dream sells greeting cards—has the improbable name of Buss, evoking the familiar, the personal, as in *buss,* "to kiss." The other, although nameless, has all the social and intellectual importance of a successful man; he is the university president. As in any dream, both Buss and the university president are aspects of Hugo himself and represent the psychological divisions that gave rise to his breakdown. With his gregarious warmth, his bartending, and his added role as a star softball player, Buss connects Hugo to his past in White Center. The president defines Hugo's present in the university: checking papers that could be poems or student themes or bureaucratic memos, but also displaying a physical weakness, a fragility that could be read as emotional weakness, even as Hugo once was strong as Buss is.

With all the deference of the poor, Buss holds the door open for the president to enter the dreamer's house. But the president "can't get through," and his physical weakness increases as Buss and the dreamer watch him through the glass, just as the poor have always watched the successful from outside.

As the president, the image of success, falls, two women come to help. Like Buss and the dreamer, they are deferential in their aid to the president, but their help takes symbolic form in an improbable tomato, which they use to try and stop the president's choking. As an emblem, the tomato has several connections to the world of Buss and the younger Hugo: it is red as blood, about as big as a softball, certainly as common and as American a vegetable as could be found, and about as far from elegance and grace as it is possible to imagine—especially when one considers more aristocratic artichokes or artistic mushrooms. With its ready juices and gregarious seeds, the tomato is part of that physical and working-class world Buss and Hugo come from, an emblem of survival brought to help a weaker man survive.

But the president, the image of success, does not survive. In his death, however, something distinctly remains: the calm that can be seen in him is reflected in the calm tone of the poem and in the emotional completeness of the simple statements that make it up. The poem symbolically embodies the choices that Hugo has made in writing *31 Letters and 13 Dreams*. In his reintegration of self, Hugo has found the emotional strength of his earlier years and the enduring calm of the imagination to be reconcilable. The isolation, neglect, and tough masculine fear have faded, with the letters and dreams, as Hugo's poetry has turned toward those essential personal connections represented by Buss and the images of survival and help that the women provide. As in the dream poem, so in Hugo's life an authoritative though not quite understood calm begins to assert itself. In that calm we see the tantalizing dream of success transformed into a workable, personal confidence not found in the earlier dreams, into an acceptance, a poise, a grace that can accept defeat, loss, and even death. With such gains, the self can imagine better dreams, turning from the impinging terrors of past failures to an inner strength, a realization that poetry creates life as well as reflects the forces that have shaped us, misshaped us, and may have burdened us with a past, a prison part of us never wants to leave.

Limiting and confining as it is in the dream poems, the past also contains those positive values by which Hugo reintegrates his identity and his life. As the dream poems organize the volume by theme and delineate Hugo's psychological obsessions image by image, the letter poems show us—in lines as expansive as Whitman's—what kind of man Hugo is as he makes tenuous, long-distance connections to old friends, fellow poets, and lovers, creating, letter by letter, a sense of community. More approachable than the dreams, the letters appear less poetically crafted[2] as their fourteen-syllable lines all too often become prose, and the detritus of too much detail, too much personal chat, seems somehow an imposition of the personal on the poetic. But unlike the poetry of the dreams, where the personal disappears in the depths of psychological surrealism, the poetry of the letters begins with personal connections, includes the residue of remembered detail, connects present with past, recalls conversations and ideas, and notices the explosion of changes, of losses that have ravaged our society and our lives over the last thirty years. What begins in personal remembrance leads to social, even political, connections as the act of making those connections also constitutes the essential basis of community. Moreover, from that entirely social matrix in the midst of the letters there arises a poetic epiphany where, for a few lines, a single image or sentiment emerges above the realistic detail, revealing briefly the essence of the letter, the connection that endures through time and space.

Hugo's letter poems are rooted in the social and societal awareness that has always accompanied American realism. The first three letters refer to his own condition: surrounded by his past in Seattle, broken down in the blur of the road from Iowa to Missoula, lost in a drunken binge in Iowa City. From there, the letters point further to the past: to the war, to that time when vast cultural and technological changes began, "never to stop." In "Letter to Matthews from Barton Street Flats," Hugo remembers a Japanese-American friend, Tada, who was shipped with his family and others "like so many pigs to single thickness walled shacks in Wyoming / where winter rips like the insane self-righteous tongue / of the times. In

Germany, Jews. In America, Japs."[3] Whether American or German, these social wounds, fascist in nature, parallel psychological scars as they became part of the emerging technology that grew out of World War II. The idea of machinery—of the state as machinery—being more important than the lives and personal connections of people informs Hugo's vision in this poem and throughout the letters. The lost farms of the Nisei take on the function of a symbolic, as well as individual, tragedy as America loses itself in change: "the war took everything, / farm, farmers and my faith that change (I really mean loss) / is paced slow enough for the blood to adjust" (p. 11). The extent of that change, of the loss the war meant to the entire society, is evident in the vision of contemporary America that rises in the middle of the poem. Hugo sees a culture paved over and cut off from those natural springs that nurtured its poorer beginnings.

> Why, faced with this supermarket parking lot
> filled with gleaming new cars, people shopping unaware
> a creek runs under them, do I think back thirty some years
> to that time all change began, never to stop, not even
> to slow down one moment for us to study our loss, to recall
> the Japanese farmers bent deep to the soil? (p. 11)

Hugo's letters have in their heart this recognition of a national impoverishment: the destruction of communities by industrial or government machinery; the loss of a sense of community because of our rapid pace of life; the loss of our small towns, regrettable in spite of their repressive and rigid isolation that worked against anything new—all because of the mass technology unleashed by the most extensive and exhaustive of wars. As that technology herded the Nisei to concentration camps, it also affected those white Americans whom it was to have helped. People have lost touch with the sense of community; things have become what Hugo calls "slick" in "Letter to Goldbarth from Big Fork." In this poem Hugo recognizes the narrowness of small towns—"a mean suspicion of anything new, of anyone different / or bright"—but he also claims his poetic roots there.

> The forlorn towns
> just hanging on take me back to the 30's where most poems
> come from, the warm meaningful gestures we make, the warm ways
> we search each other for help in a bewildering world,

a world so terrifyingly big we settle for small
ones here we can control. (p. 59)

He goes on to call the people of such Montana towns, "my women, my men." Like most of the letter poems, "Letter to Goldbarth from Big Fork" has moments of poetic tension and prosaic relaxation. The poetry of life is tied to the prose of experience and the language of the letters reflects that tie. Moreover, merely seeing the stuff of ordinary human life, of essential human connections, has become, in a culture marked by more and more fantastic creations of technology, a poetic act in itself. Stable human connections have become a rarity. Hugo looks to the thirties not out of some nostalgia for simpler times—he has no desire to return to poverty—but for the force of human sentiment that became essential for survival in times of economic depression.

It is from that base in the poverty of the 1930s Depression that by far the most compelling—and genuinely angry—poem in the book is written. The poem immediately preceding "In Your Dream on the Eve of Success," "Letter to Levertov from Butte," is nothing if not an expression of the rage that is the inheritance of poverty. Although Denise Levertov may be far away in some glamorous place like Moscow or Montreal, Hugo is and always has been "in a town where children / get hurt early. Degraded by drab homes. Beaten by drunken / parents, by other children" (p. 54). And with an echo of "what endures is what we have neglected," he enters upon a description of this essential Hugo town by means of language at once direct and simple as prose but alive with the tensions of imagery and sound that are always the mark of his best poetry.

What endures
is sadness and long memories of labor wars in the early
part of the century. This is the town where you choose sides
to die on, company or man, and both are losers. . . .
On the one hand, no matter what my salary is
or title, I remain a common laborer, stained by the perpetual
dust from loading flour or coal. I stay humble, inadequate
inside. And my way of knowing how people get hurt, makes
my (damn this next word) heart go out through the stinking air
into the shacks of Walkerville, to the wife who has turned
forever to the wall, the husband sobbing at the kitchen
table and the unwashed children taking it in and in and in

until they are the wall, the table, even the dog the parents
kill each month when the money's gone. On the other hand,
I know the cruelty of poverty, the embittering ways
love is denied, and food, the mean near-insanity of being
and being deprived, the trivial compensations of each day,
recapturing old years in broadcast tunes you try to recall
in bars, hunched over the beer you can't afford, or bending
to the bad job you're lucky enough to have. (pp. 54–55)

This, then, is the evidence of hurt, the pain of need that lies behind Hugo's poetry. It gave him that "certainty of failure," which he has mined like "a tyrant for its pale perverted ore."[4] The effect of this hurt can go two ways; one way is hate: "How, finally, hate takes over, hippie, nigger, Indian, anyone you can lump / like garbage in .. pit, including women." But that is not Hugo's choice. His most natural impulse is to survive, not to kill; to preserve, not destroy; to work against, in whatever small way his words can, that machinery of our society that numbs the soul, that takes the lives of people as numbers in its economic or technological plan: "we have been told / too often by contractors, corporations and prudes that / our lives don't matter" ("Letter to Oberg from Pony," p. 63). Again, in "Letter to Matthews from Barton Street Flats": "we look hard for the broken toy, / the rock we called home plate, evidence to support our claim / our lives really happened" (p. 12); and again, in "Letter to Peterson from Pike Place Market": "that's nobility of blood, a recognition / by those who matter that in special moments / we are together facing the brute descent of the sun / and that cold brittle star we know already burned out" (p. 26); and again, in "Letter to Wagoner from Port Townsend": "we don't take / others by the hand and say: we are called people. The power / to make us better is limited even in the democratic sea" (p. 32); and to a former lover, in "Letter to Kathy from Wisdom": "please know / old towns we loved in matter, lovers matter, playmates, toys, / and we take from our lives those days when everything moved, / tree, cloud, water, sun, blue between two clouds, and moon, / days that danced, vibrating days, dance poem. . . . because you were my lover and you matter" (pp. 57–58).

Because our lives *matter*: this is the basic, instinctual level of feeling that has always helped the poor survive. The calm that integrates the self, that seems to follow success, is a surrender not to technology or to power but to humanity. Our connections to other people are the embodiment of this essential emotion, this instinctual level of feeling that the poor know well. The minimal, essential human bonds of family, of neighborhood, of town, have diminished with the rise of urban sprawl, fast food, and mass media. What is strange and poetic in our lives now is human speech, honest and uncluttered by jargon or governmental bureaucratese, which has given us words like *inoperative,* political rhetoric such as *anti-forced-sterilization activist,* or technological verbiage such as *implement* or *parameters.*

The preservation of the human is an essential struggle, and it puts behind us those divisions of race and politics that our government and media have fostered. In "Letter to Hill from St. Ignatius" this essential struggle appears in a town in Montana where a priest once mixed Catholic and Flathead Indian chants to form a Good Friday liturgy. In the light of such a place, Hugo says he has resented Roberta Hill's telling him "how I'd never know / what being Indian was like. All poets do. Including / the blacks. It is knowing whatever bond we find we find / in strange tongues" (p. 30). He goes on to mention his new wife, Ripley, who "chants when she talks in the strangest of tongues, the human." We find speech to be song when our world comes together, when the essential human connections between ourselves and with society are made firm.

"The strangest of tongues, the human" is the language in which *31 Letters and 13 Dreams* is written. The human tongue, strange to the forms of our technological newspeak, strange to our understanding of ourselves and our unquestioned belief in progress, works from the prose of experience to those moments of poetry that matter, that create a "just poem under an unjust sky" ("Letter to Annick from Boulder," p. 20). What makes the human tongue emerge from the vast stretches of technological complacency and numbness are those small elements of the personal connecting us to ourselves through moments of remembered style, when we are most human, finding success in the midst of our failures—something technology cannot allow—as in these lines from "Letter to Mantsch from Havre":

> I want to tell him style in anything,
> pitching, hitting, cutting hair, is worth our trying even
> if we fail. And when that style, the graceful compact swing

> leaves the home crowd hearing its blood and the ball roars off
> in night like determined moon, it is our pleasure
> to care about something well done. (p. 21)

Without style and grace, words are numbers or facts, tokens to be placed in the machinery of information. Hugo's letters begin as information but work against the machinery of fact to find the connections that make us human, that are part of the machinery of our lives, our remembrance, but that rise above it. In some poems, those connections are overtly humorous, as in "Letter to Bell from Missoula," where "a religious nut" offers "unqualified salvation / if I took a year's subscription to Essential Sun Beam" (p. 5); or in "Letter to Stafford from Polson," where a "new heavy kind of posse" chases a "new wolf" into the mountains, only to find "he's green with red diagonal stripes / and jitters in wind like a flag" (p. 28); or in "Letter to Snyder from Montana," where the advent of the California poet influences the weather: "Should have warned all western Montana, / a warm force is coming. Snows will run off. The rivers / will scream and crack their banks. Winter will take a breather" (p. 45).

In all the letters—as in the dreams—the small, essential connections create the poetry as Hugo shifts quickly from image to image, in the dreams, and from fact to heightened realism, in the letters. Together the letters and dreams enact a poetics with the equivalent of that theme of minimal social connections that we find in Hugo's poetry since *A Run of Jacks*. In the letters particularly those minimal connections fill the American landscape as they overcome vast physical and ethnic differences and even succeed in recovering from that extremity of distance in American culture, the past, values that informed what were perhaps our greatest tests as a society: the Depression and World War II. Hugo sees us as a people atomized and isolated by our successes: we write to each other across the vast distances of American space, making our lives a rush of space, making our experience of time entirely present. Hugo's letters ultimately face the overwhelming space and isolation of technological society not with anger—although there is a strong undercurrent of proletarian rage—but with the realistic recognition of the necessity of human community in the face of anything huge, be it wilderness, Montana weather, economic desolation, or technological isolation. His poetics is based not on the traditions of culture but on the facts of American society. Like Williams, Sandburg, and Whitman, Hugo finds the American poem not in the great empty dream but in the small, local reality that rises above the avalanche of facts, perceptions, and the changes of the ever threatening newness of America. In that locality, Hugo finds his home and fittingly returns to that desolate home of his childhood, White Center, for his next book. Moreover, Hugo raises that same impulse to greater cultural importance as he traces its historical resonances in *The Right Madness on Skye* (1980).

10

"Some Continuum of Song": From *White Center* to *The Right Madness on Skye*

By returning again and again, in *31 Letters and 13 Dreams,* to the emerging problems of identity and stability and the rapid accumulation of losses from a rapidly expanding technological society, Richard Hugo demonstrates how important understanding the societal aspects of his poetry is to understanding the whole of his work. Even as he grew up in the thick of social and economic calamity, the Depression, so each of his books of poetry is marked by some social aspect: the odd and outcast, the poor, the desperate toughness of young soldiers, the equally desperate toughness of the western hero, the isolated town, the regressive tendencies of male sexuality, the advancing losses in a technological society. This is not to say that Hugo's poetry is a sociological or a psychological document, but it is impossible to read Hugo's poetry without noticing the nuances of social class and of economic need, and how these forces create psychological dynamics within the growth of the poet's mind and in the mind of man.

My choice of those last two high-sounding phrases is intentional: both are from Wordsworth, and both define the argument of his monumental work—much praised, less read—*The Prelude.* All American poetry derives, through Emerson, from Wordsworth and Coleridge, from the "Preface" to *Lyrical Ballads,* "The Idiot Boy," and "Frost at Midnight" as much as from *The Prelude,* "The Rime of the Ancient Mariner," and *Biographia Literaria.* Since the elevation of Wallace Stevens's poetry of the mind, much has been said about this second strand of Wordsworth, the high romantic Wordsworth of the "spots of time" and the "Intimations Ode"; witness, for example, Geoffrey Hartman's fine critical study, *Wordsworth's Poetry, 1787–1814* (1964). This is the Wordsworth of imaginative power, fixated, according to Hartman, on the "omphalos," fascinated by and tied to specific spots that liberate the mind from the "realia," the hard, necessary facts of nature, and discover the mind's full power.[1]

The problem with Hartman's study (not a problem at all for Hartman, considering his turn to deconstructionism) is that it demeans the social aspects of Wordsworth's poetry and poetics and demeans the high degree of morality in his writings, his insistence on the correct education of the imagination throughout *The Prelude* and on what he saw as the necessity of a society like that of the rural Lake District for the maintenance of imaginative powers (as opposed to the wasting of imaginative strength in hectic cities like London). This Wordsworth is, at best, often overlooked or, at worst, dismissed along with his real sins: his wordiness, his increasing tide of sentimentality and conventionality as he became ensconced in his role as poet laureate. Clearly Wordsworth wasted himself in later years by writing "ecclesiastical sonnets," but even that part of his career outlines a primal concern: the morality of the poet, his or her connection both to the divine and to the community of man, of whom the poet is always one, "a man speaking to man." This is the earlier Wordsworth, a regionalist like Burns (whom he admired, although it is hard to imagine any connection between two poets so dissimilar—Wordsworth was abstemious; Burns profligate), a man governed, often hamstrung, by the conflicting impulses of romantic dream and realistic fact—even to the point of measuring an important pond in "The Thorn" ("'Tis three feet long and two feet wide").

Although he had moments of cosmic vision—such as the "Characters of the Apocalypse" and the ascent up Mount Snowden—Wordsworth had a crotchety desire to stay put in Grasmere, hiking through the bracken and the wind; making poems out of everyday, minimal occurrences; seeing, with his sometime sentimental eye, the daffodils instead of the sheep droppings. But his reclusiveness was tied as much to his rural community and the rhythms of nature as it was to the wedding of his mind with the greater forms of nature. And it is this earlier Wordsworth who wrote the following in the "Preface" (1800) to *Lyrical Ballads:*

> Low and rustic life was generally chosen because in that situation the essential passions of the heart find a better soil and speak a plainer and more emphatic language; because in that situation our elementary feelings exist in a state of greater simplicity and consequently may be more accurately contemplated and more forcibly communicated; because the manners of rural life germinate from those elementary feelings; and from the necessary character of rural occupations are more easily comprehended; and are more durable; and lastly, because in that situation the passions of men are incorporated with the beautiful and permanent forms of nature.[2]

"Essential passions of the heart"; "elementary feelings"; "manners of rural life germinate from those elementary feelings" and are "more durable"—these phrases are not claims for transforming imaginative power, nor need they be read as sentimentalizing rural life. The passage incorporates the fundamental, essential social feelings that hold a rural society like the Lake District's together. As with Burns and his Scotland, Wordsworth wrote *Lyrical Ballads* in part because he sensed the loss of this society, a sense that increased with the years and became an overriding fear that man would lose touch with nature altogether in an increasingly urban society. It is not hard to see a comparison with Hugo, especially the Hugo of *31 Letters and 13 Dreams*. Their differences are due to different historical periods: where Hugo sees human connections as being more and more tenuous in a technological society, in later years Wordsworth believed that the essential bonds between man and nature—to create and keep a humane society—were similarly more and more tenuous. That belief lay behind Wordsworth's addition, in the 1850 "Preface" to *Lyrical Ballads,* of this extraordinary definition of the poet:

> He is the rock of defense for human nature; an upholder and preserver, carrying everywhere with him relationship and love. In spite of differences of soil and climate, of language and manners, of laws and customs: in spite of things silently gone out of mind, and things violently destroyed; the poet binds together by passion and knowledge the vast empire of human society, as it is spread over the whole earth, and over all time.[3]

This may be grand "organ music" rhetoric (to borrow Eliot's description of Milton), but it also includes some obvious parallels to Hugo: things lost silently or violently; the importance of relationships, of binding things together "by passion and knowledge." Wordsworth's "Preface" clearly establishes the social aspect of the poet as at least as important as the more highly praised imaginative aspect of higher romanticism. Indeed, Wordsworth seems to carry within himself both the overarching idealism that Emerson and others translated (borrowing also from Coleridge and Carlyle) into transcendentalism and also those seeds of the antiromantic that realist and naturalist writers nurtured to fruition, especially in America. To be Wordsworthian, then, is to be in a line that includes, among others, Bryant, Emerson, Whitman, Robinson, Sandburg, Hughes, Frost, Jeffers, Williams, Gwendolyn Brooks, and Lowell—as well as the highly imaginative Stevens. To be Wordsworthian is to be concerned with the poet's relation to society and, in American poetry, to be concerned with the problems of American society.

Like Wordsworth, Hugo has his dreams—more often in the currents of trout streams than on mountain tops; however, Hugo is much more successful than Wordsworth in writing about those thorns and idiot boys in his life, writing with greater finesse and integration of the realistic facts of society and the dreams and songs of the imagination. "The Swimmer at Lake Edward," "The Freaks at Spurgin Road Field," "Ghost in a Field of Mint," "Neighbor," and other poems about the outcast, the underside of America's glitter, the isolated lives lived far from London or New York or Los Angeles—these are as much a part of the Wordsworthian tradition as any meditations on nature. This is the part of Wordsworth that Hugo has resurrected from the mixed successes of Masters and Williams. More, indeed, than is healthy for his reputation in an American critical environment enamored of the "irreducible" (Marjorie Perloff's critical touchstone)[4] or the oblique and interpretatively "evasive" (Harold Bloom's critical pet), Hugo writes a poetry that not only opens landscape to dreams but also opens the tragedies of isolated lives to point to the failures of human community.

Since *A Run of Jacks* (1961) Hugo's poetry has been marked by two constant currents: the Wordsworthian landscape opening to dream, and the more realistic images of fragmented, isolated individuals. These two currents reach their furthest possible extensions in *31 Letters and 13 Dreams* (1977), where the poet shows those landscape-based dreams opening still further into his own haunted psyche and those fragmented lives as being one composite portrait of our alienation in the wake of the accelerated technological advances of American society. *31 Letters and 13 Dreams* is, in some ways, a cry *de extremis,* a more social and societal rendering of Roethke's psychological cry *de profundis,* "the edge is what I have." After the edge, where next? For Hugo, the answer had to be home, to White Center, his working-class neighborhood outside Seattle. It is entirely characteristic of Hugo, however, that there were two responses to his extremity, that the working out of his need for humanity should take both a realist and a romantic turn. Therefore, Hugo first publishes a book based on the facts of his home, even entitling it *White Center* (1980), and then publishes a book far more resonant, evocative, and suggestive of a spiritual home, *The Right Madness on Skye* (1980). Together, the two books locate and measure the dimensions of that home to which Hugo's poetry has been tending since the trout streams of *A Run of Jacks.*

It is a home that takes seriously the past and the confining imprint of necessity. However, in that home, Hugo knows the mind's tendency to lie, to say the not-quite-truthful thing, or to keep the hurtful past alive so that we can simplify wrongs to sentimentality. In *White Center* the facts of the past all too often slide toward half-truths, and the speaker catches himself up short: "No. Let me try again."[5] Moreover, all too often the imagined dream—by this time in Hugo's career tied only loosely to landscape—slides from the dream world to become frighteningly realistic. Such is the effect of "Museum of Cruel Days," which starts the volume and which, with the title poem, "White Center," frames the book in a vision of enduring human cruelty.

The beginning of "Museum" is tentative, half-real, half-dream: "It's not you, this dead long moan from the past, / the whip coiled, not just for display but to fit tight / in the case . . . these mementos seem ancient. Seem recent" (p. 1). As the effects of ancient cruelty persist, cruelty takes on the dimensions of all history, a history in large part unwritten because it belongs to the victimized: "This volume of grief / that crawls down the ages dissonant in its demand. / A Turk whip is no grain of sand." The Blakean allusion is bitter and antiromantic, based not on a vision but on those blank facts of peasant lives that have infused so much of Hugo, nowhere more so than in "Letter to Levertov from Butte." But there is, in this hardfisted dream, an opening to mitigating facts: "Peasants are free and still peasants. . . . And if inside you / a fist waits to beat back the bad man you are / that hand opens in hunger" (p. 2). The vision of historical cruelty, the dreams of peasant history—the entire museum of cruelty fades as Hugo's constant vision of peasant necessity rises clearly: hunger is more real than cruelty, and peasants must "buy whatever hunger / looks good on the stand." That last line of the poem takes the harsh reality into deeper areas of the psyche: peasants don't buy food, but hunger; they learn to stay alive on little, to live without real nourishment or material growth ("peasants start eating. Not well"). They buy their dreams as they buy their food—and a poet does no less.

White Center develops this interrelation between dream and need, between imagination and stark detail, through a wide array of modes and styles. Following "Museum of Cruel Days" come first a glimpse of the Hugo town—"that town hanging wherever / you are, whatever you do" ("After a Train Trip, One Town Remains," p. 3)—then a poem dedicated to Philip Levine (and written in a line much shorter than Hugo's standard), and an evocation of Stevens in a poem entitled "Scene." There is no hope of realism in this latter poem; all is surreal, comic, joyous in the creation of a rural paradise: lovers inside a barn, a creek nearby, the green sky "dotted with silly clouds / that looked like dimes." Hugo, poet and painter, enjoys this newfound imaginative strength, which is rooted in his earlier poem "The Art of Poetry" and in some of the happier letters and dreams.

> And let's say let's say woman and man.
> One barn at a time. One moon.
> The dimes are dark monsters
> ignoring the lovers. The horses
> who are also lovers and asleep.
> Deep inside deep that is the scene
> and I never wake up. (p. 7)

This poem is quite different from "Museum of Cruel Days": "Scene" is pure romance, a romance of romances, playfully shifting perspectives as in much of Stevens's poetry, although Hugo only rarely brings himself to number each of those "ways of looking at" some blackbird or scene.[6] Throughout *White Center* the moments of romance punctuate the accumulations of memory and cruelty much as in *31 Letters and 13 Dreams* but without the overriding order of that earlier volume. In these dreams, moreover, Hugo is more willing to act, to create, to enter fully into the world of his art instead of using that art to react, to judge, to try and make sense of his life and the cruelty he has seen. In fact, two of his poems, "How to Use a Storm" and "How Meadows Trick You," focus on using the world for art instead of using art as a way to relieve the harshness of the world. In both poems the element of belief—of our response to natural conditions as being willed—guides the poem and lays out alternative readings of the landscape, even turning to advice as in "Storm" ("Better we plan our kitchen to trap / whatever light arrives") and to comic literary poses in "Meadows" ("If I say thistle and the glint is tin / and picnics never happened, you can believe / something in me is modern").

But more representative of his gains in imaginative authority are the several shorter romances, like "Scene," that shift in dream to create sheer delight—as in "Snow Poem," "The Carnival Inside," or "Bay of Recovery"—each one deeply indebted to Stevens and that blackbird. In "Snow Poem" there is no blackbird, but a "snotty owl," a warm wren, and a vengeful hawk, and—after forgetting "that damn fool lecture / I gave last winter"—the mixed terror and beauty of "outside, the dead dove drifting." Another dream poem, "The Carnival Inside," indicates Hugo's imaginative growth since "Degrees of Gray in Philipsburg." Once more the speaker is in a strange town, but instead of rage, he finds music, dancing, and pleasure and promises himself "I'll never go back." In the next stanza, however, the music dies, and the police explain the religious reason—"we give thanks for fun"—as the speaker is left "empty in the empty square." He leaves, works, and then one day decides to go back to town; it has been destroyed, but now the speaker takes the carnival inside himself: "I sing in the fields and I've decked the scarecrow / in satin. The moon is a grand comedian. / I laugh so hard I hurt" (p. 56). The allusion to Stevens is blatant; so is the final, bittersweet qualification. Beneath the satin, beneath the grand comedian, is hurt. The knowledge and creation of romance goes only so far. Romance, like the knowledge of nature—of meadows and storms—resolves eventually to the mind's growing awareness of itself as perceiver, shaper, as well as respondent to reality. Always in *White Center* there is, if not the shock, then the slow tide of recognition as Hugo circles and addresses the many sides of home, taking its dimensions not only from the museum of cruel days but also from the pleasures of romance and the carnival inside.

Through most of the book, in one mode or another, Hugo's use of dream-shifts and memory is more deliberate than ever before. It is as if he were trying to put something right, to get the right perspective for the correct vision of some landscape or some past experience, the total truth of which seems always to slide out of reach. Sometimes there is someone else present, and the speaker acts as interpreter or intermediary, as in "With Ripley at the Grave of Albert Parenteau" and "With Melissa on the Shore." Here, the levels of experience overlay each other. Past memory and present connections make response and judgment that much more important and make it difficult to get at the whole truth. Similar instances of reconsideration, changes in perception, memory, or landscape, occur in "Medicine Bow," "A Good View from Flagstaff," "Changes at Meridian," and "Guns at Fort Flager." If Wordsworth was right that we both half perceive and half create the landscape around us, then Hugo wants to be as honest as a man can be in his sight of things, in his being part of the making of the scene: "What nags is / loss of loss, the desperate way I brought farms back / because I wanted the pastures always slanted gently / into the lake, warm reflection of willow and cow" ("Changes at Meridian," p. 48). If he sees too much cruelty, he can unsee it:

> A good view here. We ignore the mean acts
> in the houses though we can't forget they go on
> daily with the soul's attrition. We are certain
> why the plowhorse limps. Spread the way it is
> by wind, the world in cultivated patchwork
> claims we travel on the right freight one day
> and the years are gone. At worst
> they're more than nothing. The best friends
> we remember took us home the way we are. (p. 40)

Although a restatement of an old romantic problem, Hugo's "A Good View from Flagstaff" is a peculiarly western American view. Wordsworth wrestled with the choice of accepting "things as they are" and infusing them with "transforming pow'r" in "Home at

Grasmere," and the poem never got finished. Hugo gives up the transcendent power in the face of the brutal realism of "At worst, they're more than nothing," a sentiment that creates vistas of acceptance as wide as Montana skies. The acceptance of that evil, the "mean acts" in the houses, is the heart of *White Center,* and it depends not on some altruistic motive or poetic transcendence but on a simple psychological fact: acceptance is not intellectual, but emotional; friendship and human contact precede intellect or judgment. Because of friends and finding home, it is possible to accept those houses of the soul's attrition as part of the "good view."

Those houses, mean acts and all, have been a part of Hugo's poetry since "Duwamish": "the smoke from the small homes / turns me colder than wind from the cold river." In *White Center,* moreover, houses form a substantial theme of the book, figuring importantly in poems such as "Beaverbank," "Doing the House," "At the Cabin," "Dwelling," "Repairing the House, the Church, Restoring the Music," and, most important, the second to the last poem in the book, "Houses," in which the realism of accumulated details and the natural inclination of the mind to dream meet:

> Some say, "where I hang my hat." Some say, "where
> the heart is beating through hurt." Whatever
> you say, make sure it's alone in a cold garage,
> the mechanic's hammer banging you mute.
> . . . .
> Make sure your car when fixed
> will not break down between the home in the sketch
> and the home you deny, the boy with your mouth
> who shouts goodbye from the roof. (p. 68)

Hugo is concerned throughout *White Center* with the morality of vision and the morality of memory: what we see we may more than half create; what we remember may be fantasy. He has no hesitation about following simple realism ("where I hang my hat") with heavier romanticism ("the heart beating through hurt") and about undercutting both with a starker realism, wise to the failings of simplicity and of romance: talk of home should be covered by loud, harsh noise so that the general effect is neither public convention nor public posturing but privacy and intimacy—that which makes a home, whatever the home's contents. Significantly, Hugo ends the poem with an image of animals "you hadn't thought of for years" living on the lawn, an ending that puts romance to the service of realism: home requires facts not romance; and those facts (the animals' names) belong to something extraordinary.

"Houses," by its placement, helps us to read the passionate complexity of the book's title poem, "White Center." Here the general scheme of "Houses" is made specific: the names of Toughy Hassin, Mr. Kyte, the Dugans, and the drunk who "fell / in our garden" (from the early poem "Neighbor") populate a town that we have seen with increasing clarity throughout Hugo's career. Even clouds, the governing metaphor of "Spinazzola: *Quella Cantina Là*," and other references to *Good Luck in Cracked Italian* (1969) show up in lines that speak volumes about Hugo's life: "But your odd love and a war / taught me the world's gone evil past the first checkpoint / and that's First Avenue South" (pp. 69–70). Hugo's companion through the poem, on this walk through White Center, is his grandmother, her agrarian patience appearing as the ghost in several poems ("The Way a Ghost Disolves," "Ghost in a Field of Mint"). What emerges in "White Center" is the sense that the whole town is Hugo's house, its people the walls he has had to face throughout his career. Those people, all too human in their failings, reflect the complexity of homes. Although his grandmother walks with him, it is to her that he says, "I am the man you beat to perversion," and the connections and ambivalences among the history of cruelty, the chance of dreams, and the morality of the poet's vision weigh heavily in this important poem.

> Because I'm married
> and happy, and across the street a foster child
> from a cruel past is safe and need no longer crawl
> for his meals, I walk this past with you, ghost in any field
> of good crops, certain I remember everything wrong. (p. 70)

That certainty may be the strength of a foster child, as Hugo was, finding safety; it may also be an indication that the violence surrounding us cannot but force us into slanted vision and half-memories, into a position from which we struggle to see the past as it was. Hugo titles a book of poems *White Center* only as he achieves some perspective on the violence within his life and within that town "where children get hurt early." He is able to see his home and his town with a realistic vision that encompasses romance, in which the shifting perspectives of a particularly romantic mode of poetry derived from Stevens play a major role in Hugo's energetic efforts toward that most Wordsworthian of goals: a moral vision that sees nature and humanity with sympathy and clarity and that sees them as truthfully as possible.

That power of his moral vision infuses Hugo's *The Right Madness on Skye* with its peculiar strength. No other Hugo book says as little about Hugo the man; no other Hugo book accomplishes so much of what his whole career has been progressing toward. The regionalism of *A Run of Jacks* and *Death of the Kapowsin Tavern* (1965), the bone-deep shudder at war and survival in *Good Luck in Cracked Italian,* the wrestling with American images of isolation and masculinity in *The Lady in Kicking Horse Reservoir* (1972) and *What Thou Lovest Well Remains American* (1975), the enactments of degradation and community in *31 Letters and 13 Dreams,* and the slow, careful reassessment of the cruelties and dreams of his hometown in *White Center* all trace the development of a man always faithful to his peasant, working-class values, a man who has not adopted the pedantries of higher criticism but has kept to the essentials of regionalism in American poetry: that quest to discover, to realize fully, what makes this land a home.

So how can it be that such an American quest for definition occurs on a misty island off the coast of Scotland full of ancient Scottish, Viking, and Celtic legends? Has the Celtic in Hugo (he was born Richard Hogan) enacted some infatuation with the "Celtic Twilight"? Hardly. There may be mist, but the tendency of the poems in *The Right Madness on Skye* is toward rock, toward that Scottish meagerness in the face of harsh north winds, toward those neolithic monoliths unchanged through centuries. What we see in *Right Madness* is a peasant American suddenly immersed in an ancient culture after generations of life in flux. Skye could be in Africa or Asia as well as on the coast of Scotland—any place stripped of the acceleration of changes in which Americans live their lives. Rather than change, Hugo seeks constancy; rather than the losses we forget as we "progress," he seeks the cultivation of poor fields, of landscapes and seascapes where we learn from failure, from age, from loss that is not mere change: "we must survive sad moments, must go on ploughing / after the invaders sail, all we love left broken / or dead: lamb, hut and barbarians' wake."[7]

On Skye, away from America and its accelerations, those peasant values that Hugo has felt all his life—and has, at times, felt ashamed of—are consistent with the place. Those peasant values find voice, find a home, throughout the volume: "We need that land of slow recovery, the grief passed / wife to daughter, some continuum of song" ("A Map of Skye," p. 12); "In any century, to stay humane we lived / in one or another kind of isolation, far as we could / from highway and harm" ("Ferniehurst Castle," pp. 45–46); "we're left with whatever / we find inside to keep going" ("The Cairn in Loch An Duin," p. 54). In "Greystone Cottage" the feeling of daily life on Skye is at its clearest: "This place, this near sacred space between people and homes" where "the clock in the kitchen reminds me of a time / few people dropped by and all mattered" (pp. 13–14). Hugo is drawn to the people who are, like the landscape, "warmer than you think on first sight, with no throw-away charm / like in cities. . . . They are most accommodating, the Scots, most given to accepting fate" ("Letter to Garber from Skye," p. 57). Hugo continues this portrait of the Scots by making reference to that history of cruelty they have endured, a history that marks the peasant heritage whether in Scotland, Poland, Mali, or China.

> To be good as these people are, you must have cruelty
> deep in your history, must have tested your capacity
> for hate long ago and know how bad it can be and what
> it can do. There are castles of the cruel in ruin.
> And megalithic forts. The blood of our mothers has dried. (p. 57)

As in *White Center,* so in *The Right Madness on Skye* cruelty, its history, its effects, and its acceptance lie behind an acceptance of home. Scottish history and legend are full of the echoes of cruelty, from the strange monoliths at Kensaleyre to the ninth-century Viking invasions ("A Map of Skye," "Clachard") to the Loch Ness monster and the less well-known waterhorse legend of "Sneosdal" ("are we out of monsters? . . . no one more interesting than ourselves to fear?," p. 27) to Celtic uprisings in "The Braes" and the last spasm of authentic Scottish nationalism in "Culloden"—the pillaging and fears, the wars and murders, are part of the landscape, part of those connections that define the land's people. In "Villager" Hugo gives us a clear picture of a peasant on Skye, a petty thief who drinks too much and whose eyes look out on the sea to say "no boat will come": "oblivion / is what he must have often to survive" (p. 59). As with other outcasts, from "Neighbor" to "The Freaks at Spurgin Road Field," Hugo is able to engage a sympathy that values humanity in all its forms and realizes that "No two hurts are the same, and most have compensations / too lovely to leave." What separates "Villager" from those other, earlier outcasts, however, is the final stanza, which throws away all ironic distance and lets sympathy sing:

> I almost forgot: he'd do anything for you. Love him
> for what you might have become
> and love him for what you are, not that far
> from him. We are never that far. Love
> everyone you can. . . . we're seldom better than weather. (p. 60)

It would be easy to call this "sentimental," except there is no penumbral glory around this latter-day "idiot boy": he drinks, he steals, and he won't listen to easy poems. The phrases "he'd do anything for you" and "we're seldom better than weather" frame the poem's sentiment in its essential gray coloring of need. This need, in the face of storms and wind, is what "holds it together" in a peasant society on a beautifully austere island off the coast of an ancient and once-proud country.

This image of society based on need is the same whether on Skye or in Montana or Seattle. On Skye the image is heightened and at the same time more romantic and more essential in its composition. The peasant society survives through song, in the occupations on land and sea, and even in the enduring shapes of the awesome monoliths at Clachard and Callanish. Those stones rivet society to the land, to an economy that does not expand but that survives wind, storm, Viking invasion, and English haughtiness. It is easy to see, then, how those stones entice Hugo's imagination. He sees "The Standing Stones of Callanish" in snow ("the shadows will take you out of yourself," p. 48) and guesses their pattern is the dawn of art, an unspoken effort to shape the world; he falls in love with the "Druid Stones at Kensaleyre," the two there standing—"woman and man, I'd guess, will age no faster / than the bay they overlook"—and he resolves to become a third: "three of us solid / forever above and one with the sea" (p. 36).

So rooted in an enduring landscape, connected to peasants, to sky and land and sea, Hugo takes aim at that cruelty hovering in the air around Skye, and he focuses on it in two poems: "Kilmuir Cemetery: The Knight in Blue-Green Relief" and "The Clearances." Hugo begins the former poem sympathetic toward the knight, Angus of the Storms, whose stone monument has been pushed around over the years—a sympathy increased by the final gesture of the first stanza: "and we've run out of knights" (p. 28). But this evident docility proves the equivalent of black "shufflin' " in the feudal American South. With Angus dead and under stone, Hugo the peasant feels safe enough to ask, "And were you really / that brave?," and the poem is off on a rousing crescendo of populist disbelief in heroes, even if those heroics are well founded, as were those of the "screwy Jew" who flew extra missions against Nazi Germany during World War II. Hugo is impressed only by the waste embedded in glory and heroism: "gulls collected to shade / your blood from drying too fast in the sun. / That was a great moment. We went on ploughing" (p. 29).

The shows of heroism do not last. Raw brutality does, with or without the patina of glory. Hugo the peasant, mock-heroic, dares this small-boned ancient knight out of his stone, out of his mail, his sword, and shield: "I'd / knee you in the balls, I'd kick your ass north / all the way to the pole" (p. 29). Such barroom bravery, however, lasts even less than the earlier false sympathy; soon the realistic peasant vision reasserts itself: "Something right goes wrong / with brutality when it loses history and style." The poem's final image concentrates on a world where, whatever the heroism, "we are sand falling home / leaving no trail," implying that our common insignificance makes brutality that much less human, that much less justifiable by presumptions of taste or tradition.

A similar moment of reflection on the overpopulated world away from Skye ends another cemetery meditation, "St. Clement's: Harris."

> I come from a monstrous age, white cliffs
> climbing and climbing out of whatever painting
> I saw once, climbing out of the frame
> and somewhere above
> issuing light that released became
> some aimless immediate plural. (p. 56)

Apart from the sources of stability—the peace that unites people and homes, those connections among people that help them to survive in the face of wind—we are aimless generations of sheer number. While celebrating the essential connections of human society, Hugo still is aware of that other history, the one without the style of Angus of the Storms, which has helped to make our world one vast dispossession, one "aimless immediate plural." That other history is not celebrated, but lives in the losses of the past. On Skye, it is the history of those peasant crofters who were dispossessed, as they were in other parts of Scotland, of home and property as they were herded on boats and given unsure futures in Australia, Canada, and America. These were "the Clearances" of the eighteenth century, a classic example of the high style of capitalism: people were cleared out to make room for more profitable sheep. Hugo is brutally bitter: "Lord, it took no more than the wave of a glove, / a nod of the head over tea" (p. 22). The image of the absentee landlord is clear: he is so abstracted from Skye that he has no conception of the reality of his edict. However, Hugo refuses to escape into sentimentality about past losses. He tries a sentimental definition, "The lovelier the land / the worse the dispossession," and discards it in the face of contrary evidence from contemporary America: blacks and Puerto Ricans cried when they were cleared out of their shacks or slums. There is a fierce, peasant equality operant here: "We've all lost something or we're too young to lie / to say we hear crofters sobbing / every high tide." When also tied to present dispossessions, the sentiment is strong and imperative: to recall the loss through the truthful lie of poetry is to keep hold on that dispossession that has made us all, as Americans, sand, "aimless, immediate plural."

Of course Hugo, as inheritor of those few Celtic chants and spells that survived Viking invasion and English conquest and American encroachments, will have the crofters back: "and say it was a mistake. The landlord was drunk. / He's happy you're here. Don't worry." But the magic is lost as the dispossessed "laugh loud as money" (p. 23) and come back "the way they left, / numbed by hard labor and grim." The poet, the master of song, is "no friend in their flat eyes." The wages of dispossession are the death of that "continuum of song," that peasant heritage so much a part of

Hugo's poetry in general and of *The Right Madness on Skye* in particular.

As if to celebrate that heritage, to resuscitate it, much of this book sings: images, specific sounds, and words circle through the poetry of the volume like some melancholy hum. Three poems, moreover, specifically celebrate singing as they divide the book into rough thirds: "Piping to You on Skye from Lewis," "Langaig," and "The Right Madness on Skye." The first of these is a near villanelle, with lines on the fading Gael and the haunting theme of dispossession structuring the poem. Gracefully, gently, the poet bends to the radio's static to find "in bagpipe overtones the drumming reason / to say goodbye to the islands only once" (p. 21). Radio music—intimate connection across vast distances — provides an important background to "Langaig," as, while fishing, Hugo recalls a modern Celtic singer, Bing Crosby: "Today I believe: fish hard and hum every tune / I remember hearing the dead singer sing / and leave believing in being like him to others" (pp. 41–42). The intimate silence of fishing parallels the intimacy of remembered songs, places, people, and events that we remember because we "hum when alone, and hum wrong." What risks sentimentality achieves greater emotional effect, and in this poem Hugo likens fishing not only to singing but also to the luck he has had "to have / a job teaching others to sing." As he reels in the trout, he "recover[s]" a dead singer from his songs, and poetry again is the making of life out of loss.

Ending the book, "The Right Madness on Skye" is a divine bit of play, with its speaker "not buried. Only cold on the slab," who protests too much piping, tosses out gratuitous one-line jokes, puns on dispossessed Indians ("Bury my wounded knee at Flodigary"), dispossessed princes (Hamlet), and dispossessed Moors (Othello). It is a remarkable *tour de force,* with Harry of Nothingham (note the spelling and the allusions to rich-versus-poor Robin Hood legend), the "absentee landlord driver," hounded mercilessly by the refrain, "Tell Harry of Nothingham slow." With each stanza, the "dead" peasant commands, warns, and pontificates, often with black humor: "Give the piper and drum five minutes / and explain to them, dead, I tire fast" (p. 61). In fact, the poem dances with wit: "let the corpse dance. Make the living lie still" (p.

62); "Just because / I've no religion don't say heaven can't welcome me back / under the new majority quota now in effect." There is deep political cynicism active here; a little too much music and the "wrong madness" for Skye intrudes: "Wrong / for dispossessed crofters who didn't want me to die / and wrong for comedians waiting for final returns." The election imagery is clear, and the play on "final returns" for politicians (comedians) and the dispossessed (who are Hugo's constituency) cuts deeper to the final return of the body to earth.

Unlike "The Clearances," in "The Right Madness on Skye" Hugo's Celtic magic works—it was all a joke, "I was holding my breath all the time." Moreover, the singer here even enters his own song with "these eyes I kept closed tight in this poem," a death mask that doubles as an allusion to other, perhaps more heroic, blind singers—Homer and Milton. Here, however, the mask, the power of songs to trick, to fool death, is all part of that peasant mother wit Hugo has celebrated since the first poem in the book, "The Semi-Lunatics of Kilmuir," which appears before the book proper begins. The semi-lunatics "were crazy like dolphins," and the foremost among them—the unpronounceably Gaelic "Gilleasbuig Aotram"—knew intimately the cruelties of need and the productivity of song: "Had you the right madness bread would be secure" (p. viii). As in the first poem of the book, so in the last. The laird "who tricked me into being a crofter" is answered by the trick of a song that eludes death, that finds "the right madness on Skye" and transforms the scene of dispossession and death into a celebration. With pipes and drums given "five days" to play (an allusion to an old Seattle poem of Hugo, "Letter to Wagoner from Port Townsend"), oxen dance, and the peasant gives a final command that folds the absentee landlord driver up like a letter: "Mail Harry of Nothingham home to his nothing" (p. 63).

As Skye is an island thick with mists of song and the brute facts of history, Hugo's poetry is woven from the two strands of the songs of dream and the pull of need. This has always been the condition of his work, from *A Run of Jacks,* where "Trout" and "Skykomish River Running" (with the prophetic line, "The river Sky is running in my hair") appear with "Neighbor" and "Duwamish" (with "this poverty / is not a lack of money but of friends"). As Hugo's poetry has grown from that first book, the channels of dream and of need have deepened, gaining depth of insight into the region of the Northwest, the ravages of war in an impoverished Italy, the isolation of American small towns, and the further isolation of American men in the myths of their tough masculinity. In basing his poetry on those twin peasant authorities of dream and need, Hugo has made a remarkable American poetry, insisting that we hear "some continuum of song" that ties mother to daughter and strengthens our grasp of what is most human: the connections among people that make up society, that join the lost generations of dispossessed peasants to those generations of sand falling into a future defined further by the losses contained in technological anonymity. At a time in our literature when poets are praised for closing their doors in self-absorption and evasion, Hugo's poetry calls us to be human in our songs and in our common need.

Notes

Notes to Chapter 1

1. Richard Hugo, "Stray Thoughts on Roethke and Teaching," in *The Triggering Town: Lectures and Essays on Poetry and Writing,* p. 29.
2. " 'The Third Time the World Happens': A Dialogue between William Stafford and Richard Hugo," p. 44.
3. Hugo, "Stray Thoughts," p. 29.
4. "To Evalyn Shapiro," in *Selected Letters of Theodore Roethke,* ed. Ralph J. Mills, Jr. (Seattle: University of Washington Press, 1968), p. 136.
5. Theodore Roethke, "In a Dark Time," in *The Far Field* (Garden City, N.Y.: Doubleday & Co., 1964), p. 79.
6. Frederick Garber, "Fat Man at the Margin: The Poetry of Richard Hugo," pp. 53–67.
7. Theodore Roethke, "Some Remarks on Rhythm," in *On the Poet and His Craft: Selected Prose of Theodore Roethke,* ed. Ralph J. Mills, Jr. (Seattle: University of Washington Press, 1965), pp. 77–78, 83.
8. Hugo, "Stray Thoughts," p. 29.
9. Hugo, "Writing Off the Subject," in *The Triggering Town,* p. 10.
10. Hugo, "The Triggering Town," in *The Triggering Town,* p. 15.
11. Hugo, "The House on 15th S.W.," in *What Thou Lovest Well Remains American,* p. 8.
12. Hugo, *A Run of Jacks,* p. 3. Further quotations from this text will be followed by page references.
13. Kenneth Burke, "The Vegetal Radicalism of Theodore Roethke," *Sewanee Review* 58: 68–108.

Notes to Chapter 2

1. Roy Harvey Pearce, *The Continuity of American Poetry* (Princeton: Princeton University Press, 1961), p. 258.
2. Richard Hugo, *Death of the Kapowsin Tavern,* p. 64.
3. Hugo, *A Run of Jacks,* p. 59.
4. Hugo, *The Lady in Kicking Horse Reservoir,* p. 18. Further quotations from this text will be followed by page references.
5. Hugo, " 'The Third Time the World Happens': A Dialogue between William Stafford and Richard Hugo," p. 41.

6. William Butler Yeats, "Parnell," in *The Collected Poems of W.B. Yeats* (Toronto: Macmillan Co., 1956), p. 309.
7. Hugo, *The Right Madness on Skye,* p. 22.
8. Edwin Arlington Robinson, *Selected Poems of Edwin Arlington Robinson,* ed. Morton D. Zabel (New York: Macmillan Co., 1965), pp. 71–72.
9. Hugo, *What Thou Lovest Well Remains American,* pp. 23–24.

Notes to Chapter 3

1. Richard Hugo, *The Triggering Town: Lectures and Essays on Poetry and Writing,* p. xi. Further quotations from this text will be followed by page references.
2. See Hugo, "Writing Off the Subject," in *The Triggering Town,* p. 10, and see the discussion of sound in Chapter 1.
3. David Dillon, "Gains Made in Isolation: An Interview with Richard Hugo," p. 110.
4. Wallace Stevens, "The Noble Rider and the Sound of Words," in *The Necessary Angel: Essays on Reality and the Imagination* (New York: Random House, 1965), p. 25.
5. Ibid., p. 36.
6. Dillon, "Isolation," p. 111.
7. Ibid.
8. Michael S. Allen, " 'Because Poems Are People': An Interview with Richard Hugo," p. 89.
9. Hugo, "Degrees of Gray in Philipsburg," in *The Lady in Kicking Horse Reservoir,* p. 78.
10. Hugo, "The Lady in Kicking Horse Reservoir," in *Lady,* p. 57.
11. Allen, " 'Because Poems Are People,' " p. 90.
12. Hugo, *A Run of Jacks,* p. 58.
13. Hugo, "The Real West Marginal Way," in *American Poets in 1976,* ed. William Heyen, p. 116.
14. Allen, " 'Because Poems Are People,' " p. 82.
15. Ibid., p. 81.
16. Dillon, "Isolation," p. 106.

Notes to Chapter 4

1. Richard Hugo, "Interview with Richard Hugo," p. 98.
2. Hugo, "Letter to Levertov from Butte," in *31 Letters and 13 Dreams,* p. 54.
3. Hugo, "The Real West Marginal Way," in *American Poets in 1976,* ed. William Heyen, pp. 114–15 (hereafter referred to as "Heyen").
4. Hugo told an eighth-grade teacher that he had had his name legally

changed, when he hadn't. When he joined the army during World War II, the truth caught up with him, and he had to go to court for a legal change. (See Michael S. Allen, "'Because Poems Are People': An Interview with Richard Hugo," p. 78.) Hugo's upbringing with his grandparents is discussed later in this chapter.

5. Hugo, *Death of the Kapowsin Tavern,* p. 41.

6. Robert Coles, *Children of Crisis II: Migrants, Sharecroppers and Mountaineers* (Boston: Little, Brown & Co., 1971), p. 7.

7. Ibid., p. 112.

8. Heyen, "Marginal Way," p. 108.

9. Ibid., p. 109.

10. Hugo, "Antiques in Elletsville," in *Death of the Kapowsin Tavern,* p. 39.

11. Hugo, *A Run of Jacks,* p. 71.

12. Heyen, "Marginal Way," pp. 115–16.

13. Karen Horney, *Our Inner Conflicts* (New York: W.W. Norton & Co., 1945), especially chaps. 5 and 6.

14. Heyen, "Marginal Way," pp. 121–22.

Notes to Chapter 5

1. Frederick Garber, "Fat Man at the Margin: The Poetry of Richard Hugo," p. 63.

2. Richard Hugo, "The Writer's Sense of Place," p. 39.

3. Hugo, "Introduction to the Hoh," in *Death of the Kapowsin Tavern,* p. 2. Further quotations from this text will be followed by page references.

4. Hugo, "Interview with Richard Hugo," p. 94.

5. Hugo, "How Poets Make a Living," p. 72.

6. Hugo, "Interview with Richard Hugo," p. 107.

Notes to Chapter 6

1. Robert Warshow, "The Westerner," *Partisan Review* 21:2 (1954): 201. The exact language is worth noting: "Why does the Western movie especially have such a hold on our imagination? Chiefly, I think, because it offers a serious orientation to the problem of violence such as can be found almost nowhere else in our culture."

2. Richard Hugo, "The Anxious Fields of Play," p. 32.

3. Hugo, "Ci Vediamo," in *The Triggering Town: Lectures and Essays on Poetry and Writing,* pp. 78–79.

4. Hugo, "Sailing from Naples," in *Good Luck in Cracked Italian,* p. 94. Further quotations from this text will be followed by page references.

5. Hugo, "Ci Vediamo," p. 83.

6. Ibid., p. 75.

7. Ibid., pp. 83–84.
8. Hugo, "The Real West Marginal Way," in *American Poets in 1976,* ed. William Heyen, p. 120.
9. Hugo, "Ci Vediamo," p. 85.

Notes to Chapter 7

1. G. Edward White, *The Eastern Establishment and the Western Experience: The West of Frederic Remington, Theodore Roosevelt and Owen Wister* (New Haven, Conn.: Yale University Press, 1968), p. 73.
2. Richard Hugo, *The Lady in Kicking Horse Reservoir,* p. 10. Further quotations from this text will be followed by page references.
3. Robert Warshow, "The Westerner," *Partisan Review* 21:2 (1954): 201.
4. Earlier discussion of "To Die in Milltown" occurs in Chapter 2.
5. Hugo, *What Thou Lovest Well Remains American,* p. 12.
6. Hugo, "The Anxious Fields of Play," pp. 47–48. Adrienne Rich's reference to Hugo's honesty appears in her column, "Caryatid: Rape, War and Masculine Consciousness," *American Poetry Review* 2:3 (1973):11.
7. Hugo, *31 Letters and 13 Dreams,* pp. 38–39. Further quotations from this text will be followed by page references.

Notes to Chapter 8

1. Richard Hugo, "Why I Think of Dumar Sadly," in *What Thou Lovest Well Remains American,* p. 14. Further quotations from this text will be followed by page references.
2. Adrienne Rich, "Caryatid: Rape, War and Masculine Consciousness," *American Poetry Review* 2:3 (1973):11.
3. Hugo, "Memoirs," in *A Run of Jacks,* p. 54.
4. Hugo, "An Interview with Richard Hugo," p. 102.
5. Hugo, "The Anxious Fields of Play," p. 32.
6. Hugo, "Interview with Richard Hugo," p. 85.
7. Hugo, *The Lady in Kicking Horse Reservoir,* pp. 57–58.
8. Hugo, "Two Graves in a Day," in *A Run of Jacks,* p. 68.
9. Michael S. Allen, " 'Because Poems Are People': An Interview with Richard Hugo," pp. 82–83.
10. Hugo, "Anxious Fields," p. 32.
11. Ibid., p. 34.
12. Ibid., p. 49.
13. Ezra Pound, *The Cantos (1–95)* (New York: New Directions, 1956), pp. 98–99.
14. George Dekker, *The Cantos of Ezra Pound: A Critical Study* (New York: Barnes & Noble, 1963), p. 197.

15. Ibid., p. 198.

16. Hugo, "Anxious Fields," p. 49.

17. A letter from Hugo to the author (4 November 1977) puts the matter more succinctly: "I guess sooner or later one has to dirty his hands a little with life, no matter how polished the Grecian urn is."

18. Hugo, "Statements of Faith," in *The Triggering Town: Lectures and Essays on Poetry and Writing,* p. 71.

Notes to Chapter 9

1. Richard Hugo, "Antiques in Elletsville," in *Death of the Kapowsin Tavern,* p. 39.

2. Michael S. Allen, " 'Because Poems Are People': An Interview with Richard Hugo," pp. 84–85.

3. Hugo, *31 Letters and 13 Dreams,* p. 11. Further quotations from this text will be followed by page references.

4. Hugo, "The House on 15th S.W.," in *What Thou Lovest Well Remains American,* p. 8.

Notes to Chapter 10

1. Geoffrey Hartman, *Wordsworth's Poetry, 1787–1814* (New Haven, Conn.: Yale University Press, 1964), especially chap. 4.

2. W. J. B. Owen and J. W. Smyser, eds., *The Prose Works of William Wordsworth* (Oxford: Oxford University Press, 1974), 1:124.

3. Ibid., p. 141. Jonathan Holden also discusses the "Preface" and its relation to contemporary poetry and Richard Hugo in *The Rhetoric of the Contemporary Lyric* (Bloomington: Indiana University Press, 1980). See also note 4.

4. Marjorie Perloff, at the 1978 Modern Language Association convention in San Francisco, characterized much of contemporary poetry as "instant Wordsworth"; then she gave an example of this malady: Hugo's "In Your Young Dream" from *31 Letters and 13 Dreams,* a poem that is hardly representative of Hugo's poetry in general and that is also hardly representative of the deep current of what is "consistent Wordsworth" in Hugo's work. Whether Perloff has read the whole of *31/13*—or much of Hugo—is still in doubt. (See Holden, *Rhetoric,* pp. 112–15.) For Harold Bloom's consecration of the "evasive" in poetry, see chapter 9 (on John Ashbery) in *Figures of Capable Imagination* (New York: Seabury Press, 1976), pp. 169–208.

5. Richard Hugo, "Bay of Recovery," in *White Center,* p. 60. Further quotations from this text will be followed by page references.

6. In *White Center* Hugo only numbers stanzas for "The Ballpark at Moiese," a poem of six parts with little Stevens and a lot of Hugo ("What

we want to save grinds down finally / to the place it happened"). But Hugo's poems with numbered stanzas include one of his first poems, "Mission to Linz" (in *Death of the Kapowsin Tavern),* which he wrote soon after returning from World War II.

7. Hugo, "A Snapshot of Uig in Montana," in *The Right Madness on Skye,* p. 11. Further quotations from this text will be followed by page references.

Bibliography

Books by Richard Hugo

A Run of Jacks. Minneapolis: University of Minnesota Press, 1961.
Death of the Kapowsin Tavern. New York: Harcourt, Brace & World, 1965.
Good Luck in Cracked Italian. New York: World, 1969.
The Lady in Kicking Horse Reservoir. New York: W.W. Norton & Co., 1973.
Rain Five Days and I Love It. (Chapbook.) Port Townsend, Wash.: Graywolf Press, 1975.
What Thou Lovest Well Remains American. New York: W.W. Norton & Co., 1975.
Duwamish Head. (Chapbook.) Port Townsend, Wash.: Copperhead Press, 1976.
31 Letters and 13 Dreams. New York: W.W. Norton & Co., 1977.
The Triggering Town: Lectures and Essays on Poetry and Writing. New York: W.W. Norton & Co., 1979.
Selected Poems. New York: W.W. Norton & Co., 1979.
White Center. New York: W.W. Norton & Co., 1980.
The Right Madness on Skye. New York: W.W. Norton & Co., 1980.
Death and the Good Life. (Novel.) New York: W.W. Norton & Co., 1981.

Essays, Articles, and a Self-Interview by Richard Hugo

"The Anxious Fields of Play." *American Review* 20 (April 1974): 27–50.
"Assumptions." *Northwest Review* 14: 3 (1975): 75–80.
"Grandfather's Car." *Ohio Review* 16: 3 (1975): 6–26.
"How Poets Make a Living." *Iowa Review* 3: 4 (1972): 69–76.
"Interview with Richard Hugo." *New Salt Creek Reader* 6 (1974): 84–109.
"A Poet's Statement of Faith." *Atlantic Monthly,* April 1977, pp. 79–82.
"The Real West Marginal Way." In *American Poets in 1976,* pp. 106–27. Edited by William Heyen. Indianapolis: Bobbs-Merrill.
"Stray Thoughts on Roethke and Teaching." *American Poetry Review* 3: 4 (1974): 50–51.
"'The Third Time the World Happens': A Dialogue between William Stafford and Richard Hugo." *Northwest Review* 13: 3 (1973): 26–47.
"The Triggering Town." *American Poetry Review* 5: 2 (1976): 14–15.

" 'The White Line': From *West Marginal Way*, an Autobiography." *American Poetry Review* 3: 4 (1974): 21–22.
"The Writer's Sense of Place." *South Dakota Review* 13 (Autumn 1975): 30.
"The Writer's Situation." *New American Review* 11 (1971): 221–24.
"Writing Off the Subject." *American Poetry Review* 4: 5 (1975): 4–5.
"Young American Indian Poets. Edited and with an Introduction by Richard Hugo." *American Poetry Review* 2: 6 (1973): 21–28.

Reviews by Richard Hugo

"Gnarled, Defeated, Victorious: A Review of *The Cutting Edge* by John Woods." *Northwest Review* 9: 1 (1967): 111–12.
"Philip Levine: Naming the Lost." *American Poetry Review* 4: 3 (1977): 27–28.
"Problems with Landscape in Early Stafford Poems." *Kansas Quarterly* 2: 2 (1970): 33–38.
"*The Waters of Light: A Miscellany in Honor of Brewster Ghiselin*. Ed. Henry Taylor." *Western Humanities Review* 31 (Autumn 1977): 350–53.

Interviews of Richard Hugo

Allen, Michael S. " 'Because Poems Are People': An Interview with Richard Hugo." *Ohio Review* 19: 1 (Winter 1978): 74–90.
Ashborn, J. K. "A Conversation with Richard Hugo." *Madrona* 3: 8 (1974): 45–71.
Broughton, Irving. "An Interview with Richard Hugo." *Mill Mountain Review* 2: 2, pp. 30–50.
Dillon, David. "Gains Made in Isolation: An Interview with Richard Hugo." *Southwest Review* 62 (1977): 101–15.
Gardner, Thomas. "An Interview with Richard Hugo." *Contemporary Literature* 22: 2 (1981): 139–52.
"The Obsessive Ear: Remarks on the Craft of Poetry." *New Collage* 1: 3 (1971).
Swinger, Susan. "Remarks by Richard Hugo." *New Letters* 37: 1 (1971): 10–16.
Williams, Norm. "Richard Hugo and the Poetics of Failure." *Yale Literary Magazine* 146: 4–5.

Essays on Richard Hugo

Allen, Michael S. " 'License for Defeat': Richard Hugo's Turning Point." *Contemporary Poetry* 3: 4 (Winter 1978): 59–74.

———." 'Only the Eternal Nothing of Space': Richard Hugo's West." *Western American Literature* 15 (1980): 25–35.

Blodgett, E. D. "Richard F. Hugo: Poet of the Third Dimension." *Modern Poetry Studies* 1 (1970): 268–72.

Bly, Robert. "Notes on Prose vs. Poetry." *Choice* 2 (1962): 62–80.

Davis, Lloyd. "Semi-Tough: Richard Hugo's 'Degrees of Gray in Philipsburg.' " In *A Book of Rereadings,* pp. 198–204. Edited by Greg Kuzma. Crete, Nebr.: Best Cellar Press, 1979.

Friedman, Sanford. "Torn Divinities." *Modern Poetry Studies* 4 (1973): 344–49.

Garber, Frederick. "Fat Man at the Margin: The Poetry of Richard Hugo." *Iowa Review* 3: 4 (1972): 58–69.

———."Large Man in the Mountains: The Recent Work of Richard Hugo." *Western American Literature* 4 (1975): 205–18.

Helms, Alan. "Writing Hurt: The Poetry of Richard Hugo." *Modern Poetry Studies* 9 (1978): 106–18.

Holden, Jonathan. "Instant Wordsworth." In *The Rhetoric of the Contemporary Lyric,* pp. 112–36. Bloomington: Indiana University Press, 1980.

Howard, Richard. "Richard Hugo: Why Track Down Unity When the Diffuse Is So Exacting." In *Alone with America: Essays on the Art of Poetry in the United States since 1950,* pp. 232–46. New York: Atheneum, 1969.

Lazer, Hank. "The Letter Poem." *Northwest Review* 19: 1–2 (1981): 235–45.

Wright, James. "Explorations, Astonishments." *Fresco* 1 (1961): 153–54.

———."Hugo: Secrets of the Inner Landscape." *American Poetry Review* 2: 3 (1973): 13.

Reviews of Richard Hugo's Books

A Run of Jacks

Kennedy, X. J. *New York Times Book Review,* 15 July 1962, p. 4.

Schevill, J. *Saturday Review,* 5 May 1962, p. 25.

Smith, R. *Library Journal,* 1 February 1962, p. 564.

Times Literary Supplement, 3 August 1962, p. 559.

Death of the Kapowsin Tavern

Choice 2 (October 1965): 483.

Fussell, P. *Saturday Review,* 3 July 1965, p. 30.

Gilbert, J. *Kenyon Review,* January 1966, p. 131.

McCloskey, M. *Poetry* 107 (November 1965): 125.

Martz, L. L. *Yale Review* 55 (Spring 1966): 454.
Rexroth, K. *New York Times Book Review,* 21 February 1965, p. 4.
Sale, R. *Hudson Review* 18 (Summer 1965): 301.
Virginia Quarterly Review 41 (Autumn 1965): cxxi.

Good Luck in Cracked Italian

Booklist 66 (1 June 1970): 1187.
Howard, R. *Poetry* 119 (October 1971): 34.
Kirkus Reviews 37 (1 September 1969): 970.
Library Journal 95 (15 February 1970): 671.
Mayo, E. L. *Northwest Review* 11: 2 (1970): 115.
Publisher's Weekly 196 (22 September 1969): 79.
Reed, J. D. *Sumac* (Winter 1971): 154.

The Lady in Kicking Horse Reservoir

Allen, D. *Poetry* 124 (May 1974): 103–6.
Book World 7 (16 September 1973): 6.
Harrington, H. R. *Ploughshares* 1 (1973): 96–100.
Jacobson, K. *Northwest Review* 13: 2 (1973): 83.
Library Journal 98 (1 April 1973): 1173.
Lieberman, L. *Yale Review* 63 (October 1973): 113.
Pritchard, W. H. *Hudson Review* 26 (Autumn 1973): 584.
Publisher's Weekly 203 (19 February 1973): 78.
Virginia Quarterly Review 49 (Autumn 1973): cxl.

What Thou Lovest Well Remains American

Booklist 72 (15 September 1975): 111.
Choice 12 (September 1975): 842.
Kirkus Reviews 43 (15 March 1975): 349.
Niatum, D. *Margins* 28–30 (1976): 154–56.
Pritchard, W. H. *Poetry* 127 (February 1976): 295.
Smith, D. *Library Journal* 100 (1 May 1975): 858.
Vendler, H. *New York Times Book Review,* 7 September 1975, p. 6.
Young, V. *Hudson Review* 28 (Winter 1975): 593–95.

31 Letters and 13 Dreams

Allen, M. S. *Western American Literature* 13 (1978): 174–75.
Booklist 74 (15 November 1977): 522.
Choice 15 (Summer 1978): 869.
Cotter, J. F. *Hudson Review* 31 (Spring 1978): 214.
Garber, F. *American Poetry Review* 9 (January 1980): 16.
Holland, R. *Poetry* 133 (March 1979): 346.
Jackson, R. *Prairie Schooner* 52 (Fall 1978): 292.

Kliatt 12 (Fall 1978): 21.
Library Journal 102 (15 October 1977): 2166.
Molesworth, C. *Georgia Review* 32 (Fall 1978): 683–84.
Ramsey, P. *Sewanee Review* 86 (July 1978): 45.
Seidman, H. *New York Times Book Review,* 19 May 1978, p. 24.
Yenser, S. *Yale Review* 68 (Autumn 1978): 83.

The Triggering Town

American Literature 51 (November 1979): 440.
Booklist 75 (1 July 1979): 1564.
Hall, D. *New York Times Book Review,* 25 March 1979, p. 11.
Kirkus Reviews 47 (1 February 1979): 174.
Library Journal 104 (15 March 1979): 730.
Stitt, P. *Poetry* 138 (April 1981): 48–49.

Selected Poems

Allen, M. S. *Western American Literature* 15 (1981): 308–9.
Booklist 76 (15 October 1979): 326.
Choice 16 (December 1979): 1308.
Gosholz, E. *Hudson Review* 33 (Summer 1980): 300–301.
Kliatt 14 (Winter 1980): 21.
Library Journal 104 (1 October 1979): 2103.
Parnassus 8 (Fall 1979): 227.
Simmons, T. *Christian Science Monitor* 71 (13 August 1979): B1.
Stitt, P. *Poetry* 138 (April 1981): 48–50.
Vernon, J. *Western Humanities Review* 33 (Autumn 1979): 352–55.

White Center

Allen, M. S. *Western American Literature* 15 (1981): 312.
Best Sellers 40 (April 1980): 29.
Library Journal 105 (1 May 1980): 1087.
North American Review 265 (December 1980): 70.
Parnassus 8 (Fall 1979): 227.
Stitt, P. *Georgia Review* 35: 1 (Spring 1981): 185–86.

The Right Madness on Skye

Allen, M. S. *Western American Literature* 15 (1981): 313.
Booklist 77 (15 October 1980): 300.
Eshleman, C. *Los Angeles Times Book Review,* 21 September 1980, p. B14.
Kirkus Reviews 48 (1 May 1980): 636–37.
Library Journal 105 (1 May 1980): 1087.
Mitchell, R. *North American Review* 226: 1 (March 1981): 57–59.

Shaw, R. B. *Nation* 231 (8 November 1980): 476.
Stitt, P. *Georgia Review* 35: 1 (Spring 1981): 186–87.

Index

Library of Congress Cataloging in Publication Data

Allen, Michael S., 1947–
We Are Called Human.

Bibliography: p. 150
Includes index.
1. Hugo, Richard F.—Criticism and interpretation.
I. Title.
PS3515.U3Z54 811'.54 81–69840
ISBN 0–938626–07–8 AACR2

Ben Patrick Johnson

Third & Heaven

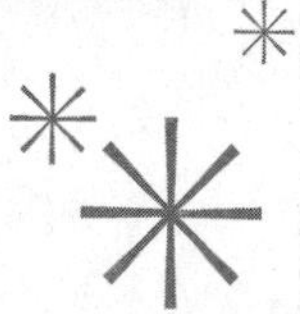

alyson books
los angeles

Celebrating Twenty-Five Years

All characters in this book are fictitious. Any resemblance to real individuals—either living or dead—is strictly coincidental.

Manufactured in the United States of America.

published by Alyson Books,
P.O. Box 4371, Los Angeles, California 90078-4371.
Distribution in the United Kingdom by Turnaround Publisher Services Ltd.,
Unit 3, Olympia Trading Estate, Coburg Road, Wood Green,
London N22 6TZ England.

ISBN 0-7394-5814-0

Credits
Art direction by Matt Sams.
Cover design by Amy Martin.
Cover photography by David Jensen.

ONE

It's Saturday morning. Freddy Ruckert is having breakfast with his three best friends. As usual they're at Noble's, a trendy diner on Third Street near the Beverly Center. The waiter has just set the food down and stepped back from their table. As Freddy grinds pepper over his omelet, he watches it fall and fleck his plate like bits of ash.

"Am I a fag hag?" Claire asks earnestly over the noise of the restaurant. Freddy sets down the pepper mill and studies her. She wears a tennis skirt that shows off legs that other women of her age regard with envy. Her makeup is light, but covers the delicate skein of scars on her face. As the air shifts, Freddy catches a hint of Claire's sweet, girly perfume. Then he glances at her brand-new haircut, a blunt crop that drops her chestnut locks flat across her forehead. She's not a fag hag, but she could certainly pass for a dyke.

"Why do you ask?" Ritchie demands. A sturdy young man with big biceps, he sits at Freddy's left. He stirs a fourth packet of Sweet'N Low into his coffee and brushes the leftover powder onto the floor with his muscular olive palm. A stooped Salvadoran with an apron tied around his midsection scurries in with a worn-out broom to sweep it up.

Freddy glances from Ritchie to Joshua, who is balancing two mini straws on the backs of his outstretched fingers, his brow tight with concentration. Freddy has always found Joshua's face handsome in a lean, beleaguered way. He is young, like Ritchie, but lack of sleep has left him with a worn expression. Joshua doesn't react to Claire's question about being a fag hag. He knows when to demur. That's what he does for a living when he's not making up lies.

"Well?" Ritchie says. "Why do you ask?"

"Remember the Third Agreement," Freddy warns. "Don't take things personally."

"Spare me the self-help claptrap," Claire snorts.

But Ritchie considers Freddy's advice and nods thoughtfully. Though it does take some of the challenge out of things, Freddy likes how Ritchie accepts what he says without much argument. Ritchie's earnestness makes him both endearing and a drag.

As Hollywood's most ambitious personal trainer, Ritchie has little to lose and a lot to gain. He lives on determination and protein shakes. He's Joshua turned inside out—he grins too quickly and sits up too straight in his chair.

Like Ritchie, Claire also sits up straight, but for different reasons. As an osteopath, she's concerned with the right and wrong way to hold one's body, and she's not shy to expound on the subject. Claire is glib in general. At the Saturday morning table, she doesn't just represent the female sex; she speaks for entire human race over the age of 35. It's a big job, but she never falls short. Claire has a steely constitution, the rigidity of which leaves Freddy constantly surprised.

And then there's Freddy himself, now slouching a bit and leaning off to one side, amused, looking from one friend to the other. As always, he's studying their mannerisms and speech, making mental notes to use later in his writing. He's glad to have his life back after an exhausting stretch of on-camera TV work that now, in retrospect, was like a long, bad flu. Freddy is not quite sure what to do with his himself, though he suspects the answer involves novels, eventually a husband of some sort, and a little house somewhere where there's no real zip code.

Claire, Ritchie, Joshua and Freddy have breakfast at Noble's every Saturday. This became habit back when the diner wasn't as popular as it is today. In the last two years the prices have risen. A small fruit cup is five-fifty—seven with yogurt—and if Freddy wants the short-order cook to sprinkle granola over his, he knows he'll need to go without fabric softener and air conditioning the following week.

The music at Noble's is less mellow than it once was. To Freddy's dismay, Ella is out and the techno beats of a Masterbeat mix CD grow louder each week. The tables inch closer together while the waiting line outside grows incrementally longer. Freddy would suggest another spot for their weekly get-togethers if it weren't for Charlie, the joint's owner, who still goes out of his way to makes sure Claire's hash browns are cooked just a little burned around the edges and the organic carrots in Freddy's omelet hold onto a bit of their crispness.

Noble's is in a neighborhood that's technically inside the Los Angeles city limits, but it oozes West Hollywood self-consciousness in every way that counts. The restaurant is small, even by hole-in-the-wall standards. The kitchen is close enough to the dining room that when the cook drops a pile of hash browns and onions onto the griddle, the sizzle roars through the room like applause, making diners have to repeat things they've just said. Clouds of delicious-smelling greasy steam billow outward each time the heavy front door whooshes.

Of late there is little room to navigate between the twelve tables (where there used to be eight), so diners and the two waiters are constantly apologizing for bumping into one other. This might be a good way to meet people, but for Freddy, that's unnecessary; the cast at his gatherings is always the same, and he's content with the fact.

Table number 6, next to the "good" mirrored wall where Charlie puts them, has a small square top. There is room for exactly four diners. Any more and someone is forced to hang off the corner and block the narrow aisle. Various fledgling boyfriends who've joined them in the past have tried gamely to fit in, but each has fallen away in frustration.

One morning, Ritchie proudly brought along a golden-tanned young man who looked like an Abercrombie and Fitch model, except for his serious buck teeth, which made Freddy think of him as Chip the Chipmunk. His real name was Chad, or Chaz, or something like that.

"So I was reading this Anne Rice novel about a ghost violinist," Freddy said once the coffee was served. "And about a hundred pages in I started to feel like a real sucker. I'm thinking, I paid how much for this book? Twenty-five bucks? And basically I'm buying Anne Rice's self-therapy."

"I don't do Anne Rice," Claire said. "I like to avoid goblins."

The silliness of this made Freddy laugh. After a moment, Joshua joined in. Claire laughed too, delighted at her own cleverness.

"Woo-o-o, goblins," Freddy shouted, tears of mirth in his eyes. Joshua and Claire crowed the word back at him, clapping.

"I don't get it," Chad said over the ruckus.

Everyone fell silent.

"That's okay," Claire deadpanned. "None of us do either."

Chad smiled gamely.

"Wow, this table is small," he said. A sheen of perspiration glistened on his forehead. "Can you scoot over a little? I can't reach the soy sauce."

"Skip it, kiddo," Claire advised. "It'll just make you puffy."

"Okay," Chad replied after a wary pause.

Claire stared at him for a moment, betraying nothing. "I was kidding."

"Okay," Chad said again. This time he didn't smile.

The next week Ritchie had the good sense to leave Chad at home, which was just as well. The relationship was over a few days after that. Maybe Claire had known it was doomed and was preparing Ritchie for the inevitable. She is always well-prepared for doom.

"Okay, here's why I ask about the fag-hag thing," she says, setting down her coffee. "I was standing at the voting booth in my neighbor's garage in my tidy West Hollywood neighborhood this week—"

"Tidy except for those guys who always cruise on your corner," Freddy mutters.

Claire ignores him. "I'm waiting to cast my ballot for all the correct candidates, supporting the correct initiatives—yadda yadda—and two of my patients happened to be there at the same time I was, both major homosexuals—"

"As opposed to minor ones?" Ritchie asks sharply. Freddy glances at him, finding semicloseted Ritchie rather improbable in the role of a gay rights crusader.

"So they waved to me," Claire continues, undeterred, "and they said, 'Hey, Dr. Claire, how are you?' and we talked a little. I started thinking about how a disproportionate number of my friends are gay men. So, does that make me a fag hag? I mean, what qualifies somebody?"

Ritchie looks ready to wail on her, but pauses and turns to Freddy for direction.

It's Freddy's job to arbitrate, to be the clan's smoother-overer. Claire might be joking, or she might be deadly serious. Whichever is the case, Joshua smells danger and decides to minds his own business. Meanwhile, poor Ritchie just can't figure Claire out.

Freddy can't blame either of them—Claire's parched humor is both deceptive and subtle. Freddy learned his lesson one evening a couple years ago when he was out for sushi with Claire and her wild-haired 19-year-old daughter Lisbeth. For some reason, Freddy was making lots of corny Yiddish jokes that night. Perhaps it was around Hanukkah, or he'd recently subjected himself to a Woody Allen movie, or maybe it was just Freddy being Freddy. He has an odd tendency to hide his macaroni-and-cheese Presbyterian roots behind Catskills shtick.

"Although I mostly do it," he has claimed, "when things are going a little *farkokhteh.*"

That evening, after they'd stuffed themselves on spicy tuna and freshwater eel, Freddy gave Lisbeth a kiss on each of her soft cheeks, dropped her off at her apartment, and drove Claire home.

When he parked in front of Claire's house, she turned to him from the passenger seat.

"Listen," she said in a grave, measured tone. "In the future, you might want to take it easy with the Jewish humor. I know you meant well, but I think it made Lisbeth a little uncomfortable."

Freddy's face went hot and he stammered a verbose apology.

It wasn't until two nights of poor sleep later, when he raised the subject again, that Claire's raucous giggling clued him to the fact that the whole thing had been a joke.

"I can't believe you fell for it!" Claire guffawed. "What a sap."

Freddy replied with a furious, mechanical smile.

When he thinks of his three friends—he's never had the need nor patience for more than three—he remembers his mother asking how he met people out in Los Angeles. There was something in her tone that tempted Freddy to answer, "In speakeasies and dark alleys." But he was gentler: "You meet people here and there."

"I read in *Newsweek* they have big drug parties where dope dealers get young people hooked by being nice to them and then—"

"Really, Mom—people are people. It's the same here as anywhere."

The truth is that the four of them—Claire, Joshua, Ritchie, and Freddy—came together through a series of benign accidents. As the hub of their wheel, Freddy supposes that if there is any responsibility to be assumed, it is his.

Yet, he thought, after hanging up the phone, his mother could rest assured that no dark alleys were involved in his encounters with his friends...at least not in the beginning.

"Here," Claire tells her dog, holding out a rutabaga she's just unearthed. She is on her knees in the long, narrow garden beside her house. The dog, a squatty black mutt named Dog, sits still and stares at Claire, panting as her purplish tongue lolls. Peeved by her dog's impassivity, Claire shakes the rutabaga at Dog like a talisman. "Hey!" she says louder.

Dog yawns broadly and lies down in the dirt.

"Suit yourself," Claire shrugs. She sets the bulbous vegetable on a piece of newspaper where two carrots and some potatoes already wait to be rinsed off and sliced for the stew Claire intends to make for dinner. "You may be a dog, but you need cruciferous vegetables too. All you want is fatty table scraps. Is that how Mama raised you?"

In her mind Claire holds a picture of a tiled, old-style candy shop in Far Rockaway, New York. She was born there on the blustery afternoon of John Kennedy's swearing-in. Her mother hadn't made arrangements at a hospital and was busy buying sour gumdrops when her labor pains began, hard and fast. As Claire thinks about it now, the circumstances seem prophetic.

Five years later, Claire graduated from kindergarten and was loosed, more or less, on the streets. At that time, Rockaway wasn't as rough and dilapidated as it looks on the TV news today. There was ease on the boulevards where Claire played hopscotch and licked Carvel pistachio ice cream. She would stand at the railing of the jetties near her house, her bare toes hanging over the edge of the cement, and stare down into the swirling tide. Little fishies swam there, and froggies, and—maybe, she conjectured—even baby sharks. They all washed up and were tugged back out to sea in a regular rhythm with which they were, apparently, content.

A few years passed. Claire grew taller and lovelier. She took up painting—first watercolors of fish and flowers, and later her fingernails. The Vietnam War flared. A couple of boys from her neighborhood were drafted, but life on the streets of Rockaway was still fairly calm as Claire learned about the birds and the bees, civil rights, and—the summer she turned 15—Mexican reefer. Her girlfriend Rachael got it from somebody who got it from somebody else who said that if you sucked the smoke in and held it in your lungs—whammo! it'd hit you hard. Claire held the joint to her lips and sucked in the smoke and coughed. She giggled, but there was no whammo!

At home, intoxication was a different story.

Claire's dad is an aging career drunk who, on benders, denies Claire is his daughter. Back when she was in school and he still occasionally left the house, he talked loudly about the domestic torment he suffered wherever he went—out on the boardwalk, at the soda counter at the corner store, and across the table at the Italian restaurant where he took the family every Wednesday night for spaghetti.

Claire's mother is a pale woman who knits endlessly and never finishes anything. Claire used to wonder if her mother was secretly making a giant comforter for a faraway daughter who knew contentment as something other than an abstract. "Maybe," she once confided to her crazy sister Elaine, "Mom's got a secret family in Jersey with more bright-colored hand-knit socks than they know what do to with."

Elaine was a piano prodigy who had a mental breakdown at the age of 11 and never seemed to move forward, either musically or emotionally. She didn't date boys—nor, as Claire now muses, girls. When Elaine came home from the hospital, things were too quiet in the house. Their father shouted at Claire to shut the hell up, already, when she sang along happily with the Monkees.

"Eat your dinner," he told Elaine at the dinner table. She ignored him, staring sullenly first at her plate, then at his face.

"Let her be, dear," their mother twittered. "She's got a *condition*."

He snorted, but conceded.

Claire tried to leave her own peas uneaten as an act of solidarity, but got hollered at so loudly that she peed in her chair.

As if she weren't getting enough attention already, Elaine developed a rare spinal disorder that nobody in the family could pronounce. She had to wear an extravagant back brace that seemed designed to simultaneously choke her and prepare her for a game of football.

Elaine was consistently cruel to Claire, who, unencumbered by hardware and madness, cultivated all the grace and popularity her sister lacked. Incensed at this, Elaine called Claire names, put gum in her hair, and stole her tampons. Claire often found the caps to bottles of her nail polish mysteriously unscrewed. One time, Claire discovered all her Beatles records except *Revolver* oddly warped. When she went to their mother in tears to protest, she got only an alarmed look, nervously pursed lips, and the merciless click-clack of knitting needles in reply.

Today, Claire enjoys telling her new patients that osteopathy "has less to do with mending broken bones and more to do with mending broken people."

Often in the mornings before she goes in to the office, she

puts on Perfetto shorts and a floppy hat and tends her garden. She knows it's good for her, those minutes spent digging in the soil and chatting with Dog about marigolds and politics. It helps Claire to start her day with things that are real before she's assaulted with piles of medical claim disputes and a squadron of pharmaceutical reps pushing trial-sized boxes of the latest anti-inflammatory drugs.

Freddy used to live around the corner from Claire. She'd see him on his morning jogs while she was gardening. She thought he was cute—though too young for her tastes and probably too gay to qualify for consideration anyhow. But he had a good energy, and Claire decided he might be good to talk to. Claire invited him in one evening to share the flank steak and asparagus she was about to throw together for her dinner.

"I'm never one to turn down a hot meal," he had said.

Once he was in the house, she decided Freddy was definitely gay. He passed on her offer of a beer, opting for a sparkling water instead. When she brought his glass out from the kitchen, he was studying the original Rauschenberg hanging in her dining room.

"It's real," he exclaimed, eyeing the artist's autograph.

"Yes," she replied.

"And big." He stepped away from the frame and backed into the dining table. "I've only seen them on postcards."

"I got it after my second divorce. Kind of a consolation present to myself."

"Did it work?"

Claire eyed Freddy cautiously.

"I put it on his credit card. So, yes."

Freddy smiled and went into the living room, where he noticed that morning's *New York Times* on Claire's coffee table.

"And you read!" he said. "The wonders never cease."

"What'd you take me for? One of those shallow Beverly Hills chicks who spends her free time shopping or at the health club?"

"Pretty much."

"Okay," she smirked. "But I also read."

The steak and asparagus came out perfectly. It seemed a shame to Claire that the meal was wasted on a gay guy with whom she had no hope of getting anywhere. Then again, he was good company, and maybe that was enough.

"So what made you decide to become a bone doctor?" Freddy asked as the two of them sat on Claire's patio after dinner. Every minute or two, the morning glory vines on the wide trellis frame over their heads dropped a heavy blue blossom to the concrete. One fell into Claire's lap. She picked it up and smelled it.

"Prom night. I went through the windshield of my boyfriend's car."

"Ouch," Freddy said, wincing.

"You don't know the half. I was messed up pretty bad. Five years in and out of the hospital. Thirty-three operations. That's how I got these scars." Claire gestured vaguely to her face.

"Huh. I didn't notice them before."

"You're just saying that." Claire never knows how to respond when somebody claims they haven't noticed her scars. To her they are huge. One starts on her chin and goes up to her right eye and another zig-zags like a lightning bolt from her ear across her left cheek. The scars used to be redder, but they have faded with time. Still, when she smiles, she feels the parts of her face shift in an uneven way and imagines it looks like she is wearing a rubber mask.

"No, honestly!" Freddy protested. "I just didn't notice. You're so pretty anyway."

"A lot of good that'll do me, coming from you," Claire replied, testing the water.

"Just take the compliment," Freddy advised.

"Anyway, I had my jaw wired shut twice. I got used to slurping up softened Jell-O. Not very feminine. Once I got so desperate that I mashed up dry Triscuits and sucked them through a straw. Which pretty much worked until I choked on Triscuit fibers and started hacking."

"So, just your face got messed up?" Freddy asked.

"All of me. I walked with a limp for a while. There was a lot of physical therapy, a lot of doctors. Some of them had great bedside manners, but other ones sucked. I mean, they were really insensitive. And lying there one day near the end of it all, it came to me. This is what I would do when I was healed."

"Hmm."

"I'd build a better mousetrap. Or short of that, a better stainless-steel knee."

Freddy and Claire fell companionably silent for a moment.

"What happened to your prom date?" Freddy asked.

"Not a scratch," Claire replied.

Joshua's ex was dying and there was agonizingly little Joshua could do for him. Rudyard was growing weak and impossibly pale.

"Truthfully," Joshua told him in tears one afternoon, "neither of us has any business sticking around."

They hadn't had sex in a long while. Rudyard couldn't digest his food. He vomited it, or if he managed to keep it down, it left him as violent, burning diarrhea. He started talking to people who weren't in the room. Joshua sat with him, holding his hand, until the afternoon Rudyard told him to fuck off and leave him the hell alone. The following morning, without a tear, Joshua packed up his car and moved from San Francisco to Los Angeles.

Two months later, on a Sunday afternoon, he walked up to the register at the Power Zone nutrition store and handed a box of vitamins to the well-muscled clerk to ring up.

It was the middle of July. The store was crowded and Joshua wasn't used to the heat. Summers weren't like this in San Francisco—nor in Salt Lake City, where he grew up. Bodies pressed close around him. Some smelled delicious while others were unpleasantly ripe. Men in tank tops and Diesel shorts sat on stools at the bar sipping smoothies and discussing circuit parties and testosterone boosters over the din of house music and protein shake blenders.

"Do you have a discount card?" the clerk hollered over the music.

"What?" Joshua asked.

The clerk pointed to the countertop next to them, where a Power Zone frequent shopper card lay.

"Sorry, no," Joshua shouted back. He didn't frequent nutrition stores often enough to deserve a card. He wasn't that serious about working out and taking supplements and using protein powders. He was too thin and too fat at the same time. Surely the clerk could see that.

"I'll give you the discount anyway," the man said, loudly enunciating his words as if Joshua was deaf or—worse—a foreigner.

This embarrassed him all the more. *Great,* he thought, *now I'm being given charity.*

"Hey," a deep voice shouted from close by, startling him.

Joshua turned to see who had spoken. It was the man nearest him at the protein shake bar. Apparently it was the guy's discount card on the counter. He was tanned and square-jawed.

"Me?" Joshua asked, sure the stranger talking to someone else.

"Yeah," the man said with a laugh. "You made a good choice. Those are the best vitamins in the store. Food-source, so they absorb completely and have all the right enzymes."

"Are you a trainer?" Joshua asked.

"Nah—a writer. But I think there's a compliment in there, and I'll take it. What's your name?"

"Joshua. And yes, that was a compliment."

"I'm Freddy. What are you doing later?"

A beat passed, during which time Joshua's eyes widened as if Freddy had just sprouted antennae.

"Are you propositioning me?"

"I'm asking you to the opera," Freddy replied.

"That's random."

Freddy glanced toward the bustle of Santa Monica Boulevard, then back at Joshua.

"A bus just went by with an ad for *La Traviata*."

"Tonight?"

Freddy shrugged and nodded.

Joshua thought about the overdue DMV paperwork on the kitchen table of his sublet bachelor apartment and the three loads of clothes spinning in a phalanx of dryers at the Laundromat down the block.

"You're in luck," he said cheerfully. "I'm free."

The opera was long and loud, but nonetheless thrilling. The fountain in front of the Music Center was lit especially for the event, and a trio of doo-wop buskers serenaded Joshua and Freddy as they waited for Freddy's car at the valet stand.

When Freddy pulled up in front of Joshua's apartment, he

shut off the engine, and they made out in the car. Joshua noted that Freddy tasted different than Rudyard—sweeter and stronger. Kissing this stranger left Joshua with a hollow feeling, as if he were cheating. But he went on. After a bit, they pulled back and caught their breath.

"Well, I should get inside," Joshua said, hoping Freddy would protest.

"Yes, you should," Freddy said.

"Can I see you again?" Joshua sputtered, dreading separation.

Freddy smiled and answered by stroking Joshua's cheek gently with the back of his hand.

A few days later, they went to the museum for a Frank Lloyd Wright exhibition. There was ease in the way Freddy joked, a canny familiarity that Joshua had never felt with his ex.

The next weekend, they ate Ethiopian food and walked up Fairfax Avenue hand in hand. Joshua's feet were light on the pavement. He could not help but skip. Over a Turkish coffee, he confessed abandoning his laundry the afternoon they met. Freddy laughed at the story, and Joshua laughed back in reply.

There was a pause.

"But, uh—listen," Freddy said. He grew quiet and looked out the window of the café.

Joshua knew what was coming. It was inevitable.

"This is really awkward," Freddy went on. "I mean, I like you a lot. And I'm not just saying that. But there's something you should know about me. I have a type. I get mad at myself because I meet guys who are totally great—like you. And it kills me that I can't get myself to feel things toward them. You're such great boyfriend material. But I always end up getting involved with darker guys."

Joshua felt a wave of shame move through him.

"And by that, you don't mean boys who went to Hebrew school—I get it," Joshua surmised, wanting very much to leave. He looked down at the table.

"Now I've hurt your feelings," Freddy moped.

"Listen, doll," Joshua said sharply. "My feelings are pretty hard to hurt at this point."

Freddy, irritatingly handsome, raised his eyebrows.

"Let me put explain it to you," Joshua said. He stirred his muddy coffee, watching the fine grounds swirl up through the brew, and began his story: "I'm a Hasidic from Salt Lake City. The irony of this was lost never lost on me."

Nor was it lost, he told Freddy, on the beaming, overwhelmingly Mormon children at school, who went out of their way to belittle him and work up rhyming nicknames using words like "kike" and "hymie." In between these pursuits, they cheerfully condemned Joshua to eternal hell along with the rest of his race.

"I don't think of myself as especially Jewish," he said. "What does that really mean, anyhow? I'm not religious at all. I haven't been to synagogue since my cousin's wedding when I was, like, 16. And I have never once in my life been hungry for brisket or latke. In December, at Hanukkah, fake snow and 'Jingle Bells' are perfectly fine."

He laughed, relaxing a bit. Freddy gave him an encouraging smile.

"Honestly, my moving to California is proof you don't have to be Baptist to be born again. In a way, after all the crap I went through, it's amazing that I don't hate blonds. Truth is, I don't really hate anyone. Somewhere along the way, I just kind of put strong feelings aside. Too much work."

"You seem to have feelings for me," Freddy observed.

"Love—my one weakness. And goddamn you, by the way."

"So I don't suppose I should ask if we can be friends," Freddy said cautiously.

Joshua considered this for a moment. He looked Freddy over and thought of the museum, of walking up Fairfax. Then he let out a brittle laugh at the humiliating situation and at his own stupidity. Finding humor always helped turn things upside down and shake loose all the shrapnel.

Ritchie catches his reflection in the long mirror in the free-weight room. He is on his way to respond to a public-address page from the front desk, but finds the image of himself so interesting that he backtracks a few steps, fixes his posture, and mugs slightly before he continues on.

People tell him he's the best-looking trainer at the gym, which is saying a lot in West Hollywood. He gets hit on nearly every day: "Can you give me some pointers on how to look like you?" Sometimes it's not as subtle: "Dude, come over to my house and sit on my face."

Freddy was already a member of the gym when Ritchie pinned on his nametag, grabbed a clipboard, and greeted his first client.

He noticed Freddy from the corner of his eye, but stayed focused on the overly tanned middle-aged man who wanted Ritchie to help him regain his lost youth. Freddy was cute, but not what Ritchie was here for—not in Hollywood, and not at this gym. Ritchie keeps his purpose looping in his head like a mantra, and it keeps him out of harm's way.

"Hey, you," Freddy said, catching up with Ritchie as he walked down the hallway one afternoon after waving goodbye to a client. "Ritchie, right?"

Ritchie looked down at his nametag.

"Yeah," he said coolly.

"I've seen you training people."

Ritchie nodded politely, but without smiling. He wanted Freddy to get to the point—ask Ritchie out, proposition him, feed him some obvious bullshit so he could shut Freddy down and leave.

"You're good." Freddy paused and looked a little flummoxed by Ritchie's stony demeanor. "That's all I wanted to say."

Freddy turned and started to walk down the hall.

Ritchie suddenly felt ashamed of himself.

"Hey," he called after Freddy. "Thanks. I appreciate it."

Freddy stopped and turned around.

"You're welcome, man. Listen, don't think I'm hitting on you, because I'm not—not that I wouldn't. But I just wanted to pay you a sincere compliment. I've noticed you."

"Same here." Ritchie smiled, caught himself, and hid his pleasure.

"How long till your next client? You want to get a cup of coffee across the street?"

"I really shouldn't," Ritchie said.

"I don't want anything from you. For real. You seem interesting, that's all."

Ritchie thought about it and sighed. He looked at Freddy's beat-up workout shoes, the sweat on his towel, the worn spiral-bound workout journal he carried. *Oh, what the hell.*

"I'll get my beeper," Ritchie said. This time he unleashed his smile. "Meet you there in five."

Freddy gave him a thumbs-up and bounded down the hallway.

A few minutes later, they were sitting over a couple of lattes, waiting for the steamed milk to cool.

"I want to read you something," Freddy said, taking some papers from a computer satchel he'd set at the side of his chair. "I'm a writer, by the way. This is from my journal: 'There is a trainer at the gym. I am drawn to this man, not so much sexually as aesthetically, the way I'm drawn to the muscled lines of a racehorse, the traces of wind in desert sand, or the symmetrically blushing blooms of bougainvillea.'"

"Wow!" Ritchie exclaimed. "That's me you were writing about?"

"Is that so strange?" Freddy replied with a smile.

"It's just that nobody talks like that back on the block."

"Which is where?"

Ritchie hesitated. He liked Freddy, but trust didn't come easily for him.

"Chicago. Cicero," he said.

"Now the accent makes sense!" Freddy laughed. "How long you been out here?"

"Three months. What accent?" Ritchie asked.

"You meeting decent people out here?" Freddy continued, ignoring the question.

Ritchie shrugged.

In Hollywood, Ritchie had decided, it was hard to tell if people were decent or if they were just feeding you a line. Back home, you knew where you stood. People spoke their minds. It wasn't always nice, but it was honest.

In the summer, when school's out, boys in the street played baseball and shouted nasty things they know they'd get their ass whipped for if their pops or moms was close enough to hear them. Plenty of times, especially in the big families on the block, their pops was working late and moms was stuck in the kitchen boiling pasta and potatoes.

In the winter, the boys on the block hung out on the corner talking about how they could kick ass and get any girl they want. When the wind made it too cold to be out in the open, the boys shuffled under the awning of the Greek grocery on the corner. They sucked down cigarettes, stomping their feet and rubbing their hands to keep warm. Sometimes they'd pass around a paper bag with a bottle of wine one of the altar boys swiped from the Parish.

Ritchie's dad was one of those late-working pops. He was in the "import-export" business. Ritchie hated it when friends asked specific questions about what his pops did because he didn't really know himself. His pops just kept quiet. Ritchie figures it was because there were parts of the job that weren't so nice.

Once, when Ritchie was 17, his older brother Frankie phoned the house, upset.

"Okay, don't tell Moms, or I'll freakin' kill ya," Frankie hissed. "I'm over at cousin Angela's house and I just found out that Pops drove to Milwaukee with Uncle Sammy to pick up—you know—a shipment. And some cops pulled them over 'cause their taillight was out and—can you freakin' believe it? They booked Sammy and they're holding Pops for questioning or some such shit!"

Ritchie wanted details, but Frankie said he had to get off the phone to go pee.

That evening, Ritchie's Moms was beside herself, wringing her hands and vacillating back and forth between cursing like a sailor and kissing her rosary. She asked the neighbors if they'd heard anything of Ritchie's Pops and where he might be. Nobody knew anything. Finally, at almost midnight, Pops came in, slouching and irritable. His clothes were rumpled and his tie was missing. Ritchie's Moms asked a bunch of questions, but Pops just waived her off.

Ritchie doesn't tell his friends much about his family, except when he's a little drunk, which isn't often. Then again, he doesn't talk to his family much either. They haven't wanted much to do with him since he told them he was going to be an actor, and not in Chicago. And that he was a fag. These mortal sins, one atop the other, form a wall that hides Ritchie from his family's view, and them from his. The Virgin Mary may be Mother of Grace;

Ritchie will be damned before he'll exit a confessional booth, grab a rosary, and hail her in a vain attempt to get back something he's lost.

No, I'm fine—it's their loss, Ritchie tells himself when the ache of missing them becomes acute.

"You're not a fag hag," Freddy tells Claire with a note of finality that he hopes will close the subject. Joshua grunts through a mouthful of scrambled eggs as if to second Freddy's proclamation. Their waiter assures a change of topic when he arrives with a pot of freshly brewed coffee. Ritchie lets go a burst of excited applause, looks around self-consciously, and puts his hands in his lap.

"Anyway," Claire says, shifting her tennis skirt after the waiter leaves, "I'm just wondering if that's why I haven't been laid in about a hundred years. I mean, it's getting pathetic. Do you know how long it's been?"

Freddy solemnly shakes his head. He really doesn't want to know.

"Let's just say most of the produce in Ritchie's salad was still seeds in wet dirt."

"And that's somehow our fault?" Joshua inquires, swallowing his eggs and squeezing a lemon wedge into his Earl Grey tea.

"Somehow...yes," she says, mocking him. "Not that I don't love you all to death. But a woman has needs. I mean, even dinner at Orso would be nice."

"We had dinner there last week," Freddy reminds her. "You ordered liver."

"I always order liver at Orso with you. You know why? Because it doesn't matter if I burp onions all night. Nobody but Dog's going to notice anyway, and if it bothers her, she keeps it to herself. I want to go to Orso and order a green salad and have to nibble it. You get me?"

"Her biological clock is ticking," suggests Joshua. He tries to be elegant as he licks lemon juice off the tips of his slender fingers.

"Are you crazy?" Claire asks indignantly. "You think I'm jonesing for rug rats? Need I remind you of my lovely daughter Lisbeth, who's presently gunning for a B average at West Valley

Tech? At my age just the sound of a baby crying causes varicose veins. I just want a guy who makes me laugh and whose eyebrows are less manicured than my own."

"She's going to transfer to UCLA in the spring," Freddy reminds her.

"Who?" Claire asks.

"Your daughter."

Claire offers Freddy a faint, pained half smile that disappears immediately.

"I thought you were getting laid all the time," Ritchie says, confused.

"I was exaggerating," Claire says defensively. "This is the truth."

"How do we know you're not underexaggerating now just for sympathy?" Ritchie asks.

"Don't be a moron, Richard."

Amidst the clatter of dishes and the banter of a dozen other patrons, a sly smile spreads across each of their faces.

"Don't call me Richard," Ritchie says, suppressing a fit of giggles.

"And don't call him late for dinner," Joshua and Freddy chime on cue. It's one of their lame group jokes.

"Anyway, how about that guy you were watching at the gym—that cute black guy with the great chest?" Ritchie asks.

"You mean Terry What's-his-name?" Claire asks as she tips milk from the little metal pitcher into her coffee.

"So you talked to him," Freddy says like a courtroom prosecutor.

"I guess I could ask him out. But he's an I.T. manager. What do we have in common?"

"Daughters," Ritchie informs the group. "He's got two of them, 10 and 7 years old. He was telling one of the other trainers."

"Besides," Freddy adds, "Who cares about conversation? You want to get married or get laid?"

"Is this a multiple-choice test?" Claire asks. "Because if it is, I refuse to—okay, I'll talk with him at the gym tomorrow. *If* he's there. And for the record, yes, he does have a great chest. If you like that sort of thing."

"You like that sort of thing," all three of her friends reply.

Ritchie has a great idea!

Claire has remarked that Ritchie has lots of ideas. Most of them are great—at least if you ask him, at least at the beginning. Never mind that a lot of his grand ideas go south between concept and execution.

It's another Saturday morning. A week has passed. The four friends are in their usual chairs at their usual table at Noble's. Steaming coffee and tea and half-eaten miniature muffins—the joint's signature starters—litter the Formica tabletop.

Claire takes a sip of her coffee. It is strong and bitter. Perfect. She is pleased with the day. Her severe haircut is starting to grow and she looks a little more relaxed. She feels feminine again.

Freddy's back is against the mirrored wall. He's just ordered an egg-white omelet with no cheese. Meanwhile, Joshua has spilled raspberry jam on the sleeve of his snappy new cardigan and is sulking.

After he orders a double chicken breast (grilled), broccoli (steamed), and wheat toast (dry), Ritchie is bursting with enthusiasm.

"Okay, guys, I was thinking," he begins excitedly. "They're doing another round of *American Idol.* And I should totally be on it. I mean, I can sing as good as any of those guys. I won't answer back to Paula and I know just how to handle Simon Cowell. I have every one of the shows on TiVo, and I was watching them last night. I kept hitting pause and running it back and I think I figured out why some of the singers get more votes. It's subtle, but I figured it out."

"Impressive," Joshua says unconvincingly. He still looks gravely unhappy about his soiled sleeve. Claire considers flagging down the waiter and asking for some soda water to dab on the spill, but Ritchie is back at it.

"Most importantly," he says, "I know what the runner-up people did wrong. Like with their hands and stuff. And how they stood there when they sang. I know what those judges want. I can totally do it."

"Wait—you sing?" Claire asks skeptically. Ritchie's scheme is just now registering.

"Like, in the shower."

"I sing in the shower too," Claire replies dryly.

"That's great, hon." Freddy cuts her off and turns to Ritchie. "So, are there auditions or something? How do you get on the show?"

"I saw a thing on the news—" Ritchie says, blooming again in the light of Freddy's interest.

"You watched the news?" Claire interjects. The story is getting a little far-fetched for her.

"I was watching for sports," Ritchie says, growing impatient. "And they came on afterward and said how the auditions were going to be next weekend at the Rose Bowl."

"Before or after the flea market?" Claire asks unkindly.

"During, maybe," Ritchie says, a little confused. He doesn't get her joke, as usual. Which is for the best, as usual. "But I better get there early, 'cause there's gonna be a lot of people. I just know it. Everybody in L.A. wants to be a star."

"Got that right," Joshua mutters, his botched sleeve hidden in his lap. "They call me every day."

The waiter arrives with their order, gingerly laying plates of food and extra saucers in front of them.

"Well," Ritchie says after the waiter departs, "if I can get on *American Idol* and stay in the running for a few weeks, I won't have to be calling up anybody. They'll be calling me. Don't you think?"

"Yup," Joshua concedes. "A few weeks of airtime can go a pretty long way in terms of endorsements and ancillary projects."

Ritchie nods hesitantly. He's lost, but encouraged by the fancy language.

"What Joshua means," Claire translates with a note of condescension, "is that if you get on the show, you're good to go."

Ritchie's eyes sparkle.

"And I'm going to be a star. I just am, and that's all there is to it."

"Hmm." Freddy nods gently, showing neither approval nor discouragement.

If Ritchie has told them once that he's going to be a star, he's told them a thousand times. Claire doesn't know, deep in her heart, if it's them or himself he's trying to convince.

For a few moments everyone is silent as they dig into their food.

"So did anything happen with that guy from the gym?"

Joshua asks Claire, clearly seeking a change of subject.

"Oh, Terry?" she asks, pointedly casual.

"Yes, Terry," Joshua replies.

"I talked to him. We got together on Tuesday night—"

Ritchie and Joshua glance up from their plates.

"And?" Freddy interrupts expectantly.

Claire shrugs, feeling a little invaded. "The date was fine."

"Details!" Freddy crows. "We need details. What's with all this vagueness?"

Claire pokes idly at her hashed browns.

"You know, that's private stuff."

"Since when?"

"What's your point?" She cuts Freddy a harsh look, irritated by his need to have the last word. "Okay, if you must know, he took me to Lucques on Tuesday. It was quiet and very nice. They had Chet Baker playing. I ordered steak, rare, and he had coquilles St. Jacques, which he pronounced properly, so he got points there. And he was pretty good with conversation for someone who fixes computers for a living. I didn't feel the need to run to the ladies room for a sanity break and splash cold water on my face. So I guess it was cool."

"And what'd you two kids talk about?"

"Interesting stuff, actually. Terrorism, tennis, his daughters—I didn't get too much into mine. We started talking about the death penalty, but thankfully the waiter brought our raspberry soufflés at just the right moment and we were spared the electric chair."

"And afterward?

"We went back to his house." Claire sees herself standing outside the door to his condominium, looking down at her shoes, while he puts the key in the lock and turns it.

"Well?" Freddy asks, gesturing broadly with his fork. "Did you sleep with him?"

Claire remembers looking at the pictures hanging on Terry's wall. He massages her shoulders, takes her hand, and eases her toward the bedroom.

"I...guess you could say that," she tells Freddy after a coy pause. She recalls the weight of Terry's chest heaving against her own, the smell the excitement on his breath mixed with the pleasant woodiness of red wine.

"Okay, then!" Freddy exclaims gleefully. "Are you seeing him again?"

Claire stirs her coffee and places the spoon in the saucer. "Last night."

"Out with it!" Freddy barks.

Claire hesitates a moment. It's none of Freddy's smarty-pants business, she decides, but can't hold in a delicious story.

"We went to the Hollywood Bowl to hear Esa-Pekka do Holst's *The Planets*," she recalls. "And this time we went back to my place. We talked for a long time—I learned he really got into martial arts few years ago—and then it was late so we went to bed."

"And the sex was..." Joshua suggests, trying to get her to spill everything.

"What makes you think we had sex?" Claire asks in mock offense, a prudish look on her face.

In her mind, the bed frame is creaking and the headboard is knocking against the wall—*bam, bam, bam*. Claire is sure the neighbors will hear it. It is cliché, but she adores aggressiveness. So she holds on to the bed sheet, a fistful of percale in each clenched palm.

"Oh, Claire." Freddy rolls his eyes.

"F you! The sex was—it was nice..." she offers, gently biting her lip. More smells come to mind, along with the glow of the vanilla candles on her nightstand, the sweet gluey taste of lube, the tickle of his whiskers.

"Details!" Freddy crows. He drums his palms rapidly on the tabletop, much to the delight of Ritchie, who grins and claps like a simpleton.

"Okay, okay," Claire concedes, shooting Ritchie a sideways glance. She's tiring of her own game. "It was fantastic, if you must know. He's nicely endowed and has that great curve of muscle that separates his lower abs from his legs like a shield, and we started off with me naked on the sheets. And he got into it by kissing my stomach and then he moved down to my thighs and slowly worked his way to my—"

"No, no!" Joshua exclaims in horror, covering his ears. "It's too much! Don't say the *p* word or I think I'll develop a tic. There's good reason why we're homos, you know."

Looking equally distressed, Ritchie nods and covers his eyes in a gesture of "see no evil". Hesitantly, Freddy puts his hand over his mouth, giving Claire a shrug of apology. She glares back at him, aghast that even her dearest supporter would turn against her. *This,* she thinks, *is what I get for hanging around juveniles.*

Then she notices the waiter standing beside the table and she clears her throat.

Everyone turns in unison.

"Are you ready for the check?" the waiter asks dryly.

The three naughty little monkeys giggle and nod.

TWO

"What?" Joshua asks irritably, shifting on the park bench.

It is mid afternoon. He and Freddy have been watching ridiculously beefy men walk their ridiculously small dogs through the quiet, shady section of West Hollywood Park. Freddy holds a pint of low-carbohydrate chocolate frozen yogurt, and Joshua is working on a Starbuck's coffee.

It's one of those lazy bank-holiday Fridays where there's not really anything to celebrate but most people in the industry have the day off anyway. Traffic on the streets is light as the talent agencies are closed. Joshua agreed, at Freddy's urging, to leave the desk and nonringing phone of his home office and come to the park for some fresh air.

Freddy turns to him. "I didn't say anything."

"Exactly! But I can tell you're thinking something."

"I'm always thinking something, Joshua. Don't trip. Drink your coffee before all the Sweet'N Low settles to the bottom like the plastic flakes in a snow globe."

Joshua smiles in a pained, forced way that doesn't show any teeth and makes it look like his cheeks ache. He's seen himself do it in the mirror and he hates the way it looks, but sometimes it's the best he can come up with.

"I can't stand it when you do that," Freddy says.

"What now?"

"Smile like that."

"Now I can't smile right?" Joshua snaps.

"I like it when you smile and I believe it. But I know you, Josh. You can't play that with me. Just be real."

"I *am* being...real," he says lamely. He tries another smile, this one even more contrived that the first. Joshua knows that he is slipping. There is a strange metallic shearing sound in his ears, a sharp whoosh that comes sixty-four times a minute that nobody else can hear. "I am being real."

"Are not." Freddy won't budge.

But Joshua can't be blamed for trying. Fakery is more durable than truth in his Hollywood. It remains as the truth falls away like pieces of roadway when the soil underneath is washed away in a flood. It gets the job done, the contract inked. And most of the time, Joshua is a great faker.

"How are you doing, overall?" Freddy asks cautiously.

"What do you mean?"

"In general."

Joshua worries the plastic lid of his cup with his thumbnail.

"Be more specific."

"In life."

"Oh, that." Joshua shrugs and stares at the ground.

"Well?" Freddy asks.

"Fine."

"'Good' fine, or 'leave me alone' fine?"

"There's a lot going on right now," Joshua replies. He feels strange inside his own body.

Freddy is quiet and watches him, which bothers Joshua. He knows his face is slightly ashen, his brown eyes sunken. He saw it in the mirror this morning. Nobody else but Claire or Freddy would notice. Nobody else would know what these signs mean.

"So, then, leave it alone?" Freddy asks gently.

"Yes," Joshua says with relief. "If you don't mind."

"Okay, but don't forget your promise to call us if—"

"Freddy! We've talked this to death. Leave it alone. *Please*."

It has taken Joshua some time to recognize when shadows are closing in on him. It's easy for him to dismiss the early signs, to work around them, to stay presentable. One night of less than wonderful sleep leaves him feeling out of sorts, but that's to be expected, he tells himself. A careless choice of words from Claire or Ritchie during a telephone call will sit wrong in his stomach, but they're his close friends and he's naturally vulnerable to their opinions. Gloomy weather may leave him tired and unmotivated to return business calls. But isn't procrastination one's right on a gray day?

Yet there is a blurry line—a stretch of no-man's-land he crosses—where it's no longer individual things that seem challenging, but living as a whole. He has discovered a place near the edge of his bed where, if he sits and cranes his neck toward the window, he can see the branches of a large old oak tree that grows in the neighbor's yard. His daily communion with this tree has become a sort of barometer for him: If he looks at it and sees the rich majesty of nature's beauty, he is in great shape. On most days, it's less grand than that. He sees a simple tree, with leaves and brown bark exactly as they should be, and that's reassuring, in its way. He knows that the day will likely pass uneventfully. Then there are times when the branches remind him of bare bones, jutting and stark. On those days the sight of the tree makes his skin go clammy.

At the beginning of a downward slide, Joshua still shows up for things, in body if not in mind. He continues to pack his gym bag each morning, walks on the treadmill, stretches on the blue mats. He knows this is supposed to help. The doctors say so; the softcover self-help books say so.

But then there are the songs broadcast over the gym's PA system.

It starts not to matter what the music is. It is all threatening—love songs that mock his lovelessness, party songs that make him furious at people for being so frivolous. And the mournful ballads are particularly agonizing.

His sessions on the treadmill become more difficult with each passing day. And Joshua is getting tired. He wants to resign from life. After not too much of this, he takes a day off from the gym—then two, then nine.

Joshua knows that it's time to make the call.

But he doesn't make the call. Not yet. Because as he sinks into his darkness, it's impossible for him to believe that he has not always been there. The good humor and vigor of a week or two earlier are forgotten. What a fool he's been to believe that he could have an easy go of things in life! The pilgrimage he must make is solitary, the way well-trodden. His friends are of little use. To call them and say, "I'm in another dark pit and I need your help," strikes him as absurd. When he's truly at the bottom, chipper encouragement from Claire or Freddy seems like a sick joke.

The pit is what Joshua knows. It's awful and it's awfully familiar. And they—his friends—are just muffled voices from somewhere outside of that dark truth. Their optimism is intolerable. Perhaps they are being patient with him and perhaps not. In their enthusiasm for his return to robustness, they scoff at his point of view. To report his feelings at the risk of having them discounted is more than he can endure. He doesn't want to hear them postulate about the roots of his terror and despair. He can't bear the notion of his friends picking casually through the junk heap he has become.

Soon, nothing feels safe. Billboards advertising blue jeans or vacations to Las Vegas, malt liquor, genteel e-mails from his mother in Utah, the enthusiastic yapping and cuff-licking from his neighbor's shaggy Lhasa apso when Joshua shuffles to the lobby of his building to grab his morning paper—all of it feels threatening.

This pit of his is slippery-sided. Getting out seems hopeless. By now, Joshua's arms and legs have lost their climbing strength. Anyway, he's tired all day, too tired to do anything. F*uck the newspaper,* he thinks. *Leave it there.*

A strange twilight surrounds him as morning and night become less differentiated. The dizzy metallic shearing pulses in his ears, sounding nothing like the blackbirds that sing, high above his slippery pit, from the tree branches in front of his building. Joshua questions the source of the sound. Is it the scything of the grim reaper?

"Please," he prays in a whisper, "come quickly or give me back the blackbirds. Don't abandon me to this purgatory."

The sweetness of night-blooming jasmine that the Santa Anas carry through his window on warm evenings can't compete with the sickly sulfuric smell that pools around him. Perhaps it comes from his moldy bedding, soiled with the distinctive perspiration of the distraught. Or maybe, like the metallic clacking in his ears, the foul smell is just a product of his misery.

And he doesn't make the call to his friends that he's promised a dozen times he will make. He stays silent. He stays in bed. He doesn't bathe. He doesn't cry. He doesn't do anything except pound gently on the top of his head with balled-up fists, messing up his hair with his knuckles.

Finally, at a time that cannot be predicted, Joshua picks up the phone with an unsteady hand and makes the call.

"Hello?"

"It's me," he says quietly, after a moment.

Or he just shows up at Noble's on Saturday morning for breakfast, looking hangdog, pale, and blinking in the sun as if he hasn't been out in a while, because he hasn't.

The thing that has made the biggest difference for Joshua recently is his fledgling public relations company. At present, the enterprise is no more than a side office and a reception desk rented from a Century City talent agency. Joshua and a slight Asian receptionist named Min constitute the entire operation. Min is a man, but he has no hair on his arms or the part of his bird-like chest that shows in polite office wear. He speaks in a disconcertingly high-pitched flute of a voice. Claire swears he is really a she—as if Claire would know about these things. Or maybe, Ritchie conjectured at Noble's one Saturday morning before Joshua demanded a change of subject, Min is a he who used to be a she, or a she who used to be a he. Such migrations fascinate Ritchie for reasons Joshua can't quite grasp.

Naming what the various clients on his public relations roster have in common is as tricky a task as guessing Min's gender. Mamie Redbird, Joshua's cash-cow, used to pose in leopard-skin bikinis for pinup pictures back when pinup pictures were the rage.

In the early 1970s, she won a Supporting Actress Oscar, the cachet of which she rode until it was thoroughly exhausted. Now, ruined by time, Malibu sun, and plastic surgeons intent on making tee time, Mamie earns her living playing dotty aunts and overburdened social workers on made-for-TV movies.

"My roster," Joshua freely acknowledges, "proceeds south from there."

Yet, for all its oddity, Joshua's PR business is his domain—a small fiefdom that gives him a sense of both pride and duty. It is a reason to get out of bed in the morning when everything else conspires to keep him stuck among his stinking pillows.

"I don't want to be too dramatic," he tells Freddy, shading his eyes and squinting at a some kids climbing on the playground equipment, "but I can honestly say my little business has kept me alive."

It's unusual for Joshua to be without sunglasses. He always has the most fashionable shades—typically Gucci or Prada. The darker the lenses the better. The accessory gives him a feeling of safety, of separation from eye contact and ugliness that might otherwise be unbearable. Just as the foggy marine layer that settles over Los Angeles in the morning hours softens the edges of the strip malls and menacing Humvees, the tint of Joshua's glasses softens the harsh sunlight that threatens to expose his world's seams and flaws.

"Look at 'em," he says, still squinting at the gaggle of kids laughing and dangling upside down from the jungle gym. "Innocent. For now. They have no idea what they're in for."

"*We* have no idea what *we're* in for," Freddy reminds him.

"Don't go Eastern on me. I get enough of that from the front desk." Joshua gestures with his head to where Min would be sitting if they were each in their chairs. He imagines Min there, delicately filing his nails. Freddy glances over at the empty patch of grass where Joshua is indicating and smiles.

"You know what I mean," he says.

"And anyway, by now I have a pretty good idea what I'm in for, thank you very much. Most days, it doesn't seem so bad."

"That's good to hear."

"Other times—"

"You've got your company," Freddy says with the sort of tidy hastiness that Joshua loathes. "And you've got Min answering the telephone for you. And even though the office is small and hot and you've yet to figure out if Min's a man or a woman, you have to make a salary and pay rent and take care of Mamie and that science fiction guy you rep, so you show up. Right?"

"I show up," Joshua says, nodding grimly.

"And that's half the battle."

"More than half," Joshua confesses. "The whole war. Normandy and the Pacific Theater in one fell swoop."

"Drama queen," Freddy says with a smirk. He scrapes the bottom of his yogurt cup with the plastic spoon, then looks up to make sure Joshua knows he's kidding.

Joshua nods back. Yes, he knows Freddy's playing around. And yes, he loves Freddy back. He finishes his coffee and drubs his fingers on the lid a couple of times before tossing the cup into a nearby trash barrel. Freddy puts an arm around his waist as they get up and walk back to Joshua's car.

Joshua feels the ease in Freddy's touch and is grateful for it.

"Thanks for getting me out of the house."

"Well, if not Min, then me. Somebody's got to."

The next morning Freddy wakes to the sound of raindrops pelting the metal cover of his bedroom window air conditioner. The color of the sky reminds him of pocket lint. He rolls over and checks the clock. Might as well get up. He has no plans for this Saturday, other than breakfast at Noble's. He stretches his legs, yawns, and shakes some odd, unconnected fragments of dreams from his head. He feels anxious about the wide-open space ahead of him. *Okay,* he tells himself. *Don't go there. It's a rainy Saturday and there's plenty to do.*

After the morning rain comes a surprise burst of sunshine that dries the sidewalk in front of Freddy's building and leaves dramatic water spots on his car. He rolls the windows down as he pulls onto La Cienega Boulevard. It is that time of spring in Los Angeles when the weather is unpredictable—not yet the endless succession of hazy summer afternoons, but no longer the thunder-crack season of downed palm trees and cars swept into the concrete channel of the Los Angeles River.

When Freddy gets to Noble's, the sidewalk tables have been put out—a wager on the part of Charlie, the owner, that the rain will not return.

Claire and Freddy breakfast alone. It's the morning of the *American Idol* tryouts at the Rose Bowl in Pasadena, and Ritchie has conned Joshua into going along to give him a publicist's pep talk in case he gets nervous. Which will not be the case, he's assured each of his friends in separate phone calls, as Claire and Freddy discover in their obligatory gossiping about whomever's not at the table. Ritchie is as thoroughly rehearsed as any Olympic gymnast sprite before her turn at the parallel bars.

His meticulous preparation annoyed the bejesus out of his neighbors. The last time Freddy was over at Ritchie's place—to take him to the Nordstrom's semiannual men's sale—he noticed an accumulation of plaster dust along the baseboard below the wall where the stern Armenian couple next door had banged late-night protests, accompanied by muffled cries of invective against Ritchie's mother, father, and ancestors. Ritchie claimed cheerily, when Freddy inquired about the mess, that he accepts this as part of his lot as an artist, no more off-putting than chilled fingers to a starving nineteenth-century writer sequestered in his unheated garret.

Freddy answers his Beethoven-beeping phone, which rings just after they've taken their first sips of coffee.

"Hello?" Freddy says, embarrassed. He knows he is displaying bad manners even before Claire scowls at him.

"It's me," Joshua greets him warily.

Standing, Freddy apologizes to nearby diners, none of whom are paying him any attention, and steps outside to take the call.

"So, yeah, we got the right entrance and everything," Joshua tells him, negotiating his worn, leather-wrapped steering wheel with one hand and holding his cell phone with the other. "There were signs all around, and cops directing traffic. We had to pay six bucks to park because we got there later than we planned. Ritchie wasn't feeling too good, and we had to stop."

"Did he barf?" Freddy asks.

"More or less."

"Is he in the car with you now?"

Joshua looks over at Ritchie slumped against the passenger-side door. Ritchie is oblivious to the brilliantly green, rain-soaked hills of Griffith Park that flash by as Joshua zips along the 101 freeway.

"More or less."

"It went *that* badly?"

Joshua considers how honestly he should answer.

"It didn't go at all," he says. "We got there and the line was wrapped all the way around the place. I mean, it was really amazing. All these kids hoping to be the next big deal, or at least to get on the air in front of Simon and Paula and the black guy who calls everyone 'dawg'."

"Jackson. Randy."

"I always block his name for some reason. Anyway, yeah. They're all there, lined up with their moms and dads and friends, and I think it was a little creepy for Ritchie because..." Joshua hesitates. "Well, most of them are pretty young, and—"

"Did Ritchie make a fool of himself?" Freddy asks.

"Um, on a scale of one to ten—"

"You want to fill me in later?"

"Maybe that's best," Joshua says with relief.

They waited in line for what seemed to Ritchie like half the day. Joshua claims it was just two hours, but he always adjusts things to fit what would sound right, so one can never quite trust him on facts. Everyone there was 17 years old. Why the hell did Ritchie wait so long to start this? He's too old now. He missed his shot. And when they got up toward the front of the line, Ritchie could see that the entrance was set up like one of those airport security checks with metal detectors.

But Ritchie looked better than them. They were all scrawny. And Ritchie was taller. This would be a cinch. Except maybe Ritchie was wearing the wrong shirt.

Finally, it was Ritchie's turn to talk to an actual human producer from the show. He stepped up to the little *x* marked on the carpet with masking tape, and Joshua moved off to the side. Suddenly, Ritchie wished that Joshua could stay beside him—not for the whole audition, maybe, but just right then, just for a minute.

There was a blond suntanned girl in an *American Idol* T-shirt sitting behind a desk. Her nose was down in her paperwork, and even though he was already standing on the right place, shifting his weight from one foot to the other, she called out, "Next!" without looking up.

"Ritchie Catalano," he announced. To his own ears, it sounded weird and sort of broken, so he cleared his throat and said it again clearer and louder. "Ritchie Catalano."

The girl finally looked up. She made a screwy face. "And you're escorting—?"

Which confused Ritchie—did he look like a male prostitute? Then it struck him what she meant, and he blushed furiously.

"I-I'm with my buddy here," he stammered. "I mean, I'm the one that I'm here for. Well, I'm here for *you*, but I'm here as me. KnowwhatImean?"

"*You?*" She blinked and stared as if she didn't believe him.

Never mind all the preparation—the hours of rehearsals with his karaoke CD until 1 in the morning while his neighbors shouted back when he hit his high notes. The bitch behind the desk made it all evaporate.

"Sir," she began, as if she wanted to be slapped, "are you aware of the qualifications for this audition?"

Ritchie nodded and his hands went icy and his stomach felt like he was about to throw up.

"And you're here to audition for *American Idol*?" she inquired skeptically. "Have you watched the show?"

"Yeah, I have," he said. But now a bit of Sicilian fire edged into his voice—he was getting pissed. "Have you?"

Which was probably not the best thing to say, and it didn't really make any sense. But everyone gets mad. Especially Ritchie. He doesn't like to, and he doesn't think his anger fits him. It's always the thing that shoves him out into life's oncoming traffic.

Then the girl went too far. She gave Ritchie a very smug look and asked, "Have you been in front of a mirror lately?"

At this point, something clicked in Ritchie's head. It was like a windup cuckoo clock that ticks and ticks until a mechanism inside springs to life and havoc ensues. All of a sudden, Ritchie was quite through with the blond girl and quite through with this supposed interview—or audition, or whatever it was. He had an itchy desire to go over and kick the girl's ass, or at least to go out and find her big brother and kick *his* ass—that would be more in line with Ritchie's upbringing. But he wanted this *American Idol* thing so badly! He just stood there steaming and ignored her rude question. Just stood there, frozen, like a moron.

For a moment, he looked desperately over to the corner where Joshua had stepped. The bright light shining on Ritchie made it impossible for him to pick Joshua out of the shadows.

After a minute, the girl smirked.

"Hel-lo?" she said.

Ritchie took a breath and pulled himself up very straight. From an unexpected quiet place inside him, he discovered the voice to say, with great control, "I have a song prepared. 'Lucky Star' by Madonna. When do you want me to sing it?"

"Look, sweetie," the girl said as if she'd just bitten into a lemon, "*Idol* is the number one show in America. We have millions of teenage girls watching. And they want to see someone they can imagine as their boyfriend. First off, you're as big as a tank from all the—*whatever* you do, bodybuilding, steroids, military maneuvers. Hon, it's all a matter of timing. And I've got news for you. Your time for something like this passed ten years ago. The girls who watch this show want to see someone they can fantasize about kissing. They don't want to see their gym teacher."

Ritchie took this in. He felt the blood pounding in his temples, his hands, and even his teeth. His hand was clenched so tight around his head shot that the picture was crackling. He was about to go dago on the girl, so he tried to let the anger get away from him, breathing in and out. Ritchie hates it when he feels like that!

After another moment had passed, he looked her dead in the eye and said, "Thank...you...very...much." Then he shielded his eyes so he could spot Joshua, and gave him a ferocious nod.

Joshua strode forward, grabbed Ritchie by the sleeve, and

dragged him toward the exit without a word. Along the way, Ritchie's crumpled head shot fell to the concrete studio floor. By the time they reached the door, the girl was already interviewing the next hopeful.

Now they are in the car, heading back to West Hollywood. The trip is cruel and will not end. The sun has bested the clouds and lazes overhead. Ritchie rocks his head slowly from side to side against the door frame of Joshua's rickety old Mercedes.

"I think Claire's going to barbecue tonight," Joshua offers after a long silence.

It takes a moment for Ritchie to realize that Joshua has said something. A distracted "mm" is all he is able to manage in reply.

"Freddy said we should be there around 7."

"I don't think I'm going to be very hungry tonight," Ritchie says slowly.

Joshua turns to him. "Sorry, kiddo, this one's not optional."

For dinner, Claire tries something new with tofu and stalks of baby asparagus she found at the Beverly Hills farmers market. She stands in the kitchen with Dog panting at her feet and stir-fries the asparagus with almonds and Bragg's liquid aminos before tossing in the tofu that she has marinated and set to the side. She feels like one of those chefs on television. Almost Martha Stewart, whose manner she quietly admires, though it's now more fashionable to scorn her. But Martha doesn't have a 21-year-old daughter who can't quite seem to find her way, and Martha probably isn't secretly terrified that any man she gets close to will consume her whole. Claire does, and is. Privately, of course. Which is how things like that are best kept.

The asparagus and tofu turn out very well, and her three dinner guests acknowledge her talent. But while Freddy and Joshua dig in, Ritchie picks at his food. This is uncharacteristic and off-putting, considering how good the meal is, how much effort Claire has put into making it, and the fact that Ritchie is usually an eating machine. He consumes a predetermined number of calories every three hours and gets more antsy than a grown man ought to when there are interruptions in this regimen.

Claire sees his food habits for him to impose a sense of order on a life that tends toward chaos. The elements of Ritchie's life are like marbles being shaken around in a shoebox—clattering, hard, each repelling the others on impact. What he needs is something to hold those marbles still and safe. A tuft of eiderdown is what he deserves, but even a pad of spun cotton would do. Claire watches him and imagines him small, all elbows and curly black hair and wild eyes.

Tonight, despite his pouting, there are no gaps in the conversation. Freddy has plenty to say about a somber Iranian film he saw in order to review it for his arts and culture Web site. Joshua has a story about going to a science fiction fan convention earlier in the week with his actor-client from the syndicated outer space show. Claire tells all about her third date with Terry—including a detailed description of a Lucian Freud retrospective at MOCA.

"I guess he wants to get serious," she says with a shrug as she comes in from the kitchen with a second platter of her asparagus concoction. "He introduced me to his girls." She sets the food on the table, and Freddy helps himself to a large portion.

"Did you get along with them?" he asks, running his finger around the rim of the serving plate to steal a taste of the sweet soy-ginger sauce.

Claire wonders why she brought up the subject.

"What's not to like about kids?" she asks sharply.

"Uh-huh," Freddy says, watching her closely.

Claire wishes he would look somewhere else and leave her alone. It's her life, after all.

Terry's two little angels are good students at school, and their clothes are very tidy. Everything in his condo is very tidy. Claire has never met a straight man who could keep a white carpet unstained. Terry lives in a big complex in Sherman Oaks with the kind of perfectly green lawn that looks like the gardeners go at it with fingernail clippers late at night. Inside, the whole place smells like paint. When people paint over their lives, it's a giveaway that things aren't as they should be.

Not only is Terry's carpet white, but the kitchen counters and blender and toaster and juicer are white too. This is all kind of ironic, it seems to Claire, considering that the family is black. The sofas are beige—almost white—and he has two salmon-colored fake marble vases on the hearth of his fireplace. Claire decides an attempt to describe the effect of salmon against white—even to her taste-conscious gay friends—wouldn't do it justice.

"So his daughters," Freddy persists.

"You had to see the vases," Claire says. "They're big. Perfectly placed. I sat there sipping my Diet Coke and I couldn't quit staring. They were like...giant fake breasts. You just can't take your eyes off them."

"Maybe you *are* a lesbian," Joshua says.

"Not like that." Claire ignores the jibe. "Just the marvel of them."

"Didn't you notice them before?" Joshua asks.

"Breasts?" Claire plays dumb.

"The vases!"

"I guess they didn't bother me," Claire says. "Or the lights were lower—this was the first time I was at his place in the daytime." She gets up to clear the table, but Ritchie, suddenly remembering his manners, scolds her and takes a plate from her hands. He makes his way quietly around the table, randomly picking up a few dirty dishes before moving toward the kitchen.

Claire sighs. "Two girls with really good posture. The older one just got braces, and her hair was in those little pigtails the way black girls do it. Or their mothers do it."

"Or their fathers," Freddy suggests.

"Yeah, well. The younger one missed her nap, I think, so she was a little crabby but still polite. She said 'thank you' at the right times and sat on the couch nice and quiet while Terry tried to explain to them what I do. He got a little lost in the part about Pilates, but overall he did a decent job. And they were patient as well as tidy. Completely nice tidy kids, I guess. If that's where your heart is. Mine was there once. Really, it was. Okay—not really. But I love her."

Claire falters. They know Claire is talking about her daughter, Lisbeth, who became the center of Claire's life for about twenty years that she could have spent doing a lot of other things.

"Lisbeth isn't tidy," Freddy muses.

Claire keeps still for a moment, her breath shallow.

"Nothing is, really," she says quietly, looking at the tablecloth.

"Huh?" Freddy says.

"Nothing is tidy."

Ritchie comes back into the room, solemnly carrying a half gallon of vanilla bean ice cream and four giant spoons as if in preparation for a religious rite.

Claire loves him.

Freddy remembers the slogan "Television is a drug" from when he was young. It spooked him. He can't recall who among his parent's hysterically liberal friends was spearheading a "turn off TV" campaign that year, but the drug reference was a particularly prophetic rallying cry for a generation of parents who were reeling from the Vietnam-era roll-your-own fist-raising panoply on the nightly news.

Freddy still finds it easy to resist the lure of TV. In fact, he is flat out irritated by most shows. Yet he is susceptible to the call of the Web. Surfing cyberspace seems to him a little like working the planchette on an Ouija board: You're never really sure if you're directing what you're watching or if it's directing you.

He plops down on the couch with his laptop to check mail, and there's a hyperlink in something he's been sent, and he clicks on it. Time shifts and it's three hours later and he's back where he was the day before, mad at himself and vowing to push away from the damned machine and get out and just *live*.

It's the personals ads that get him the most—the haystack where he goes searching for a needle to rip at the Kevlar that surrounds his heart. He also spends a lot of time looking at vacation destinations—far-off islands that he knows he'll probably never visit.

In the aftermath of his last break-up, Freddy finds himself spending an exceedingly large amount of time in front of the computer, logged on via DSL to all the trouble a boy can find at 2 A.M.

Traffic on San Vicente is bad even at this late hour. Whoever said Los Angeles goes to bed early didn't know what they were talking about. Freddy feels somewhat satisfied, windows down on his car. Tonight, over the course of three decaf lattes, he finished his review of the Iranian movie. If pressed, he would have to admit the article is somewhat slapdash and he really had to stretch to make the requested 1,500 words. Which is a lot of words. His heart just wasn't in the work. His heart isn't in anything he's writing right now. He has an editorial essay due in three days on how reality television is changing the landscape of entertainment, but he doesn't give a rip about reality television. Or entertainment, really. He only took the assignment because his editor seemed desperate to get the story written and Freddy was too absorbed in his sudden, fresh pining for a boyfriend to notice that the article was being dumped on him.

Now he's in the carport. Now he's getting his computer satchel and gym bag out of his trunk. Now his key is in the lock of the back door. Now he grabs a quart of nonfat milk from the fridge, sniffs to make sure it's still fresh, and drinks it as he walks down the hall into the darkened second bedroom he uses as an office. Now he's out of his shoes and dress shirt and sitting in front of the computer monitor, surfing. He's restless.

He had a little flicker of inspiration recently in regard to finding a new boyfriend *hurry, quick* via some other means than the personals ads, which have grown dreary. He sees the same desperate people over and over again on site after site. Their blurry pictures remind him of mug shots of orphaned dogs at the pound waiting to be adopted or put to sleep.

His plan is quite ingenious. The guys with a lot to offer probably aren't advertising themselves, at least not with Web cam photos of their shaved pectorals. Since so many people are putting up personal Web sites nowadays—complete with descriptions of themselves and poems and photos of their pets—why not use a search engine to look for someone who fits his criteria for a mate? Then again, he remembers the saying "Never join a club that would have you as as a member."

Freddy is drawn to artists—singers, dancers, musicians, occasionally fellow journalists if they're sufficiently unbookish—and is especially turned on by young men with good teeth, eyes that sparkle, and a breathless way of saying what they're thinking that makes you want to go along for the ride. In Los Angeles they call it "star quality" or "that certain indescribable something."

At about half past midnight, some carefully chosen keywords and the tireless indulgence of Google.com lead Freddy to the official fan site of a singer and actor named Justin Salvatore. When Justin's picture pops up, Freddy feels a familiar flutter in his stomach. Justin is brown-skinned and breathtakingly beautiful. He has full lips and liquid, almost androgynous brown eyes. He's the star of the Broadway musical *The Jungle Book*. On the main page of his Web site he's posed in a loincloth costume. His lean body is firm, and his gaze is fixed on a far-off horizon as he stands in front of a jungle motif. It's clear from just that one publicity shot that he's as sparkly as Freddy could wish for.

Freddy is beside himself. It is well past polite phone hours, but he calls Claire anyway. Luckily she's still up, sitting in bed in her old chenille bathrobe, doing last week's *New York Times* crossword puzzle with Dog snoring beside her.

"Take a look at this site!" Freddy squeals as she makes her way to her computer, sighing heavily. He reads her the Web address and waits impatiently during the click-click-click of her hunt and peck typing.

"Okay, so he's cute," she says, sleepily nonchalant. "Who is he?"

"Justin Salvatore," Freddy says indignantly, as if it's a household name.

"And he's wearing such a nice leather skirt—"

"Claire, it's a loincloth. You know, as in *The Jungle Book*?"

"It's a skirt," Claire insists.

"I just want to kiss him," Freddy gushes. "I wonder if he's got a boyfriend? It says on the bio page that he's lived in Manhattan ever since he graduated from the Brooklyn School of the Arts."

"Which was about five months ago, by the looks of his picture," Claire remarks. "Isn't that a little young for you?"

"Age is relative," Freddy says, a little injured. "Anyhow, do you see the section with the sound clips? Click there."

There is a pause. Freddy fears Claire has fallen asleep.

"What's a six letter work for *escape,* starts with *e,* ends with *s*?" she finally asks.

"Are you paying attention?"

"Never mind. I got it—egress."

"Click on the link, will you?"

Claire grumpily complies, and through the phone line, Freddy hears the same sound that came through his computer speakers a moment earlier. Justin's voice is a clear, theatrical tenor, heartbreaking, faltering at moments, then confident and riffing at the refrain.

Claire interrupts the song several times with comments, but Freddy shushes her.

"Nice," she admits when the song is over. "So what are you going to do?"

"Write him an e-mail," Freddy declares.

To: Justin2479
From: FreddyWrites
Subject: Your Web site

Dear Justin,

I feel a little foolish writing this, but I know I must. I'm sure you get lots of fan mail and requests for autographs, etc. I also assume you get hit on rather often. So, approaching you blind like this, as a complete stranger, I face the challenge of how to make my voice rise above the noise.

I figure my best shot is to be blunt:

I don't know if you're into men, but I think you're extremely attractive.

I don't know if you're single, but I'd love to find out.

I don't know what you like in a partner, but-all humility aside-

I promise I'd give you a run for your money.

I live in Los Angeles, but would fly to New York for the chance to take you to dinner.

I'm enclosing a picture so you know I'm for real. If your curiosity is piqued (hopefully!!) and you want to know more about me, check my online profile.

Quite fondly,
Freddy Ruckert

Freddy reads his note a half dozen times, making small changes and substituting words—"gay" for "into men," "clutter" for "noise"—before saying a little prayer and clicking the "send" button on the screen. When a dialogue box opens on his screen announcing "Mail sent 1:32 A.M.," he claps his hands and giggles and knows it will be a while before he is able to fall asleep.

Ritchie has another great idea!

It comes to him as he sweats on the Stairmaster at the gym. He doesn't know whether he's out of breath because of his brilliance or because he's working on level 9. He's also not concerned that his enthusiasm might ebb once he comes down from his endorphin high, has a protein shake, and changes his socks. Right now, he needs all the excitement he can muster.

The argument in his mind simple:

There is a catch-22 to becoming a successful Hollywood actor. Unlike Broadway—where unknowns can and do walk into cattle calls and wow their way into shows—on the West Coast casting often happens over the telephone, with agents pitching their actors to producers, who then package movies and TV pilots with actors already attached. If you're not in the loop, he's been told, you're screwed. The attractiveness of the package has nothing to do with the performer's talent or suitability for a role, or even the assembled cast's collective chemistry. It's merely a question of which actors are hot and saleable at a given time. Notoriety is beneficial, being at the right parties and pictured in the right magazines is good, and the key player in the whole circus is the actor's publicist. Right! A resourceful publicist can parlay near-nobody-hood into Wilshire Boulevard cachet with a few well-placed calls. They can book space on the couches of late-night talk shows and secure tables at tip-top restaurants. They can make careers out of pixie dust and flimflam.

Ritchie has watched Joshua and his peers work magic and turned green with envy at the results.

It's surprising, he thinks as he drips sweat on the gym equipment, that it has taken him this long to realize Joshua holds what he needs to make him a success. Perhaps he was restrained by shyness or Midwestern propriety, though he knows he's too ambitious for the former and too Sicilian for the latter.

"So," Freddy asks over the din of techno music after Ritchie has laid out the logic for him. "You think you're going to get Joshua to handle you?"

The two of them are shopping at the trendy clothing store on the first level of the gym. Freddy is fussing with the French cuffs on a paisley shirt he's trying on.

"It's a no-brainer," Ritchie exclaims. "He's always getting those faxes about parties and art openings and stuff, and I'm done with clients here by 8 most nights. I just need to get my picture taken in the right places—you know, have those producers get used to seeing me—and then it'll stick. Like, "Yeah, I know that guy." He winks, clicks his tongue, and points a thick finger like a pistol in Freddy's direction.

"Uh-huh." Freddy says noncommittally. "So are you just going to ask him?"

A skinny sales clerk in a tight T-shirt and distressed jeans walks over and offers to help Freddy with the cuffs.

"Saturday after breakfast me and him are going hiking," Ritchie tells him. "I figure that's a good time to talk about it. You know, I'll have his attention for a while and all."

The sales clerk tugs at the back of Freddy's shirt, trying to make the collar lie flat on his shoulders.

Ritchie smiles and nods at his own excellent idea, and Freddy beams back, though his smile is a little wan.

Freddy intends to spend Saturday night home alone. Claire won't hear of it. She drives over with her car alarm blaring its dopey singsong warning.

"The battery in my remote must be dead," she shouts into her cell phone, "or else the alarm's short circuited."

The call ends abruptly while she's still fretting, but Freddy can already hear her alarm echoing from a couple of blocks away. He leaves an instant message on his computer screen unanswered, grabs a pair of flip-flops and his hardware-store tool kit, and hurries down the stairs to meet her. He wouldn't be in such a rush if it weren't 10:30 at night and if his neighborhood wasn't so quiet and otherwise undisturbed.

He is standing out in front of his building as Claire careens around the corner, the hood of her car bouncing as if she's in a chase scene on television. He directs her into a parking space. She is already starting in with apologies as she scrambles out of her car, but Freddy puts up his hand to silence her and takes her keys to open the trunk. He remembers the technician putting the horn there on the day the alarm system was installed. He and Claire sat on a Naugahyde couch in the stereo store waiting room, reading magazines and eating trail mix. The guy kept coming in to assail Claire with questions about wiring and polarity and electronic serial numbers. The one thing Claire was able to answer definitely was yes, put the horn in the trunk if that's where it will be the loudest. And now, in front of Freddy's building, it is as loud as rapture.

"Do you know how to make it shut off?" she shouts over the noise, plugging her ears and hopping as if she has to pee.

"Sort of," he hollers back, opening the trunk and feeling around the inside lip for wiring.

"Well, make it quit," she begs.

He hesitates a moment, then takes the pair of wire cutters from his tool kit and decisively snips the dangling cable running to the plastic horn. The alarm falls silent mid yelp. He hears crickets. Claire hugs him.

"Is it fixed now?" she asks too loudly, as it the racket has not ceased.

"Sort of," Freddy replies, looking warily at the dangling wires.

She presses the clicker on her remote. Nothing happens. She presses it again. Still nothing.

"It's supposed to chirp," she says, confused.

"Not anymore," Freddy offers delicately.

Claire's visit is short, and for that Freddy is grateful.

The second surprise call of the night comes from Ritchie. Freddy is standing in the kitchen making a turkey sandwich when the phone rings.

"Are you home?" Ritchie asks. Freddy leaves it alone. "Can I come over?"

"I guess."

"No, I can tell you're busy."

Freddy sighs and marvels that his friends' neuroses tend to mirror his own.

"Am not," he tells Ritchie.

"It's too late to come over, never mind."

"Ritchie!"

"It's almost midnight."

"Your point being?"

It isn't until Freddy hangs up that he realizes how glum Ritchie sounded. Freddy licks the mayonnaise knife, sets it in the sink, brushes the telltale crumbs and meat into the trash, and wonders what the trouble is.

There was a time—a year or three ago—when Saturday night would never find Freddy home to answer the phone. Friends would know better than to call expecting him to answer. Not that he had that many friends, anyhow. It was a transient rotating group—guys he'd slept with and kept around for laughs and racy memories, a funny lesbian from an office where he used to work, an oddball guy with thrift-store pants who wiped down counters in the rock-and-roll coffee house at the end of Freddy's block. The guy was forlorn and thin and occasionally he asked Freddy out to dinner at a strip-mall Chinese place for which he seemed to have an unending supply of two-for-one coupons.

But on Saturday nights none of them would call because they assumed Freddy was out dancing at the Catch One Disco or driving around alone listening to a Philip Glass CD turned up loud. They knew he liked to hit the review button over and over again to listen to the part in Anthem Three where the celeste and choir of alto voices signal the climax of the work's whirling musical dervish.

The time alone wasn't really all that enjoyable, for Freddy hadn't yet explored the simple pleasures of his own company, nor had he come to appreciate all the drama that could be avoided by the simple condition of solitude. He still forgets, more often than he likes to admit, that he doesn't need to be around constant jingle-jangle in order to feel okay. But at the same time he is starting to discover that great beauty can bloom in unexpectedly cool, shady moments. It's in the famous space between the notes in the jazz of things where the indescribable "it" gently waits.

Freddy dislikes things like fearless love and the ability to play tennis. He doesn't trust them. They frighten him. To make it worse, he's also afraid of fear, and the knowledge of this terrifies him in the night—in those bramble-filled patches of thought that he wishes were filled with serenity.

He wants the world to promise him things and then follow up in short order. Three turkey sandwiches and a pint of Häagen-Dazs equals a stuffed belly, sleepiness, and self-loathing—appalling when he jots down the menu of his binges in his journal before bed, but predictable and reassuring. A familiar story line.

Nowadays his friends know it's pretty likely he'll be home on a Saturday night. And on this chilly evening he finds himself at a delicious crossroads.

He and Ritchie lie together on the wicker sofa on his balcony, spooning almost. Ritchie's head rests on Freddy's chest. The late evening is damp, and dew is settling. An old orange yarn blanket Freddy's mom knitted before he was born covers their legs, and their stocking feet poke out. Freddy notices a hole in the end of his sock.

They are quiet. Freddy realizes this is the closest he's ever been to Ritchie. He wonders if Ritchie is thinking the same thing. He is momentarily in love with his friend.

"The conversation with Joshua went really crappy," Ritchie says abruptly. "Maybe I was too blunt."

"You? Blunt?" Freddy smiles and rests his chin on crown of Ritchie's head, which tips back slightly as Ritchie looks up at the sky.

"It seemed like a great idea. I mean, didn't it?"

Freddy hesitates. *Don't spoil the moment.* "You were very enthusiastic—"

"Right!" Ritchie says defensively. "And I figured he would be too. But he thought I was shitting him. For real. He thought it was a joke. I get done telling him how it would be perfect if he was my publicist, and I list off all the reasons why, and then he nods and starts laughing. So what do I do? I start laughing too, like some freakin' idiot. Like, of course I was just going for a laugh all along. That Ritchie, always good for a joke, you know? Some freakin' joke."

Ritchie pulls away and sits up straight, but Freddy takes him by the shoulders and eases his muscular frame back down. *I love you.*

"It's okay," Freddy says soothingly, but Ritchie is still tense. "Let it go."

"I don't want to freakin' let it go," Ritchie nearly shouts.

A dog barks from a few houses down. Freddy softens his grip.

Ritchie continues, quieter. "That's why I came out here, man. Every day I go to that gym and kiss ass—and I'm not saying it's beneath me. It's an honest day's work. But it's not why I'm here. I left my mama and my brothers and sisters and cousins and everything I know to come to Hollywood and become somebody. I don't need to be no movie star, just some-freakin'-body. Not to be the butt of a joke."

"Nobody thinks you're a joke," Freddy assures him. "It was just a misunderstanding. I'm sure Joshua would feel awful if he had any idea. If you want me to talk with him—"

"No!" Ritchie says, sitting up again abruptly. "I'm embarrassed enough as it is."

This time, Freddy lies still, watching him. After a moment, Ritchie turns around, gives Freddy a meek smile, and settles back into the hollow of his shoulder.

They are silent for a bit.

"The stars..." Freddy guesses cautiously when he notices Ritchie gazing skyward again.

"Yeah..."

"A zillion of them. A man could start counting them now and never be done."

"That's the beauty of it," Ritchie says, reaching up to trace the outline of the big dipper with his index finger.

"How do you mean?" Freddy is intrigued.

"You gotta have something you can chase that's just a little farther away than you can reach. To keep you going."

"And what do you do if and when you finally catch it?"

Ritchie opens his palm a gestures to the night sky with a sweeping movement.

"I'll let you know when I get there."

Freddy waits for word from Justin Salvatore. He vows not to log on to his e-mail account too often, but then does it anyhow, hoping there will be at least a return receipt in his inbox.

He grows bored. The week has passed uneventfully. Since he turned in his movie review for the arts and culture Web site, he has spent a lot of time writing in his journal about birds and traffic and making up little scenarios involving the customers he spies on from his corner seat at Starbuck's in West Hollywood. It is busywork, but it keeps him out of trouble—both Joshua's bleak brand of struggle and the more debased kind Freddy used to get into. *Those were the days,* he thinks, then realizes the folly in this.

The necessity of change finally dawned on Freddy in the middle of the night about six months ago in the parking lot of the Pavilions supermarket on Santa Monica Boulevard. Freddy sat in his car, windows rolled up and doors locked, eating half-frozen sheet cake with his hands. The bakery department was closed when he got to the store, trembling, and the only sweets available to glut his intense craving were the cakes waiting to be decorated the following day with flowers and balloons and happy-birthday wishes. There was no greeting in swirling calligraphy on the one he was scarfing down—just bland gooey frosting that he got all over his hands and steering wheel and then on the radio knob as he searched around for a station that would make him feel a little less horrible.

Freddy had parked his SUV well apart from the other cars, beneath the buzz and orange halo of a security light. It was well past bar closing time, so the sidewalk at the far edge of the lot was empty except for a couple of weary-limbed hookers trudging past in high heels and snagged panty hose. Freddy slid a little lower in his seat when he saw them, hoping the streetwalkers wouldn't come any closer and mock his humiliated debauchery.

His mouth tightened. The streetlamps and neon of the supermarket blurred as tears made everything go watercolor. How far had he fallen that he was worrying what a couple of strung-out streetwalkers thought of him?

Freddy looked down at his hands, at the sugary green and white frosting beneath his fingernails. He tore a strip of waxed paper from the cake box to wipe them clean.

"Please," he whispered. "May I never be here again."

Before Noble's on Saturday morning, Claire takes an extra long shower, singing an old nursery rhyme as the bathroom fills with steam. She had quite a night last night. She wonders if she's glowing in the way people supposedly do after that sort of thing. It's been long enough since she was properly laid that she can't quite remember.

As she passes the kitchen, she considers a climb on her old stair-stepper machine, but continues toward the front door with a laugh. She got her workout last night.

She is the first to arrive for breakfast. The busboy is still dragging tables out onto the sidewalk and arranging the chairs and flower vases. Claire flirts with him—just a few words in Spanish, but enough to make him blush, and to make her feel powerful and electric. She gets *The New York Times* from the vending box on the sidewalk to occupy herself as she sips coffee and waits for the others to show up. Page 2: There is a debate in Queens over enforcement of a law limiting how far sex offenders can live from schools and playgrounds. The controversy holds her attention for about three paragraphs. Then it's on to the exploits of a Central African dictator with a propensity for stockpiling toxic substances and imprisoning suspected homosexuals. This article she finishes in a cloud of anger. After a few more stories on a few more pages, she begins to wonder where they hide the happy news.

The waiter comes by to replenish her coffee. A little spills over the rim of her cup and splashes into the saucer. Clucking his tongue, he lifts the cup and wipes up the spill with a small rag from his apron. As he snaps the fabric in the air with a *thwack* and tucks it back into his pocket, a smile of apology appears on his gentle, wrinkled face. Claire smells the coffee, strong and dark, and remembers—why does she always seem to forget?—that the good news she seeks is not in the newspaper; it is in the sunlight that falls against the windowpanes whether or not she opens the blinds to let it in.

Now, she closes her eyes and breathes in deeply, remembering last night. When she opens her eyes and sees the room again, Joshua is standing in the doorway. He waves hello.

"Are you okay?" he asks as he takes his seat.

"Oh, I'm quite fine," she assures him with a smile.

Joshua laughs, not understanding. He's wearing a new red sweater—cable knit, very soft. Claire indulges him with generous oohs and aahs.

"And by the way," she says dreamily as the waiter fills Joshua's cup, "the coffee's extremely good this morning."

Freddy and Ritchie are close behind Joshua. They walk in together, arguing. They take their customary seats, still debating the subtler points of a traffic law.

"A double white line is the same as a double yellow," Ritchie insists.

"Only between 7 A.M. and 7 P.M.," Freddy counters. "I remember it from the written test."

"Which you failed twice," Ritchie reminds him.

"So I ought to know it all pretty well now."

"Says who?"

"Okay," Claire interrupts. "Hello to you two."

"Yes, correct, hello," Freddy grouses, knowing Ritchie has bested him, and not at a bench-press marathon this time.

Menus are passed around, though the gesture is just a formality. They all know the selections by heart, left side of the menu and right, and they each order the same things every week, except on the rare occasions when Ritchie's had a beer the night before and chooses fruit salad over his customary toast and egg whites. He read in a book on skin care that melons rehydrate the body after one has consumed alcohol. Claire knows better, but correcting Ritchie is seldom worth the energy.

The waiter comes and takes their orders, only half listening as he scribbles on his little pad. Just as his patrons know the menu, he knows what they're going to order.

"Very good," he says decisively once they've finished. He leaves for the kitchen, and Claire yawns.

"Are we that entertaining?" Freddy asks.

"No, I just..." Claire pauses and yawns again, putting her hand over her mouth and scrunching up her nose. "Sorry. I was up late last night."

"And at the office," Joshua exclaims. "I couldn't believe I found you there at 11 o'clock on a Friday night. I was just calling to leave a crank message. How late did you stay?"

"Late." She looks around at them and considers whether to fess up.

"Claire..." Freddy says admonishingly.

"Later than 12," she purrs.

"Claire!" he exclaims.

"Okay," she says, not wanting to play this game again. "I locked up about a quarter after 1."

"You had that much paperwork to catch up on?" Joshua asks, clearly not getting it. "How long can it take to transcribe a week of medical dictation?"

"I didn't work straight through. I took a break to—I-I went and got something to eat," Claire says. She feels a blush rising and is determined to stop it. She fails.

"Alone?" Freddy asks.

Should she tell them? She wonders.

Claire clears her throat and smiles. She looks at Freddy, who smiles back expectantly. She decides there's really no harm in providing a few details—probably no harm, anyhow. Besides, it's her life. She can live it how she wants to.

"There was this electrician working on the fire alarm," she says. As soon as the words are out, she wishes she could have them back. But she has already started, and Freddy would never leave her alone if she didn't say more. "The guy was supposed to come yesterday morning, but he had an emergency at some other building, so he didn't get to my office until the end of the day. I'm at my desk, working on insurance reports. He's on a stepladder reaching into the ceiling, dragging around wires and insulation. I shoved the computer over as far as I could, but I had to get the reports done, and none of the files are on the receptionist's machine in the outer office, so I couldn't go work out there. I just had to sit with stuff falling on my desk. It was very distracting. It's only natural that I was looking up a lot, right? Anyway, he was wearing these khaki shorts that were loose around the leg, and he had on a jock strap—"

"Athletic supporter," Ritchie says, correcting her.

Claire looks at him. It is sometimes amazing how his mind works.

"Why do I feel like I'm hearing the script of a porno movie?" Freddy asks.

"Trust me, there's no horny pizza delivery guy in this story," Claire says with a twinge of irritation, trying not to get defensive. "I was hungry and I just found it hard to concentrate on what I was doing, what with the falling insulation and all—"

"And all," Freddy echoes dourly.

"So I asked him to have some dinner with me," Claire says hurriedly.

"You went on a date with the wiring repairman?" Joshua asks.

"What date? We just went to get some Thai food over on Melrose in his crappy old pickup, which—trust me—was not romantic, unless dented fenders and crumpled Carl's Junior bags turn you on. Oh, and busted shock absorbers. I got to hear all about the Green Bay Packers, his favorite team in the world. He asked the waiter for a burger and fries. At Tommy Tang's. Trust me, he is *so* not someone I would get involved with."

"Sounds like you were on a date to me," Freddy says.

"I had green onions and smelled like a dragon."

"What did *he* smell like?"

Claire looks at him, surprised for a moment. "Honestly? He smelled like a real man. He *is* a real man, which is refreshing."

"What's that supposed to mean?" Joshua asks. "That being a slob and having bad shock absorbers defines manhood?"

"That's not what I said." Claire is genuinely peeved.

"Sure sounds like it," Freddy insists. "What about a guy who likes the theater? Or smells clean? Is he less of a man?"

"Well, for instance, the only thing Terry has ever smelled like was April-fresh fabric softener. And he never held me tight when he kissed me."

"Aha!" Freddy nearly shouts, clapping his hands at the revelation. "So you kissed the repair guy too?"

"Well—" Claire hedges.

"What else?" he demands.

Claire sees her in basket being shoved off the desk. In one sweeping motion, medical file folders and loose papers cascade everywhere and the telephone falls to the floor. The stepladder is pushed aside. Strong hands lift her hips and set her down on the calendar blotter. She tips her head back and sees the ceiling panel out of place as she tries to find somewhere to hook the heel of her shoe. She feels his weight pressing on top of her.

"I'm not saying another word," she tells her friends.

"So, wait. Does this mean you're all done with Terry now?" Ritchie seems offended by the apparent failure of his match-up. "You're pulling a hit-and-run?"

Claire looks at her coffee for a moment, then into Ritchie's eyes, then back down at her cup. Just in the nick of time, the waiter arrives with their food.

THREE

"Listen, I've got a favor to ask but I don't want you to get the wrong idea."

There is silence on the other end of the phone. Then Freddy hears a sharp burst of television static and the sound of Joshua banging on something.

"Hello?" Freddy asks hesitantly.

"You know I'd do anything for you," Joshua promises flatly.

"Thank you," Freddy says quickly, eager to press forward before Joshua has a chance to qualify the pledge.

Freddy's never thought of himself as a patient person. For him, anticipation is oversold. He wants things now and he wants them loud. Too much time has passed since he sent his e-mail to Justin Salvatore. He can no longer check e-mail, see no reply, and remain cheerful about the rest of his day.

It's Sunday morning. Freddy woke today, as he has for many days running, with a picture of Justin in his head—his lips, his liquid amber eyes. Freddy knows it's just infatuation. He's starstruck, but he doesn't care. Justin is not merely a glowing image on Freddy's computer screen. He's flesh and blood and Freddy's determined to know what it feels like to kiss him on the mouth. Maybe even with tongue.

"So? What's the favor?" Joshua asks and there is another squawk of static, some voices for a moment, then more static.

"Never mind, I—" Freddy fumbles.

"Sorry. No, I'm trying to get this satellite dish receiver to work in the den. My neighbor gets it fine in his apartment, and I thought if I ran a cable in here—what does it mean when it says 'Signal Strength EEQE'?"

Freddy is about to conjecture, but opts for the truth instead: "Like I have any idea."

"Well, I was getting some British TV channel just fine and then it went all screwy."

"Maybe the wind blew the dish."

"Hey, yeah," Joshua says thoughtfully.

"Or aliens—" Freddy imagines saucer-eyed Martians making mischief on Joshua's roof.

"Please! What do you need?"

"You remember my mentioning Justin Salvatore?"

"You haven't shut up about him—"

"I've been that bad?"

Joshua sighs, and Freddy can feel his resistance soften.

"Actually, it's nice to see you so inspired—"

"I want to meet him *now*," Freddy blurts. "I-I don't know how, exactly. I was hoping that maybe you could—you've got listings of agents and things like that—"

"You want to cast him in a movie," Joshua asks skeptically, "or sleep with him?"

Freddy stews. "Don't make this difficult."

"What's difficult," Joshua says with a bit of exasperation, "is me calling up William Morris and asking for a client's home phone number because I know somebody who wants to get into his pants."

"So he's with William Morris, then?" Freddy asks hopefully.

"Freddy—"

"Look, I know it sounds fishy. But you're a publicist. I mean, maybe there's some benefit coming up that he should sing for?"

"The Freddy Wants A Boyfriend society?"

"If need be, yes. Or handicapped children. Guide dogs for agoraphobes. Whatever—we can figure that out later. For now, can you just find him?"

Joshua is silent. Freddy hears his satellite TV cutting in and out in the background.

"I don't know," Joshua finally mutters.

"You already said you would," Freddy insists.

"I also said I'd marry Sally McKenzie from down the block. But I was 6 at the time and didn't know what it would entail. Same as this."

"But Justin is so...*beautiful*," Freddy pleads.

"Oy," Joshua sighs. "I just don't know. But I refuse to listen to you debase yourself like this."

Joshua goes quiet again, and though Freddy is dying to respond, he knows well enough to hold his tongue. He counts in his head as several seconds pass.

"Fine," Joshua says after a moment. "I'll do my best to track him down. But so help me, you better handle this with discretion if I find him. Keep it professional or you'll embarrass us both. And remember, he may not be out."

"I'll be very professional," Freddy assures him. Even as he makes his promise, he's wondering what the nape of Justin Salvatore's neck might taste like. For some reason, fresh peaches come to mind.

All day long Ritchie has had a craving for low carbohydrate frozen yogurt. Carbolite is a pale substitute for sweet, buttery vanilla ice cream, but it bears enough resemblance to the real thing to appease his yearning. Though he's more of a skinless-chicken-breast-and-dry-potato kind of guy, Ritchie revels in the knowledge that he can slurp down a pint of fluffy yogurt and only have run himself 142 calories in debt.

He has discovered that Carbolite isn't always good. There are several variables involved, including which flavor of syrup the guy at the store has mixed into the froth as it cools and thickens, the temperature of one freezer machine versus another, and how hard the goop gets shaken around. If things are really going Ritchie's way, the chocolate–peanut butter is a perfect consistency. On the other hand, the fruity flavors make it hard for him to convince himself that eating Carbolite is a treat and not a punishment. Those who frequent the Cultured Class on Santa Monica Boulevard—"the regulars" the guy behind the counter sneers as if it were an insult—have taken to calling each other, in a sort of ad hoc phone tree, on evenings when the flavor and mix are in harmony. This makes it imperative to get to the shop early, before they run out of the good syrup and refill the machine with some cruel mix like toffee-tangerine.

Tonight the feature is fluffy, well-frozen German chocolate. Ritchie, ranking high in the low-carb yogurt social order, gets a voice mail message early and extends an invitation to Freddy to meet him at the Cultured Class after Ritchie's last client at the gym.

It turns out to be a good thing that Ritchie chose Freddy as his Carbolite date, because Ritchie has issues he needs to discuss. He dashes out the door still wearing the purple nylon warm-up suit that he usually changes out of as soon as he's off the clock. All the way from the gym to the yogurt shop, he rehearses what he's going to tell Freddy.

"You won't believe what just happened," he brags to the traffic signal on the corner. "I was talking to this guy at the gym..." A woman waiting for the light looks at him oddly, but he ignores her.

When he walks up the stairs and under the awning of the Cultured Class, his excitement has made him short of breath.

Freddy is at a table waiting. He sees Ritchie, stands up, and comes at him for a hug and a kiss. This is far more affection than Ritchie feels two men should show in public. His arms go stiff. *Get off me*, he thinks. Embarrassed by Freddy's effusiveness and not sure how to act, he glances around, first at the guy behind the counter, then at a straight couple sitting near the window looking bored. Realizing that nobody in the place gives a damn, he relaxes a little into Freddy's hug.

Though Ritchie's eager to launch into his news, he waits until they order. He gets the sugar-free chocolate chips on top of his yogurt and Freddy opts for hot fudge sweetened with fruit juice. They grab a stack of napkins and head for a little table in the corner with a chipped orange Formica top.

"Okay. So I was just starting my 7 o'clock client," Ritchie begins once they're settled. "She's this assistant mortgage broker lady. Anyways, I notice this dude sizing me up from across the way. At first I didn't think anything. I mean, it's a cruisy gym. But he kept staring. And I though, Christ, this dude's got a lot of balls. But the thing is, he wasn't cruising exactly. More like staring. So I'm having the lady do some narrow-grip presses and we're closer to the guy now and he's still checking me out, so I give him a 'Whassup?'—not rude, just kind of cool. I figure that'll shut him down. But it does the opposite. He takes it like some kind of invitation and he starts talking. He's a photographer, he says, and he wants to ask to me about a project.

Ritchie starts to rub his nose with the back of his hand but stops himself, remembering his Pops scolding him and smacking him on the back of the head.

"Yo, Ritchie!" his Pops would say. "What kind of rude behavior is that? You're a Sicilian, boy. We're the finest people on earth. Get some manners."

Ritchie drops his hand into his lap.

"So anyways," he continues. "You know me. I don't get too excited 'cause I figure he's talking about porn. It's always freakin' porn. These guys come up to me at Starbuck's, in the market, wherever. It's just one of those things I've gotten used to, living in West Hollywood. They all got some video they're shooting, or a Web cam, or they're starting a club and want me to dance there."

"Some guys'd be flattered," Freddy says as he steals a chocolate chip off Ritchie's yogurt and pops it into his mouth.

"Yeah but no," Ritchie replies, shooing Freddy's hand away when he reaches for another chip. "Don't get me wrong, man. I'd kill to be in show business. I want it more than life itself. But not like that, you know? So anyways, I figure the guy's got funny business in mind so I just kind of laugh it off and tell him I'm pretty busy with another project right now. And I'm not lying. I'm in the middle of training. And he's cool with that but asks what time I'll be free. So I'm thinking, damn, this dude won't give up! So I look at him again, really look into his eyes. You know I'm a pretty good judge of character, right? And he seems cool. So something in me just figures, what the fuck, pardon my French. So I tell him to talk to me at 8, even though I'm supposed to be here to meet you at 8:15, right?"

Freddy nods. He has finished his yogurt already and holds his spoon like he wants to hijack some of Ritchie's.

"Did he stick around?" he asks.

"I didn't think so at first. I got my stuff from the personal training office and I was heading down to the executive lockers to change and I didn't see him. I gotta admit I was a little, you know, disappointed—just a little. But then, there he was around the corner in the lobby and he came up to me and, uh..." Ritchie reaches into his pocket. "Well, basically, he's a photographer and he's got a card."

He takes out a brightly colored high-gloss business card and slides it across the table for Freddy's inspection. The card is a small, sensuous portrait of a woman standing in an arched doorway. A long, crepe scarf around her neck catches the breeze so that it covers her breasts and parts down south. Her belly button is hidden by the name "Aldo X" which is stamped across the card in ornate gold foil lettering along with the world "photographer". The phone number has the same prefix as the low-rent voice mail Ritchie had when he first moved to town.

"Uh-huh," Freddy says after inspecting the card. He slides it back to Ritchie.

"It's not porn or anything like that—what he does, I mean," Ritchie says, anticipating suspicion. "He said he's been watching me at the gym for a while—"

"Who hasn't?" Freddy observes wryly.

Ritchie has to work not to smile.

"Anyways," he says, "he's been hired to do this campaign for the city, for the big billboard at Santa Monica and La Cienega. Kind of a 'Welcome to West Hollywood' thing. And he asked me to be the model for it. He wants a smiling picture of me in a Speedo with my arms spread out wide. Kind of like I'm a greeter inviting everyone in."

"That's great," Freddy says cheerfully. He's still preoccupied with Ritchie's yogurt.

"No, it isn't." Ritchie winces. A pang of anxiety grips his stomach.

"Okay, it's not great," Freddy admits, turning his full attention to his friend.

"Everyone would see it!"

"Yes...?" Freddy doesn't understand the problem.

"I mean, *everyone*," Ritchie says. He imagines his cousins and nephews standing at the busy intersection, staring up at the billboard in disgust. "A rainbow flag logo and me with my stuff practically hanging out and, well—I mean, the background would probably be pink. Do you know what that means?"

"It means you probably shouldn't wear a green bathing suit for the picture?"

"It means everyone will think I'm gay!" Ritchie announces. The guy behind the counter looks up. Ritchie's face feels hot.

"News bulletin, sweetheart—"

"I mean, they'll think it just automatically."

Freddy clears his throat and looks down at his empty cup.

"Okay," Ritchie says. "Let me explain it like this. I'm cool with being who I am, I mean, when I'm home in my apartment or when I'm hanging out with you guys. I can just do me. But when I go back to the block, none of my friends there know I'm gay. Not that they ask. They just know I'm off in Hollywood and they assume I'm running some sort of angle out here. That I'm a made man. They're just livin' the same as they always did, running deliveries, hanging on the stoop if it's not too cold—you know, Chicago wind, she gets brutal in the winter. Even then, when I go back, we get in my boy Angelo's car and cruise Lakeshore and everything almost seems right. Things fit."

Ritchie leans back so that his shoulders touch the wall. He looks out the window.

"Like when we were in high school," he remembers. "We used to get stoned when my pops wasn't around, and talk about girls from the next block, you know—who we'd give it to, and who was a whore, and just laugh our asses off. But now? If I told Angelo I was a freakin' homo, or if he saw me checkin' out a guy or something—I don't even want to think of what he'd do. It's deep. And my family? My Moms? Forget it. *Finito*."

He picks up his yogurt cup and licks some of the melted yogurt pooling along the rim. In the process, it drips on the knit cuff of his jacket.

"Clumsy boy!" he hears his mother scold. "Always messing things up! You disappoint your father. You will bring shame to this family yet."

"Ritchie?"

"Yeah, sorry." He dabs at his sleeve with a napkin. "So every time I go home, it's like jumping into cold water and I can't breathe. Then I get back here to L.A. and I freak out for the opposite reason. Here am I into this new life, but I can't ever really break away from all the old shit—the fucked-up things I'd hear behind my back on the playground. Before I learned to fight, I can't tell you how many times I got beat up because I was too pretty, or my eyelashes were too long and curly, or I liked to dance. Get into that—I taught half the boys in my neighborhood to dance! I'd spy on the girls from my cousin Matteo's block. They'd be hanging out between the cars and doing little steps to impress each other. Then I'd go home and practice it in the mirror. I'd work that shit over and over until I could do all the turns and snaps about a hundred times better than those girls."

Ritchie sat forward and made an elegant "vogue"-like gesture. His arms are now too thick to pull off such maneuvers with the cat-like grace of a dancer, but his body holds the memory of leaner days.

I'd be at these house parties over in the corner by myself, just doing my own thing, and people would stop and stare at me—in a good way, I mean. And pretty soon the boys on the block heard how I could move, and they'd pay me a few bucks to show them some steps so they could impress the girls I got the moves off of. It's pretty funny when you think about it—the same guys who'd smack me around on the corner to impress their boys'd pay me their lunch money to show 'em how to dance so they could maybe get to third base."

Freddy watches Ritchie's gaze.

"But they never figured out you were gay?" he asked gently.

"They said that shit all the time," Ritchie replies coldly. "They kicked my ass over it. It got to where I was scared to go out of the house. I'd feel sick. But they didn't mean it, me being a homo, not in a literal way. They were just looking for a reason to call me out. If they talked trash about my pops or one of my brothers, they'd get their ass kicked because it would get back to the family and one of my older cousins would shut them up fast. We're like that, Sicilians. Always. But the boys on the corner could say whatever they wanted about me personally, and it was up to me to defend myself. I was too smart to call stupid, I didn't wear glasses, so they called me a *froso* and it just stuck. Lucky me, huh? Nobody knew it was for real. Shit—I didn't even have a clue back then. I was just doing my thing, you know?"

Freddy smiles.

Ritchie realizes he's said too much. "Anyways," he says with a sigh of summary.

"So?" Freddy asks. "Are you going to do it? If it's on the up-and-up, I mean."

Ritchie looks out the window again at the traffic. At the church across the street an AA meeting has let out and a bunch of men are standing around passing each other cigarettes and drinking coffee from little foam cups. The guy behind the yogurt counter flashes the lights off and on a few times, signaling that the place is about to close.

"I might as well give it a spin," Ritchie says, looking back at Freddy. "The idea, I mean."

He grins and Freddy smiles back.

Half an hour later, Ritchie is at home sitting in front of his computer, his face lit by the glow of the monitor. He picks up the phone and presses a speed-dial button.

"Whatcha doing?" he asks when Freddy answers.

"Sitting here wondering why you still haven't gotten your caller ID fixed."

"Okay, yeah," Ritchie bristles. It's been a year and a half since he moved into his apartment, and he still hasn't complained to the phone company and made them fix it. Freddy and Joshua have nagged him about it a thousand times. But whenever he thinks of it and calls 611, he has to listen to a long menu of choices and press a bunch of buttons and wait on hold. And in the half dozen times he's tried, he's never had the patience to wait it out and talk to an actual person and get it changed.

"So what's up?" Freddy asks.

Ritchie is looking at Aldo X's Web site. The guy seems like enough of a pro. He gives Freddy the address and hears him typing it in.

"But click on the gallery," Ritchie instructs. "There's this one picture of a naked dude, pretty cute, and he's got his dick pressed into this rusted metal kitchen door. The skin's all squishy through the little squares of the screen and he's got the cord from the shade wrapped around his dick and balls. There's no freakin' way in I'm doin' something like that!"

"I'm sure the photographer won't ask you to," Freddy says, sounding not at all sure.

"Really?"

"Okay. Truth is, I've been asked to do some strange things on shoots. Like even just for a head shot for a writer's magazine. No, I didn't want to be covered in glitter, and no, I didn't feel that dropping ecstasy would help me reveal my truest self for the camera."

"Yeah, well, Aldo X better not try that shit with me," Ritchie says, imagining the photographer from the gym trying to put drugs up his nose, or under his tongue, or however a person takes ecstasy—Ritchie is not sure. Then, he is small again and back on the block in Chicago, his body tense, squared off in a boxer's stance in front of Vinnie Gallitano, who's just called him a *froso*. Ritchie feels his little boy hands tightening into fists and rising in defiance for the first time.

He gets up, walking with the cordless phone out the front door of his apartment and down to the hall to the front door, where he sits on the front steps. The cordless connection grows a bit crackly.

"Can you still hear me?" he asks.

"Loud and clear," Freddy assures him. "And for what it's worth, all you have to do is stay in control of the situation. You set the tone and let him follow, rather than vice versa."

"Well," Ritchie says, "there's no way I'll—"

"I know. No screen doors and string wrapped around your—"

"Right!"

"If you want Joshua and me to come along for the shoot, just to make sure things are okay, you know we'll be there for you."

"Nah, I'm cool," Ritchie says, suddenly wanting get off the phone. "I'll see you later, okay?"

"Okay," Freddy says, sounding surprised. "Are you okay?"

"Yeah." Ritchie wants to be left alone, for real. He reaches for the hyacinth bush that grows next to the front steps and pulls off a blossom, twirling it between his fingertips.

"You know," Freddy tells him, "I used to get offended by the way you deal with things. But I figured it out. You stick around for just enough reassurance to feel safe, then you're out of there."

Ritchie hesitates, not sure if he's been paid a compliment or gently put in his place.

"Yeah?" he says cautiously, looking down at the flower.

"It used to bother me," Freddy goes on. "But then I began to realize the point, which is that you come back. You always come back, because you need more. And you've got more to give."

Now Ritchie understands, and he relaxes.

"Thanks."

"You just don't like to acknowledge it," Freddy said with a smile. "It's been beaten out of you, sweet little *froso*. Goodnight."

"Goodnight," Ritchie echoes and hangs up.

He shifts uncomfortably. Even the mention of the word *froso* makes something inside of Ritchie knot up. He looks out at the traffic, waiting until the light changes and the line of cars in front of him proceeds before he takes the flower in his hand and cautiously smells it. It is rich and lovely.

He looks around to make sure nobody is watching, then drops the blossom onto the pavement, hoping a gust of wind might pick it up and blow it out of sight.

After he hangs up the phone with Ritchie, Freddy sighs and pulls off his shoes and socks, leaving them in a pile next to his desk. He clicks on the keyboard to launch AOL and check his e-mail, hoping for anything from Justin Salvatore. He finds a long list of spam for porno sites—"Banned animal sex via discreet credit card transaction!"—and get-rich-quick schemes—"Dear Sir or Madam, Begging your pardon, I am the consul to the deposed Secretariat of Keyna, and your assistance is urgently needed in the transfer of one million dollars U.S. funds into a private account overseas." It's hard for Freddy to believe people are actually snared by those ploys, but there must be some poor suckers in cyberland who clean out their bank accounts, or the charlatans wouldn't keep at it.

He deletes a series of messages. There's nothing from Justin. More messages are highlighted and removed. He arrives at a note from his mom. Freddy scans it hurriedly, then sighs and clicks the new mail button again in the hope that Justin has written in the minutes since he logged on. The little icon spins, then returns nothing. Compulsively, Freddy clicks it again. Still nothing. Again, he clicks it. The computer beeps at him.

"Fuck off," he tells the machine. He spins in his chair, stands up, and walks over to the window, looking at the sidewalk and the apartment building across the way. On the street, a man is walking his dog. Two lovers are kissing in a convertible at the red light on the corner. The palm trees in Freddy's front yard are swaying slightly in the breeze. None of it moves him. If Justin were here, he would feel all better. None of this ridiculous loneliness. Justin would cure that. Justin would cure Freddy.

That's all that's going on, Freddy decides—a little loneliness. Alone in a crowd. Lonely Avenue. If Justin were there in the apartment, Freddy would grab the Mexican blanket off the arm of the sofa and sit with Justin under it on the front stoop like two little Indians. They'd make out and laugh about secret jokes. And Freddy would smell him. Freddy bets he smells like cologne and soft leather. No, wait—peaches. That fits better. Freddy thought of peaches the first night he saw Justin's picture. Standing at the window, Freddy smells his own forearm, hungry.

He doesn't think he should be blamed for fixating on boyfriends, though Claire does. Right now it's Justin Salvatore who can do no wrong; before that it was a porn star, and prior to that the failed writer who Freddy convinced to move back to New York where the guy started his career (thereby dooming the relationship, an eventuality Freddy was too myopic to predict at the time).

In each instance Freddy ended up alone, disguising his voice to leave a message on a dating chat line, surreptitiously cruising the waiting area at the car wash, or closing down Starbuck's on a school night. He doesn't like to think of how many times he's been tossed out at last call along with two or three other oddball fugitives, reluctantly carrying their screenplays or doctoral theses tucked under their arms. On those nights, Freddy sits in the parking lot, shivering behind his steering wheel, pained at the thought of going home to an empty apartment with more books to be read, more articles waiting to be written, and that seductive spider web of loneliness, the Internet.

He falls asleep on the sofa. When he wakes with a start, the sun is shining through the blinds. Disoriented, he checks his watch. It's 8:15 in the morning. He looks over at the phone on the end table and notices the voice mail light flashing. He picks up the phone, dials, and enters his code. He has two messages.

"Hey, it's me," Claire says anxiously in the first. "You must not be up yet. Call me back, okay?"

Freddy presses 7 for delete, yawns, and stretches his legs. There is a crick in his neck.

The second message is also from Claire, and she sounds even more distressed.

"Freddie, I've got to talk with you. There's this stupid thing with Lisbeth. I know she's a kid—well, she's 21. But she got herself into trouble a couple of weeks ago, and I'm just finding out about it now. So call me."

Freddy sits up, yawns again, and scratches his stomach, then dials Claire's office number. After a wait, her receptionist puts him through.

"Right," Claire launches in, forgoing the perfunctoriness of a greeting. "So Lisbeth goes to this party for some girl she went to high school with. And she's standing in line to use the bathroom, and some friend of the host cuts in on the line. And the girl says something or other to Lisbeth and the two of them have a little standoff. And then, I guess, Lisbeth slapped her."

Freddy's eyes grow wide. "That's not so good."

"So now the girl's parents are filing assault charges."

"What?!"

"Lisbeth just faxed me the papers—"

"She didn't mention this before?"

"Which part?"

"The part where she—the whole thing!"

"She says she didn't remember."

"Was she drunk or something?"

"You know Lisbeth."

"So yes," Freddy surmises.

"Give or take."

"How hard did she slap her?"

"Slap, smack, assault..." Claire clears her throat. "It's...you know...different ways of saying the same thing. Lisbeth swears it was no big deal. In fact, some of the other kids there saw it and laughed. But the fact she forgot the whole incident—I've been sitting in my office asking myself, *Is this what I raised? A batterer?*"

"Jesus!" Freddy is flustered. "Does she need a lawyer? Have you called anybody?"

"I called *you*," she says quietly. Without seeing her, Freddy knows her jaw has grown tight and her eyes have softened. "But yeah, I called my ex-brother-in-law Jerry at his big office over in Century City. After leaving me on hold for ten minutes, he comes on and says the charges aren't that serious but he'll show up at her deposition and make sure everything goes right."

"Deposition!" Freddy exclaims, getting up from the couch.

"And he said that she should get her story straight."

Freddy walks to the bedroom and picks up his wristwatch. "Listen—can you meet me downstairs over your lunch break?"

"No, no. I'm okay, really," Claire insists. "You don't need to—"

"But I've got an idea."

"Really, I—"

"Twelve-fifteen." Freddy hangs up.

His next call is to Joshua.

"Two things," he says when Joshua picks up.

"Make it quick," Joshua says. "I've got Mamie holding on the other line, and if I make her wait too long, she forgets why she called and threatens to fire me because of it."

"Okay," Freddy says, rifling through his dresser drawer for a fresh T-shirt. "First off, you hear anything from Justin Salvatore?"

"Like I told you the last seven times, I'll call you the moment I do."

"Bitch! Second—can you cancel whatever you've got booked for lunchtime?"

"Freddy, I—"

"Listen, we've got a situation. I'll pick you up in an hour, okay?"

Joshua sighs. Freddy hangs up before Joshua can protest further.

By the time the two of them reach the lobby of Claire's office building, the line at the coffee shop stretches almost to the stainless steel elevator doors. Through the crowd, Freddy sees Claire waiting at a table in the middle of the room. She offers an apprehensive smile and waves weakly. Joshua waves back.

"She doesn't look so good," he says under his breath.

"Well, if you consider..." Freddy offers in her defense, but they are already at the table, so he lets it drop.

"Okay, here's the plan," Joshua says, taking her hand as he and Freddy sit down.

Freddy delights in watching Joshua grow from hapless to powerful in one breath. He takes command of a situation and shepherds it to a familiar pasture with astonishing ease.

"It's simple," Joshua assures Claire, though fifteen minutes earlier in the car he himself was puzzled when Freddy suggested the strategy. "We're going to prep Lisbeth for the deposition. You know, coach her."

"We, who?" Claire sounds unconvinced.

"We, us," he says. "You still have that camcorder, right?"

"You mean the one that takes funny-sized tapes that don't fit anybody's VCR?" Claire asks. "I think it's in the closet somewhere. But really, I don't think it's the best idea to—"

"And we've got what—two weeks, Freddy said?"

"Fifteen days."

"Two weeks and one day." Freddy nods with excessive cheer.

"This is going to be such a cinch," Joshua promises. "We start by sitting her down and going over the details of what happened, then—"

"Wai-wait," Claire interrupts. "Look, guys," she says, pulling back from Joshua and laying both her hands in her lap. "I appreciate both of you coming over here through traffic. Really—you're the best friends I could ask for. But this is something the lawyer should handle. I mean—no offense, but what you guys know about is show business."

"And what do you think a courtroom is?" Joshua demands. "Didn't you see *Chicago*? What kind of fag hag are you? But don't answer that. Like Richard Gere said, it's all about razzle-dazzle, knowing how to talk to people."

"We all saw *Chicago* together," Freddy recalls. He's looking over to the sandwich counter, eyeing the bagels and coffee. It's well past his usual caffeine and eating time. His temples are pounding and he wishes the conversation would finish. He imagines standing up at the next pause and snatching a bagel.

"I...didn't raise her like this," whispers Claire, her brow furrowed.

Freddy nods, snapping back to his previous thought. "Yeah. *Chicago*. Wasn't that right after Christmas?" The food would have to wait.

"It's showmanship," Joshua assures them. He seems to be speaking to an audience larger than just his two friends. "Plus, people are so used to reality TV now, you have to make real life into a show for them if you want them to believe you."

"There was a pianist," Freddy remembers, trying to ignore his insistent headache. "He was playing in the lobby next to a big cardboard cut-out of Renée Zellweger. We had to wait in line forever at the concession stand. Ritchie pissed everyone off by making the popcorn guy dig through the case to see if any of the brands of candy had less than ten grams of sugar."

"I've always been a pacifist," Claire insists quietly, "even during the '80s when it wasn't cool. After we split, her father even became a Buddhist. She didn't learn this from us."

"The movie was sold out," Freddy continues, "and you guys gave me a hard time because I keep looking at the Latin boy taking tickets who you said was about 12, and why didn't I just go cruise a junior high school?"

"You've got to talk in sound bites or you'll lose their attention," Joshua says, trying to corral the conversation. "The line is blurring more and more. Entertainment's getting more real, and real life is becoming more ridiculous."

"Must have been that school we sent her to," Claire laments. "I never should have taken her out of private, not even for Beverly Hills High. The Académie had such gracious teachers."

"I loved *Chicago—*"

"But after her father got all blissed out, there wasn't as much child support coming in."

"Hey!" Joshua says. He claps twice to get their attention. "Here's the plan."

"But it was a difficult time. I was still in my residency and didn't have two dimes to rub together."

"Are you guys listening?" Joshua shouts, red-faced.

Claire and Freddy stare at him in surprise.

"Of course!" Claire says. "We always listen to you."

Freddy nods his injured agreement.

"All right, then," Joshua says, rapidly regaining his composure. "Can you have Lisbeth over at your place tomorrow night? Don't tell her too much ahead of time, or she might not show up."

"That's not how I raised her," Claire says shaking her head. "To shy away from responsibility. Oh, God."

"Make your flank steak or something. It'll be a little party. We can all come. Then when it's show time, she'll have an audience just like when she gets to the actual deposition."

Claire pauses and turns to Freddy for direction. He stares back at her, eyebrows raised. She looks over at the people standing in line for coffee and weighs the proposal before speaking.

"Okay, okay," she says in a rush. "But not until 8-ish. I've got to clean the place before you come over, and I won't have time tonight."

"When have you ever cleaned for company in the past?" Freddy asks skeptically.

"But I do now, that's why." She shrugs, kisses Joshua on the cheek and Freddy on the forehead and retreats toward the elevators.

Once she's out of sight, Joshua turns to Freddy.

"Um, okay," he says, suddenly dropping his publicist's smile. "You were just a big fat zero in the help department."

"What do you mean?" asks Freddy, who glances enviously at patrons walking away from the coffee shop with steaming cups and little paper sacks heavy with baked goods.

"*Chicago*? You were supposed to be the voice of reason while I laid out the plans. Look at the state she's in."

"Hey," Freddy says defensively, "I got us here, didn't I?"

Joshua gives Freddy frosty look.

"And it was my idea to begin with, right?"

Joshua stands and picks up his sunglasses and keys from the table.

"Okay," he shrugs. "Point taken."

Claire has lit a lot of candles. This is one of her habits, especially on evenings when there are people coming over. It makes her feel as though the house is dressed. But tonight, she realizes, she may have gone overboard, especially considering it's just family. There are votives lined up along the mantle and, on each stereo speaker, a big aromatherapy candle reeking with the essences of patchouli and seaweed. A cluster of dripping tapers stands in an antique candelabra in the middle of the coffee table.

"What is this, a séance?" Freddy asks, flopping down on the couch next to Ritchie and poking at the melted wax with his finger.

Annoyed, Claire crouches and drags the candelabra out of his reach. She eyes him suspiciously as she heads back to the kitchen to tend the stove. The sound of her friends' conversation begins to mingle with the steamy burble of a pan of sauce simmering on the front burner. An aluminum lid rattles atop the Dutch oven Claire uses to steam asparagus. The homey clatter makes Claire happy. She notices that the window above the kitchen sink is steamed over tonight, even in the warmth of summer.

She opens the cabinet and takes down a container of raw almonds to offer Freddy and Ritchie. Almonds are full of healthy oils and fiber and protein and make a great snack food, but probably not in the quantity Claire consumes when she doesn't stop herself. There's a tub on her office desk, another wedged between the driver's seat and the parking brake in her car, and always a few spare containers in the kitchen cabinet.

"I should practice on the video camera before we do this for real.

I mean, like, focus and stuff," Ritchie says as Claire walks into the living room to set the almonds on the table. "I kind of suck at that."

"I wouldn't get too twisted," Freddy says, scooping a handful of nuts and swallowing them almost without chewing. "Nobody's going to watch the tape but us. And we've all seen you unfocused plenty of times."

Ritchie smiles amiably and lets go a single "ha!"

Claire heads back to the kitchen. She's noticed, many times, how everyone's digs seem to pass Ritchie without scathing him. He sunbathes in life's brighter patches and avoids the chill of its shadowy slopes. Does he simply not get it? If so, there's a part of her that's envious. Then again, maybe Ritchie is completely aware of what's being said around him and makes a conscious choice to ignore the venom. If he has *that* ability, Claire decides, she should covet it all the more.

"Ten minutes on the vegetables," she announces. "Are Joshua and Lisbeth here yet?"

Clearly they aren't. Her friends tease her with their silence.

"Well, okay then," she shrugs.

"She's in her element," Freddy chuckles as Claire fusses in the kitchen. She smiles to herself because he is right. She runs the tap to rinse a cutting board and continues to eavesdrop on the conversation in the living room.

"So, are you going to do that shoot?" Freddy asks Ritchie, his mouth full of almonds. "For the billboard, I mean?"

"Yep," Ritchie says. "I'll be doing no carbs for ten days starting Saturday after Noble's. I got to hit L.A. Sporting Club to pick out a Speedo. The photographer guy said to bring a few, but I think I'm basically going to give him blue, white, or black—Jesus, I hope I'm doin' the right thing here."

"If you're not sure about it—"

"I'm sure. 'Course it may look different after day 5 of no carbs."

Claire opens the fridge and twists the top off a jar of capers. The vacuum seal opens with a snap. On Joshua's request, she's leaving sardines out of the salad tonight, but it will need something to take the sardines' place. Capers and peppercorns will help.

Dog barks and Claire hears the front door swing open. She

wipes her hands on a towel and rounds the corner to see Joshua and Lisbeth, who have arrived at the same time. They laugh as they come in, and the room feels full. Claire walks over and gives them each a hug.

"Anybody want a glass of wine?" she asks, pointedly avoiding looking at her daughter. Everyone declines, as they always have, except during the brief stint when Joshua tried to solve his depression through social drinking.

Claire is not a member of their little sober club. She doesn't drink often, but when she does, her memory goes fuzzy. The next day, her friends grouse about how she behaved. The last time she had more than a glass of wine was during her birthday dinner at Celestino's. That evening, Freddy claims, she took off her shoe and banged it on the table like Kruschev.

Tonight, the wine bottle doesn't even make an appearance. Everyone has seltzer water except Ritchie, who read somewhere carbonated beverages rob the body of calcium.

Claire herds them into the dining room. She's lit even more candles there, giving the room a warm glow, and has laid the table with bright-colored plates and cranberry napkins.

"We should take a picture of it!" Ritchie effuses. Claire's still camera is broken. There is a video camera at the ready, but Claire thinks that fact might be better kept from Lisbeth until after dinner.

"Shall we say grace?" Joshua asks. Freddy, an agnostic like Claire, snorts his disapproval of the idea. They roll their eyes and abide a moment of silence while Joshua communes with the Almighty.

Everyone digs in, talking with mouths full, laughing, knocking silverware on the floor, slipping scraps to Dog despite Claire's longtime insistence that people food gives the dog gas. Claire is delighted at the speed with which the dishes are emptied, but keeps an eye on Lisbeth, who is uncharacteristically quiet.

There is an unfamiliar cast to Lisbeth's face—a gravity Claire has never before noticed. Her hair is pulled back severely into a ponytail that disappears into the hood of the shapeless, oversized sweatshirt she keeps zipped to the neck. Lisbeth pokes at the mango salad with her fork. She's taken tiny servings and, unlike the others, she doesn't reach for seconds of anything. Several times, Claire begins to say something to Lisbeth, but awkwardness stops her. More than that, she knows she must let Lisbeth be.

"So," Joshua says, setting down his fork and smiling briskly, "I go to pick up Mamie Redbird at the salon the other day—"

"What're you, her driver, now?" Freddy asks.

"And I walk into the place," Joshua continues, ignoring Freddy, "and it's like the end of the world in there. Everyone is running around frantic. And then I see Mamie coming out of the back room, banging her purse on her head. I try to find out what's going on, but she's too crazy to make any sense. All she keeps talking about is 'that goddamned Mexican.' She keeps pointing over at Carlos, the guy who does her hair. And he's looking pretty pissed too. His smock is flapping all over the place and he's dragging the owner of the salon toward Mamie and pointing at her and saying all kinds of bad stuff in Spanish, which of course the owner doesn't understand, because he's Persian. Mamie runs to the back again, still caterwauling and smacking herself with her purse, which is something you just have to see."

Claire smiles, grateful for a rest from her own thoughts.

"So finally I get the owner to talk—he's the calmest of the three. And it seems that Mamie and Carlos got into a fight over what shade of purple rinse to use on her hair. She kept insisting that he watered it down and her yellow was showing through. So Carlos made her stand in this light, then another light, and over by the window, and finally she goes to the manicurist's table and puts her head down under the desk lamp and the bulb is so hot that her hair spray starts to smoke."

"For serious?" Ritchie asks, a forkful of flank steak poised before his lips.

"Oh, yes!" Joshua insists. "She's screaming, and Carlos is—well—beside himself, and the owner is bowing at the waist and apologizing to everyone in Farsi—even to me! Then Mamie comes back out and I grab her and drag her out of there; I assume there's no charge for the burned-up hairdo. And my biggest challenge is getting this hysterical woman to the car without anybody recognizing her. But this is Santa Monica Boulevard, if you know what

I mean, so of course everyone in L.A. Sporting Club sees her, and the people across the street at Starbuck's. And it doesn't help that her car is an '82 Rolls with license plates that say THE BIRD."

Everyone laughs except for Lisbeth, who is in some faraway place. But even she manages a half smile. Then the table falls quiet and a sickly feeling passes through Claire's chest.

"You know what?" she offers, snapping to attention. "You are my four favorite people on the planet. So how about that?"

"Four out of two billion? Pretty impressive numbers," Freddy muses. "Wait, is it two billion total, or two billion Chinese?"

"Not sure," Claire says. "But in any case, two billion Chinese aren't here for dinner tonight. They wouldn't all fit in the living room, and I'd run out of forks and napkins pretty quick. Though I usually cook enough steak to feed a billion or so."

Then Ritchie gets up, to Claire's surprise, and starts clearing the table. She tells him to stop; she'll take care of the dishes. But he hushes her. She shrugs and relents.

Claire is eager to serve dessert. As a rule she doesn't bake, leaving the cookies and double-crusted pies to Freddy, who eagerly takes to preparing them around holiday time. For tonight's dinner, Claire picked up French roast coffee and some kind of phyllo-crusted pastry at Trader Joe's. She follows Ritchie into the kitchen and cuts broad slabs of the dessert, sets them on plates, and tops each serving with a drizzle of chocolate sauce and a small handful of crushed macadamia nuts.

She walks the food into the dining room, balancing the dishes on her arms like a waitress and places one plate in front of each guest. Freddy compliments the dessert, making a play on words at which Claire laughs, though she isn't paying close attention. Instead, she is listening to the movement of the conversation, waiting for a pause.

Finally, a moment arises when everyone is eating. Claire looks over at her daughter.

"Lisbeth, honey," she says, smoothing tablecloth in front of her, "Joshua has this great idea for the deposition."

Lisbeth sets down her fork. "Okay..." She hesitates.

"What we were thinking is this," Joshua launches in, using his hands as he speaks—a salesman at work. His delivery is succinct and well-rehearsed. He nods in the direction of Claire and Freddy as he mentions, in turn, each of their roles in the can't-lose brainstorm. He closes with a tidy summary. "So? What do you think?"

"Not on camera, though," Lisbeth says.

"It's important you see how you look," Joshua replies. "Your eyes, your body language. That way you can have it all smooth for next week."

"Okay, then," Lisbeth says weakly.

Joshua nods and smiles at Claire and Freddy. The deal is closed. Ritchie hops up and heads to the closet of Lisbeth's old bedroom for the video camera. The boys move to the living room for their little video shoot.

Alone now with Lisbeth, Claire blows out the candles on the table and watches as the spires of smoke climb through the air. Lisbeth is playing with her napkin.

"Honey?" Claire says, and Lisbeth looks up. "It's going to be okay."

"I know," Lisbeth replies quickly and without much confidence.

"C'mon." Claire leads her to the other room.

Brown extension cords snake across the carpet, one plugged into the next. Joshua being Joshua, the sofa pillows are fixed just so, plants moved so none of them will look like they're sprouting out of Lisbeth's head, and Claire's reading lamp has been repositioned to throw light onto the draperies behind the furniture.

"It'll add depth to the shot," Joshua assures Claire when she balks. He takes Lisbeth's hand and draws her to the sofa.

"Sit down," he suggests softly.

"Should I put on lipstick?" Lisbeth asks from where she's been placed, looking anxiously from face to the next for guidance. "I don't usually."

"You're fine, baby," Claire assures her, backing out in the way. "Just be yourself."

Joshua sits down next to Lisbeth. "Tell what really happened and say exactly what we tell you to say—you know, your take on things."

Lisbeth nods earnestly.

"And rolling," Ritchie says from behind the camera as he fumbles with the little buttons that control it. He is hunched over and squinting into the viewfinder.

"All right," Joshua begins, the consummate talk show host. "Why don't you tell us what happened on the night of the party. Were you there alone?"

"I was with my two friends, Leigh and Chantal," Lisbeth says, as slowly and deliberately as a defendant on an old Perry Mason rerun.

"Were you with them the entire evening?"

"Yes, except when Chantal was making out with this guy in the bedroom. So, no."

"But they pretty much knew you were calm and sober the whole time?"

"How much is pretty much?"

Joshua's smile fades a bit. "More than not?"

"Sober? Or calm?"

"Do we have to choose?" Joshua asks, sounding slightly irritated.

"They had caramel apple martinis with little chunks of chewy candy."

"Aha! And you'd never seen Ms. Shahan previously?"

"Prior to my smacking her? Only when—"

"Let's not say, 'smacking'," Joshua interrupts gingerly. A pained expression tightens the edges of his face.

"Well, then, no," Lisbeth flusters. Her upper lip is shiny with sweat and she swipes at it with the back of her hand.

From her vantage, Claire wants to rush over and stop things, but she holds herself in the doorway to the kitchen.

"I mean," Lisbeth explains, "she was kissing someone at the party too. Not in the bedroom and not her boyfriend either. So it was pretty trashy."

"And then she cut in front of you in line?"

"I think it was her boyfriend's friend," Lisbeth says mischievously, "which makes it even worse. They all came in the same car. At first I was confused as to who was dating whom, but Chantal explained it to me after she came out of the bedroom. With the guy, I mean."

"And after the altercation with Ms. Shahan?"

"I'd have to say yes." Lisbeth nods. "Definitely. Probably."

Joshua looks as though he doesn't feel well.

"And where was Leigh at this point?"

"I'm not sure," she says with great assurance. "Outside smoking? Yes, smoking. Or she might have gone down to the liquor store for more ice."

"So neither of them were with you in the hallway?"

"Not technically, but she was drunk."

"Leigh?" Joshua asks, perplexed.

"No."

"Chantal?"

"No."

"Miss Shahan?"

"Yes. I personally saw her have at least three martinis, although she did spill one of them on a giant teddy bear that the girl having the party had since she was twelve. And other people said she had more."

"And she was in an agitated state?"

"She looked like she had to pee."

"So she was aggressive toward you—rude, physically blocking you."

"They're all so rude anyway," Lisbeth says with a distant look.

"Who?"

"Persians," she whispers. Her eyes gleam with the joy of divulging a naughty secret.

"Let's leave that out of the deposition too," Joshua suggests nervously.

"It's true, though." Lisbeth shrugs. "The women especially. I think it's because they had to wear those dark, creepy dresses and hoods for so long—and the Birkenstocks. Kind of like nuns if they had to do what their husbands said. Not God, I mean. But here in America, the Persian women just drive white Mercedes sedans and dye their hair orange and smoke too much on restaurant patios and are mean to the busboys at the Ivy. Really, you can ask anybody."

"At the party, though—" Joshua prompts.

"She was cutting in line, and I told her she couldn't. And she just looked at me in that way. You know, *that* way. And I said she'd better move it or lose it; at least I think that's what I said. And she says that *I'm* the loser. And that was just, you know—it was too much."

"So, then you—"

"She was asking for it," Lisbeth says grimly.

"Not literally though."

"Might as well have."

"Okay..." Joshua says. "How about this—maybe she didn't understand American customs and was acting in a way that made you feel threatened?"

"She grew up in Brentwood," Lisbeth replies.

Joshua seems disappointed. He asks a few stray questions, then settles on a strategy:

"We can't do much with the facts here," he says. "But facts are only the sticks and stones, and they won't break your bones. Not in this town. So be as sweet as possible to everyone at the deposition thing. Even the girl's lawyer, if he shows up—I'm not sure if they have the other lawyer come—and let them see that someone as sweet and nice as you could never have done something like this."

"I'm not sweet—"

"Of course you are, baby," Claire interrupts hastily.

"Only if I like somebody."

"You're not only sweet," Joshua assures Lisbeth, "you're shy."

"Me?"

"This whole thing was a big misunderstanding."

Silence falls for a moment as everyone tries to wrap their heads around that one.

"Is it all going to be okay?" Lisbeth asks, suddenly fragile again. She looks hopefully to Joshua, then Ritchie, and finally to Claire.

"Of course," Claire insists after what she realizes is a bit too long a pause.

"Are we done, then?" Lisbeth wonders aloud.

Ritchie stops the recording because Lisbeth must leave; she's meeting up with a girlfriend to go to the movies. She kisses them each goodbye on the cheek—Claire last—gets her jean jacket and purse, and leaves. After Lisbeth pulls the front door shut behind her, Dog trots to the door and sits at attention, wagging her tail as if Lisbeth might fling the door back open and shout, "Surprise!"

They all stare at Dog for a moment.

"Well, she did great," Joshua says. Freddy and Claire both look at him as though they're not sure whether he's referring to Dog or Lisbeth.

"Yeah," Ritchie agrees, squinting at the little buttons on the camera to find the right one to rewind the tape. "And she looked good when I zoomed in and out. Stayed right in focus."

"Which is an art in itself," Freddy remarks.

"I really should get her a lawyer," Claire says worriedly.

"Nah," Freddy replies with unconvincing casualness. "She'll be fine."

"I want to play back the tape and see if there's anything I missed," Joshua says.

Claire nods anxiously.

"How about we all watch?" she asks.

"I don't see why not."

"I'll make the popcorn," she says. She means it as a joke, but when Ritchie's face lights up, she shrugs and heads back to the kitchen to hunt for her cast-iron popcorn kettle.

"Shall I assume you'll want trans-fat-free margarine on that instead of butter?" she shouts.

"And low-sodium salt if you've got it," Ritchie hollers back.

When they put in the tape and Lisbeth appears on the screen, her expression seems more grave to Claire than it had in real life. Maybe it has something to do with the way Ritchie zoomed in tight so she was cut off at the chin and forehead. Lisbeth starts answering Joshua's questions. Claire is surprised at how funny Lisbeth's responses are the second time around—even when she's being perfectly straightforward.

"What time did you get to the party?" Joshua asks from off-camera.

"I'm thinking," Lisbeth answers, looking up and sticking out her lower lip as if in great concentration, "around 10:30, maybe?"

Claire chuckles. Feeling bad about this, she looks over at Freddy, whom she discovers is stifling a laugh of his own.

Next, Joshua asks something inaudible on the tape. Lisbeth looks perturbed. She clears her throat and looks around the room as if she's watching the bumbling of a bee.

"Wait! Run it back," Ritchie says with a snort, a bit of popcorn flying from his mouth. "That was priceless."

Joshua presses the remote control. Lisbeth's expression is even funnier this time. They rewind the tape yet again. By the fourth pass, they anticipate Lisbeth's throat clearing and applaud it when it comes. Claire feels bad about enjoying herself at her own kid's expense, but it's liberating, like setting down a heavy parcel after a long walk up a hill.

With many stops and starts, it takes them an hour to make it through the interview. They laugh until there are tears in their eyes. Even Joshua is chortling.

"She just looked at me that way," Lisbeth says from the television screen, staring into the camera and raising her eyebrows dramatically. "You know, *that* way."

"*That* way," they all repeat ominously, turning to raise their eyebrows at each other. Ritchie has come over and is sitting on the floor in front of Claire, resting his back against the sofa between her legs.

"You people are incorrigible," Joshua says, sliding from the sofa onto the rug, almost knocking over Freddy's Diet Coke.

"Watch out, pal," Freddy warns with a pugilist's snarl, rescuing his soda can. The videotape runs out at about the same time the popcorn does. Claire looks down at her watch and can't believe it's nearly midnight. She announces the hour gravely.

"Mark it down as just another rip-roaring night in West Hollywood," Freddy proclaims. At this, they all have one more laugh.

Claire's guests gather their keys and cell phones and Tupperware dishes full of leftovers and head to the door en masse.

"But she'll do fine," Joshua says gently as he stands in the threshold. "Really."

FOUR

Mamie Redbird calls.

Joshua sits at his desk, looking with dread at the display on his phone. He doesn't have to pick up the line right away; that's Min's job. But once Mamie's call is answered and Min's had a brief chat with her, she'll be sent through and Joshua will have to contend with her.

This is the third time she's called today. Or is it the fourth? Joshua loses track. Conversations with Mamie have no definite beginning or end, so the precise number of times she's bothered him is less relevant than his lingering feeling of irritation. Each of the facets of her odd life has rough edges, and she relies on Joshua to smooth them all.

"Mamie on 2," Min announces crisply.

"I can see that," Joshua grumbles.

"Well, then."

"Yes, dear," Joshua says to his prize client, picking up the handset.

"The guy just left," she skulks, "And now the house smells funny."

Mamie's voice, trained at the Actor's Studio, has grown ragged and deep with the help of Pall Mall 100s. She says "house" like an elongated "hows" that trails off into gravel.

"Who left?" Joshua asks. This is how their conversations go.

"The ex-*ter*-minator. It smells like he sprayed Mexican pepper in here."

"Maybe he did."

"You must get them to fix it."

"How?"

"Threaten them or something."

"The exterminator? Mamie, that's not my job."

"Sure it is—"

"Is not."

"I pay your rent—"

Joshua considers this. "I'll make a call."

He glares through the open doorway at Min as if it were Min's fault that Mamie is impossible.

"By the way," she purrs like Satan's house cat, "have you heard anything back from that producer we met at that charity function last week?"

"You know I'll find you the minute I hear from him."

"Yes, but—"

"Mamie, I will."

She is quiet.

Joshua imagines her sitting on the wide sofa in her peppery-smelling living room, lined lips drawn tight as a tied-up duffel bag. She's probably wearing a dressing gown with no bra and the sort of expensive flip-flop sandals that might just as well have been purchased for three dollars at Sav-On.

Mamie doesn't hurt for money. Fred Segal sandals and dinners at Patina don't worry her. What does worry her is her mortal enemy—time—and the damage it has wrought on her body and career. She makes no secret of this. She hisses the bitter truth on the phone to Joshua each day and blurts it out in the interviews he books for her with *Southern California Senior* and *The Palm Desert Courier*. Joshua wishes he could get her *Entertainment Weekly* or even *People*, but the calls he makes to that sort of magazine go unanswered. Two and a half years into selling Mamie, Joshua doesn't try much any longer. Like Mamie, Joshua takes everything personally. He knows that's risky in the publicity business, where nothing is personal and allegiances mean little. It's a big part of what makes him good at his job and lousy at life.

"Mamie? Are you still there?"

"Yes," she sighs.

"You sound...down."

"Look, sweetie," she says with a sharp, affected *t*, "I'll call you later."

She hangs up without saying goodbye. Joshua sets the phone in its handset and waits. Mamie will call back shortly. He gives her two minutes—five if she has to pee or fix herself a cocktail.

He steals another glance at Min, who is humming to himself and folding a sheet of copy paper into origami triangles. Joshua makes a mental note to find his receptionist more to do.

There's not enough time to start a new call before Mamie will return with the continuation of her crisis, so Joshua waits quietly.

Min waits quietly too, having completed his paper crane.

Through the plasterboard wall, Joshua hears the sound of phones ringing, calls being transferred, agents making deals. Though the hubbub makes him angry, he has nothing to complain about. The back office he rents from the ICA Talent Agency has a good Century City address, and it's cheap. He and Min each have a window. They get to use the photocopier and water cooler down the hall, and have keys to the private men's room with chromed toilet seats and cakes of French soap next to the washbasins. But it's difficult, on slow days, to sit at his desk and hear all the muffled activity just a few feet away. Joshua's back wall adjoins the bullpen of the ICA on-camera commercials department, where various agents and assistants field a hundred calls an hour, finessing deals at double- and triple-scale—or so Joshua imagines. In any case, there are a lot of phone calls and a lot of commotion. At present, he'd give his eyeteeth for a bit of that frenzy.

Min's phone rings. Joshua looks down at his watch. Four minutes have passed.

"Mamie on 1," Min declares.

"Joshua here."

"Okay—why I was really calling. I have a big idea. It was a dream that came to me. In the night, naturally. You know I went to the doctor last week."

"And everything went smoothly."

"Except for the part about my implants developing scar tissue."

"He said that was nothing to worry about."

"For now. But there's no telling what it'll mean next year, or the year after that. So I was thinking—I could get them taken out. The implants."

"Mamie—"

"I didn't tell you right away because it seemed like a bad idea. But then last night I had this dream—"

"Dreams are metaphors—"

"I was standing outside the hospital talking to the press. And the reporters were asking me questions and saying how courageous I was."

Joshua is silent. Mamie's idea is ghoulish. It is also brilliant.

"You want to have your implants removed for the publicity it would generate," he muses.

"*You* would generate, my Jew-boy. Think of all the damned pink ribbons you have me wear and breast cancer walks you make me show up for. Which I do, even though I don't see the point. The only person they ever put on the news is that dreadful Jamie Lee Curtis, who's never won an Oscar in her life and never will—"

"Mamie!" Joshua exclaims.

"Well, it's true," she sniffs.

"So if you took your implants out—"

"I'd make the 11 o'clock news on all three channels—"

"Six channels, now—" Joshua informs her.

"And maybe the suits at the networks would see fit to give me the series I deserve."

Joshua drums his fingers on the desktop. "You're serious about this."

"Do I ever joke? About anything?"

"Well, no."

"Of course I do," she says dismissively. "Dean Martin said I was the funniest girl he ever met, including Lucy. I think Dean Martin is a better judge of character than you."

"Dean Martin's dead. But the sick part," Joshua considers aloud, "is this could finally get you *People*. My friend there says they're looking for a heroic Hollywood recovery. It's been about a year."

"You get cracking on that," Mamie commands huskily. "I'm

calling the surgeon to set up an appointment. I hear the good anesthesiologists at Cedars book way in advance."

The line clicks and goes dead. Joshua is silent for a moment before he bursts out laughing. Once he starts, he can't seem to stop, even when Min swivels around and stares at him suspiciously.

The weather forecast was a lie. It was supposed to be warm this morning. Ritchie shivers in his bathrobe and flip-flop sandals on the roof of an apartment building off Sunset Boulevard. He holds a venti decaf from Starbuck's and pulls off the cardboard sleeve so he can get extra warmth from the cup. When he moved here people told him that cold weather in Los Angeles is unlike cold weather anywhere else. He laughed at this; he is from Chicago, where winters are epic and deadly. But now, squinting in the morning sun and checking if he can see his breath, he gets it. The cold in California is cunning, coming at the end of days that have been balmy. The wind picks up and although the temperature may only drop to 50 degrees, in shorts and a T-shirt, a poor sucker is left with chattering teeth and goose flesh.

"You about ready?" Ritchie asks hopefully.

"Yeah," Aldo X says, crouching over his bag of photographic equipment a few feet away. "If I can get my medium-format to trip the strobe. The contacts must be dirty."

"Hmm," Ritchie answers, not knowing what else to say.

"We may end up shooting with natural light, which isn't the worst thing in the world."

"Right," Ritchie agrees. Again, he has no useful comeback.

"Let's see where we are with things now. Come stand over here, away from the AC pipes and all those wires. I want to see all you, no distraction."

Ritchie steps into position. The photographer has him take a few steps to one side, a step back, a step forward. Ritchie feels awkward. He probably should have cancelled the whole thing. Forget the dieting he's suffered getting ready for this shoot—the tuna fish and water and lettuce, the extra hours on the treadmill. He doesn't have to be at work at the gym for three hours. He could be home in bed right now, asleep and warm.

"You want me to keep my robe on?" he asks, not sure what to do.

"For the first shots, sure. I'm just getting lighting and angle right. Whatever makes you comfortable."

What would make Ritchie comfortable is not being here. But he knows he has to do it. Not because of anything Freddy or Joshua said; his own gut told him to go through with it—to do this billboard.

"Nah, I'm cool," Ritchie lies. He loosens his waist tie and lets the robe fall to the tar and gravel roof at his feet.

Aldo looks up from behind the lens of the camera and smiles. "Wow!"

Ritchie stands a little taller. He knows he looks good. His diving suit is bright red and his chest and stomach are shaved and his skin is dark from several visits to the tanning salon across the street from the yogurt shop. After his shower this morning, he mixed a splash of baby oil into his lotion so he'd have a slight glow.

"What do you want me to do?" he asks.

Aldo laughs. "Man, you don't have to do anything. Just stand there."

So Ritchie does. The camera shutter pops several times.

"Take a half step to the right," Aldo instructs. "Good. Turn your shoulder toward me and give me your eyes."

Ritchie stares into the lens, seeing a slightly distorted reflection of himself in the camera's filter. He tightens his abdominal muscles and flexes his biceps.

"Oh, yes! Nice," Aldo says.

Ritchie grins.

"Keep it serious."

Ritchie glowers.

"Not that serious."

"Sorry."

"Look out at the horizon."

Ritchie turns and sees the Ralph's half a block down. In the entrance to the parking lot, a homeless woman in baggy, brown thermal underwear is dancing with her arms raised in the air. Traffic is backed up onto the street, and drivers take pains to avoid her.

Ritchie wonders if he put too much gel in his hair this morning.

When he turns his head a little to show more of his good side, he can no longer see the homeless woman; now he confronts a billboard advertising breakfast sausage sandwiched between pancakes. Ritchie would love some breakfast sausage. In order to look trim for the shoot, he has consumed nothing but a few sips of water since lunchtime yesterday. This is what professional fitness models do, according to a magazine article he read. But now his lips are dry, he has an odd sort of heartburn, and he feels faint.

"And give me your eyes again," Aldo coaxes. The shutter clicks repeatedly.

Ritchie contracts his stomach muscles. His legs are starting to cramp. He wants to sit down. He wants to eat. He feels himself starting to break out in a cold sweat.

"Great," the photographer says, stepping away from his tripod and clasping his hands together.

"Huh?" Ritchie wonders what he's supposed to do now. Is this where the guy offers him drugs or tries to tie him up?

"We're done."

"We're—"

"I have what I need. I don't believe in overshooting. It's a waste of time and money."

"Really?"

"There's a standard release form downstairs in the apartment for you to sign."

Ritchie feels somehow cheated. He was just warming up.

It is just after dawn. The air in chilly. There is dew on the grass and the windshields of cars. Ritchie can see his breath in the thin morning light. He sits beside Freddy in the front seat of Freddy's car at the corner of La Cienega and Santa Monica. Both of them have paper cups of coffee. The engine is off and Freddy has the radio tuned to the public jazz station at the bottom of the dial. He yawns and shivers, zipping up his sweatsuit jacket so that the edges of the hood join at the base of his neck.

"You don't have to stay," Ritchie says, feeling a little embarrassed.

"Are you kidding? Where else would I be?" Freddy counters, clucking like an old woman.

"I'm just saying—"

"I always yawn at 5:30 in the morning."

"Not when you're sleeping, I bet," Ritchie figures.

A garbage truck goes by, huge and squatty. Ritchie holds his cup for warmth and cranes his neck to look up at the billboard across the street. There is a giant ad for light beer.

"All the same, though, you're sure it's this morning?"

"Yep." Ritchie nods. "He said the crews head out as soon as the sun is up."

"Well." Freddy shrugs and points at the coppery sun, which has just begun to appear over the low apartment buildings on the eastern horizon.

A city bus pulls up in the lane in front of them, full of people with headphone radios and newspapers and expressions that seem unduly weary for so early in the day. The traffic light turns red. The bus stops.

Ritchie takes a sip of his coffee: a half-caf venti brevé vanilla latte in a double cup, extra hot, no foam, four packets of sugar in the raw. The barrista who works mornings at the Starbuck's across from the gym has taken to referring to this as the "Sicily special," which suits Ritchie fine. While he was dieting for the photo shoot with Aldo X, he suffered through sugar-free lattes made with Sweet'N Low, which became known as the "evil Sicilian special." This didn't suit Ritchie as much, but he put up with humor at his temporary humorlessness.

The light changes. The bus lumbers through the intersection. When it has gone, Ritchie sees that a yellow service truck has pulled up across the street. A man in a hard hat has gotten out and is looking up at the billboard overhead.

Ritchie claps his hands in excitement.

"Here we go!" Freddy says.

They watch as the worker and another man go up in a cherry picker and climb the billboard's scaffold toting wide rolls of paper. They start at the top right corner and unroll the new advertisement one strip at a time. There are the tops of some letters, then a piece of Ritchie's head blown up to gigantic proportions. The next strip reveals WELCOME TO WEST HOLLYWOOD, CALIFORNIA along with Ritchie's face and neck. His chest follows, and finally his abs and crotch appear, along with the tagline ONE OF AMERICA'S BEST CITIES TO GET INTO centered directly below the bulge in Ritchie's swim shorts.

"Well, that's a little suggestive," Freddy observes.

Ritchie shrugs. He is entranced by the oversized image of himself. His teeth are white and he is smiling broadly. The advertising company has obviously retouched parts of the picture; his body looks ridiculously toned and chiseled, and the birthmark near his belly button has vanished.

"So?" Freddy asks. "What do you think?"

Ritchie can only nod. Freddy looks at him and smiles.

"Well, okay then. I think I hear some pancakes calling our names."

"IHOP?" Ritchie asks.

"None other."

Freddy starts the car and pulls into traffic. Two blocks later, when they arrive at the International House of Pancakes, Ritchie steps out of the car and gets a better perspective on the billboard. It is gigantic. He looks really good. A middle-aged man walking his dog in front of them turns to cruise Ritchie then glances up and sees the billboard. He nearly walks into a lamp pole before craning his neck around to stare at Ritchie again. His dog yelps as the man stops short, yanking the leash.

"That's you!" the man exclaims, pointing to the billboard.

"Yeah," Ritchie acknowledges. "Me."

"And you're real! I mean, you're here. Can I have your autograph?"

"You want my autograph?" Ritchie can't quite believe it.

"Here," the man says, dragging his dog toward Ritchie and Freddy. He reaches into a leather shoulder bag hanging across his chest and fishes out a beat-up notebook and a Sharpie marker.

Freddy laughs. Ritchie blushes, but he is thrilled. It feels like someone has given him a shot of adrenaline, but with no needle prick. He signs the notebook—"Best wishes, XXOX Ritchie Catalano," and shakes the man's hand.

Freddy grabs Ritchie by the elbow and drags him into the restaurant.

"Did you see that?" Ritchie asks excitedly once the waitress has brought them menus and a bottomless pot of world-famous coffee.

"Yeah," Freddy says excitedly and nods. "You're a star now!"

"Nah! I'm just—really?"

"Don't let your head get too swollen up, though. It's a tough town."

Ritchie nods and stirs his coffee as he dribbles creamer into the cup so that it makes a swirling, beige tornado. It is indeed a tough town—tougher than Chicago, no matter what his uncles and cousins might think. They don't know. All they know is how to listen to orders from a fat old guy who wears big sunglasses in the middle of winter and rides around in a Caddy. Punks are what his cousins are. Delivery boys. They may run cash and guns instead of pizza, but it's all the same.

After their orders arrive, Ritchie mops up syrup in his plate with a forkful of pancakes. He has ordered the kind with whipped cream topped by chocolate chips and banana slices in the shape of a smiling face. He's eating like a man on death row, though there's no gas chamber waiting for him—just a strict carbohydrate-modified diet. He lets Freddy pay the check and gives him a quick peck on the cheek as a show of thanks.

Later, at the gym, everyone has a comment about the billboard.

"Ladies and gentlemen, Mr. Abs," announces the skinny guy behind the front desk when Ritchie comes into the building.

"Can I touch you?" asks a woman with thighs that bulge out of her leotard. She pokes Ritchie's triceps with a porky finger before he has a chance to answer.

"When I grow up," a slight-built blond twink in basketball shorts gushes, "I want to be you, if the job isn't already taken."

Ritchie laughs and jokes with each of them, warm in his belly from pancakes and admiration. His words are effortless, his humor graceful. He has found his calling.

Claire is on her lunch break. In fifteen minutes she will be done with her workout. She checks her watch often. Today is cardio day, which entails a grueling half hour of uphill hiking on the treadmill and another half hour on the elliptical machine. She feels like she's skiing through pudding. Her hair is stuck to her forehead. Sweat trickles down her shoulders and chest and drips from her elbows and the bottom band of her sports bra. It gathers in puddles on the long pedals of the machine.

Claire forgot her Walkman at home today, which makes the exercise especially dreary and leaves her open to the assault of well-intentioned conversation from the people working out around her. She doesn't mind it much if the interest comes from a cute guy, though most of the guys at this gym are gay.

One young man—at least ten years her junior—has smiled at her a half dozen times in recent minutes. He is walking on the treadmill across the way from her and she has to turn her head slightly to see if he's still looking. She wants his attention but doesn't want him to know that she does. He ought to keep looking at her and then approach her—an overture to which she will be polite but noncommittal. He will leave the gym in pleasant frustration. Once she's sure he's gone, she will leave, feeling victorious. If she never sees him again, she has succeeded. If he happens to be waiting downstairs on the street for her, pretending to browse the windows of the hair salon, she will fuck him in his car.

Claire is tired of straight men. They don't pick up their things or take care of their hair. They neglect their dental work. They only want to talk about things that go fast and light up, like race cars and wireless Bluetooth devices. Some of them will broach more interesting topics—politics and art and psychology—but in that case they are didactic and prone to deadening soliloquy. She tends to take from men what they're good for—sex—and count on her friends for the things that really matter—the heart part.

The guy on the treadmill smiles at her again. This one will be a cinch. He's cute, with big biceps and consciously careless scruff on his face. Claire looks down at the display on her machine. Six minutes left. She checks the television monitor in front of her where a CNN anchor talks silently about the day's news and a stock ticker crawls by underneath.

Then she looks back to her cute guy—but he's gone. Claire is startled. There is a tangible vacuum in the room in the space he'd just occupied. She looks around, but he is nowhere, not at the drinking fountain, not in the corner of the gym with stretching mats and a ballet bar. She feels a flash of panic, of abandonment. How dare he?

The last few minutes of Claire's workout are as agonizing as the last period of third grade before summer break. She can't wait to get to the locker room and out onto the street. Maybe he will be waiting there for her, fidgeting with his cell phone, adjusting the zippers on his gym bag, trying to look inconspicuous. The gym lobby would be a more comfortable place for him to wait, but it would be too blatant.

She throws her things into her gym bag and hurriedly sprays one squeeze of perfume down her underpants just in case. She pulls her hair back into a bun and slams the locker door. Breezing through the lobby, she barely pauses to wave hello to Ritchie, who is biding time between clients by chatting with one of the gym's giggly membership sales girls.

There are several passers-by on the broad sidewalk, but there's no sign of Claire's guy. She squints to see if perhaps he has wandered up the block toward the Koo Koo Roo restaurant. She sees someone who might be him and takes a few tentative steps in that direction. But then she realizes she was mistaken and feels foolish. Did he think she was too old? Was it her haircut? The way the thin skin has begun to sag a bit at the tops of her elbows and ankles? Or maybe he is gay after all. Yes, that's probably it. She tries to put the embarrassment out of her mind and heads for the parking deck.

Claire needs to get back to the office and deal with some insurance claims because she is leaving directly at 5 so that she can get ready for an ACLU event to which she is invited. As she waits for the elevator, she decides she will wear her black and white polka-dot dress and a pair of black flats that don't make her excessively tall. There's nothing worse than being seated at a banquet next to a short Jew, which is likely at an ACLU function in Beverly Hills. Few of the men she meets are taller than her, and many are as much as a head shorter. Claire finds this off-putting enough that she has intentionally not developed usable skills at ballroom dancing to avoid the spectacle of towering over a partner. "No thank you," she can tell a man's forehead if asked to waltz or salsa, and honestly add, "I don't dance."

Her afternoon at the office goes smoothly. She sees several patients, one of whom is a precocious 6-year-old with a hairline fracture in her wrist from a playground tumble.

"What's that for?" the girl asks, pointing to Claire's stethoscope.

"This? For listening to you heartbeat and your breath," Claire explains, holding it up and tapping on the diaphragm.

"How about I just breathe loud and then you won't have to use it?"

"Why didn't I think of that?"

"I'm for real!" the girl insists.

"Okay. But you've got to make your heart beat extra loud too," Claire replies. She opens the examination room drawer to get a lollipop.

Once the waiting room is empty, Claire goes over the insurance forms. Providers now balk at claims they used to pay automatically. Claire takes it personally. It's as if the company is questioning her value. Claire would like to believe she's worth plenty.

She likes this quiet time at the end of the day. Her assistant has gone home and the phones are forwarded to the answering service. She looks out the window of her office where, to the east, she sees the top of the Beverly Center and, beyond that, downtown. It is late afternoon. The city lights are just coming on. Traffic is jammed in all directions, tail lamps and headlights aflame. From her perspective, all is silent and still, except for the way the glowing tail lamps dance like a Van Gogh sprung to life in the shimmer of heat rising from the pavement and the hoods of cars. Claire smiles at the thought of Van Gogh painting the Los Angeles traffic. She closes the top of her notebook computer and reaches around the back of her chair for the jacket to her pants suit.

Traffic has never bothered Claire much, even if she's running late. She can call Freddy or Joshua and lose herself in the conversation for five minutes—or fifty if necessary. In fact, she get so involved with their discourses on politics or dentistry that the hard part is remembering to navigate lanes and turn at the right intersection.

"What?" she asks when Freddy picks up.

"How should I know? You called me."

"That's no excuse."

"No, it isn't," Freddy admits, "but it's all I've got. Are you in the car?"

"It seems. And you're on the computer again. I hear you typing."

"It's what I do for a living—"

"Chat rooms?"

There is a beat of silence, and Claire imagines Freddy seething cartoonishly.

"Haven't you got that ACLU dinner tonight?" he asks. "Shouldn't you be getting ready? I want to go see *Whatever Happened to Baby Jane?* at that revival theater on Beverly by La Brea."

"Yes, I do. And thank God for the ACLU, if that's the alternative—"

"ACLU and God shouldn't go in the same sentence—"

"Neither should Easter and disco, but that's never stopped you."

"What's the latest with Lisbeth?"

"Fine, thanks."

"Well, then—"

"I'll call after the thing if it's not too late."

"I'll be back here on the computer. Typing."

Claire hurries when she gets to the house, letting Dog do her business in the back yard. She goes into the small second bedroom that used to belong to Lisbeth and takes her polka-dot dress from the dry cleaner's bag. Claire reaches behind her back to zip it up, once she's shimmied inside, and is dismayed at how her underpants leave a small bulge of skin on either side of her lower back. Perhaps it is just the angle she's looking from. She turns around in front of the mirror and sneaks a look over her shoulder as if to catch her body in the act of betrayal.

Half an hour later, Claire drops her car off with the valet at the Beverly Hills Hotel and makes her way through an obstacle course of palm fronds and flashing cameras to the main ballroom. She finds table number 112, which matches the vellum reservation card in her handbag. It is in the back and off to one side. Claire will have to crane her neck to see the keynote speaker, but this doesn't bother her. The point is to be here among like-minded people who care about the same things she does.

"Excuse me, is this seat taken?" she asks a man whose complexion, hair, and eyes are all the same hue of watery gray.

"Not at all," he says, standing to be polite. He smiles and Claire notes that his teeth, large and shaped like hominy, match the rest of him in shade. If only he were wearing a gray suit, Claire thinks, it would be possible to squint a little and make him disappear entirely.

She smiles back, takes the napkin from the plate in front of her, and sets it in her lap. The table seats a dozen and there are still a few spots open, likely soon to be claimed by some of the crowd still milling around exclaiming about President Bush's imbecilic graft or how rudderless the Democratic Party has become.

"I like to come to these things," Claire tells the man beside her, gesturing at the room. "But not usually alone." This is true, but not an accurate portrait of things. She doesn't like to come alone, but most often she does. Her friend Larraine, a fellow politico, has a shrinking fear of crowds and confrontation and is quite prone to making plans with Claire then begging off at the last moment with the excuse of a sudden, dubious-sounding illness. Freddy cares about social politics but doesn't well tolerate public events that embrace calla lily and Rolls Royce liberalism. As for the other half of Claire's familiar foursome, Joshua's usually at an opening for some movie or restaurant or hair salon, and Ritchie couldn't possibly be a worse date.

"Me too. I like to keep involved," the man says. "And you get such a better perspective at this kind of dinner than you do just reading about it all in the *Times*."

Claire notices a depth to his eyes, a quick flicker there that she finds interesting.

"Not that that's saying much. I'm no fan of the *L.A. Times*."

"No kidding," Claire agrees. "They should just send out the supermarket circulars and car ads leave well enough alone."

"Maybe the Sunday real estate listings."

"Not even," Claire disagrees. "People should stay put."

"I'll second that," the man says. "I got my place off Mulholland Drive ten years ago, and I think I'll probably keep it until they haul me off to the geezer farm."

Claire laughs heartily.

"Claire," she says, extending her hand.

"Bob," the man says with a smile that, like his eyes, draws her. His jaw is a little crooked, dented on one corner from what looks like an accident—Claire is suddenly self-conscious about her scars—and his smile is crooked in a way that makes his seems at once sly and kind. He is perhaps 50 years old, and trim without being thin. His suit is dark and unassuming, and he wears a blue linen shirt unbuttoned at the collar.

"You're very lovely," he tells her, which strikes her as bold. They will presumably be seated next to one another for the rest of the evening, and such an advance would leave him in an uncomfortable position if it were not well-received.

"You probably say that to all the angry left-wing girls," she replies.

"Not so much the angry ones."

"Good decision."

"But you are. Lovely, I mean. And presumably left-wing."

"I'm a card-carrying member of the ACLU," she says with pluck.

"Which will get you a discount on coffee mugs at the table out front."

"You're funny," she admits aloud.

"One step below handsome, but it seems to work with the left-wing girls."

"You've got all the angles figured, huh?"

"Mostly I stay home and read. I save a lot on dinner bills and dry cleaning."

Claire laughs again. She decides that she's going to sleep with Bob. She usually knows how far things are going to go within the first few minutes of meeting a guy. She was right with the electrician at her office and right with Terry from the gym, though that one took a while.

The evening is long and the guest of honor talks for almost an hour about the rights of Middle Eastern suspects in terrorism investigations. Claire is interested at first, but after a while she finds herself studying the drapes and banquet trays and the patterns in the carpet around the table where she and Bob are sitting. She tries to smell him but she can't. She finds herself wishing the room were a bit warmer so he would perspire a little.

She gets her chance to smell him once the evening is through. They go back to her house and, once she quiets Dog's discomfiture at a stranger being in the house at such a late hour, they make love on her bed.

"Made love," is how she describes it to Freddy the next day, for that is what it felt like.

"Are you going to see him again? Is he a keeper?" Freddy asks.

"He's a detainee, at least," she replies.

"What's that supposed to mean?" Ritchie asks worriedly when she repeats the joke the next morning at breakfast at Noble's. "Is this guy in some sort of trouble?"

"Only if you count me," Claire surmises. "Pass the marmalade, will you?"

"Hmm!" Ritchie retorts.

"There's something really great about having sex with a man who's seasoned."

"I thought it was making love," Freddy interjects.

"That too. It's just that as I get older, I don't get older inside, you know? I still feel like a girl. I don't know if that's normal, but that's how it is. So on the one hand, I feel weird even hanging around someone like—"

"Terry?" Ritchie asks, apparently still sore on the subject.

"Because he's old enough to be someone's dad, which weirds me out. But then I meet someone like Bob and it clicks. And it feels—I don't know. Appropriate, I guess."

"How old is he, actually?" Joshua chimes in. "And pass the cream."

"Fifty-four."

"So when you were in kindergarten," he calculates, "he was in—"

"—decisive about who to take to the junior prom. I'm telling you, it feels right."

"Well, sweetheart, that's what matters," Freddy says, taking the little pitcher of cream from Joshua and lightening his own coffee. "We are all just protective of you."

Claire smiles. She knows her friends are loyal when it comes to her romantic life—except for Ritchie, who seems oddly protective of Terry. Then again, there's no figuring Ritchie, so she smiles anyhow.

The next night, she sees Bob for dinner. She puts on lipstick in the bathroom mirror while he's waiting in the living room drinking a glass of seltzer. She smiles and makes kissy faces, making sure none of the lipstick is bleeding into the tiny vertical crevices that have begun to appear above and below her mouth over the last couple of years. She notices that one of her upper teeth feels a little odd. Or maybe it's her sinuses; it's hard for her to tell the difference.

"Are you ready?" she asks, making her entrance with a deliberate flourish of skirt.

"Sure," Bob says. He doesn't look at Claire right away, which disappoints her. He's glancing over the collection of books that line the narrow shelves on either side of Claire's fireplace. "Have you read all of these?"

"Not the encyclopedia, entirely."

"I love Dostoyevsky," he says, tapping the hardcover spine of the book as if to pay it acknowledgment directly.

"College," Claire admits.

"And Arundhati Roy. I think the Indian expats are the romantics of the new century. *The God of Small Things*...such attention to detail amid the climate of repression—"

"I liked the fucking. With the mom and the guy."

"But I have to tell you, Claire," Bob says, laughing. "You lose me on the Patricia Cornwall and Michael Crichton."

Claire laughs at his joke. But he is not joking. And she knows it. She moves outside of her body and looks at herself, chuckling stupidly, standing in her dress with her lipstick on, over the hill, a desperate soul who will do anything to have someone like her.

The rest of the evening passes—they go to dinner, they drive along Mulholland to look at the city lights—but Claire isn't there. She's watching the goings-on from a perch atop her own shoulder. At one point, she wonders if she's the Angel of Mercy or the Angel of Death. Perhaps for the moment their voice is one.

Claire reminds herself that she doesn't believe in angels. They are fictions created by people miserable with the options offered by real life. Claire is miserable too sometimes—okay, often—but she doesn't resort to hocus-pocus for consolation. If such things as angels existed, how could they have let her go through the windshield on prom night?

"He said what?" Freddy exclaims the next day when Claire recounts the evening for him on the phone. "I can't believe you're serious."

"I'm serious," she assures him, wishing she hadn't brought it up. She is sitting on the sofa next to *The New York Times*, still in her flannel nightgown. Dog is on the floor beside her. The blinds are drawn except for the one nearest her, which she has opened for reading light.

"What a louse," Freddy concludes. "You're an intellectual. I bet he's intimidated."

"He's not the timid sort."

"He's a louse!"

"Well, he's a bold louse then," Claire figures, "one who reads a lot and makes me feel little."

"Did you tell him?"

"That he reads a lot?"

"That your books are your books and they're precious to you."

"I'm not all that married to *Jurassic Park*, really—"

"You're missing my point," Freddy interrupts.

"No, really."

"Okay." Freddy sighs. "You're not seeing him again, are you?"

"I don't know," Claire admits, curling her feet up under her and tucking the hem of her nightgown around her knees. "I forgot what I said at the end of the date."

"Then the answer is no." Freddy is adamant. "Absolutely not. Forget him. Rip up his number."

"He has mine—"

"Again, you're missing my point."

"I think I told him not to call me," Claire remembers sketchily.

"Well, good."

There is a pause. Claire hesitates.

"Freddy?"

"Yes?"

She waits another moment then quietly says, "Thank you."

"What is so urgent that you have to call me three times in half an hour?" Freddy demands irritably when Joshua answers the phone.

"It was three messages," Joshua corrects him. "I actually called about seventeen times."

"Well, then?" Freddy rubs his eyes. It's late afternoon. He has been napping for a while; he's not sure how long. After lunch there was simply nothing to stay awake for.

"I found him," Joshua says gleefully.

"Who?" Freddy asks, kicking at the covers and trying to imagine what new client Joshua would need to brag about so urgently.

"Justin Salvatore."

The name is like a gentle kiss against Freddie's ear. It makes his toes tingle and his fingers curl around the cord to the antique phone that sits on his nightstand.

"What?" he coos.

"He's hiding out in Boston. I tried his agent and publicist in New York and none of them have heard from him for a couple of months. I guess he had a record deal that got dumped at the eleventh hour. He got himself fired from *The Jungle Book* because he was spending too much time and energy on his recording career for the show producers' comfort, and when it all blew up he just fell off the earth. Then, yesterday, I had a brainstorm—I pulled a 'who is' ID for his Web site and came up with a New York voice mail number. I left him a message and he just called me back."

"You actually talked to him?" Freddy feels like he's floating.

"For like fifteen minutes. Nice guy. He's taking some time off at his mom's place on Lake Gichi-whozit and regrouping. I guess it hit him pretty hard—getting fired off his show and dumped from his record contract. But I told him about you—"

"What'd you say?" Freddy resists admitting the fact that he sounds like a giddy schoolgirl.

"Just that I have a client that wanted to talk with him about a benefit performance—"

"You're my hero—"

"And I asked if it'd be okay for you to call him directly."

"He didn't get my e-mails?"

"He's in a cabin made of Lincoln logs. I don't think they've got broadband. Do you want the number or what?"

Freddy reaches to the nightstand for a pen. He overextends his arm, loses his balance, and tumbles onto the bedside rug. The phone handset is wrenched from his hand, springs on its coiled cord, and strikes his chest with a painful thud. He cries out.

"Hello?" Joshua's voice crackles.

"I'm here," Freddy says with a slightly dazed laugh once he recovers the handset. "That literally knocked me off my feet."

He takes down the number and listens to Joshua's cautionary words with no intention of following the advice that he be professional about things and wait until tomorrow to call Justin.

"I owe you one," Freddy says, searching for a polite way to hurry Joshua off the phone.

"You owe me more than one. You owe me, like, a jumbo pack. I think you should be careful with this because I'm not sure that—"

"Oh—can you hang on a second?" Freddy lies. "I've got another call."

"Okay, but—"

Freddy reaches and depresses the button on the phone cradle. The line goes dead.

"I'm sorry, Joshua," he whispers, "but Daddy's got needs."

He dials the number he has just taken down and waits as it rings twice, three times, four times. At last comes a "hello."

"I'm looking for Justin Salvatore."

There is a pause.

"That'd be me," says a young, sweet voice.

"My name is Freddy Ruckert. You just talked with my friend Joshua—"

"Oh, yeah. He seems like a great guy—"

"I-I saw your Web site, and I had to find you. I think you and I have a lot in common. I know I'm just some stranger calling out of the blue, and this sounds kind of stalker-ish, but I feel like we are supposed to meet—professionally, I mean. You're really talented and...well, I have my moments...but it hasn't been an easy road for either of us, and..."

Justin laughs. "Are you nervous calling me?"

"Petrified," Freddy admits.

"Why?"

"Because you're Justin Salvatore, and I've been looking at your pictures on my computer for weeks, and I'm a little starstruck."

"How do you know I'm not star-struck about you?"

Freddy considers this. "Because who am I?"

"If your publicist is for real, you're practically a household name."

Freddy imagines Joshua's trademark boasts. "He said that?"

"And you're putting together some sort of a benefit?"

Freddy panics. "Yes—kind of. It's still in the discussion stage. But it's dear to my heart and I definitely want you involved."

There is a pause. Then, with a smile in his voice, Justin says, "Tell me more."

"Are you serious?"

"I haven't hung up on you yet."

"This is true," Freddy says, clearing his throat. "And this is the weirdest experience for me right now because I like you so much and I know I shouldn't say that in this call and I'm totally blowing it, and—"

"Freddy? Relax!"

Freddy takes the phone away from his ear and hugs it to his chest for a moment. He can't help but laugh. He turns to the full length mirror on the back of the closet door and, pulling the comforter over the top of his head with his free hand, mouths a silent scream at his reflection.

"Hello?" Justin says after a moment.

"Sorry! I'm here."

"Which is where, exactly?"

"I'm sitting on the floor of my bedroom. In Los Angeles. With my comforter over my head. And where are you?"

"I'm in a big wicker chair on the porch at my mom's place on the lake. The sun fell below the trees across the water just before you called. There are stars in a clearing of the clouds, and they're reflecting down on the water, which is really smooth because there's no wind tonight."

"You talk like a romantic," Freddy muses.

"You listen like one."

"How can you tell?"

"Well, *you* haven't hung up on *me* either," Justin reasons.

"Can you see the big dipper?"

"I'm looking at Orion's belt. It's about a size 28, which has always irked me."

"I think Orion takes spinning class," Freddy offers.

"Or purges. Which would be very un-Greek of him, but there's no accounting nowadays."

"In any case," Freddy surmises, "no Big Fat Wedding for him. If he's straight."

"I hear the goddess Artemis was sweet on him, but it ended badly. Not the sort of thing to talk about in our first phone call."

"You could hang up on me and call me back."

"I don't want to hang up on you. I like you."

Freddy feels a flutter in his stomach. "Already?"

"I'm a good judge of people. I had to learn."

Freddy thinks about Justin, possibly the most beautiful man on earth, sitting in a wicker chair talking with him on the telephone. He thinks about the smell of peaches, about the nape of Justin's neck.

"I'm older than you," Freddy hears himself say.

"By how much?"

"Seven years, I think."

"Nah, we cheated my age in my bio by three years, so it's really more like four. I was a freshman when you were a senior. I'd have looked up to you. Especially if you were in the school play."

"I was always in the school play," Freddy assures him.

"Look how much time we've wasted!"

"So let's quit. Are you going to be in New York anytime soon?"

"I hadn't planned to." Justin hesitates. "But I could. I've got to record some voice-overs for a Disney movie."

"Or Boston."

"New York's better," Justin says decisively. "Where I am now is just—I needed a break. But why do you ask? What's going on in New York?"

"I am," Freddy decides with glee. "For as long as you'll allow. A couple of hours, the afternoon maybe—I'm sure you'll get bored."

The broad smile returns to Justin's voice. "Not at this rate."

They decide to connect twelve days later. It will be Saturday evening of the Fourth of July weekend. It's difficult for Freddy to hang up, but he knows he will see Justin soon and likely talk with him even sooner.

Later, Freddy and Joshua pick up Claire to go to Real Food Daily, a macrobiotic restaurant a few blocks from her house. Ritchie came along with the rest of them for an outing a few weeks after the restaurant opened, but he was spooked by the lack of meat or fish or even reasonable amounts of soybeans on the menu.

"I really apologize for hanging up on you," Freddy tells Joshua as they walk from the car to Claire's front door. "But I was a man possessed."

"And you still are, clearly." Joshua rings the bell. "Did you even nail down if he's gay? I mean, under what pretense are you meeting him?"

"No pretense at all. And I don't care if he's gay."

"Your conversation was that good?"

Claire opens the door, tapping on her wristwatch. "Finally here? You guys are ten minutes late. There's daikon sprouts and sesame paste a-waistin'."

"Okay, grumpy," Joshua says. "Come on."

They walk to the restaurant, shoulder to shoulder on the broad sidewalk. Freddy's feet are light. Joshua and Claire persist in debating Justin's sexual leanings.

"How about that loincloth picture on the Web site?" Claire asks. "No self-respecting hetero would be photographed in that pose."

"Please!" Joshua scoffs. "For an eight-show-a-week over-scale Broadway contract with Disney, even Charlton Heston would. Most actors I know would wear fruit on their heads and dance the mambo to be in a Disney show."

"But come on—Justin's head shot, then. He was wearing lip gloss, for Christsakes."

"He has the most kissable lips..." Freddy says half under his breath.

"What?" Claire asks skeptically.

"Never mind. Look," Freddy concludes, "whether or not he's gay, he paid me lots of attention. And I'm in love. So don't rain on my parade."

They enter the restaurant and are shown to a booth by a skinny waitress with long hair and a tribal henna tattoo on her wrist.

Claire orders a noodle salad, Joshua tries a mushroom burger, and Freddy goes out on a limb with the evening's special, a chipotle pepper seaweed casserole. They finish the meal with an order of tree twig tea and questionably healthy chocolate cookies.

Freddy buys dinner. They leave the table, laughing, with a lot of crumbs to brush off their laps.

FIVE

A woman is admiring some fake jewels in the plate glass window of the bric-a-brac shop next to Noble's. Ritchie studies her from the doorway where he is waiting—he arrived first today for Saturday morning breakfast. The woman is pretty, probably 40 years old, but is trying to look as though she is fresh from high school, and in the process has lost any charm she might have had. She wears a short denim skirt with a leather motorcycle jacket over a thermal shirt silk-screened with a yoga symbol. She is overly tanned and overly blond. Her breasts are bulbous and look rubbery, as do her lips and the pointy tip of her nose. On her feet are wedge-soled tennis shoes with glittered vinyl uppers. If she were standing on Sunset Boulevard instead of Third Street, Ritchie thinks, she might be mistaken for a hooker. Here, she is just one of a thousand aspiring actresses, never quite successful, clinging by her acrylic nails to youth and possibility, each angry at God for allowing her to age.

Ritchie both pities and reviles her. He would like to look away, to simply not see her, but he is drawn to her as he is drawn to the cautionary spectacle of ambulances and crushed glass at a traffic wreck.

At last she moves on, and Ritchie is relieved.

He starts to go over, in his head, the brilliant idea he intends to share with his three friends when they arrive. Soon, Joshua rounds the corner and greets him with a hug. They take their usual table inside, complaining about the crowd and the overcast marine layer in the sky and the surprising perils of shaving with an electric razor. Claire comes in, boldly wearing shorts that show off a big purplish-yellow bruise that she got when she slipped on a rock while she was hiking earlier in the week. Freddy arrives last. He acts jumpy, with a quick flicker of a smile that goes away almost immediately. He's been this way ever since he heard from Justin Salvatore. According to Freddy, he and Justin spent seven hours on the phone in three days, which must make Sprint very happy.

"So, I have an idea," Ritchie tells them once everyone's settled in and has ordered their coffee. "And this time it's a really good one."

Claire gives a smirky look to Freddy, who's too lost in goo-goo land to notice.

"Did you know Marissa Reese has started working out at the gym?" Ritchie asks.

"Who?" Claire makes a face.

"Who!" Ritchie retorts, almost insulted by her ignorance. "Only the star of *Catch Me, I'm Falling*."

Claire shrugs.

"The top-rated sitcom on the WB!"

"Is that the channel with the crippled frog?" she asks. "I avoid networks with amphibian mascots."

Ritchie ignores Claire's dig, which is usually the best plan when dealing with her. She's too clever and too mean to mess with.

"Well, on the show she's just broken up with her boyfriend and—hel-*lo*—the whole point of the show is that she's in love. So what I figure I do is next time she's at the gym, I'll be extra nice to her, and she'll see right away how perfect I would be to play the new boyfriend on her show, and she'll tell the producer or director or whoever, and then I'll be a star!"

For this brainstorm, Ritchie expected to receive immediate bravos from Freddy and Joshua. He knew Claire would be tougher. She always is. But now, none of them is saying anything. Freddy is looking down at his plate. Joshua clears his throat and appears to need to go to the toilet. Claire is tapping the back of her coffee spoon against her palm.

"Neither of you are going to tackle this?" she says to Freddy and Joshua after a moment.

Freddy raises his eyebrows and lets out a little snort as if something were funny, but keeps looking down at his place setting.

"Fine," Claire says irritably. "Make me do all the dirty work. Look, Ritchie—that idea is harebrained. And desperate. As usual, you deserve points for creativity, but sometimes I wish you would just plant your feet firmly in reality and *look* at yourself."

Ritchie dislikes her intensely. "So what do *you* think I should do?" he asks with an edge of challenge in his voice.

"You could start out by getting a real job."

"Hoo-kay," Joshua says under his breath.

"What?" Claire demands. "Am I not just saying what we all think but the two of you are too nicey-nice to tell him?"

"Claire, take it easy," Freddy warns.

"Okay. Well, I'm done then."

"Thank you," Ritchie tells her vaguely. He's not sure how he feels nor how he is supposed to feel.

Claire waits for Lisbeth in the outer office of a law firm in Westwood near the UCLA campus. It strikes her as ironic that Lisbeth would be deposed here; it seems a taunt aimed at Lisbeth's lack of academic prowess.

"What time is it?" Claire asks the crisply dressed man at the walnut reception desk across from her.

"Eleven-thirty," he says with a smile that looks more like a tic.

Claire looks at her watch. It says 11:30 also. It's the second time she's asked the man what time it is and the twentieth time she's checked her watch.

There is a queen palm plant in the corner of the room and an orchid on the coffee table. Claire imagines that the receptionist takes care of them. Next to his bank of telephone switches, he has a spray bottle that reminds Claire of the one she once used to discipline Dog when she was housebreaking.

There is the sound of voices in the hallway. She recognizes one as that of Lisbeth. The voices sound calm. She looks at her watch. It's 11:40. She doesn't know if it's good or bad that the deposition ran the better part of an hour. Perhaps they didn't start right away. Or maybe there was an emergency call for the lawyer—the phones certainly have been busy up front—and the question-and-answer session was interrupted. Or maybe Lisbeth choked, said all the wrong things, and admitted to something she didn't do.

A pair of glass doors open, and Lisbeth is there with the two lawyers. They are in suits and Lisbeth wears a drab, overly starched outfit Joshua chose at Ross Dress for Less. Her hair is braided in back so that she looks like a little girl going to her confirmation.

The lawyers, one from each side of the case, are full of thank you's and polite chitchat about SUVs and golf. Claire puts down her *New Yorker*, rises from her chair, and takes Lisbeth's hands.

"Can we go?" Lisbeth asks, looking from Claire to her former uncle Jerry.

"Yes. You did well," Jerry says, winking at Claire as if to reassure her.

Lisbeth nods and walks toward the exit, tugging to adjust to the sleeve of her ill-fitting gray sweater.

Jerry leans in to Claire and gleefully says, "Home run! Opposing council's going to advise his client to drop charges within twenty-four hours. There's just no case here."

Claire smiles to herself as she and Lisbeth walk to the car.

"So?" she asks. "How do you feel?"

"Like I never want to drink again in my entire life. And slap someone."

"Fantastic."

"I gave all the answers Joshua told me to, except the part where the girl's lawyer asked me about whether you and Dad hit me as a child."

"We never hit you!"

"That's what I told him."

"Once...twice at the most. You were really a handful."

"I didn't know what to say, so I just cried and said I didn't believe in violence."

"Brilliant."

They go back to Claire's house, where mother and daughter spend the afternoon splayed on the couch watching a Jennifer Lopez movie and eating red grapes from the plastic bag.

That evening, Lisbeth takes a long, cool bath. Claire lies on her bed and hears her daughter singing quietly to herself down the hall. She closes her eyes and hums along.

When Lisbeth is done, she comes into the bedroom. Claire, already dressed to go out, has laid out one of her own party dresses for Lisbeth, who dons it gingerly and puts on a pair of her mother's heels.

"Whoa," she says, wobbling at first as she inspects herself in Claire's full-length mirror. Claire realizes Lisbeth is quite unused to wearing anything other than sneakers. She brushes her daughter's hair and mists each of them with two puffs of Angel perfume.

"There," she says with satisfaction, tucking her hair behind her ears and giving both of them a final look-over.

They drive to a karaoke bar on Sunset Boulevard where Ritchie and Joshua are waiting at the valet stand at the corner of the parking lot.

"Hey!" Joshua calls, waving exuberantly. This is his and Lisbeth's evening, really, a celebration of their success—or lack of failure. He and Ritchie walk toward Claire's car as an excited man in a red jacket and bow tie takes the keys from her.

"I knew she had it in her," Joshua brags. "It's natural poise."

Everyone hugs each other, even Ritchie, and Claire feels a warmth in her stomach. It's a little like drinking red wine, less thrilling than being in love, about on a par with sleeping in on Sunday morning. They walk inside and get a booth. Ritchie pulls up a vinyl chair for Freddy, who arrives shortly.

"I hear you dogged it out of the bark," Claire hears Freddy tell Lisbeth over the loud music.

"What?"

"I hear you knocked it out of the park," he shouts.

Claire laughs hard at this.

The room is filling up with an odd assortment of USC frat boys, Japanese, and a couple of groups that seem to be celebrating someone's birthday.

Claire orders drinks—hot sake for the girls and lemonade for the boys—and passes around a three-ring binder full of karaoke song choices.

"What are you singing?" Claire asks Ritchie, who blushes and shakes his head.

"I'm not going to get up in front of you guys and make a fool of myself!"

"Like hell you're not. Pick."

Ritchie grins at her, and she sees why the boys fall madly for him. Suddenly, her sometime object of scorn is a beautiful creature, all blue-black hair and dimples and sparkling eyes.

"I love you," she blurts.

He looks confused and picks up the karaoke book. "Is that an '80s song?"

"No...never mind." The moment has passed. Claire blushes.

Thankfully, it is loud in the bar and there is no awkward silence. Freddy launches into a fresh story about his new long-distance love, and Claire relaxes. The waitress, petite and dopey-eyed, brings their drinks, and Claire takes a sip of her sake. On the small stage across from them, the host of the karaoke show announces it's time to begin. He holds a stack of note cards where patrons have written down what they want to perform.

"First up," he leers in what Claire figures to be an impression of an American talk show host, "Ah-nold singing *Only the Lonely*."

One of the frat boys lumbers onstage, amid howls encouragement from his friends, and butchers the song. A few patrons clap.

"Next person," the host effuses, reclaiming the microphone, "we have Ree-chee."

Claire looks over at Ritchie in surprise. He winks at her and slides past Lisbeth to go to the stage. Claire can't figure out how he got himself signed up; he certainly didn't do it at the table. She realizes it must have been planned in advance. She feels a stab of resentment at being left out of a surprise, but quickly recovers and looks over at Lisbeth with wide eyes and a shrug.

Ritchie stands in the middle of the stage. He seems too large for the space and fidgets while the host punches buttons on the CD player. The track begins. At first Claire doesn't recognize the song, but after a couple of lines, she realizes it's "Smooth Criminal" by Michael Jackson. The recording is hopelessly out of Ritchie's key and he jumps up and down an octave before settling into a sort of tuneless patter-reading of the lyrics. He shuffles his feet, warming as the crowd warms to him. At the first chorus, he flashes a smile and manages a serviceable moonwalk, pointing at Lisbeth as he barks out, "You've been hit by—you've been struck by a smooth criminal."

Freddy leaps up and joins him onstage, though he's no more lucky with the key than Ritchie. Still, they are a winningly hammy duo, and at the end of the song, Claire gives them a standing ovation, cheering so loudly that she knows she will be hoarse tomorrow.

"Your girl is here," says Lombard, the queen at the front desk. He nudges Ritchie, who's standing beside the counter chatting away a break between clients, and gestures toward Marissa Reese, who's just breezed in. She pulls her gym membership card through the scanner and drops it back into her satchel before adjusting her Jackie O. sunglasses and sashaying through the lobby toward the locker rooms. Ritchie watches her pass.

"You look like you want to fuck her," Lombard says.

"Maybe I do." Ritchie shrugs defensively.

"What-ever." Lombard rolls his eyes and forms a W with his thumbs and forefingers.

Marissa is pretty. But Ritchie would no rather sleep with her than with his own sister. And while he's on a gay billboard and works in a gay gym, there's a big part of him that still recoils when his masculinity is assailed—especially by a queen like Lombard, who has stripes of color in his hair and a scarecrow body that makes his uniform polo shirt look as though it is still on the hanger.

"I'll talk to you later," Ritchie says coldly. He wanders toward the lobby without waiting for a reply. He goes to the doorway of the women's locker room and stands there a moment, not sure what to do next. He wasn't expecting Marissa today. He wasn't expecting her *any* day in particular, but today he woke up late and didn't have time to fix his hair right. Maybe she won't notice. He'll have to be extra clever.

He is so intent in his deliberation that he doesn't notice her rounding the corner to leave the locker room.

"Oh!" she says, startling slightly as she nearly runs into him in the doorway. She cowers for just a moment, put off by Ritchie's size and closeness, then raises her chin slightly and passes without another word.

Ritchie goes queasy. He has blown it. Right out of the gate, she's on edge. *Don't panic. Keep breathing.* He shakes his hands a little like he learned to in high school drama class. When he looks across the lobby, Lombard is watching from the front desk.

"Motherfucker," Ritchie whispers under his breath before he heads to the stairs to follow Marissa to the workout floor.

He finds her climbing onto a stair-step machine and adjusting her headphones. She looks smaller than she does on TV, especially next to the oafish man laboring on the machine next to her. Ritchie hesitates in the doorway, unsure of what to do next.

"Excuse me," someone says from behind him. He realizes he is blocking the way.

"Sorry," he mumbles, stepping aside. He stands and watches Marissa. Maybe he should go tell her a joke. That might be a good way to break the ice:

"Did you hear the one about the canary who fell out of the tree?"

No. What an idiot he is! Flattering her is probably the best way to go. He walks over to where she has begun to work out and stands in front of her machine.

"I just love your show," he says.

"Huh?" She pulls one side of her headset out of her ear with a sour expression. She hasn't heard what he said.

"I love your show."

"Oh. Thanks." She puts the headset back in her ear. She is done with him.

"Your character has really grown this season," he says.

"What?" She switches her headphones off, now clearly annoyed. Ritchie knows he should stop, give up, but he has ventured this far and feels compelled to see his endeavor through to the end.

"Your character. She's grown a lot."

"I'm working on that right now," Marissa says, switching her headphones back on. She gives Ritchie a dismissive smile.

Her music plays. Ritchie is frozen in place. Several seconds pass.

He should walk away, go back to the personal trainers office, read a magazine until his next client. Instead he stands, listening to the *whir-whir-whir* of Marissa Reese stair-stepping. She is doing her best to ignore him, which he knows is not a small task, considering his size and the fact that he is directly in front of her. Yet she seems intent on the blinking lighted display of the machine and the television monitors off to one side playing music videos from the '80s and a Mexican Western film.

"Hey." Ritchie goes for broke, tapping on the readout of her machine in a way that clearly startles her. "Who's the casting director on your show?"

She stops stepping and takes her headset off. "Look, dude. It's all in the phone book. Anything you want to know about the show, you can look it up there."

She picks up her headset and towel and retreats from Ritchie, almost running into a mirrored column in the process. Once she's about ten feet away from him, she makes a beeline for the stairs.

Ritchie stands, heavy with despair. He shifts his weight from one foot to the other as if he might loosen the yoke on his shoulders, but it does nothing. He looks to see if anyone else in the line of treadmills and bicycles has witnessed his shaming, but each person seems completely absorbed in his or her own sweaty work.

Slowly, Ritchie walks to the trainers office. He wishes there was someone there to talk with, someone's dumb jokes to listen to, but it's just him and a cheap metal desk and some motivational posters with large-breasted girls showing off their abs. He drops into the chair with a sigh. He knows he's blown it. He should have stopped and walked away, come up with a better approach. But he's stubborn—that's what the problem is, his stubbornness. And he's no good at any anything he does, never has been. If he weren't so goddamned stubborn, he would get a clue that what he was doing was wrong, all wrong, but instead he just keeps on the same losing streak. And he always will.

It is one minute past noon and time for his next client, a 50-ish litigator with AIDS who visits the gym on his lunch break three days a week so Ritchie can keep his stomach reasonably flat. Ordinarily he's a bit of a drag, but today he's a welcome distraction.

"Hi," Ritchie says, finding him flat on his back in the stretching area attempting some sort of sit-up movement that makes it look as though he is trying to climb under low-slung barbed wire in a prisoner of war camp.

Ritchie listlessly takes him through his workout.

"Is something wrong?" the man asks at one point, but Ritchie is so distracted that he doesn't realize until several minutes later that the question has been asked.

When they are done, Ritchie walks him downstairs to the lobby, as is his custom, and tells him goodbye. As Ritchie turns around to head back upstairs, he sees the gym manager standing in front of him.

"May I see you in my office?" the manager asks coolly.

"Sure." Ritchie knows this can't be good.

"Do you want to tell me what happened this morning?" the manager asks, shutting the door behind them and walking around to sit on his desk.

"Are you talking about the girl who—"

"The well-known actress who was in here not an hour ago complaining about your behavior. Ritchie, if there's one thing that's important around here, it's discretion. We've lost enough business to Crunch and Equinox without you sending the few celebrity members we have left running out the door by fawning all over them."

"It was a misunderstanding."

"It was a lawsuit waiting to happen. Do me a favor—if you want to keep working here, pay attention to your clients and forget everything else. You're a trainer, nothing more. The sooner you get that through your head, the better off you'll be."

Ritchie nods and can't think of anything to say. He's mad and itching to knock the guy square in the jaw, but he can't. He needs this job. The manager is right—he's a trainer, nothing more.

"Go on, then," the manager says, now awkward and looking away.

Ritchie leaves, walking past the locker rooms and out onto the fire exit steps where employees loiter and smoke on their lunch breaks. God has paid Ritchie a small favor and there is no one on the stoop. He waits until the fire door swings shut behind him before he sinks to the pavement and bursts into tears, pounding his forehead with balled up fists.

Joshua has saved his friends a table immediately in front of the stage. He figures they're likely to laugh a lot, which will encourage the performers. Political satire isn't a big seller in this town, especially when it's sung by drag queens on a cabaret stage. Most publicists would simply have passed when they got a phone call from the Term Limits, who are seeking representation. But Joshua is not most publicists, nor is he in a position to turn away clients. He met the four drag queens at the Coffee Bean. Over lattes, they agreed to Joshua's monthly fee, and that—as far as Joshua is concerned—was that. They're signed. And now they're making their Sunset Strip debut at the Viper Room.

Joshua has invited development people from Fox and DreamWorks, selling the idea of a sitcom with four outrageous women, played by men, living in an apartment together and talking politics...a lot. He pitched it as *The Golden Girls* meets *Face the Nation* at *The Birdcage*. Both executives he talked to this responded with silence. But maybe they'll come anyhow.

He checks his breath with the palm of his hand and finds it salty and a little ripe. He must find chewing gum before he talks to anyone up close. It's a quarter to 8 and there are only a dozen or so people in the club, not counting the bartender and Claire, who's just arrived with Freddy and is making her way across the room. Joshua doesn't have time for gum now. He greets them with hugs instead of kisses and turns his head to the side a little as he speaks with them. They take their seats.

Last to arrive is Ritchie, who was just glum enough last night to agree to stand at the corner of Santa Monica and San Vicente and hand out flyers to the crowd meandering from bar to bar. He comes in, now, like a gay Pied Piper, followed by a half dozen middle aged gay men who seem to be collectively entranced.

"Are they with you?" Freddy asks cheekily as Ritchie comes up to the table.

Ritchie turns around, not realizing that he has been followed. He seems panic-stricken for a moment, then embarrassed, then he reverts to yesterday's degree of glumness. He takes his seat without answering.

"What's with him?" Claire whispers loudly.

"Don't ask," Joshua advises. The night before, his inquiry into Ritchie's state of mind launched a convoluted narrative about television actresses and stair-step machines.

Joshua looks around. The room is starting to fill up. He calms, which he recognizes by the way his left temple ceases to throb. He quits fiddling with the red cocktail napkin he's been folding into tiny triangles and stuffs it into his pants pocket.

"Ladies and gentlemen...and the rest of you," the club DJ announces over the thump of generic acid jazz, "please take your seats for the show."

The crowd complies, more or less, and the lights go down. Joshua makes his way to the side of the stage. He scans the audience to see if the development people have come, but it is impossible to see. He checks his breath again. It has gotten worse.

"Condoleezza," a falsetto voice sings a cappella in the dark. "You're the girl I wish I could be, Condoleezza."

A spotlight opens on the one black member of the Term Limits, who is dressed in a vivid red Mexican frock. He wears a wig that looks as though it was stolen from a second-rate production of *Carmen* and holds a pair of maracas, which he shakes several times as the other members of the group join him on stage.

> Dub considers you a pal,
> An old-fashioned classy gal.
> Though you're colored, so was Colin
> And we're fallin' hard for you.

Joshua keeps looking over at his friends, wanting them to like the show. Freddy is laughing. Joshua laughs because Freddy does.

But Claire looks bored and Ritchie remains unmoved, or else he just doesn't get the references.

The Term Limits finish their ode to President Bush's cabinet and get a polite smattering of applause before they start in on a snappy swing tune about immigration. The audience likes this song better. Even Claire smiles once or twice.

The set goes well, and the audience applauds politely and laughs at the appropriate moments. Maybe signing the group was a stroke of genius on Joshua's part. True, he needed the money, but he had foresight and knows a good thing when he sees it. He is a master publicist in the making, albeit one with halitosis.

To close the show, the oldest member of the Term Limits appears solo, dressed in reverse drag like Marlene Dietrich—gray hair slicked back and a yellow flower in his lapel.

"If I kissed Jesse Helms, would it be a crime?" he croons in a warbly voice. "If it was, that's okay. I can take hard time."

At the end, he tips a top hat to the audience and blows a palm full of glitter at them.

The group gets a standing ovation from much of the house, including Freddy, who seems taken by the cleverness of the lyrics.

"So?" Joshua asks expectantly, turning to Claire as he rejoins his friends.

She makes a face. "Been there, done that."

Joshua sighs, then notices her beaded black purse lying on the table.

"Have you got any gum?" he asks.

There is something wrong with the light over Freddy's desk. The bulb flickers. He can fix it sometimes by running the dimmer up and down. Other times, it has a mind of its own. Lately it's been getting worse, and he leaves it off, letting the glow of the computer screen light the room.

"Oh, my God, he's naked," Claire exclaims, drawing her chair up closer to Freddy and adjusting her reading glasses.

Freddy clicks a few more keys and other pictures of the same man load on his Web browser. There is one where he wears a cowboy hat and chaps, another where he is lying on a bed showing off his butt.

"And this is just some regular Joe who put his pictures on the Internet?" she asks.

"Some Joe who spends ten hours a week at the gym."

"Clearly," Claire agrees wholeheartedly. "But what if somebody out there saw this? Like his boss or his mother?"

"I doubt his mother is cruising m4msex.com. If so, she's got her own issues."

"But this is just for gay people?"

"No! That's my whole point."

Freddy closes the site and opens a new browser page, navigating to a straight dating portal. He realized a few days ago that it was time for Claire to get back into the mix. She's been ornery and restless, shrill when she calls. It came to a head when Freddy was telling her breathlessly about his most recent conversation with Justin Salvatore. Right in the middle of it, Claire said she had to go and hung up the phone. Clearly, something was amiss. Romance is not dead—not in Freddy's mind—and especially now, he can't tolerate any such implication from those around him. Claire needs to get laid, or kissed, or at least taken to dinner and a movie by a straight man who can make her laugh. She needs a reminder of what can be, if not what is.

"You just type in what you're looking for and it searches for you," Freddy says as he demonstrates. "Like if you want a redheaded guy, you click this box here."

"I don't care what color his hair is. Really."

"Greater or less than seven inches?"

"The hair?"

Freddy gives her a dour look and before selecting "seven-plus" on a pull-down menu. Claire clears her throat but doesn't make Freddy change it.

"Height?" he asks.

"Taller than me."

"Income?"

"Not on welfare."

"Level of education?"

"He has to be smarter than me, or I'll be rude. But not too smart."

Freddy leaves the "education" field blank and moves on.

Sometimes the circumspect approach works best with Claire, who is not the easiest person in the world to work with.

"So it just sifts through available men?" she asks. "Like a yenta?"

"More like you're in a singles bar with bad lighting."

"Bad lighting isn't always my enemy. You're talking to scar girl."

"Bad lighting on *them*."

"Well."

"But it helps a lot if you have a profile and picture of yourself online. That way if you send them a message, they're more likely to respond. Or so I hear."

"I'm not putting my face on some Internet dating site."

"Fine. You don't have to."

Claire taps her foot several times on the hardwood floor of Freddy's office.

"Do you still have that little digital camera?"

Freddy positions her beside the fireplace and has her rest her elbow on the mantle. She looks wooden and a little pained, but it will have to do.

"Undo your blouse one more button," he instructs.

"What? I'm not going to...." But she does, then offers a broad grin that makes her eyes crinkle into little slits.

"Eyes," Freddy reminds her.

She opens them too wide, and she looks a little maniacal. Freddy snaps several pictures in rapid sequence.

"Good," he says, pulling the tiny plastic media card out of the camera and sticking it in a little device hooked to the computer. Claire's pictures pop up on screen.

"Oh, hell!" she whines. "Do I look that old?"

"Not after a little Photoshop." Freddy is already resizing the pictures, clicking digital samples of Claire's skin tones to blur and erase her wrinkles. "By the time I'm done you'll be younger than Lisbeth."

"God willing. But if we're screwing with the pictures like this, how do I know the guys who send me snapshots of themselves aren't doing the same thing?"

"They are. It's like taxes. Everyone takes a few extra deductions."

Freddy walks Claire through the process of filling out her

own online profile. They quarrel over each point, but Claire concedes them one by one. At last, Freddy clicks "update profile" and it's a done deal. He switches off the computer and the two of them go have dinner at Real Food Daily.

"So how's that short story about the cop coming?" Claire asks between bites of macrobiotic sushi.

Freddy wishes she'd leave the subject alone.

"Fine, I guess," he lies. He hasn't done any writing work for many days. All he can think about is Justin Salvatore. He feels frustrated, living half a life. Everything hinges on his trip to New York to meet Justin face-to-face.

"When do I get to see some pages?" Claire asks. As bitter as she can be, Freddy's found her a thoroughly supportive reader. Her comments are incisive and insightful. She sees into his characters' intentions and asks questions that Freddy sometimes struggles to answer.

"I don't get why he gives his fiancée the ring," she complained after reading a piece Freddy was preparing to send to *Atlantic Monthly*. "I mean, if she treated him so badly, why wouldn't he just leave?"

In truth, Freddy had made the character give the girl an engagement ring because she'd need to have it later in the story, not because the action matched the character's personality. Claire's question spurred him to go back and rewrite the scene.

He sits poking at his pickled ginger with a chopstick.

"Are you going to eat that?" Claire asks, her hand already on Freddy's last piece of sushi.

"Yes," he says, trying too late to shoo her away.

"Sorry," she says with a full mouth and a shrug.

They finish their chai tea and head home on foot.

"They say nobody walks in L.A.," Claire observes.

"I believe there's a song to that effect."

"Yeah, well, I do," she says, stepping decisively into the crosswalk. Freddy follows.

"You're from New York," he reminds her.

"Long Island."

"Same difference."

The next evening, Freddy and Claire meet up again, this time at Claire's house. They sit down at the computer together and log on to the Web site where Claire placed her ad. Freddy has spent the day somewhat idly, the fact of which he does not reveal when Claire asks.

"Nothing much," is the answer he gives. Actually, he has taken two naps, jerked off to the thought of Justin Salvatore kissing his stomach, and pushed a grocery cart up and down the aisles of Ralph's on Sunset without buying anything.

"Okay, put in your ID and password," he instructs. Claire types the information, adjusting her reading glasses before she hits the ENTER key.

The Web site hesitates for a moment then opens her personal mailbox. There are eighty-six responses to her personals ad. Claire nearly falls out of her chair.

"Eighty-six," she marvels.

Freddy laughs. "Face it, you're one hot number."

"Eighty-six is a hot number," Claire chortles.

"And you're fresh meat."

"You make it sound so romantic," she says, giving him a wry look.

Freddy opens his mouth to offer a comeback, but the look on Claire's face stops him. She is gleeful, the most popular girl at the dance. It is a Claire who probably existed before she went through the windshield of her boyfriend's car on prom night. Rolling his chair around to position himself behind her, Freddy leans in and gives her a gentle peck on the cheek.

SIX

When Freddy wakes each morning, it is with one thought in his mind. In the evening, lulled to sleep by the sound of traffic, he is led to dreams by the same preoccupation. In the middle of the afternoon, in front of his laptop computer at Starbuck's, with the cursor blinking on a blank page, Freddy is robbed of prose by his sweet tormentor. He'd be angry at the way he is frozen were it not so ambrosial. He is drunk, and he's okay with it.

It was not like this with the porn star, nor the opera singer who preceded him. Both men brought Freddy distraction, but neither left him so ravaged as this. It is as if the code of his being—the DNA twisting through every cell of his body—has been modified to require the presence of another, particular person, without whom Freddy is useless.

He gets in from a walk around the neighborhood and sees the voice mail light flashing on his phone. Excitedly he dials in. Maybe it is Justin who has called. But no, he discovers, it is the editor of a European newspaper syndicate for whom he writes on occasion. It seems the Continental cultural elite are become fascinated by the Park Avenue–Beverly Drive obsession with plastic surgery. The editor wants Freddy to write an essay about what drives the "crazy Americans" to be anaesthetized then lasered, mangled, and bruised in the name of beauty. Freddy has typed a few expositional sentences on the subject, and even went as far as to call a plastic surgeon acquaintance to set up an interview, but he can't seem to find any momentum on the piece. It's just not interesting to him. There is no beauty in the depths of the artifice the editor seems so ravenous to have him plumb. Freddy presses the key on the phone to delete the message. No, he hasn't got an outline for the article. No, he doesn't have a tag line yet. No, he has no sample paragraphs to send the editor.

Freddy shouldn't be working on this sort of stuff anyway. He should be writing a novel. He cannot explain his world in 750 words. Freddy has many ideas for a first novel, only a few of which he has committed to paper. But he does finish short stories, on occasion, and he's had two published. His mother likes them tremendously.

It is a quarter till 5—fifteen minutes before his scheduled phone date with Justin. It's not a date, really—Justin had suggested, when they last spoke, that he'd be home to take a call after 8 o'clock Boston time—but Justin was likely so casual about it only because he still hasn't sussed out the situation with Freddy and doesn't know whether it's cool to reveal his true feelings. Freddy is not overly committal yet either, though each time they connect, he wishes he could catapult through the phone wiring and plaster Justin with kisses.

Tonight, things will change. Freddy will make his move.

"Hello?" Justin says tentatively when Freddy's call connects.

"Guess who?"

"Hmm." There is a smile in Justin's voice. "I was hoping I'd hear from you."

"For real?"

"Don't get too excited—there's not much else going on around here. But yes, as a matter of fact, I was looking forward to it all day."

Freddy, lying on his back on the sofa, scissors kicks his legs in the air with glee.

"And you have no idea what I look like or anything," Freddy marvels aloud.

"There's no computer here. But I go on intuition—"

"Which is twenty times faster than dial-up."

"And a lot more reliable." Justin sighs. "Hi, there."

"Yeah...hi."

There is a wonderful silence before Freddy speaks again.

"I keep thinking of the Fourth of July weekend," he says.

"It's not long now."

"Eight days. I can't wait to be in Manhattan."

"Just *be in* Manhattan? I thought I was part of the lure."

"We could get something to eat on the park and then watch the fireworks. We'll talk about, uh, ideas for the benefit thing. You know what I mean."

Justin laughs. "I know what you mean."

"Then I'm in big trouble."

"I may be too."

Freddy is unable to speak.

"Did I say the wrong thing?" Justin wonders coyly.

"No, but you're right. We're in trouble."

"A girl in my tenth grade class got in trouble and didn't come back after Christmas break."

"That's a different kind of trouble," Freddy laughs, "but sign me up. And while you're at it..."

He falters.

"Yes?"

"I don't think I can wait eight days to meet you. Can we make it next Friday night?"

"You want to fly in early?" Justin asks.

"I'd fly in tonight if it wouldn't cost me three thousand dollars."

"Yeah, don't be crazy!"

"Too late."

"Friday, then," Justin agrees. "A week from tonight."

"I'll see you in Manhattan."

"I'll see you in Manhattan."

Ritchie doesn't want to go out of his apartment. Really, he doesn't want to go out of his room, but he has to pee and eat and grab the mail and, even if he's moping, he must wear fresh clothes, which necessitates trips downstairs to the laundry room in the basement. And he must have protein shakes. This is depression, not starvation. Luckily the Power Zone is just two blocks away.

On a Tuesday afternoon, Ritchie goes there in his ball cap and sweats and nobody bothers him except the guy at the counter who tells him his credit card won't go through, which forces Ritchie to dig in his pocket for a couple of wrinkled, balled-up twenties. The moment reminds him of the stories he's heard about otherwise perfectly good-hearted guys who end up putting ads in the back of the gay tabloids and hustling to make ends meet. Ritchie won't be one of them. He *won't.* He doesn't know how he'll prevent it from happening, but something good will come through soon. He thanks the guy behind the counter, scoops up his change and receipt and heads home.

When he gets there the phone is ringing.

"I've called you four times," Joshua blurts when Ritchie picks up. "What's the problem?"

"Nothing. I've just been here. Taking care of stuff."

"You know you can bullshit some people. You can bullshit Claire. But you can't bullshit me."

"I can't bullshit Claire," Ritchie says. It's true.

"Anyway, I know what's going on and I'm not going to let you sit around and wallow in things and shut yourself off from the world."

"I'm a grown-up," Ritchie says, bristling.

"Hardly. And this evening, I'm babysitting you."

"I don't need a babysitter."

"Say, 7 o'clock? My house?"

"I don't need a babysitter," Ritchie growls.

"Pack an overnight bag."

Ritchie sighs. "Seven o'clock."

He hangs up and takes a long nap during which he dreams several of his teeth have come loose from his head and he cannot find them. When he wakes, with a start, the first thing he does is reach to his mouth to make sure his dental work is intact.

When he gets to Joshua's front door, backpack slung over his shoulder, Ritchie is greeted with a kiss and a hug, which sets him off balance and makes him take a step back into the apartment hallway. Maybe coming over wasn't such a good idea.

"Easy there," Joshua laughs, taking Ritchie's hand and leading him inside, where it smells like popcorn. "I hope movie night works for you."

"Yeah, fine," Ritchie says, realizing that he is hungry. He follows Joshua to the living room where the TV is showing financial reports in some Asian language. He sits on the sofa and takes a sip of the water Joshua brings him.

"Do you have pajamas with you?"

"I usually sleep in boxers."

"Well?"

"Yeah. And my toothbrush and running shoes for in the morning."

"Excellent!" Joshua claps, heading to the bathroom for a moment then reappearing with a couple of towels and an apothecary jar full of something that looks like wet dirt.

"It's a cucumber and seaweed facial I picked up at Aveda."

"It looks like mud."

Joshua squints at the writing on the label. "Clay, actually. But the girl there said it would tone our skin and tighten pores."

"I'm in," Ritchie says. He acts like he's not a fan of lots of fussy spa products, but he secretly loves the smell of chamomile lotion, mint foot cream, and botanical masks. Sometimes he smears a little aromatherapy oil on his chest under his trainer's shirt. It melts a little when he sweats and the aroma rises, ever so gently, so that he alone may enjoy it.

Joshua sets a towel over Ritchie and tucks it in around the collar of his shirt. "You're supposed to put it on thick."

Ritchie laughs, sticks his fingers into the wet clay and lifts a palm full to his cheeks. The cool sensation extends as he spreads the mask to his nose, his forehead, and the tip of his chin. Joshua mimics Ritchie's actions.

"A little more over there." Ritchie points to a patch near one eye that Joshua has neglected. "Smear it a little...perfect."

They race to the bathroom to wash off their hands and admire themselves in the mirror.

"But don't make faces because it's supposed to dry," Joshua warns.

Joshua has rented an old black-and-white movie, which he should know Ritchie doesn't really get into, but Ritchie acts like it's okay. He's not happy, however, when he discovers that the film is not only old but is in a foreign language, which means subtitles. Ritchie doesn't do subtitles. If he wanted to read his way through a story, he'd buy a book. And considering that there are exactly five books in Ritchie's apartment that aren't about fitness, anyone who knows Ritchie should have made a better pick.

"Just give it a chance," Joshua insists. "It's a classic."

Ritchie huffs but agrees, settling in on the sofa and noticing that the mask on his face is getting stiff. It smells like a green garden after the rain and, for some reason, that makes Ritchie feel like crying. There is some memory there—something from when he was very small—involving a rainstorm and lightning and running down the block with his soggy tennis shoe slipping and twisting off his foot. But that's all—just an image.

"Are you okay?" Joshua asks, pausing the DVD.

Ritchie looks up. "Yeah. Of course." He shifts his weight so that he is leaning slightly on Joshua, who smiles and lets the movie play again.

It is something called *Blue Angel* and stars Marlene Dietrich, who Ritchie's never heard of but Joshua insists was a big deal in her day. Certainly, Ritchie decides, she knew how to give sultry looks, even if she was a little butch. He crunches on popcorn and sips lemonade Joshua made with lemons he bought from immigrants on the corner.

They stop halfway through the movie and wash off the masks, each remarking on how tingly and fresh their skin feels. Ritchie buries his face in one of Joshua's thick cotton towels and breathes in deeply. He is calm.

"Thank you," he says. Joshua shrugs and smiles, not knowing what Ritchie is thanking him for.

Afterward Joshua, who is used to getting up early to go to the office, yawns broadly, covering his mouth and giggling. Ritchie laughs with him and follows him into the kitchen, where they get more lemonade and popcorn.

"Let's go outside," Joshua suggests. It is a warm evening, and the Santa Anas stir the palm trees as they sit down on the giant upturned wire spools Joshua uses as chairs on his balcony. Ritchie unbuttons his shirt a couple of buttons. He leans back against the wall and closes his eyes. The wind moves across his tingling face.

"It's good to see you like this," Joshua says. "How you are right now, I mean. Not how you've been this week."

"Nobody gets how hard it is for me," Ritchie replies after a bit. "This is a whole different world out here. Back on the block they would beat me down and beat me down, and after a while I just started believing their bullshit—that I would never amount to anything. And after you take that in, it's insane trying to get rid of it. It's there with everything I do, driving down the street, talking to clients at the gym, everything."

Joshua nods sympathetically.

Ritchie's shoulders scrunch and he sucks in a sharp breath without intending to. He realizes how nuts this must appear and he turns to Joshua to apologize.

"I do that sometimes when I feel real pent up," he explains.

"I know," Joshua says. He puts his hand awkwardly on Ritchie's back. "I've seen you do it a lot of times."

"Yeah, well, I wish I didn't."

"Me too," Joshua agrees. He tousles Ritchie's hair. "Me too."

"Hey, watch the hair, buddy," Ritchie warns in vain.

"Queen!" Joshua teases him with a smile.

Claire finds an excuse to walk from the lobby of the clinic back to her office. She tells the patient waiting out front that she can't find his file and it might be on her desk. As she passes a giant potted orchid in the hallway, the flower brushes against her white smock and she has to dab at the lapel to get rid of the sticky orange pollen.

The patient's file isn't on her desk, as she knew it would not be, and she shuffles several folders around as if to be able to say she'd honestly looked. But while she is sliding the folders over the desktop, her attention is on her computer screen, where a Web page from the dating site lists the most recent replies she has received. Twelve men have sent her messages in the past hour. She claps her hands with excitement. Twelve messages! She weighs, for a moment, the idea of not opening any of the e-mails, leaving them like foil-wrapped chocolates, mouthwatering in their potential.

But then she deems the notion foolish—why delay, perhaps permanently, bursts of gratification that could be enjoyed right now?

She takes a look around her beige Ikea office as if to make certain she's alone before clicking on a message from a man with the handle StellarSeller:

> Dear Lisbeth:

(Claire hopes her daughter wouldn't be appalled by having her name temporarily poached for the sake of her mother getting some romance.)

> I am the number-one residential real estate agent in Brentwood and Santa Monica. I'm the kind of guy who sees what he likes and always gets it.

Claire clicks on the picture button and he appears on her screen. Apparently, the guy also likes the dessert tray and always gets what he sees, because even in a Hawaiian shirt she can tell he has a belly and man boobies. Claire shivers with displeasure and clicks to close the window.

Her patient in the lobby rings the bell at the front desk, and it lets out an anemic ting.

"Coming," Claire calls, quickly clicking on another message.

> Dear beautiful young lady:
>
> I want to rub your breasts against my cheeks and sing songs of passion in your ears and tie you up and make noisy love to you in the dark...

Claire lets go a closed-mouth, unladylike grunt and deletes the message without finishing it. She stands, and feeling a little violated by the last e-mail, slaps the side of the computer screen, which wobbles and almost falls over on her desk.

"Are you okay in there?" the patient calls.

"Yeah, I just tripped," Claire lies, laughing unconvincingly. "Let's put you on the roller table."

She walks the man down the hall to one of the add-on treatment rooms she shares with a Pakistani chiropractor who works half days in the same office. It's a positive collaboration, Claire thinks, and particularly beneficial at times like this when Claire needs to mollify a patient for a while. The roller table is Claire's favorite. She believes it does good things for the spine. But she can't bring herself to add a line-item fee in a patient's bill for a treatment that was administered largely so she can have an extra fifteen minutes to finish her lunch or return a phone call or look at love letters from strangers on the Internet.

"Is it too deep?" she asks the patient as he shifts his shoulders in response to the slow, grinding mechanical action of the table. Lying flat on his back, he shakes his head no, but he grimaces slightly as the big machine's rollers make their way up his spine. He is a typical man, Claire thinks as she lowers the roller to a more shallow position. They pretend to be so tough. But it's all an act. They're all one grimace away from being whiny little boys—spineless, useless to her. And as if that weren't bad enough, they leave. At some point (Claire has never understood how and when it begins) men grow restless in the circumstances they've vowed they desire. It's a cruel joke, really.

Claire watches her patient for a moment, then reaches down and cranks the roller control to its highest setting.

"You'll be fine," she assures the man as he moans his displeasure at the machine's invasiveness. Claire hurries from the room before he has a chance to protest further.

When she reaches her desk, there are already three new responses to her ad waiting on the computer. Claire clicks on the most recent.

> Dear Lisbeth,
>
> You are luxuriant. I am Chinese-American looking for a large, tall white woman to bear me children. I can see from the picture on your advertisement that you have the kind of hips and breasts that would make childbearing and rearing possible. I urge you to consider the possibility of—

"Christ," Claire whispers under her breath. She deletes the message with a shudder.

The next two e-mails are milder and more palatable: successful, middle-aged men from the West Side who want to date Claire and show her a good time. One includes a picture. The man is a little saggy but trim and has a nice smile. She saves the message to her desktop before heading back to the treatment room to release her patient from his peculiar punishment.

The man is grateful for her return. After Claire helps him off the table, he rushes to lace up his shoes and get out of the office. Loose change falls from his pockets when he stands. Claire follows him toward the door and holds out a handful of pennies and dimes she has scooped from the carpet. But before the man notices her, he is gone.

Claire looks at the coins in her hand, shrugs, and dumps them in a pile on the waiting room counter next to her business cards and the oversized wooden restroom key. Someone will need thirty-seven cents, she decides, and it'll be there waiting for them.

It is lunchtime, so Kitty is gone for an hour and a half. Actually, Kitty often takes two hours. Claire knows it's her fault for letting Kitty slack off and for not saying anything when she comes back late.

From the hallway, Claire hears her computer announce new e-mail. She hurries in to check it:

> Dear Lisbeth,
>
> As a child psychiatrist, I am more at ease treating little people's phobias and maladjustments than my own. Though, in truth, the greatest unpleasantness of my life is that I go through my days alone, with no special someone to laugh with and enjoy the little successes and foibles. My likes include fine dining, theater, crisp air on a Sunday morning hike, the warmth of the sun while driving up the coast in a convertible. I'd love the opportunity to experience one or more of these with you.
>
> Sincerely,
> Hugh

Claire reads the message a couple of times before she clicks the RESPOND button.

"Okay, Hugh," she types, "you're on. When and where?"

Claire hits RETURN to send the message, then considering what she has just done, she makes a crazy face.

There are no patients for another thirty minutes, so she calls Freddy, who goes on at length about his abdominal fat and the calorie count of oatmeal versus wheat bread and how insanely wonderful Justin Salvatore is. He doesn't ask about Claire's ad and its responses, but after they hang up Claire forgives him for his preoccupation. He's just a man, and that's how men are.

The computer makes a harp-strum sound. Claire looks down. There is a reply message from Hugh:

Dinner. Sunday, 7 P.M. Cicada. I'll drive.

Claire is pleased. She jots the date in her book before typing Hugh a reply to accept his invitation.

For the next three days, she and Hugh trade e-mails frequently. They ask each other what books they have read lately. They debate stories from *The New York Times*. On Saturday morning Claire sends a message to explain that her name is not actually Lisbeth, and in the next sentence asks for help with her crossword puzzle: "What is a fourteen-letter word starting with *p* that means 'charity giver?'"

Hugh answers swiftly: "I believe the word you are looking for is *philanthropist.*"

"Thank you, my dear," she tells the walls and tall windows of her home office. She finishes her crossword and gets ready to go to meet her friends for breakfast.

"Wait, so you haven't actually spoken to him?" Ritchie asks after the waiter pours their coffee. Claire shakes her head no. Joshua rolls his eyes.

"Leave her alone, you two," Freddy insists. "The Internet is a perfectly legitimate way to meet people."

"It's a perfectly legitimate way to get ass," Joshua suggests. "As far as meeting real people, I'd try the supermarket or a twelve-step meeting."

"I don't have any addictions," Claire says.

"Not that you admit to, which is the first step," Joshua replies.

"Gymoholics maybe?" Claire suggests.

"For starters. You'd find more as you went along."

"Maybe you can be my sponsor," Claire smirks, hoping sarcasm will sidetrack Joshua, "and help me find my serenity."

"Sounds like you already found it," Freddy says, "and it answers to 'Hugh'."

"We'll see tomorrow night."

"Can we come watch?" Joshua wants to know.

"No."

"Spoilsport."

"Freak."

Joshua crosses his arms in a huff. Claire is pleased her diversionary tactics seem to have worked. Freddy is poking Ritchie like a 5-year-old trying to get a rise. The waiter arrives with more coffee. Suddenly, everyone is grown-up and polite, easing their cups forward for another dose of Noble's famous dark brew.

As Claire sips her coffee, she imagines what tomorrow will be like. Through the afternoon and evening, she dwells on thoughts of Hugh as she reads the paper, gives herself a pedicure, takes Dog for a hike, and puts medicated oil on several hot spots where Dog has bitten herself. Romantic obsession is the domain of Freddy and Joshua. Claire is more sensible than this.

She reads Virginia Woolf in bed before she goes to sleep, sipping wine and munching on what she calls "ghetto bruschetta," a loaf of sourdough bread with olive oil and chopped tomatoes. Crumbs fall in the sheets, but Claire doesn't care. They're her crumbs. If she rolls over in the night and they're still there, it's her own doing. She forgives herself. Solitude, she decides, is underrated.

Bougainvillea and jasmine grow outside the French window that separates her bedroom from the garden. Their vines press against the glass. But instead of being menacing, the enclosure gives Claire a feeling of comfort. The whole bedroom is cozy—her cream-colored comforter, the candles by her bed, Dog huffing contentedly nearby on the floor.

She finishes the bottle of wine and announces broadly to the mirror on the closet door, "Solitude is underrated."

Claire knows she will have a hangover in the morning, but

doesn't care much. She will sleep soundly tonight and she will not dream. Enough wine takes away Claire's dreams, and she's fine with that. Dreams are for dreamers. Claire is sensible.

The next afternoon she tries on several pairs of shoes before deciding that the black ones with the bows and low stiletto heels work best with her dress. She turns this way and that in the mirror, checking out her backside, the curve of her waist, the slight droop of the skin on her upper arms. In the end, she is satisfied. She wears her hair up in case Hugh drives his convertible—he told her he has a 1966 Jaguar.

At 6:30 sharp the doorbell rings and he is there, standing on her doorstep in Dockers pants and shoes whose soles seem a little worn at the outside edges, giving Claire the impression that he is bowlegged. She welcomes him in and opens a bottle of medium-priced champagne for mimosas. He sits on the couch a little nervously, as if he is waiting for her father to appear around the corner and start asking him questions and telling him what time to have Claire home. He doesn't touch his fizzing drink.

"So this play is supposed to be really good, huh?" Claire calls from Lisbeth's room as she gets a black shawl from the closet.

"That's what the paper said," Hugh assures her, rising from his seat and meeting her in the foyer. "You look lovely."

He did bring his convertible. It starts rough and coughs clouds of bluish smoke that follows them up the block. The engine is noisy. Claire wonders what the neighbors might be thinking. *Well, fuck them,* she decides as she lifts her shawl to cover her hairdo as Hugh peels out with a neck-snap of acceleration.

"I must confess," Claire tells him once they hit Beverly Boulevard, "I've never been much of a fan of August Wilson. But I'm willing to try anything."

She smiles and realizes she is lying. She tries what she knows she likes and leaves the rest. It makes her cross and impatient that, halfway through her life, she is still expected by strangers and loved ones alike to go to animated movies, try nouvelle cuisine, and wear colors she knows are wrong for her. Why does nobody give her credit for knowing herself? They treat her like a child who won't eat her spinach, clucking and shaking their heads.

"He puts in too many words sometimes," Hugh agrees. "But it's kind of like jazz. You have go beyond the individual notes to find the real music. It's less about the melody and more about where it's pointing you."

Claire nods and thinks about this. "Okay," she replies.

They have reservations at Cicada, a trendy gold and black restaurant on the street level of a Byzantine art deco building a few blocks from the Music Center in downtown Los Angeles. They arrive five minutes before their reservation but the maitre d' seats them right away. Claire has to strain a little and put on her reading glasses to make out the fine print on the menu.

"Will you be going to the theater this evening?" the tuxedoed waiter inquires as he pours them water from a lead glass pitcher.

Claire smiles and nods, looking at the waiter's shiny, slicked-back hair and wondering how long ago it was that Hugh lost his mane. She glances over at her date as if she will find an answer there, but his attention is lost in the menu. His reddish shiny head reflects the glow of the candle on the table.

"Are the truffles black or white?" Hugh wants to know.

"White truffles, sir, only the finest," the waiter assures him. "And the lobster today also has truffles."

"Sold," Hugh squeals like a piglet.

Claire looks down at her napkin for a moment. "Me too. Except—no—I'll have the risotto."

"Very good." The waiter takes their menus and disappears.

"So you're a hiker?" Hugh asks, breaking a piece of bread and spreading it with a knife full of butter from a pat impressed with the logo of the restaurant.

"Yes. With my dog. But even without her, yes. I like an uphill challenge." Claire laughs at her own wordplay, though she's not quite sure what she meant by the joke. Hugh laughs too.

"I like to hike but I get shin splints," he says.

"Well, maybe you should come see me in the office. We could do a trade—I'll fix your shins and you can fix my inner child." There is a pause. "You being a child psychiatrist, I mean."

"Oh, yes. Yes!" Hugh laughs again.

The waiter brings their food. The smell of truffles is one of

Claire's favorite sensory pleasures, along with cinnamon candy and the aroma of freshly laundered towels hung out to dry in the sun. This particular preparation looks promising—the truffles are sliced paper-thin and steam in their bed of rice, olive oil, and onions.

Hugh is already wrangling with his lobster, ripping off pinchers and digging for meat. Claire pokes at the risotto and tries it. The rice is undercooked and the onion is still sharp.

"How is it?" Hugh asks, his mouth half full.

"Great. Really," Claire says with a smile. Why should she lie? Just call the waiter over and send the food back. There's still plenty of time before the play starts. But she cannot. She looks at Hugh, at the pleasure he seems to be taking in his own dinner—albeit a bit aggressively—and feels both jealousy and a longing for his say-so.

"You look lovely," he says as if she has prompted him.

Claire beams and sits a little taller in her chair. She takes another bite of the risotto. Maybe it's not so underdone after all.

SEVEN

The crew from channel 7 has to restart their taped introduction several times after they are interrupted by the wailing of emergency vehicle sirens.

"Standing here on what some hope will be a historic day for women across America—"

A passing ambulance lets off three shrill blasts as if to stymie the efforts of the reporter, who stops, knocks her microphone against her forehead, clears her throat, and begins again. "In three...two...one."

"I mean, it is a hospital, after all," Joshua says to calm Mamie Redbird. The two of them stand outside the main entrance to Cedars-Sinai, waiting for the crews from channel 2 and Lifetime to finish setting up their cameras and microphones. Joshua has arranged for a hospital spokesman to issue a statement before Mamie speaks. There is a boxy lectern set up. Its wood grain veneer is chipped along the bottom where it has been dragged many times for press conferences such as these.

Everyone who's anyone dies at Cedars—or has their baby here. It would be gauche to leave or enter the world at County or UCLA. USC will work in a pinch, but it's further from the television stations and fewer reporters are likely to show up. Joshua had to sweet-talk the dispatcher at channel 2 to get a crew today; there is a wildfire in Temecula, and every available camera is focused on plumes of smoke and some hillside homes that are threatened if the wind shifts. Joshua doesn't care about the fire in Temecula. He cares about Mamie Redbird. Or rather, he cares about her publicity. And today is Mamie's day.

She looks better from her surgery. There is color in her cheeks and she has done her hair for the first time in a week. Joshua got her gay nephew to send over a dress for the event, but her matronly shoes do not match it. Joshua wonders if she is aware of this. If she is, she's a good faker. At her own insistence, and over Joshua's objection, she has topped this outfit with a scarf tied at the neck.

"It makes you look like Rosalynn Carter," he insisted, "or a stewardess." But she waved him off.

"Thank you all very much for coming today," the spokesman says, approaching the lectern when Joshua nods at him. "We are pleased to be releasing a very special patient—a true Hollywood legend. A team of our finest physicians has successfully removed breast implants for Ms. Mamie Redbird. This was done purely as a precautionary measure following scans that indicated the presence of what could be pretumorous tissue. Ms. Redbird is in excellent health and after a short convalescence will be back making the movies America loves. Thank you."

Joshua and Mamie applaud, Joshua praying that none of the commentators airing the footage will remark on the fact that the last movie Mamie Redbird made that America loved had a soundtrack that was released on eight-track tape. He gently pushes her forward, and she takes her place at the microphone. There is a moment of quiet before she begins. Miraculously, there are no ambulances on the go in the vicinity.

"I stand before you not as one woman," Mamie says in a very dignified manner, her near-baritone suddenly modulated. "But rather as an emissary to women everywhere. There is nothing so fleeting as beauty, and nothing so precious. For as long as time can remember, women have gone to extraordinary lengths to make themselves beautiful. I have, and you have."

Mamie looks earnestly from one camera to the next. "Sometimes that beauty comes at a price. But I am here to make sure you know that price need not be your life. Every year, two million American women will get breast cancer—"

Joshua cringes. Mamie has botched the statistic, inflating it by a power of ten. But her speech is fantastic, better than he had hoped. She is on fire, her voice steady.

"So I implore you—see your doctor. Get screened regularly. Stop cancer before it stops you, and we can all be truly beautiful."

She smiles magnanimously and offers what appears to be a diva's half bow. Joshua steps forward and leans into the microphone.

"Thank you," he says and shoves her aside. There will be no question-and-answer. Actors speaking without scripts are disasters waiting to strike, and although Mamie has done a fine job, Joshua is not pressing his luck today.

Within moments, the cameramen begin disassembling their tripods, and technicians coil microphone cables. Mamie watches the proceedings silently with a far-off smile on her face and a slight mist in her eyes. Joshua finishes giving one reporter the correct spelling of the hospital spokesman's name, then turns and looks at Mamie. She is lit with delight, a starlet again. Her nephew is waiting to drive her home. As she gets in the back seat of the sedan she waves goodbye to Joshua and blows him a kiss.

Later, Ritchie comes over to watch the 11 o'clock news. Freddy is too enraptured with his future husband Justin to answer the telephone or reply to an instant message, and Claire is on her third date with the bald child psychiatrist, so it's just the two of them. They watch channel 2 and 11 while TiVo records channel 7.

All of the newscasts lead with the fire story. At the first break, channel 2 teases more fire coverage, while 7 sells a story about the rape trial of a basketball star, and 11 has discovered that pretzels are fat-free.

"I'm sure it'll be in the second news block," Joshua assures Ritchie and himself, switching between commercials. But when the anchors return, there is no mention of Mamie. A cat has been stranded in the fire. No Mamie. Gene splicing could make tomatoes stay ripe longer. No Mamie. There was a car bombing in Israel. No Mamie.

Sitting on the sofa, Ritchie watches Joshua warily. Joshua feels the weight of his glance but won't make eye contact.

"It's got to be next," he says, withering.

Finally, at 11:28, one of the stations—by now Joshua has lost track of which—introduces their grinning entertainment reporter, who appears with a picture of Mamie over his left shoulder.

"Just when you thought you'd heard it all," he begins, smug in his starched shirt, "along comes a story like this." The television cuts to pictures of Mamie talking, but they do not play her voice; the commentator continues. "Giving new meaning to 'utter desperation,' onetime Oscar nominee Mamie Redbird went public about a recent breast implant removal today. Why, no one's sure. She does look smaller, maybe? But no more talented. Moving on to the rape trial, cameras outside the courtroom happened to catch this footage of a squirrel—"

Joshua switches the television off. Ritchie mumbles something about being sorry and having to leave. Joshua nods and sits silently staring straight ahead while the blood pounds in his temples.

The telephone rings. Joshua looks down at the display. It's Mamie. He can't talk with her now. He can't do anything now. The phone finishes ringing and goes silent. After a moment, it begins again. Mamie again. Joshua still can't talk.

He sits and looks at the cracks in the plaster where the ceiling meets the wall, cracks that have likely been there since the 1994 earthquake but he is just seeing for the first time.

Joshua is motionless for a very long time. He falls asleep sitting up and wakes with a start just past dawn when the gardener from the apartment building next door starts his leaf blower. Joshua's neck is pinched. His clothes are rumpled. There is a bad taste in his mouth. He looks down at the phone. The light is not blinking; Mamie did not leave a message. Slowly, he rises and walks to the front door, his neck and legs as stiff as if he'd been in a car crash.

He turns the lock and goes through the dim hall to the entryway of the building where the morning papers are waiting. He picks up a copy. The fire is all over the front page. Joshua flips to the Calendar section. What he sees makes him fall back against the wall in surprise: there is an oversized color photo of Mamie that goes down below the fold, taken from a low angle so that she looks angelic. The large headline reads "A Survivor's Story."

The rest of the paper falls from Joshua's hands to the floor.

He hears the phone ringing from inside his apartment. He hurries back. It's Mamie. This time he picks it up.

"Hello?"

"Home run, kid," she wheezes.

Ritchie felt bad about leaving Joshua in such a sorry state, but he was responding to a call almightier than that of friendship. There was a guy involved.

The guy works behind the bar at Rage and looks out at Ritchie often as he walks along the Boulevard after work. He has short brown hair and usually wears no shirt. Ritchie has noticed how beautiful his stomach muscles are, lit from beneath by the glow of neon lighting that runs along the bar. He has looked at Ritchie through the open patio and Ritchie has looked back—unable not to—smiling and nodding slightly. Several weeks of noticing each other went by before they talked one afternoon at Starbuck's.

"We should hang out sometime after I get off," the guy said, introducing himself as Tristan over the whoosh and din of the espresso machine and blenders. He nodded "yes" to his own idea as if he'd just cemented a deal.

Ritchie put Tristan's number in his cell phone and watched him leave through the big glass front door of Starbuck's, his gymnast ass perfect in dorky blue jeans.

Last night, at the time of Joshua's shaky showing on the evening news, Tristan was preparing to get off early at midnight. He and Ritchie met at Norm's for twenty-four-hour bottomless coffee and pancakes. Neither of them ate much; both claimed to be watching their waistlines. They kissed for a while in the parking lot as they leaned up against the door of Tristan's Jeep. Ritchie licked at the taste of mint chewing gum and clove cigarettes in Tristan's mouth, darting his tongue to explore Tristan's lips and teeth. They pressed their hips against each other, each of them feeling the other's arousal.

It was Ritchie who finally broke away.

"Okay," he said breathlessly, looking down at his watch and seeing that it was 2:30 in the morning. "I've gotta go."

Tristan put out his lower lip in a pout and tried to pull Ritchie back in for another kiss.

"Stop it," Ritchie laughed, resisting. "I'm for real."

"When can I see you again, then?" Tristan demanded.

Ritchie looked at Tristan's melon-shaped shoulders and tiny waist. "Tomorrow night?"

"Excellent. I can get off by 1, I think."

"You're going to keep me up past my bedtime two nights in a row?"

"If I have my way, that'll be the least of my sins."

Ritchie stood and watched as Tristan pulled out another clove cigarette and lit it, climbed into his Jeep, and waved "goodbye." He waited as the glow of Tristan's taillights traced the empty lanes of La Cienega Boulevard and disappeared around the corner onto Santa Monica before crossing the street and heading home with heavy feet.

This evening, he takes a nap after work, setting his alarm for just before midnight. He showers, scrubbing all his parts especially well—hoping this attention to detail will have been time well-spent—and dresses in Papi underwear and a pair of khaki shorts. He sprays himself with cologne and checks his hair in the mirror several times before leaving the apartment.

"Hey, how ya doing?" he asks the mirror. He winks. "How ya doing? Hey, there."

Satisfied, he puts the key in the lock and goes.

The Boulevard is busy as he makes his way to Rage, where he is meeting Tristan, the taste of whom he has been anticipating all day. There is music coming from the doorway to Micky's. By the time it reaches the street, it is just a thumping rhythm. A claque of queens giggles and pushes past Ritchie. Their hips sashay and their fingers snap as they gossip loudly about some unfortunate friend who's not with them tonight.

"Hey," Ritchie says amiably, but they are gone and have not noticed him.

A man in a jogging suit stands on the corner walking a little dog on a leash. He leers as if he'd like to cut his pet loose and drag Ritchie into the nearest parked car.

"Hey," Ritchie says to him too, but he hurries on his way and doesn't make eye contact.

As he comes up on Rage, Ritchie sees that it is a happening

night; there are go-go boys dancing on boxes at either end of the bar, and patrons stand waiting in a small line to get their IDs checked so they can go inside and drink. Ritchie scans the crowd for Tristan. After a moment, he spots him working behind the bar—chest bare, T-shirt tucked into his back pocket. Ritchie feels disappointed; he had imagined Tristan would be waiting for him when he arrived. Now Ritchie feels unimportant.

But Tristan looks up and sees Ritchie, who's standing on the patio with his hands in his pockets, and waves. He puts up one hand, fingers outstretched, to say he'll be done in five minutes. Ritchie smiles and nods, giving him a thumbs-up.

Ritchie waits. It is uncomfortable standing on the sidewalk with everyone passing, but he doesn't feel like going inside and joining the crowd. Five minutes become ten, which become fifteen. At last, Tristan waves to Ritchie and points to the back of the bar. Ritchie walks around the corner, behind a bank ATM and past some Dumpsters, to the bar's rear entrance. When he gets there, Tristan is waiting, a clove cigarette lit, popping a stick of mint gum in his mouth. Ritchie sees that he is wearing khaki shorts that match his own.

"Get over here," Tristan says, and Ritchie obliges.

"Twins," Ritchie notes before planting a kiss on Tristan's lips. "You ready?"

Tristan nods and picks up a nylon backpack at his feet.

They walk on the emptier side of the street past the city bus terminal and toward the gym. Tristan grabs for Ritchie's hand and Ritchie lets him take it. For some reason, it feels good. Maybe it's because Ritchie is horny, and this makes him bold.

They near the corner of the gym building and Ritchie looks at a cement truck that has parked for the night along a side wall where the outdoor pool is undergoing construction.

"They're loud all day," he says, pointing toward a pile of bricks and rubble.

"What are they doing?" Tristan asks, coming up alongside Ritchie and putting his arms around his waist.

"Redoing the pool. It was leaking and some of the neighbors with houses on the other side of the wall were complaining.

They just finished the Jacuzzi and filled it this afternoon."

"Yeah? How does it look?"

"Great. The tile is imported and it's a hot color. Come here," Ritchie says, pulling Tristan over to the wall. "If I give you a boost you can see it."

He laces his fingers together to make a stirrup for Tristan to climb. Tristan obliges, hopping to grab the top ledge of the wall and peer over while Ritchie steadies his torso, feeling the smoothness of Tristan's skin where his shirt rides up over his stomach.

"What do you think?" Ritchie asks.

"Awesome. Was it that big before? It's dark but I can see it steaming...hang on."

Ritchie is surprised as Tristan pulls himself up to a sitting position on the top of the wall, the toes of his tennis shoes scuffing as he climbs to scale it.

"What do you think you're doing?" Ritchie asks, nervous for a moment. He turns to look at the boulevard, half expecting to see a sheriff's patrol car waiting to arrest them for breaking and entering.

"Well?" Tristan says, turning so that his legs drop on the far side of the wall. "Are you coming?"

Ritchie looks up and him for a moment and scratches his head. This is a really bad idea. Even Ritchie knows it. But Tristan is beautiful. The way the sculpted curve of his triceps disappears into the sleeves of his T-shirt is driving Ritchie crazy.

"Here," Ritchie says, reaching for Tristan's hand. Tristan helps him up the wall, almost losing his balance in the process. Once he's on top beside him, Ritchie laughs and grabs hold of Tristan's waist to steady himself. They look into each others' eyes, then kiss deeply. Ritchie tastes Tristan's delicious flavor again.

Minutes pass, the two of them sitting atop the wall like a couple of Humpty Dumptys, before Ritchie looks down to the darkened pool area and sees the faint vapor trails of steaming water rising from the Jacuzzi. Tristan notices him watching it.

"So nobody's used it yet?" Tristan asks.

"Nope. The chemical guy was there this afternoon while I was training clients. I think they're opening it day after tomorrow."

Tristan nods in the direction of the Jacuzzi then gives Ritchie an intense look. Ritchie smiles and feels himself blush. He looks out to the street, which is empty, then back at the pool area, which is empty too.

"Okay," he says in a stage whisper and lets himself slide down the wall so he lands inside the pool area with a gentle tennis shoe thud.

Tristan is wide-eyed and giggles. "You're for real?"

"Why not?" Ritchie says and shrugs, though he immediately thinks of several good reasons why not.

Tristan hops down beside him and pulls him into a kiss. Each of them giggles and shushes the other. They kiss again, pressed against the wall, then gently make their way, lock-lipped, down into a reclining pool chair beside them, until they are lying facing each other with their legs intertwined. Ritchie reaches under Tristan's shirt and runs his hands up his chest, feeling the smoothness of his stomach and the points of his nipples. Tristan moans, quickly helping Ritchie pull the shirt off. Ritchie sits back and admires the view for a moment before he takes his own shirt off.

Now they are half naked and bursting with potential. It is chilly outside in this night air. Ritchie pulls Tristan close again, giving him a bear hug so that the sides of their faces meet and their lips are at each others' ears. Tristan kicks off his shoes and socks, somewhat awkwardly because Ritchie is holding him so tightly. He reaches to Ritchie's crotch and feels the bulge there—no surprise to either of them. He moans again as he rubs it.

Ritchie tries to remember the last time he felt this wound up. It was probably when he was 17 and exploring the myriad variations on the art of the blow job with a guy from the swim team at his school. They were in the basement of Ritchie's house late one afternoon, back behind the furnace, and there was no lock on the door that led down from the kitchen where his mother was making pasta. They had to be silent when gasping, and the boy actually put his hand over Ritchie's mouth when Ritchie came in order to stifle the sound that accompanied Ritchie's orgasm.

Now the danger feels just as close, and the excitement too. Tristan is not 17. He has the skills of a man, slipping his hand behind the small of Ritchie's back to press their hips together and using the other hand to unfasten Ritchie's belt and pull it free of his pants in one long, fluid movement. Ritchie's shoes are off his feet now. He's not quite sure how it happened, but there are soft lips and nibbling teeth everywhere, hands everywhere, Tristan everywhere.

The top button to each of their pairs of khaki shorts is undone. Tristan rubs the head of Ritchie's dick through his underwear, and the soft fabric is getting moist from Ritchie's excitement. For a moment, Ritchie feels as though he might come just from this, but the wave of pleasure subsides into a more stable feeling of arousal.

Ritchie thinks he hears a noise. It is sharp—something scraping against concrete. He freezes. Tristan, not having heard anything, continues undeterred for a moment before he notices Ritchie's posture and stops.

"What's the matter?" he asks.

"Shh!" Ritchie looks in the direction the sound came from. They both lie still, awkward now. But there is no further sound, just the burble of the Jacuzzi and the faint rumble of a car passing on the Boulevard.

"Didn't you hear that?" Ritchie asks.

Tristan shakes his head no and looks at Ritchie for a moment before pulling him back into a kiss. At first Ritchie can't relax, but when Tristan starts rubbing the head of his dick again, he submits. Sensing victory, Tristan shimmies out of his own shorts. Unlike Ritchie, he wears no underwear, and Ritchie sees a striking tan line visible even in the faint light that spills over the wall from the city around them.

Ritchie's pants are off now, along with his underwear. He and Tristan get to their feet and move toward the Jacuzzi hand in hand.

"We'll christen it," Tristan whispers, reaching for the railing and taking a step down into the water. Ritchie is just behind him, feeling the wet warmth on his ankles, his knees, his thighs as he descends the steps. Then he throws his weight on Tristan and the two of them are floating naked, making out, both fully erect and pressing against each other. They roll in the water, splashing though Ritchie knows they shouldn't; it could attract attention. But they don't care. They are enraptured. Ritchie's tongue explores Tristan's mouth and Tristan returns the query, sending

Ritchie into shivers of ecstasy as his tongue leaves Ritchie's mouth and meets his cheek, his neck, his ear.

"You are so fucking beautiful," Tristan whispers.

It couldn't get any better, but it does. Tristan reaches below Ritchie's waist and starts playing with him gently in the water. Ritchie feels a wave of orgasm coming and he fights it.

It is then that he hears the scraping sound again, and this time it is undeniable. Something is being dragged across the pavement next to the pool. He and Tristan let go of one another, Ritchie's hands moving instinctively to cover his blatant arousal.

The lights switch on. It is a midday flood of illumination.

"Oh, shit," Tristan whispers.

Ritchie blinks and squints. The scraping sound was a plastic trash barrel being dragged by a member of the gym's cleaning crew, the rest of whom now descend the steps toward the pool. They are polite Mexicans, and Ritchie knows three out of the four of them reasonably well.

When the members of the crew see Ritchie and Tristan, they stop and stare. Ritchie and Tristan stare back.

"*Buenas noches,*" says the man with the trash barrel. He is large-limbed and has a heavy gray mustache that droops at either side of his mouth. His uniform T-shirt is soiled. A woman, whom Ritchie remembers to be his wife, stands near him holding a rake, her mouth agape.

"*Buenas noches,*" Ritchie echoes weakly, horrified, realizing that although his nakedness is partly hidden by the fact that he—along with his raging erection—are underwater, he has no towel nor any polite means of exit.

One of the men on the crew is holding a stack of small rag towels and has a large spray bottle of industrial cleanser hooked on his belt. He lets out an awkward twitter of a laugh, stomping first one foot and then the other.

Ritchie points to the stack of towels. At first the man doesn't understand; he stops laughing because he is confused. Ritchie points again, wishing he knew enough Spanish to ask the man to come over.

Finally he gets it and sets down the towels. He holds one up, waving it like a bullfighter. He laughs again, amused at his own joke, until he looks over at the man with the trash barrel, who is apparently the crew foreman. The foreman is not laughing. He gestures toward the Jacuzzi. The other man reluctantly picks up two towels and walks them over to Ritchie and Tristan.

The towels are no larger than a foot square, but Ritchie looks at them gratefully. He takes one from the man, mumbles a "thank you," and holds it directly over his crotch as he climbs out of the hot tub with his back toward the wall. Mercifully, his erection has subsided.

Tristan follows, reaching out for a towel and climbing out, slipping a little on the top step and hurrying to recover his footing.

Each of them pulls up his underwear and shorts. All the while, the crew stands and watches, clearly amused, with the exception of the foreman, who doesn't seem to find any of this funny.

"I can't wait to get out of here," Tristan says under his breath as they make their way toward the gym building, shoes and shirts in hand.

"Then let's go," Ritchie says, pulling open the fire exit door and stepping inside. He may never see Tristan again after tonight, and Tristan may never again meet the cleaning crew. But Ritchie will see them tomorrow, and the day after that, and the day after that. It is probably for this reason that, although he feels like throwing up, as soon as he and Tristan are on the street again, he starts to laugh uproariously.

Freddy is sitting in first class. He has managed an upgrade using frequent flyer miles. *Not bad,* he thinks, considering he bought the ticket a few days ago at a deep discount. It is a long trip to New York City, one that he has made many times in varying states of excitement. Regardless of the purpose of the trip, he knows that he will be happiest with himself if he forgoes the cookies and ice cream and extra dinner rolls that are foisted upon first class passengers. He also knows he will say yes to the treats today, as he always does. If he has a single curse, Freddy has decided, this is it. But he also figures it's a small concern compared to the liquor and gambling others put themselves through to find a measure of calm.

He is trying to read a book, but he can't concentrate. He looks at his watch every few minutes—which, on a five-hour flight, is a tiresome endeavor. Somewhere over the Grand Canyon he gets drowsy from the rich food and falls asleep in his seat, but the respite is short-lived; he is too keyed up to doze for long.

He is going to meet the Justin Salvatore, the most beautiful man in the world. He has plucked a star from the firmament to hold in his own hands. It is almost beyond his comprehension, this thing that he's doing. He has flown to meet a man before; he did it with the porn star. But this is different, larger, legitimate—or as legitimate as such a project can be, given the circumstances.

"Ladies and gentlemen," the flight attendant finally announces, "in preparation for landing, the captain has requested that passengers discontinue use of electronic devices and return all seats to their upright position."

Freddy checks his watch. It's almost 10 o'clock, and he has plans to meet Justin at the Hilton on Avenue of the Americas at midnight. Can he hold himself together for another two hours? He will have to, though he feels like spinning apart—like taking the next flight back to Los Angeles, like finding some stranger for a quickie in the airport restroom—because there's no way Justin can live up to Freddy's fantasies. He might as well get some carnal consolation prize for all the energy he has expended.

At baggage claim, a bored-looking man in a yellow necktie holds a little sign that says RUCKERT in block letters. This is a holdover from Freddy's days working on-camera at a television entertainment news program; he got used to being escorted in and out of town and still enjoys the privilege, even though he now has to pay for it himself. It gives him one less thing to worry about when he travels.

In the car with his hastily packed bag, Freddy checks the time. It's 10:30; he will get to Manhattan well before midnight. All the better, he thinks. He can see Justin as soon as he arrives. Maybe a quick stop in the men's room of the hotel to freshen up...

"Hello?" he says into his cell phone, plugging his free ear. There is a lot of noise in the background of the call.

"Sorry," Justin says. "I was just watching a movie on TV."

"So I'm early."

"Great," Justin says, sounding a bit panicked. "How early?"

"I should be there just past 11. Can you be ready?"

"For what?"

"For me."

"I've been ready for you for days."

"Then put on a clean shirt and meet me downstairs. We can walk. I'll call you when I'm there." He hugs the phone to his chest and rocks back and forth in the car seat with glee.

"You catch the game tonight?" the driver asks.

"Can't say I did," Freddy admits gladly. He replays the phone call in his head. Did Justin seem hesitant when he said he was getting there early? Is Freddy intruding? Is this rude of him? Maybe he should wait until midnight. No, Justin said he'd been ready for days.

"Just go," he whispers for his own benefit. "Dive in. Be yourself."

There is little traffic. The driver gets Freddy to the hotel at five past 11. He pays the man and takes his bag, stands for a moment looking at the marquee, then glances over at the big Bulova clock on the corner of Sixth Avenue. Yes, he is here. Yes, he is doing this. Yes, he is ready.

He pushes through the revolving door into the lobby.

"Already?" Justin sounds genuinely distraught on the house phone.

"Yeah...like I said—"

"No, it's okay. I'll just..." There is a muffled sound as Justin shifts the handset and drops it.

"Hello?"

"Sorry!" Justin apologizes, recovering. "I'll just—give me twenty minutes, okay? I'll meet you in the bar."

"Sure," Freddy says, trying to sound buoyant, though he is a bit put off. Twenty minutes? *Okay*, he tells himself, *I'm still ahead of schedule. Of course Justin seems harried.*

Freddy takes his things and sits in the bar. There is a convention going on at the hotel, and a dozen or so rowdy men in suits and nametags are at the bar drinking domestic beer and throwing back handfuls of the salted party mix the hotel is pushing instead of peanuts. Freddy waits. This is a giant moment in his life; there's no denying it. Five minutes pass. Then it's ten. The men at the bar are getting drunker and noisier. Freddy wonders why there are no women. It would make sense if the guys at the bar were gay, but they are obviously, dully straight, mumbling on about football and their last vacation in Las Vegas. He gets up and stretches, but he is too anxious to walk around. He also doesn't want to give up his comfortable seat in plain view of the bank of elevators. Each time the bell rings and one of the elevator cars opens, Freddy expects to see Justin emerge. What will he be wearing? How will he act toward Freddy? The doors open. Everyone gets out. There is no Justin.

Now it has been twenty minutes. Freddy realizes he's posing slightly, stomach knotted, hoping to look casual and cool when Justin sees him. Is his hair okay? He could check it in the large mirror across the lobby, but that would involve getting up. Twenty-five minutes now. The conventioneers are getting obnoxious, hooting and bothering the cocktail waitress weaving among them. But she sounds like she's from Queens and seems perfectly capable of standing up for herself. Another elevator car comes. There is no Justin on it. It's been a half an hour—no, thirty-two minutes. Freddy has to go to the bathroom but he decides to hold it for another bit. Surely Justin will be down. He plays with the paper napkin the waitress brought with his Diet Coke.

At forty minutes, he can't stand it. He goes to the house phone and dials Justin's room. The line rings five or six times before going to voice mail. Freddy hangs up and dials again. The same thing happens. Maybe Justin is on his way down. Freddy hurries back to his chair and looks casual. More minutes pass. Several elevator cars arrive and empty. Justin is nowhere to be seen. It's been fifty minutes now. Freddy is starting to get a little irritated. He tries Justin on the house phone again. Again, no answer. He goes to the bathroom and pees, splashes water on his face and fiddles with his hair, then hurries back to the lobby, sure that Justin will be looking around for him. But all Freddy finds are drunken men in blue and brown blazers. Another call to Justin's room yields the same results as before.

At this point, Freddy starts to panic. What if this is all a setup, a cruel joke? What if Justin has been stringing him along and has no intention of meeting him? It's been an hour now and Freddy is livid with frustration. He doesn't know whether to cry or shout. One of the elevators dings. The doors open. Standing inside is Justin Salvatore.

He steps out into the lobby and looks around. He's got sunglasses on, a tight T-shirt, torn up jeans, and Army boots. Both his arms are covered with wristwatches and trinkets. His hair is blond and cropped haphazardly short. For a moment, Freddy questions whether it's really Justin. But then they see one another, and Justin beams his trademark toothy grin. There's no mistaking him.

"Well, hello," Freddy says, standing and walking toward him.

"And hello to you, sir," Justin says, pulling Freddy into a generous hug. Freddy feels Justin's body pressed against his, just for a moment, and it thrills him. Justin in thinner and a little frailer than Freddy imagined, but he is still Justin Salvatore, star of Broadway, most beautiful man on the magazine covers. The jewelry and knickknacks poke Freddy in the chest and arms. He lets Justin go.

"Sorry I took so long," Justin says, grinning. "I was in the bath and time got away from me."

"It's okay. It was worth the wait."

"So what are we doing? You want to go for a walk? It's really humid out, but I love the air in New York in the middle of summer. It reminds me of when I first came here."

"I can't deprive you of that," Freddy says.

The two of them stand back and look at each other for a moment. Freddy is delirious. He is standing in a hotel in New York City face-to-face with a beautiful, famous young man whose picture he pulled off a Web site a few weeks ago. This is not how real life happens; this is make-believe. But no, it's not. Justin is actually standing before him. Better yet, the night is just beginning.

"Shall we?" Freddy asks. Justin's smile broadens, if such a thing were possible.

They walk from the hotel to a bodega on the corner of Broadway where Freddy buys them each a small fresh fruit salad for six dollars. From there, they stroll the few blocks to Central Park, where they find a spot on a low stone wall to sit and eat. It is the thick of the night, half past midnight, and probably 80 degrees outside. A trickle of sweat runs down Freddy's chest and he feels his underarms dampen.

Justin is impossibly handsome. Or maybe it's not that he's so handsome, but rather that he's so *Justin*.

"Take off your sunglasses," Freddy tells him. Justin hesitates for a moment, then does. His eyes are pale and a little wide, like those of a nocturnal creature who hasn't been out of his burrow for a while.

Freddy spears a forkful of blueberries and holds them out to him. "Here."

Justin leans forward, closes his mouth around the berries, and pulls them off the fork with his teeth, all the while looking at Freddy.

"And you had no idea what I looked like?" Freddy asks, not quite believing.

"I know this much: When I was sitting talking to you on the deck at my mom's that first time, I was wearing a pair of sweatpants, and they ripped at the crotch when I went to move. So I took that as a good sign."

"You're loony," Freddy decides.

"I'm artistic," Justin counters, getting up and taking Freddy by the hand. "Come on."

He leads Freddy down a path into the park. It is dark and for a moment Freddy is anxious for their safety, but he relaxes as Justin leads him past a softball dugout and out onto the field.

"It's the only place in New York I've found where you can see the stars well," Justin says, sitting down on the grass and easing back into a reclining position, propped on his elbows.

Freddy sits down beside him cautiously, not wanting to soil his pants legs with grass and dirt. Justin studies the stars and Freddy studies him. He looks at the curve of Justin's cheekbones, at the way they carve his cheeks into an almost permanent smile. Freddy moves closer to him, to his lips. Justin eases himself to the ground so that he is lying on his back on the grass. Freddy lies on his side beside him, close enough so that each can feel the other's breath. He looks at Justin's lips again and leans forward to kiss him gently.

"Wow," Justin whispers.

Freddy doesn't know how to interpret this. But when he sees Justin's eyes are closed, he takes it a good sign. He kisses Justin again, a little longer this time. Justin definitely kisses back. Freddy eases his arm under Justin's neck and pulls him closer so that they are face to face. They make out with abandon, running their hands through each other's hair and exploring the contours of each others' faces. Freddy's head is speeding like a runaway locomotive, swaying this way and that, threatening to fly off its tracks at each curve. They kiss for many minutes.

At last they pull back and lie on their backs, looking up at the stars and holding hands.

"Did you think it would be like this?" Freddy asks after a moment.

"What do you mean?"

"Us. When we met."

"I can't say that I had any idea. I was just taking you as I found you."

"And how do you find me, at this point?"

Justin is silent. Then he laughs quietly. "Let me ask you a question," he says. "What if I told you that tomorrow morning you will wake up and there'll be an envelope in your mailbox. And if you open that letter and read it, it's going to say that everything you've experienced in your life so far is fiction; it's a waking dream. And what is real is entirely different from that—not better or worse, but entirely different, everything you know, everybody you love. That whole world is illusory. Would you want to get that letter? Would you open it if opening it meant knowing?"

Freddy thinks about it for a moment and wonders where the question is coming from.

"Yes," he says hesitantly. "I would open the letter. As a matter of fact, I got that letter some time ago and I've been working since then to reconcile that world with the one I know."

"What do you call that world?" Justin asks excitedly. "Does it have a name?"

"I call it God," Freddy says matter-of-factly. He is surprised at his own words, though he's speaking honestly. "And everything else is, like you say, illusory."

"Are you real?" Justin asks and looks over at Freddy in dead earnest.

"Pardon me?"

"Are you real? I want to know if you are real or if I'm making you up."

Freddy leans forward and places a kiss on Justin's forehead, a kiss on his nose, a kiss on his soft lips. "I'm real."

"We shall see," Justin says, sitting up and brushing himself off. "You ready?"

Freddy smiles and gets up. They walk across the softball diamond and back along the trail to the edge of the park. He is in New York City. It is the Fourth of July weekend, Friday night at two in the morning. The air is sticky. It makes Freddy's clothes cling to him. He is walking down Broadway with a Broadway star, brushing against each other to hold hands, awkwardly at first then with greater assurance. This is definitely real.

"Do you feel it?" Freddy asks, taking a risk.

Justin waits a few paces before answering.

"How could I not?" he says.

Freddy smiles at this, for it is not a real answer, but leaves him no room to question Justin further on the subject.

"Well, I'm glad," Freddy manages. "Because if it was just me, I'd have to throw myself under a bus."

Justin stops in front of a Times Square electronics store and holds up their interlaced fingers as if for evidence. Then he leans forward, almost pressing Freddy against the plate glass window, and kisses him lightly on the lips.

"How could I not feel it?" Justin asks. Freddy's legs go weak.

They keep walking. Justin wants to go to a club on Eighth Avenue for a drink. Freddy doesn't drink and doesn't like being around alcohol but right now Justin can do no wrong and anything he might come up with Freddy would greet with a sort of woozy glee.

It takes effort to move through the thick air. The foot and car traffic around them is about as sparse as it gets in New York other than during a blizzard. They get to the bar and Justin greets the bouncer; apparently, Justin's a regular. Inside, the room is minimalist white with dark wood accents, but the lights are very low so that the whole place has a warm, amber glow. The crowd is a stark contrast to that of the hotel bar. It is mostly men here too, but they are gay, demure, too stylish for cackling and back pounding. They wear summer Prada or Abercrombie & Fitch.

"I need to freshen up," Justin says, patting the little shoulder pack Freddy has not even noticed he's been carrying since he came down from his hotel room. It is as ragtag as the rest of Justin's appearance, decorated with pins from several '70s punk bands.

"I'll be right here," Freddy says, following him to the restroom and stopping outside by the pay phone. There is a chair and Freddy takes a seat. He feels the need, unexpectedly, to catch his breath.

A cigarette girl walks by, a flat box of smokes and chewing gum hung around her neck in the traditional manner. She looks as though she has run off from a burlesque show—her platinum blond hair is curled into ringlets that dangle beside her cheeks and her bosom is trussed in a velvet bustier. Seeing the prospect of a sale, she sidles up alongside Freddy.

"Say, I thought there was no smoking in bars in New York City," he says.

The cigarette girl titters and covers her lipstick-reddened mouth.

"That's the *law*," she says in a cayenne-laced drawl. "But in a joint like this, in the middle of the night, people do as they please. Ain't nobody watching but the angels."

"You're not from here," Freddy guesses.

"Neither are you," she counters. Then, realizing that she is not going to make a sale, she rolls her shoulder away from him flirtatiously and continues on her way. But after a few steps, she stops short and turns back toward Freddy.

"Here," she says, holding out a matchbook.

"Thanks..." Freddy says, confused. He takes the matches.

The cigarette girl nods and sashays off into the crowd.

Freddy looks down at the matchbook in his hands. It is shiny and black. On the back is an ad for the Chelsea Hotel. He stares at it for a moment, thinking of an old Joni Mitchell song, then sticks the matches into his front pocket of his jeans. He gets up and examines a display of flowers on a glass table across from him. A guy passes, going into the men's room, and checks Freddy out. Freddy nods and acknowledges him but he is not excited, as he might otherwise be, because he is swirling in Justin's very broad wake. Freddy checks his watch. Has it been fifteen minutes? It's nearly three. What is Justin doing in there?

After twenty minutes, Justin emerges, smiling as before.

"That certainly took a while," Freddy says. "Is everything okay?"

Justin looks surprised. "Fine. What do you mean?"

"Never mind. What can I get you to drink?"

"J&B on the rocks," Justin says rapidly and comfortably, as if it's something he says all the time. "And do you mind if I smoke?"

"Of course not," Freddy says, although he actually does mind both the liquor and the cigarettes. It all reminds him of his father back before he was sober, back when things were out of control. But he has the cigarette girl's matches, which he offers and Justin accepts.

He goes to the bar and orders, watching Justin take a place at the ledge running around the outside wall. Carrying over Justin's drink and his own ginger ale, he sees that Justin has pulled something out of his bag. He assumes it's a pack of cigarettes. As Freddy sets down the drinks he sees that Justin has indeed lit a cigarette with Freddy's Chelsea Hotel matches, but has also taken out a couple of pencils and a sheet of scratch paper that he is tearing in two.

"Let's try something," Justin says, pushing a piece of paper and pencil forward on the ledge for Freddy to take. "Turn away from me so you can't see me, and in three minutes, make a sketch of me tonight from memory. I'll do the same of you."

Freddy agrees and turns his back slightly to Justin, putting the lead of the pencil to the paper and moving it. What comes out looks less like a person and more like an abstract with a series of rounded shapes and some precipitously jagged edges. He labors at it, afraid he's made a mess. Coils of smoke from Justin's cigarette creep around him and over his shoulders and tickle his nose.

"Time," Justin calls.

"I suppose it's not too hard for you to call time," Freddy notes, turning and indicating the series of watches that line both of Justin's forearms.

"Yeah. I always know what hour it is. Though they don't all

work. Some are rusted because I don't take them off in the shower. Another couple have dead batteries and one is busted from when I got in a fistfight with my ex."

"Wow," Freddy says. "So why do you wear them all?"

"I don't know exactly. I always wore one. The second was a bit of a lark. Then after that, it just kind of grew. Eventually, they started feeling like home to me. They were what I knew."

"Do they protect you?"

"In a way, yeah. From feeling like I don't belong. But that's so boring. Show me your picture."

Freddy slides his piece of paper toward Justin, shy about what his latest, greatest crush will say about the odd portrait. Justin takes it and holds it up, wide-eyed. He turns it one way and then the other, looking at it close and at arm's length.

"What?" Freddy asks after a moment.

"It's spectacular," Justin decrees. He looks as though he doesn't want to set it down.

"Can I see yours?" Freddy asks and takes the picture Justin has made. It's a clear, art school sketch of his face. Justin's pencil is studied and polite to Freddy.

"I'll keep this forever," Justin says, delighted, folding Freddy's doodling and tucking it away.

"Can I ask you a question?" Freddy wants to know.

"Sure," Justin says, relighting his cigarette, which seems to have gone out.

"Do you consider yourself a romantic?"

Justin takes a long drag on his cigarette. "I consider that I have a big soul. If someone wants to call that romantic, that's up to them."

"I think you're a romantic."

"Suit yourself." Justin shrugs. He drains his drink and gestures toward the front door.

Freddy nods and takes Justin's hand, leading him through the crowd and out onto the street.

They hold hands without any hesitation now, leaning against each other as they walk down Ninth Avenue, deep in conversation, going nowhere in particular in no rush whatsoever.

"This is a dream," Freddy sighs.

"I thought you said this was reality and the rest was a dream."

"I want to keep on dreaming this. Don't wake me."

"Nobody understands, but you do," Justin says, getting excited. "I try and explain it to people but either they just don't get it or they look at me like I'm crazy. They don't see the patterns in things."

"There are patterns in everything," Freddy says, looking at the traffic lights blinking and changing color, then envisioning the designs of microchips and the way cornfields look from the window of a plane.

"You get it," Justin whispers, seeming genuinely amazed.

They walk a little while in silence before coming up on an all-night diner.

"Hungry?" Freddy asks.

Justin shrugs.

They find an empty booth. Both of them are sweating now and heavy in their bones when they drop to their seats. Freddy faces the street, reading and rereading the neon sign that brags, backwards, "The Finest Cup of Coffee in the World."

Freddy orders a sandwich. Justin just wants coffee. Freddy is entranced but can hardly keep his eyes open, so he orders coffee too.

Justin plays with empty sugar packets after emptying five into his cup. He folds the little paper envelopes into homemade origami shapes and pushes them around the tabletop with his pointer finger. He sings quietly, much to Freddy's pleasure.

Freddy realizes he's been quiet and apologizes:

"I never stay up this late. You?"

Justin laughs. "Sometimes. It's New York. I'm in the theater. We stay up."

Freddy looks down at Justin's hands. As if to compliment his bedecked arms, Justin has rings on each of his fingers. They are mostly trinkets, not fine jewels. One is in the shape of a snake and looks like it belongs on a Hell's Angel. Another could have come from a bubble gum vending machine.

"My rings too, huh?" Justin asks, noticing Freddy examining them. "They've all got stories, like the watches."

"Sometime—"

"Oh, I'll tell you all the stories." He lays his hands palms up on the table. Freddy gently lays his own hands on top, face down.

They look deep into each other's eyes like they're having a staring contest, but it is much more than that.

"I know what you've been through. With the record label and all." Freddy says after several minutes pass.

"Everyone knows. They might as well have rented a billboard in Times Square to announce it."

"No, I mean I *know*. I went through the same thing with a TV show I was on. One minute I was the next great thing, and the next I was an embarrassment they had to get rid of. It tore me up inside. I'm still dealing with it."

Justin smiles sadly but doesn't say anything.

Freddy's attention is distracted by a very bright light outside. He hasn't noticed it before.

"Are they filming something down the street?" Freddy asks, thinking he's seeing the spill from a movie crew's arc lights.

Justin laughs again. Freddy gets up and walks toward the front of the restaurant. What he was seeing was an illusion. The light was actually a shaft of dawn sky between two buildings across the street. He has been talking with Justin all night. He can't remember the last time he's stayed up all night talking. Probably not since with his first boyfriend. Fatigue suddenly hits him. He looks back at Justin, who is humming contentedly to himself and playing with his sugar packets, still wide awake.

"I better get another cup of coffee before we go," Freddy says, flagging the waiter. Justin gives him a thumbs-up.

Freddy pays the check and they walk out into the light, blinking a little. Now Justin has use for his sunglasses. It is early Saturday morning and the city feels empty.

"I should walk you back to the hotel, huh?" Freddy says.

Justin takes Freddy's hand and leans his head on his shoulder. "Yeah."

They pass an empty lot where Justin stops and points at where the dripping from a window air conditioner on a high floor of the building next door has left a rainbow-hued mark on the broken pavement. He walks over to it and stands staring at the ground for what feels to Freddy like a long time.

"What do you see?" Freddy finally asks.

"A rose," Justin tells him in a voice quiet with emotion.

Freddy takes a few steps back, a little dizzy with fatigue, and leans against the rough wall, looking at the vacant lot with its dirt and broken glass, spires of weeds, and Justin Salvatore staring at found beauty on the ground. Freddy laughs: Justin is *his* found beauty.

From somewhere, an old Elton John song comes to Freddy. He sings a few lines softly, but loud enough so that Justin can hear: "I thought I knew...but now I know that rose trees never grow in New York City."

When he finishes the song, as well as he can recollect it, Freddy closes his eyes and rests. A kiss on the lips from Justin wakes him.

"You sing beautifully," Justin whispers. "Walk me home."

Freddy smiles sleepily. Back on Avenue of the Americas, it does not take them long to reach the Hilton.

"Shall I see you up to your room?" Freddy asks.

Justin looks down at the pavement for a moment. "Maybe not."

Freddy is startled by Justin's sudden hesitance.

"Really?" he asks before he can stop himself.

"But can I see you later? You look like you could use some sleep."

"What about you?"

"I'm just going to watch some television. I've really enjoyed tonight." He slips through the revolving door and is gone, leaving Freddy alone on the sidewalk.

EIGHT

It is almost 9 o'clock when Freddy arrives at the downtown apartment of his ex, Timothy, where he is staying for the trip. Timothy is eating breakfast when Freddy arrives.

"You could have called," Timothy scolds once he's buzzed Freddy up to the apartment and Freddy has set down his things in the front hall.

"It was so late and I didn't want to wake you," he says, falling onto the couch, exhausted. "And besides, I forgot."

"At least you're honest."

Timothy is trim, slimmed down in the years since he and Freddy broke up. His belly has tightened and he wears his hair in a tight-cropped Caesar cut. Freddy resents this a little, wondering why Timothy didn't work harder to make himself attractive when they were together. But it is all for the good—Timothy is dating an Italian from New Jersey named Joe Something-or-other, and Freddy is happy for them.

"So? I assume you met the Justin guy, considering you were out all night."

"I said I was sorry."

"It was that good?"

"I think I'm in love."

Timothy laughs at this, finishing his breakfast and gathering his things to go to the production office of the TV show he's writing for. "The good news is you'll have the apartment to yourself for the day. You can sleep in as late as you like—"

"I'm supposed to meet him back uptown later."

"Sleep, princess. The boy will still be there when you get up."

"This one's no ordinary boy. Will you have dinner with us tonight?"

Timothy looks surprised. "I guess we can. I'll ask Joe."

"Well, I haven't asked Justin either. But I need you to meet him. I need to know if I'm totally nuts."

"Trust me, I will let you know if and when you lose it. It will be my pleasure to inform you."

Timothy leaves and Freddy tries to get comfortable in Timothy's bed; the sofa is his by rights, but with Timothy gone, there's no good reason not to sleep in his bed. Besides, the air conditioner is in that room, and though it's still early in the day, the July heat is already rising, making the streets of the Village smell of piss, shawirma, and rubbish. With the cool air blowing on him, Freddy falls into a gleefully fretful sleep, shallow and wakeful because of the cups of coffee he's drunk and the flush of new love.

At 3, he wakes and, after using the bathroom, follows his next urge, which is to call Justin at the hotel. The front desk rings Freddy through, but there is no answer. Freddy gets up and pokes through Timothy's refrigerator for something to eat. He finds fat-free muesli and a carton of soy milk. Timothy was always an odd eater. He cited lactose intolerance and difficulty with spicy food as reason to eat a small, bland assortment of food. This bored Freddy at home and infuriated him at restaurants when Timothy insisted that his food be prepared just so. In truth, Freddy believes, Timothy is persnickety because he is a director and needs to feel in charge, even if at a given moment all he is in charge of is soft-boiled eggs.

Freddy calls Claire's cell and finds her away for the weekend in the northern California wine country.

"If it's that good with Justin," she tells him, "I suppose you could just let go."

"And what?"

"Free fall."

Freddy laughs at this, a little giddy. "So have you been talking with Hugh?"

"Every day. He's got all these fascinating stories. He can hold my attention for hours."

"Which is a remarkable thing."

"And he puts up with Dog."

"Which is remarkable too, considering her flatulence."

"That was me. I lied."

"So what are you doing in Sonoma?"

"Staying at a bed and breakfast and taking a tour of wine country."

"With Hugh," they say simultaneously.

"You say it like it's a bad thing," Claire protests.

"You say it like it's obvious," he counters.

Claire pauses. Freddy can hear horses in the background.

"It is," she says decisively.

Her phone connection goes bad and they lose the call. Freddy decides he will try her tomorrow.

Four o'clock finds Freddy fed, showered, and restless. He plays with the buttons on his shirt in the mirror. Should he leave just one open at the neck, or two? He licks his teeth in the mirror. They could be whiter. He considers brushing them again. Justin still doesn't answer the phone; Freddy leaves him voice mail with the address of the restaurant where he wants to have dinner, along with a request for a call back as soon as possible. He wants to see Justin before dinner. Freddy wants to see Justin *right now*, see him and touch him and talk with him, now and nonstop until further notice.

At 5 o'clock, Freddy leaves another voice mail: "Hey, it's me. I hope you're getting this. Like I said before, we're eating at 7 at Josie's. I left you the address before. I hope everything's okay." He pauses. "So, yeah. See you there."

He hangs up with a frown and sinks into the foam cushion of Timothy's mid-century sofa. *No*. He forces doubt from his mind. Everything went remarkably well last night, even though Justin made him wait. Justin likes Freddy. He likes him a lot. There's no question of it. Freddy just needs to relax. He sighs. He sits. This is foolishness. Dinner is two hours away. Even with an extreme amount of primping and ample time for the cab ride, he still has over an hour to kill.

Maybe Timothy has some interesting videos. Freddy rummages through the cabinet beneath the television, hoping he will not find porn; he does not. There are only some old episodes of *The X Files* and a Goldie Hawn movie Freddy has never heard of.

Disappointed, he goes and brushes his teeth again, though they don't need it.

"I was expecting to hear from you by now," he reprimands the mirror, then softens his wording: "I had hoped you'd call by now." But even that sounds clingy, so he abandons it.

He checks his e-mail on Timothy's computer and, bored, goes into a chat room for a few moments before clicking the window closed and slamming down the screen of the laptop computer, disgusted with himself. He has no business in chat rooms.

He leaves Justin another message, wondering now if he and Timothy will be eating alone.

During the cab ride to Josie's, Freddy is tense. His right cheek twitches slightly. He feels like putting his face against the cool of the car window. The sun is just setting and it casts an amber glow across the city, interrupted by the regular, jagged shadows of skyscrapers. Instead of putting his face against the glass, Freddy holds his cell phone there, in case Justin calls and the antenna signal is weak.

"Just drop me off at the corner," he tells the African cabbie when he discovers that they are on a one-way and will have to go around the block to put him directly in front of the restaurant. Freddy pays and takes a receipt—this is a business trip, after all, and he can deduct it—before slamming the door and heading toward the restaurant.

Timothy is waiting at a table on the patio when Freddy gets there.

"Hey, where's your boy wonder?" he asks, looking up from his menu.

"Running late, I guess," Freddy answers glumly, sitting down. "Yours?"

"Had to work late."

"You got lemon?"

Timothy smiles and holds up a small dish. Freddy takes a couple of slices, dropping them into his water glass so that it matches Timothy's. This is one small dietary fetish they share, and it makes Freddy feel a little calmer to indulge in the ritual.

"You have to come back into the city for the opening of my new play," Timothy says. "We have Phylicia Rashad playing the mother, and she's amazing."

Freddy nods and smiles as Timothy goes on about the show, the rancor he's had with the play's producer, the giant banner advertisement that hung in Times Square for a week. Freddy smiles and nods appropriately when Timothy pauses, but he is not really listening. He sneaks glances at his watch and he checks, over and over, to make sure the squarish lump of the cell phone is still in his pants pocket and it has not vibrated.

It is dark now. After waiting for fifteen minutes, the two men order appetizers and the waiter lights the candle on their table. Someone next to them begins to smoke a cigarette, and Timothy leans forward to complain in a loud, forced whisper that anyone on the patio could hear. It seems to Freddy a good opportunity to excuse himself, which he does, and heads to the men's room. It's been well over a half hour since he got to the restaurant. He stands outside the restroom door and phones Justin for what he promises himself will be the last time this evening. As has been the case all day, the call goes to voice mail. Freddy hangs up without leaving a message. He feels like crying. He has come to the city for nothing.

Freddy is in no hurry to get back to the table, but as he walks back through the restaurant toward the patio, he sees in silhouette someone standing next to his and Timothy's table. His heart jumps and he draws a sharp breath. When he gets closer, he sees Justin has arrived.

"He-e-ey," Justin greets Freddy broadly, pulling him into a lazy hug. "Sorry I'm late. But I thought I should bring some music."

He slips the worn backpack off his shoulder and pulls out a couple of dime store tambourines, handing one each to Freddy and Timothy.

"So you met one another—" Freddy says.

"I recognized Justin from the *Jungle Book* posters," Timothy says with an uncomfortable smile. For a moment, he holds the tambourine like a power tool he has no idea how to use. Then he sets it on the floor next to his chair. The tambourine makes a muffled clatter, as does Freddy's when he sits down and follows Timothy's lead.

"Sorry," Justin says again, taking a seat. He then grins so broadly his eyes almost shut and it looks as if he is trying to show off all his teeth at once.

"Did you get my messages?" Freddy asks, noticing the accusation in his own voice.

"I got one. Then I think I left my phone somewhere. I'm almost out of minutes anyway so it doesn't really matter."

"I called you a bunch of times..."

Justin just smiles in response. Freddy sees that he is sweating, beads of perspiration moistening his forehead and making his tie-dyed T-shirt cling to his shoulders. He sits and they order, though Justin seems to have some trouble deciphering the menu.

"The appetizers are on the left-hand side," Freddy advises.

"I just want French fries."

"I don't think they have that here. It's a health food restaurant."

"Okay." Justin sounds as if he as been scolded.

"But let me ask the waiter."

Freddy flags their waiter, who is standing off to the side admiring his well-greased, jaw length locks in the plate glass window.

"Can we get French fries?" Freddy asks as sweetly as he can.

"We have some baked sweet potato sticks—"

"And French fries?"

"I'll check with the cook." The waiter says with a sigh, bested. "It shouldn't be a problem."

Justin goes to the bathroom. Once he has left, Timothy leans in to Freddy.

"He's on something," Timothy whispers loudly.

"Like what?" Freddy hisses back, as if they are keeping a secret.

"Some street drug—I don't know the names."

"Crack?"

"Something. But he's high as a kite. I'm serious."

Freddy nods uncomfortably. "You think he's on something?"

"Not think—I know. And another thing I know is how gullible you are."

"Timothy, just stop."

Timothy shrugs. "You want me to tell you these things or not?"

They sit in silence. Freddy pokes at the butter pat with his fork, making a set of wiggly parallel lines where the tines imprint the soft surface.

It is many minutes before Justin returns, singing quietly to himself, seemingly unaware of the length of his absence.

Timothy cuts Freddy a look. Freddy glances away.

"I know what you're thinking," Justin launches in, cutting off his own song mid verse, "and I think I should explain."

He leans in and speaks more quietly. "There are people after me. I don't know what they want, but they bugged my computer in my old place on 46th Street, and now they keep track of what cabs I take. I try to lose them. But they always find me."

"There are people following you—" Timothy says sardonically.

"You have to believe me."

"No, I don't," Timothy corrects him. "And frankly, I want you to stay away from my friend."

"I thought he was your ex," Justin says, riled.

"That's none of your business! And whatever our history, I care about him a lot and I'm not going to see him taken advantage of by some cracked-out chorus boy."

The waiter shows up with the French fries along with Timothy's nut patty and the seitan tacos Freddy ordered.

"I don't think we're going to need this," Freddy apologizes. "And Justin, maybe it was a mistake us all getting together. I guess it was just too soon."

The waiter stands back, looking puzzled, unsure whether to set the food on the table.

"Can I get a Jack Daniels?" Justin asks nobody in particular.

The waiter puts the food down and makes a hasty retreat.

Timothy pushes his chair back and stands up.

"Thanks for inviting me," he says to Freddy.

"Timothy, look," Freddy flusters. "This wasn't supposed to happen."

"Tell *him*," Timothy spits, gesturing toward Justin without looking at him. He picks up his phone and keys and walks toward the patio exit.

"Timothy!" Freddy calls after him, but he is already hailing a cab. Freddy knows there'd be no stopping him now anyway. Timothy's stubborn like that.

After he is gone, Freddy and Justin sit silent for a moment.

"That went badly," Freddy remarks acrimoniously. He hates making a scene. But more than that, he hates Timothy's disapproval.

"Hmpf," Justin remarks, picking at the fries the waiter has left. He examines a slice of potato, blowing off a few flakes of parsley that cling to it before popping it in his mouth. He chews then looks over at Freddy. His face drops when he sees the disappointment there.

"I'm so sorry," Justin says, and sounds for the life of him as if he really means it. "I love you. I don't want to fuck things up."

Something tugs at Freddy's insides. He sees Justin as two people, the picture-perfect hero from the Internet and the lost child that sits before him. Suddenly, Justin's words echo in his head. He is in love with both halves.

"Just tell me one thing," Freddy asks quietly. "And be honest, okay?"

Justin half shrugs but nods ever so slightly, looking away.

"What are you on?"

There is a long pause before Justin answers.

"Some people call it Tina."

"What do you call it?"

"Survival."

"Get on the next plane!" Joshua insists.

"The thing is—"

"The thing is, there is no thing. You get home. I am not asking. I am telling."

Joshua stares at the speakerphone in his home office. It is Sunday afternoon. There is a half-eaten bowl of Shredded Wheat in front of him, cast off after the cereal soaked up all the milk and got mushy. He is still in his pajamas.

Freddy, on the other end of the phone, sounds worn. "Anyway, I planned to be in New York for four days, so I will."

"You don't have to prove anything," Joshua says.

"He's really amazing. I mean, fucked up—yes, but wow! I've barely slept in two days. He keeps talking and it's like I can't look away. We had to move hotels."

"*We?*"

"It's a long story."

Joshua shakes his head in dismay. Two of his three best friends have lost their minds to love. Normally sensible Claire is bananas over a man who whisked her away for the weekend. Meanwhile, Freddy is giving his heart to a drug-snorting singer. It is almost more than Joshua can tolerate.

"Really," he insists, "you can't do this."

"Too late. And the Four Seasons is nothing less than Justin deserves. Besides, I get miles."

"You put the room on your credit card?" Joshua is apoplectic.

"Their smallest room. The guy at the desk upgraded us to a corner suite when he recognized Justin. I'm telling you, he gets VIP treatment in New York—"

"On your credit card."

"You're not helping."

"*You're* not helping," Joshua shouts. "You're in way over your head."

"Well, I'm not coming home until tomorrow night."

"Are you sure he's gay, at least?" Joshua asks, grasping for an angle.

"After last night," Freddy says lasciviously, "I'd say there's no question. He sat on top of my—"

"I don't need details!"

"Tell the truth—if it was you, you'd be all up in it like—"

"Like nothing," Joshua snaps. "I'd have to good sense to leave."

Joshua says goodbye, gets off the phone, and holds his head in dismay.

He calls Ritchie. At least Ritchie is sane now, or as sane as Ritchie gets. The two of them spend the afternoon shoe shopping in Beverly Hills. There is a sneaker store that is close enough to Rodeo Drive to make them feel as though they are shopping with the wealthy set, but still sells Chuck Taylor's for twenty-nine dollars plus tax. They buy matching jogging shoes. Joshua knows Ritchie's will wear out faster than his own, but for the moment the two of them look like twins. As they go to Jamba Juice and wait in line for a smoothie, Joshua imagines that he and Ritchie *are* twins. Joshua will never be raven-haired and six-foot-one. But now, he stands tall and pulls his shoulders back and imagines.

NINE

Claire takes a long shower. When she picks up the bar of soap from the chromed dish, there is a curly gray hair stuck to it, obviously Hugh's. She makes a face and holds the soap up to the showerhead so the water will wash the hair away and she won't have to touch it. She's had enough of Hugh for the moment. He's a perfectly nice guy, but Claire is used to doing things on her own, and Hugh doesn't seem to get it.

"You're giving me a 10," she explains on the way back from Sonoma. "I need a 7."

Hugh nods and listens, but the evening they get back, he has a dozen roses and a greetings card couriered to her house. Claire is angry when she signs for the delivery. After the guy with the clipboard leaves, she mumbles "Leave me alone" under her breath.

The card that came with the flowers is creepy. It's a picture of a mulberry tree and is inscribed "here we go round" in fountain pen ink in Hugh's slightly shaky writing. What is this supposed to mean? Claire opens the card and a check falls onto the floor. She picks it up and turns it over. It's made out for $5,000, and on the memo line he's written "for the care and feeding of Dog and Lisbeth, my new family."

Claire throws the check back on the floor and stares at it as if it is contaminated with anthrax spores and will sicken her. It does sicken her, actually, but only in her gut, where she feels that something is badly amiss. She wishes she could undo Hugh, take back the dates and feelings she's felt, erase the kind things she's said.

She sits on the sofa to contemplate what to do. More than anything, she wants to take another shower to get this icky feeling off her skin. She takes off her shoes and socks and walks heavily toward the bathroom with Dog panting along beside her. When she reaches the bathroom door, the phone rings. She looks down at the display. It's Hugh. She throws the phone at the floor. Thankfully it misses the hardwood and catches the edge of the carpet, where it glides to a stop against the upholstered leg of the sofa. She stares at the phone while it finishes ringing.

"Fuck," she tells Dog.

The phone rings again. This time it is at Joshua's house. It is late in the night. Joshua is asleep. He reaches for the clock, picks it up, and holds the green display to his face to see the time. It's a quarter after 2.

"Hello?" he coughs into the phone. "Excuse me."

"It's okay. Can you hear me?" The voice is tinny and far away. There is commotion in the background, voices arguing, the sound of a security buzzer.

"Christian?" He recognizes the voice of his ex.

"Yeah, it's me. Listen, I need your help."

Joshua sits up. Hearing Christian's voice is something of a shock.

"I haven't talked to you in how long? A year?"

"Two," Christian says. "But let's catch up another time. Right now I need you to come over to the Hollywood Precinct."

"What?" Joshua turns on the light, squinting in the glare of the bulb. He imagines Christian standing at a pay phone in one of his circuit boy tank tops. Even a goatee, a tribal tattoo around his arm, and a constantly lit cigarette don't make Christian look older than about 16.

"There was this misunderstanding. I was out in front of my building having a cigarette and—you know they bust people for loitering in this neighborhood—"

"That's why they call it Vaseline alley," Joshua remarks.

"And I didn't have my ID, so the cops brought me in. I'm scared."

"But why are you calling *me*?"

Christian sighs. "I figured you'd have the five hundred to get me out."

"Five hundred dollars!" Joshua explodes.

"I'll pay you back next week as soon as I get it from my mom."

Joshua shakes his head. "I don't know, hon."

"Please, baby," Christian begs in a small voice. "They took away my shoelaces."

Joshua sighs, scrunches up his face, and smacks himself on the forehead.

"I'll be there quick as I can."

A few minutes later he sits in his parking garage alone, waiting for his engine to warm up. Maybe, he thinks, if he waits long enough, the fumes will suffocate him and he won't have to go. But it's a big garage, with three levels and hundreds of parking spaces, so it would take too long. Besides, Christian wasn't worth the trouble.

Outside the police station on Wilcox Avenue, Joshua recalls the two times he's been to this squat Cold War brick building—once to turn in a ransacked purse he spotted in the bushes near his apartment, and a second time with two neighbors to turn in a petition against a noisy old lady next door who wouldn't keep her cats under control. Never has he come here because anyone he knew was in real trouble with the law.

The officer at the front desk is a heavy black woman whose braided hair has begun to come undone. She speaks without looking up from her *Wired* magazine. Joshua feels as if he's being scolded by the directions she gives: "Jail. To the right and down the hall. You'll need the last name of the detainee."

She gestures toward to a buzz-locked set of doors with no windows. Joshua follows her instructions, discovering a hallway that smells like an animal shelter. The tiled floor is worn and scratched. He reaches a window, behind which sits an elderly uniformed man with a voice that should be selling jelly on TV:

"Yes?" the old cop asks slowly and deliberately, a lopsided smile on his face.

"Here to post bail for Johannsen. Christian Johannsen."

"Johannsen," the officer repeats, but doesn't do anything.

"Yes," Joshua says, shuffling uncomfortably.

A moment passes. Then the old man looks down at a clipboard on his desk, and says a third time, "Johannsen."

"Christian. I'm here to post bail."

"Five hundred dollars," the man reads, sliding a hooked finger from left to right across his printed page.

Justin pulls out the thick ATM deposit envelope he's just gotten at Bank of America. It's his grocery money for this week and half of next. He taps the envelope for the man is if to say, "Here it is."

He slides it across the sill and the man takes it, handing him a release form in exchange for cash.

"Here," the officer points at two places Joshua is supposed to sign, "and here."

Joshua scribbles his signature then waits as the old man gets up and creeps across the back office.

Several minutes pass. Joshua hears the muffled sound of men fighting. He notices, from the clock on the wall, that it's ten minutes till 4 in the morning. He slouches against the wall, then pulls himself into sharp posture, wary of what awful germs he might be getting on his sweater.

A buzzer at the end of the hall sounds. There is a click, and a battered door swings open. Christian stands behind it, a smirk of his face. He is bedraggled, holds his shoes in one hand, and has clearly dirty stocking feet.

"Johannsen," Joshua says.

"Christian," his foolishly handsome ex corrects him, walking forward.

"You're Johannsen to me now," Joshua says sternly. "We're on a last-name basis."

Christian gets close and tries to give Joshua a hug and a kiss, but Joshua gently pushes him away.

"You smell," he remarks. "And what's with the shoes?"

"They wouldn't give me back my laces. I'm hungry."

"I'll buy you Denny's. But that's the end of my charity."

They leave and go to the restaurant. It is almost dawn. They share a pot of coffee. Christian spends most of breakfast looking out the window at the cars passing on Sunset Boulevard. Joshua stares at him. There are lines on Christian's face that weren't there before. Occasionally Christian notices Joshua staring and smiles, but even his teeth don't look like they should.

"Are you doing okay?" Joshua asks eventually.

"What do you expect?"

"I mean, before that. In general."

"Money's been tight. Everything's been tight."

"Are you behaving yourself?"

"Was I ever?"

"That was why I broke up with you."

"*I* broke up with *you*."

"In your dreams, crackhead," Joshua laughs. "And listen, are you telling me the complete truth about how you got arrested? Because as I was driving over to the station, I kept going over it in my head and something just felt wrong."

"Well..." Christian makes an impish face.

"Oh, Lord."

"The cop was really cute," Christian blurts. "Okay?"

"You had sex with him!"

Christian looks away for a moment then turns back at Joshua with a glint in his eye.

"You always assume the worst," he says edgily. "That's why you get depressed. And you act like you're not as horny as the rest of us. But we both know you are, and that you take it up the ass like a champ—"

"This is *so* inappropriate," Joshua fumes.

"And you're self righteous too. Look at you," he laughs. "If we went to the car right now and I made a move on you, I could have you in thirty seconds."

Christian slides his hands across the table and tries to lay them on Joshua's, but Joshua pulls back and shakes his head in disgust. Christian has a lot of nerve, and if he thinks he can get back on Joshua's good side by making a cheap pass, he's got another thing coming. Joshua is livid. He takes a big gulp of cold water, excuses himself to use the restroom, and tugs the bottom of his T-shirt past the waist of his jeans to hide the outline of his arousal.

A waitress with a big tray of food is in the aisle and Joshua pushes past her, staring straight ahead.

Two days later, in another restaurant, he is much calmer. It is Saturday morning at Noble's. Claire, Freddy, Ritchie, and he are together in the same room for the first time in weeks. Joshua is bringing them up to date about the dramatics with Christian.

"So did he?" Claire asks, pausing in the middle of a sip of coffee. "Fuck the cop?"

"He says he offered to blow the guy for forty bucks."

"Is that a good price?" Claire wonders.

"For Christian, I'd have to say yes," Joshua muses. "He's got serious skills."

"But they didn't do it?" Ritchie asks, picking at a bowl of blueberries and shifting in a muscle T-shirt that looks two sizes two small.

"No, the cop arrested him."

"For loitering?" Claire asks.

"For pandering."

"Would you have bailed him out if you knew the truth up front?" Claire sounds like a TV talk show host. Joshua feels ganged up on.

"No. Yes," he blunders. "Probably. I know where his mother lives. I can get my money back even if he totally fucks up. So yes, I guess I would have. I'm codependent."

"And you still like him," Freddy digs.

"No! He's got skills. There's a difference." Joshua feels himself blush. The truth is about to come out.

"You didn't!" Freddy sounds aghast. "After all that, you had sex with him?"

"Listen, don't *you* judge *me*," Joshua hisses.

Freddy is quiet. He's told all of them about Justin, and now Joshua's blatantly turning the calamity against him. Realizing he's gone too far, Joshua winks at Freddy, but it comes off badly. Freddy rolls his eyes.

"The worst part," Joshua admits, "is as we were sitting there talking about it at Denny's, he tried to make it better by saying he would've blown the cop for free. As if that excuses what he did."

"Did you buy him shoelaces?" Ritchie asks.

"Please! My charity ended at eggs sunny side up."

"And sex," Claire reminds him.

"And sex," Joshua admits.

"Okay, listen," Ritchie interrupts, his tone completely changed. "I have something to tell you guys."

They turn to him. He grins, then blushes and instinctually brushes a curl of his locks, which he has been growing out fashionably long, behind his ear.

"So this guy came up to me at the gym—"

"Oh, Jesus," Claire mutters.

"No, no. He's for real. In show business. He makes movies that go on HBO and a couple of other channels I forgot."

"Makes them?" Freddy asks, equally skeptical.

"He's a producer. I seen him on the credits of a movie he told me to watch on cable last night. It was good. About this girl who finds out she has cancer. And he was asking me a bunch of questions at the gym. Like what I want to do with my future, stuff like that. He goes by J.W.—just initials—which is very sophisticated."

"Did he ask for your pager number?" Joshua questions.

"C'mon, you guys. He's totally legit," Ritchie insists, getting upset. "Just be happy for me, okay? I don't know where this will go but it's a real producer asking me real questions and it just feels like—like I'm a real actor."

Joshua looks down for a moment, turning repentant. "I'm sorry, Ritchie, you're right. That is really good news. And who knows what'll happen."

"Yeah," Claire adds, not as convinced. "You could be the next Brad Pitt."

"Can I have your autograph?" Freddy asks, fishing for a pen and sliding it across the table along with a clean napkin.

"As a matter of fact, yes," Ritchie says, looking delighted. "And you better save it. Because it's going to be worth a lot someday. Mark my words."

"We always do," Joshua reminds him, patting Ritchie on the wrist so gently that, even for all his stiffness, Ritchie can't refuse the gesture.

TEN

Freddy digs around in the front pocket of his jeans and pulls out the cell phone that is ringing an electronic rendition of Rimsky-Korsakov's *Flight of the Bumblebee*. It's a 212 number. Someone is calling him from Manhattan.

"Hello?" he says, putting up a polite hand of apology to Claire, who is sitting next to him in her Mercedes. She is driving the two of them to the movies.

"Hey..." the voice says hesitantly. It takes Freddy a moment to realize it's Justin.

"Oh, hey!" Freddy is pleased. "What's going on?"

"You remember you said you wanted me to come out to L.A.?" Justin asks. "Well, I'll be there on the 10 A.M. flight."

"Are you serious?"

"I've got a bunch of boxes and stuff and it's not all holding together well, so if you have a big car like you talked about, that'd be good."

"Yeah, of course." Freddy swallows hard and glances over at Claire, who gives him a quizzical look. "Um, I'll be there to pick you up at 10, then. You need anything?"

"Just you."

"You're so sweet," Freddy swoons.

"Oh—and some Marlboro Reds," Justin adds hastily.

"Sure..." Freddy hesitates. "So meet me at baggage claim?"

Justin says something that sounds like a "yes" but the phone is cut off abruptly and Freddy hears a single beep tone. The call must have been from a pay phone and Justin didn't have any more change.

Freddy closes the cover of his phone and waits for it to ring again.

"Who was it?" Claire asks.

"Him," Freddy says ominously.

Claire snickers.

The phone doesn't ring. Freddy stares at it. He thinks of kissing Justin, of feeling his closeness. But Justin is too much to manage.

The phone still doesn't ring.

"Sometimes," Claire says like a schoolteacher, "you get what you ask for."

"I didn't ask for *this,*" Freddy protests. He reaches over in a huff and switches on the radio. Claire grabs the knob and turns it back off.

"Like hell you didn't," she counters. "You've been flipped out over him for *how* long? And you yourself invited him—"

"But not to come in four days."

"Did you get a sense of how long he's staying?"

"It seems like he's...staying."

"Unless you're about to marry him, you can't put him up. Does he have other friends in LA? Money for a hotel?"

"I really don't know," Freddy admits, panicky. "What am I supposed to do?"

They reach the parking ramp for the Arclight movie theater. Claire takes a ticket from the machine and pulls up the driveway.

"Treat him kindly," Claire suggests. "Beyond that, it's your call."

They see an art film about a middle-aged British woman writer who goes away for holiday and meets a girl who, through a series of circumstances, is staying at the same house she is. There is a love triangle with a man from the town, whom the girl ends up killing. She and the writer lady bury him in the pool house. Then the writer lady realizes it was all just a dream.

Freddy feels cheated by this ending, and complains about it loudly on the way home.

"You don't get that the girl is an amalgam of all the parts of the writer that were never allowed to be," Claire explains. "It's her repression."

"Mostly I get that she killed the cute pool guy, somebody's going to find out, and then she's screwed."

"You're missing the nuance, and you're anxious about Justin tomorrow."

"I'll give you one out of two—should I make up the guest bedroom? Will he be fucked up or sober?"

"Like I'd know."

"You have more experience with these things—"

"The hell I do!" Claire snaps. "But I'd guess fucked up, and only one bed necessary."

Freddy doesn't sleep well that night. In the morning, he sits at his computer and tries to write, but he keeps getting one faltering paragraph done, then deleting it. He's not clever and he has no discipline—he doesn't like to sit for long spells. He doesn't have much of an imagination. Often, all that comes to him is the dialogue of TV shows and movies he's just seen. It is clear—he should not be a writer.

He closes the word processor window then checks his e-mail a half dozen times, clicking the "refresh" icon compulsively.

At lunchtime he is outside baggage claim, pacing. The passengers from Justin's flight come down the escalator from the gates, hover around the baggage carousel, pick up their suitcases and duffels, and disappear through the glass sliding doors into the parade of imbroglio and honking horns that rings LAX. But none among the passengers is Justin. Freddy feels for the phone in his pocket. Yes, it's on.

Finally, after twenty minutes, his phone vibrates.

"You're not going to believe what happened," Justin says before Freddy can even offer a hello. "They put me standby, then when they were calling out names they skipped over me. I was listening the whole time."

"So you're still at JFK?"

"Can you get me on the next flight? I'm here with all my boxes and I haven't eaten since yesterday."

Freddy squeezes the phone tightly and purses his lips. He stomps.

"Hello?" Justin asks.

"I'll go up to the ticket window and work it out," Freddy says reluctantly.

"Great!" Justin is exuberant. "I'll head my stuff down to that gate."

"Question, though—why were you on standby?"

"I was late. The cab took longer than—you know."

"I'll get the ticket," Freddy mopes. "Call me back in a little while."

Five hundred and forty dollars later, Freddy is sitting at a Mexican cantina in the International Terminal. It's too long before Justin's flight arrives to sit around comfortably, but if Freddy drives home, he knows he won't get anything useful done. So he sits and waits. And the longer he waits, the more irritated he gets with Justin.

The cab wasn't late. Justin was. And God knows how many suitcases he's lugging. Or not even suitcases, cardboard boxes. This is what Freddy fears—boxes and paper bags tied with yarn.

What arrives, many nachos and Diet Cokes later, is Justin, sporting five days of stubble, a giant ear-to-ear grin, and a rumpled dress shirt whose sleeves are made bulky by all the strange jewelry and tchotchkes he wears. He is at the base of the escalator at baggage claim when he and Freddy spot each other.

Reluctantly at first, Freddy hugs him. But as Justin has his drug of choice, so, Freddy discovers, has he. And he's embracing it. He draws in Justin's smell, sour and smoky and ominous, and is uncomfortably turned on in front of a crowd of people. He pulls back from Justin a few inches to allow himself to settle. He shakes the leg of his jeans.

"Here I am!" Justin announces in a tone that is as ominous and arousing as his smell.

Together they get his things, which include two suitcases, three boxes, and a couple of industrial-duty garbage bags into which the hotel cleaning staff probably emptied Justin's belongings before tossing him out on his ear.

It's a heavy load for Freddy to lift into the back of his SUV.

"They made me pay extra because of the weight," Justin distresses, looking over his assortment of property as mother duck would her quacking ducklings. "But it's all I own, so I couldn't leave anything behind."

Freddy gets Justin's fidelity to his odd lot of junk. Empathy is what makes Freddy a decent person, but condemns him to scenes such as this.

He knows his friends would handle things better.

Claire's tough. She says "no." She can walk from craziness and wash her hands of it. Ritchie is either smart or dumb enough to keep focused on his own needs and aspirations. Joshua gets bent out of shape over boys. But, like Ritchie, he's driven enough by his own struggle to disallow such egregiousness.

Back at the house, Freddy carries Justin's suitcases to the bedroom and leaves the boxes and trash bags in the hall to put into his storage locker later.

"Help yourself," Freddy calls out, referring to the fridge. The clinking of jars and bottles attest that Justin is already doing so.

"Is this a Picasso?" Justin asks.

"Yeah." Freddy walks into the room and stands beside Justin, who is staring at a small framed lithograph Freddy bought online during one of his periods of feeling wealthy. It's murky-colored, which is probably part of why Freddy got it for four hundred dollars, but is clear enough to show a circle of musicians dancing around under a tree with a goat, playing their instruments for the benefit of the moon and a wary owl watching from the branch of a tree.

"It's amazing," Justin exclaims with his winning smile, not taking his eyes off the picture.

Freddy feels a rush of pleasure and he heads back to the bedroom to make room in the chest of drawers for Justin to put away his things. When he returns to the kitchen five minutes later, Justin is still staring at the picture.

"Sweetie?" Freddy interrupts gently.

"Huh?" Justin is startled. "Oh—hi."

Freddy holds out the pack of Marlboros he bought at a convenience store on the way to the airport. Nimbly, Justin opens the pack and pulls one out, still entranced by the lithograph.

"Got a light?" he asks out of one side of his mouth, holding the cigarette between his lips.

"Actually, no," Freddy admits.

Justin shrugs, goes to the stove and turns on a burner, leaning down perilously close to the blue flame while the tip of his cigarette catches fire.

Freddy watches silently. Nobody has ever smoked in his apartment before. He has no ashtray. What will the place smell like now? Should he ask Justin to go outside? He considers this, starts to come up with a polite objection, but can't make himself say it. All he can do is watch Justin smoke, the cherry of the cigarette glowing orange-red as he inhales, the smoke leaving his lips and pooling into a cloud that hovers beneath the kitchen light.

In a few minutes, the cigarette is gone.

"Can I take a shower?" Justin asks. Freddy shrugs and walks him toward the bathroom, pausing at the hall closet to get him a clean towel.

"It takes a while for the water to get hot. Old building," Freddy explains.

Justin returns a blank expression and shuts the door in Freddy's face. Freddy stands in the hallway, hearing Justin undress, mutter to himself, and clink and clatter as his jewelry slides around and catches on his clothes. Justin turns the shower on and Freddy hears the plumbing through the walls and ceiling.

"Whoo!" Justin exclaims loudly when he opens the shower door and steps into the spray.

Freddy falls gently against the wall in the hallway, momentarily overwhelmed.

Justin starts to sing. At first it is tuneless, bits of scales that climb atop the other until the window panes rattle back his full-out high tenor. Then the scales evolve into a song. It takes Freddy a moment to realize he's hearing "Prepare Ye the Way of the Lord" from *Jesus Christ Superstar*. Justin is genially slaying the song, carving it up and serving it in delicious slices. Freddy smiles. He should be paying good money for a front row seat like this. His fears abate. With his weight against the wall, he slides slowly down until he is sitting on the hardwood floor. He knows Justin will not stop the concert until all the hot water in the building is used up.

Ritchie doesn't expect much when he calls the number from a photocopied flyer he sees posted on a lamp pole outside the Cultured Class advertising EXTRAS AND MODELS WANTED. He assumes it's another porn Web site or something equally as dead-end. So he's surprised when a perky young woman's voice answers the phone.

"Hello, Extras Plus."

"I'm calling from the ad looking for models."

"Sure," she says gleefully, "let me get your name and number and we can set you up for bookings."

"Excuse me?" Ritchie doesn't think he's heard her correctly. "You don't want me to send in pictures or something?"

"Not really. Just show up on time."

"For what?"

"Today, we've got..." She pauses and seems to be reading something. "Can you be at Hollywood and Vine at noon?"

"You don't even know what I look like—"

"It's a photo shoot for a political magazine—"

"Or how old I am."

"It's seventy-five an hour plus a fourth hour if you go past three. One hour minimum."

Ritchie does the math in his head. He clears his throat. "Okay."

At noon, he is showered and shaved and nervous, standing in the hallway of a drab office building. He straightens up and checks the zipper on his pants.

Just as Ritchie reaches to push the intercom buzzer, the door swings wide. A fat man with hair like yellow pillow stuffing is standing there, sweating and ruddy and dressed for the beach. An expensive-looking digital camera hangs from a strap around his neck.

"You here for the Fallujah shoot?" he asks Ritchie.

"I, uh—" Ritchie pulls a piece of paper from his pocket and tries to read his own handwriting. "Yeah, is that something to do with Iraq?"

"Come in," the fat man says with a nod. "I'm Bob. I'll be shooting this spread. Your costume's in the back office. You can change in there."

He tosses a paunchy shrug toward a second doorway behind him. Ritchie peers cautiously around his corpulent profile to the lobby. All the chairs have been pushed back against the wall, and a coffee table is wedged in the corner, so the space seems almost empty. Furthermore, it is quiet. There doesn't seem to be anyone besides Bob in the office.

"It's budget cutbacks," the fat man explains. "They work three days a week. Except me. For some reason, bad political parody is a full-time job."

He follows Ritchie's glance around the lobby, turning to inspect it himself.

"Oh," he offers in explanation, "we're going to shoot on the floor."

Ritchie's eyes travel down to the ratty and pilled carpet, stained from years of coffee spills and footfalls. Then he looks back at the fat man and doubts the smarts of going on.

"Don't worry," the photographer chuckles. "You'll be in a burka and we'll Photoshop out the stains on the rug."

Ritchie attempts a smile and nods. "Um—a burka?" It sounds like a candy bar or a kind of sandal.

"It's in the back."

Bob steps aside and Ritchie walks hesitantly past him to the back office, his paper full of notes and directions gripped so tightly he can feel it dampening in the sweat of his palm.

A sign over a small, unattended reception desk reads *New Left Magazine* in greenish 1970s type. An almost-dead rubber tree languishes in the corner, shoved beside the upturned coffee table. There are old-fashioned computers and stacks of newspapers and magazines everywhere—it seems as though nobody's tidied up here for some time.

At least, Ritchie thinks, it doesn't seem like this gig has anything to do with porn. He wonders if he'll get paid now or if he'll have to wait for a check to come in the mail. In the meantime, he feels twitchy, as if the photographer, now behind him, is about to pounce and any moment and Ritchie will have to fend him off.

In the small rear office, Ritchie finds a hanger with a black robe and what appears to be a wimple like the nuns at St. Sebastian wore when he was an altar boy. His anxiety redoubles.

There is still hope. Perhaps, if he makes a dash for it, Ritchie can make a clean exit through the front door before the fat man can raise an objection. Ritchie will skip the elevator and take the stairs so Bob the photographer can't catch him. He'll be in his car and heading home in three minutes. He'll change his cell phone number so the cheery agency girl can't reach him.

"You want some privacy?" Bob the photographer calls from the doorway directly behind him. Ritchie spins around, startled. Now he is boxed in and can't run away.

"What exactly is this shoot for?" Ritchie asks weakly.

"It's a mock ad," the fat man explains. "It's a giant box of detergent marked FREEDOM and it's crushing a woman in a burka."

"Okay." Ritchie blinks a couple of times. "I don't get it."

"You're the woman!"

"No, I'm not."

"Nobody will be able to tell," the photographer blurts. "We just needed someone—"

"Not me."

"It's a big burka," he whines. "We needed a guy. Your face is almost completely covered. Don't make me call the talent agency again. I'm supposed to have this done by 3 o'clock."

Ritchie examines the costume a second time. He thinks of next month's cell bill and the forty dollars he owes Joshua from the last time they went out and Joshua paid the cover at the Catch One disco.

"Okay," Ritchie says dejectedly, kicking off his shoes to change. "Close the door behind me."

Five minutes later he is lying on the dirty carpet in the magazine office lobby, flat on his back with his legs twisted to the side, trying to method-act pain and suffering.

The photographer gives him directions, but Ritchie doesn't hear much of what the man says because his head is covered by the costume.

Ritchie works the paycheck math again in silent humiliation.

"How long do you think this will take?" he asks the photographer, whom he cannot see.

"What? You're all covered up."

"How...long...will...this...take?" Ritchie hollers from within his fabric confines. He is claustrophobic and starting to itch.

"We're done," the man says.

Ritchie sits up and twists the cloth off his head, spitting wool fluff and wiping his mouth with the back of his hand.

"We're done already?" he asks, incredulous.

"I just needed a couple of shots."

"Oh." Ritchie does quick multiplication. Seventy-five dollars minus parking equals—"Do you validate parking?"

"Sorry," the fat man says, and offers a ruddy faced, toothy grin that makes Ritchie squeeze and unsqueeze his fist in a long-buried, automatic compulsion to smack the guy in the face.

The bedroom phone rings at Freddy's place. He rolls over and picks it up. It is dusk and he was half asleep, alone in his apartment.

"You told me to call you," Claire says flatly after Freddy greets her. "So I am."

"Okay."

The line is silent.

"Is that it?" Freddy asks.

"Pretty much. Are you writing?"

"No."

"How come?"

"Him. We were talking a lot. He just went out to get more cigarettes."

"So write now," Claire instructs.

"Can't."

"How come?"

"Claire! Leave me alone," Freddy says uncomfortably.

"You were the one who said to check in—"

"I'm busy. Call you later."

Freddy hangs up before a fight can start. He goes to the bathroom and wonders how it could possibly take an hour and a half for Justin to go to the end of the block for Marlboros. He returns to the bedroom and picks up the phone. Claire answers after the second ring.

"What's the matter with you?" Freddy asks before she even says hello.

"What's the matter with *you?*" Claire's voice is edgy.

"Look, I'm coming over."

"What about Justin?"

"I gave him a key."

"I don't really feel like company."

"I'll be there in ten minutes."

Freddy grabs a ball cap and jacket and heads out.

Claire opens the door without a smile when he gets there. She's got on the men's pajamas Freddy bought her two Christmases ago, which he would take as a compliment if she wasn't also wearing such a sour expression.

"You look like your dog died," Freddy informs her.

Hearing her name called, Dog barks cheerily and bounds across the room to greet Freddy. She licks his hand with her purple tongue.

Claire goes to the sofa and sits heavily. The coffee table is littered with newspapers, dirty plates, and cups. There is an empty wine bottle and an old chipped Peanuts mug that Freddy recalls having belonged to Lisbeth.

Claire drinking merlot from Snoopy's head is not a good sign.

Next to the mug is an old hardcover book titled *Satyagraha: Finding Your Peace*—another bad indicator. Freddy follows Claire, moving aside last week's *New York Times Magazine* from the cushion to make space for himself.

"Is it Hugh?" he asks delicately, sitting down.

"He won't leave me alone," Claire starts in. "I mean, can't men take a hint?"

"Well, you're so subtle—"

"I accidentally smacked him in the mouth the last time we were together, and on purpose I didn't apologize."

"I'd think he'd get it."

"But the worst thing is I called my mom and told her about it all. According to her, I'm leading Hugh on—"

"No!" Freddy feigns shock.

"And she said I've always been a vixen." Claire is getting worked up. "I mean she actually used that word."

"When was the last time you saw Hugh?"

"I'm not a vixen," Claire insists. "Because I sleep with a guy, she assumes—I saw him two days ago."

"*Why?* I thought you were trying to distance yourself—"

"I went over there to ask him politely to stop calling me," she says defensively.

"That's not a mixed message, is it?"

"My own mother says this is my fault. If anybody's going to take my side, it should be her."

"How long were you at his house?" Freddy is appalled and can't move beyond this. "Please tell me you didn't you have sex with him—"

"Then she hung up on me. My *mother*!" Claire looks pained. "And of course I didn't have sex with him! What are you, crazy? I was there maybe half an hour, forty-five minutes tops."

"Claire, you should just ignore him—"

"So then he keeps calling." She is feels herself begin to ramble. "And I try and be nice and tell him to stop, but—"

"Don't answer the phone," Freddy enjoins.

"My mother said I've been this way since high school. She dismissed me. She *hung up*!"

"Take a deep breath."

Claire looks at him, injured.

"This is my own mother we're talking about. *You* take a deep breath."

Freddy mulls how to proceed.

"She may have been harsh," he says more quietly. "But that's how mothers—"

"When I needed her to be there, she dumped me."

"Because she thinks you didn't dump Hugh," Freddy says, steering in a more sympathetic direction, "when in truth you did."

"Not the way she wanted me to. Which is always how it works with her. If I don't do things like she would, it's no good at all. But she's never hung up on me."

"Claire..." he says softly, taking her hands.

"I don't think I want to talk to her ever again."

"Be reasonable," Freddy begs.

"That's her job."

"Fair enough. But I love you too. What can I do?"

Claire's eyes well with tears.

"Don't hang up on me," she whispers. "Don't leave me."

"Never," Freddy promises, pulling her into an embrace and rocking her gently.

The next evening, Joshua parks on the street in front of Claire's and puts on his flashers so he won't get a ticket while nabbing one of the parking permits that hang on a nail inside her front door.

As he approaches the house, he smells garlic and cooking meat. Claire must already be deep in the preparation of flank steak. Everyone has their own therapy, their own shortcut to Zen. Cooking is Claire's way of getting sane.

Before Joshua can get to the door, Ritchie pulls in and parks behind him—their timing is always impeccable—and honks to signal Joshua that he's there.

Once they are inside and the issue of parking passes has been settled, they help themselves to almonds from a bowl on the table. Ritchie exclaims over a giant vase of stargazer lilies that make the living room smell sweet.

"They're from Freddy," Claire brags, brushing the hair out of her eyes and wiping her hands on the dishtowel she's carrying. She seems happy, if a little manic. Freddy told Joshua that Claire's having boyfriend troubles and family troubles at the same time, so Joshua figures it's understandable for her to be a little cockeyed.

Lisbeth is here tonight, smiling, flushed, and reticent about what's going on in her life.

"I'm fine, thanks," she replies when Joshua asks.

"How fine?" Joshua probes.

She shrugs. "Fine, I guess."

Dinner is supposed to be at 7. When 7:15 arrives, all the familiar food is set out and steaming. But Freddy still isn't there. Claire suggests they start to eat.

"He'll get here when he gets here," she says as if tardiness was in some way normal for Freddy. To the contrary, Freddy is the kind of guy who would show up an hour early for his own funeral.

Ritchie shrugs, needing no more encouragement than this, and starts loading his plate with steak, grilled corn on the cob, and mango salad. Obviously he is carbo-loading. Slivered scallions tumble off his strips of pink-centered steak and various juices pool deliciously in the middle of his plate. He digs in, making exaggerated closed-mouth *mm*s of appreciation. Joshua smiles, imagining Ritchie as a kid doing the same thing with his mother's Italian cooking.

It is 8 o'clock when Freddy arrives with his new boyfriend Justin in tow. This is the first time Joshua's seen Justin in person. Any oddness Claire may be exhibiting is immediately overshadowed by the enormous peculiarity of Justin's demeanor. He enters the room flashing a wide smile and shaking everyone's hand. But as soon as it seems nobody is looking at him, he takes on the appearance of a hunted animal, eyes darting, fingers fidgeting as if he'd as soon leave his own body if it were possible.

"What is this?" he asks, cocking his ear toward the source of the music Claire is playing.

"Norah Jones," Claire replies, handing him the CD case and gesturing toward the stereo. Joshua approaches it cautiously and stares at the display on the CD player.

"Yes," he says, transfixed. He picks up the remote and holds down the "review" button for a moment so the song's chorus repeats.

"Yes," he says again.

Having seen enough craziness the moment, Joshua turns his attention to dinner. He loads his plate and pokes at the salad, which is just starting to wilt in the pleasant way it does once the lettuce begins to absorb the balsamic vinegar. For all of Claire's ups and downs, there is little variation in the quality of her cooking—it is always great.

Joshua sits in a large, white-painted Cape Cod chair on the concrete porch outside Claire's dining room. It is dark out, and the back yard is faintly illuminated by the glow of the lights from the house. Soon, the weather will turn and it will be too cold to stay outside for any length of time in the evening without a jacket. Even now it is cool. Joshua balances his plate on his lap, and tucks his napkin into the neck of his open shirt. Gingerly, he cuts his steak with a serrated knife and tastes it.

Through the open French doors, he can see Justin, who has found the remote control for the CD player and is standing by himself in front of the stereo, riveted, letting the same snippet of music play again and again before scanning the disc backward in jerky bits and reviewing it. Someone has given Justin a glass of red wine, which he holds in his free hand and swallows in gulps in between the fragments of song. After repeating this series of movements several times, he holds down the back-scan button and begins to rewind the whole album. A few moments later Lisbeth walks into the living room, silently takes the remote control out of Justin's hand, smiles at him, and goes back to whatever she had been doing. The music plays normally again. Justin looks up at her for a moment, hurt, then is absorbed once again in the workings of the CD player.

"Come sit with me," Joshua instructs Freddy, who is standing just beyond the open doorway, loading his plate. Freddy comes out on the porch and drags over a second chair that matches the one Joshua occupies.

"How have you been?" Joshua asks, noticing that Freddy looks a little pale, even in this light.

"It's been a tough few days," Freddy admits with a little smile that tries to make everything okay but can't quite. "Yesterday I came over to talk to Claire and left him alone to go to the market on the corner. When I got home he was outside the door waiting. He lost his key. I don't think he knew what time it was. You know what I mean?"

"Freddy," Joshua begins cautiously, unsure of how much he should say. "You know you're one of my best friends, right?"

Freddy nods.

"And you know I'd do anything to protect you."

Freddy nods again, this time adding a shrug.

Joshua considers how to proceed. Feelings must be spared, but Freddy's got to know the truth. Another of Joshua's exes used crystal meth, among other things, when he was sick. It made him crazy. Then, along with AIDS, it made him dead. Joshua does not feel kindly toward the drug.

"I've been around meth before," he says. "It's no joke."

"What do you want me to do?" Freddy asks.

"It doesn't take a Ph.D. to see that your new boyfriend is messed up." Joshua starts to get emotional. "Or let me be more specific—he's not just using crystal, he's a bona fide junky."

Freddy is taciturn, staring down at his plate. He drags a scallion around in a little circle with the tip of his steak knife.

"I don't know what I'm supposed to do," he says at last. "He's amazing."

"There's no good end to this story," Joshua warns, torn between saying too much and not warning Freddy of inevitable consequences. "You have to get him to quit."

"That's too big. Even the little things are tough right now. You can't imagine how hard it was to get him over here. He doesn't want to meet new people. He's scared, I guess. He was sitting in the corner of the room, and I had to trick him to get him to come—I told him we were going to get cigarettes then go to the Ringling Brothers circus where there are lions. Once we left, I conveniently remembered we were supposed to come over for dinner."

They both look in at Justin, who has made friends with Dog and is patting her rhythmically on the head in time with the music.

"Then when I got here, he said he would wait in the car for however long dinner took. So I told him there were cigarettes inside. Actually, I'll bet Lisbeth has some."

Joshua sees the humor in this, but the whole situation doesn't sit right with him.

"Freddy, you have to be careful."

Freddy nods, but clearly the conversation is done. Claire comes out and reprimands them for sitting outside.

"You'll catch a cold."

"That's an old wives' tale," Joshua objects.

"I'm a doctor," Claire reminds him. "And it's almost time for Scrabble."

Scrabble is Claire's favorite game. The rest of them tolerate it well, but none derives the sort of overwhelming pleasure from it that she seems to. She loves words. More correctly, she loves big words. And she seems to know lots of them. She usually wins by a large margin, which may be the key to why she is so passionate about the game.

"Finish your dinner," she instructs.

"It's delicious," Freddy says obligatorily, though it's very true. He takes a large bite of salad as if to demonstrate his appreciation. Claire is pleased.

Ten minutes later they are all gathered around the dining room table, except for Justin, who begged off hoarsely and is sitting to the side, staring intently at the tree branch cracks that Claire's wall earned in the last good earthquake. Lisbeth has had too much to drink. Claire seems to have as well, which doesn't perturb Joshua at this point, because it will give him a better handicap at the game.

They hand around the trays and each player pulls seven letters out of the velvet bag that came with Claire's deluxe Scrabble set. She is very proud of the set—both its quality and the bargain price for which she acquired it—and sometimes lords it over her friends. Joshua forgives her, as does Freddy. Joshua's not sure if Ritchie notices her pridefulness.

Joshua gets the Q which he knows is useless without a U and will sit in his tray like a canister of toxic waste until he gets a lucky draw and can spell *queen* or *queer. Quiet*—that would be good also.

Freddy goes first. He puts down the word *battle.* Claire keeps score, tallying on a narrow pad that also came with her game set. Joshua looks over his letters, coming up with *loyalty* and nearly clearing his tray. Claire congratulates Joshua but doesn't actually seem pleased. It is Ritchie's turn. He frets a bit, then spells *top.* Claire likes this. Lisbeth branches off Freddy's word and lays down *ambush.*

Justin seems discontent, gets up, and starts wandering the living room and hallway like a ghost. Freddy looks up after him warily, but his attention soon returns to the game.

Finally, it's Claire's turn. Tile by tile, she spells out *amasatoy,* laying the final letter atop the Y from Freddy's word.

"Uh-*mass*-uh-toy," she says, delighted.

"What does that mean?" Ritchie asks unexpectedly.

Claire's eyebrows rise and she looks slightly panicked.

"It-it's a Thai cooking term," she assures him. "But it's in common usage now."

"I've never heard of it," he persists.

Freddy looks as though he's about to fall out of his chair with surprise.

"Are you challenging me?" Claire wants to know, her voice suddenly deeper. Her eyes dart down to the dictionary for a moment then are back on Ritchie. Her face is growing red, and it's not from the wine.

"Perhaps you mean *satay*—s-a-t-a-y," Ritchie suggests in a baffling display of bravado.

Claire shakes her head resolutely no, and asks again, "Are you challenging me?"

Everyone is silent. There is an appreciable tension in the room. Claire and Ritchie stare at each other for a moment. Then he lets out a little cough.

"No," Ritchie says, backing down. The standoff is over. Claire smiles, tallies her own score, and pulls new letters from the bag.

A number of rounds and three quarters of a chocolate truffle cake later, Claire is the winner of the game, as usual. She is quiet in her victory, composed, almost smug.

Joshua helps her clear the table from dessert and follows her with the plates and forks to the kitchen, where Claire starts washing dishes.

"You cheated," Joshua says once he's certain they are alone.

"I don't know what you're talking about," Claire says so offhandedly that it's clear she does. Her rubber gloves are soapy and steaming.

"That word—the Thai thing. You made that up."

"It's not cheating, it's strategy."

"Claire—"

"Look," she says shrilly, "if he's too dumb to realize he's been had, then he deserves it. It's like taking candy from a baby—one too stupid to realize his lollipop's missing."

Joshua watches her for a moment. "Are things that bad for you?" he asks.

Claire puts down the plate she's scrubbing and turns to him, her gloves dripping dishwater on the floor. Her face is hard. Neither of them moves until Joshua picks up a sackcloth towel and hands it to her slowly.

She takes it, wiping her gloves.

Her jaw is set but her eyes give her away—they are rimmed with damp redness.

She turns her face from him and plunges her hands back into the sudsy water. Joshua knows she will not answer his question.

"Dinner was lovely," he says, turning to go.

Lisbeth and Ritchie are laughing in the other room. For some reason, Justin is barking like a puppy. Maybe he's trying to rile Dog. If so, it's not working.

It is late. Joshua stifles a yawn. He has a conference call at 7 A.M. tomorrow with a cable network in New York about Mamie Redbird appearing on a celebrity hobby show he's never heard of. It should be interesting trying to get her to plant crocuses or visit sick children for the cameras. Hearing Justin yapping and panting from the other side of the house, Ritchie is reminded of the difficulty of teaching old dogs new tricks.

He is at the kitchen doorway. He pauses there, changes direction, walks over to Claire and gives her a gentle kiss on her shoulder.

"Goodnight," he whispers.

"I love you," she says softly, but will not turn around.

ELEVEN

"Girls glow. Boys perspire. Horses sweat."

Joshua thinks of his seventh grade gym teacher's dictums on hygiene as he stands in line at Koo Koo Roo to buy skinless chicken breast and baked yam. He has just finished working out at the gym and has definitely perspired. He is uncomfortable with sweat, or "perspiration," if one is to accept old Mr. Henson's terminology. Joshua gets damp when he works out, and the funk of his armpits and private parts reminds him grimly of puberty and sitting in the car with his mother when he was wearing shorts.

"Look!" she exclaimed. "You've got big-boy hairs on your legs!"

He wanted to be invisible then, or perhaps be the victim of a sudden, steel-shearing collision in which his side of the car was ripped from the other and somehow, magically, he would survive and never see his mother again.

Now he smells himself, not funky but clearly mannish, and tries to focus on the menu board in front of him. He is third in line. There are two registers with pleasant high school girls in bright red aprons taking orders and dispensing change.

"Next?" one of the girls in front of him finally says. Joshua steps forward.

"I'll have two breasts and two side orders, um..." He looks over the steaming glass display case at potatoes, green beans, macaroni and cheese, trying to decide.

"Next customer?" the other counter girl says. A man steps from behind Joshua to start ordering.

On instinct, Joshua turns to look at him. The guy is tall—maybe six-foot-five—lean and muscular. He has almond-shaped eyes, a somewhat aquiline nose, absurdly clear skin and jet-black hair tousled in precise disarray. Joshua is aware that he is staring and makes no effort to stop himself. It would be pointless anyhow.

"Rotisserie chicken breast," the man tells the counter girl in front of him. His voice is a sweetly husky tenor with clean, nicely developed consonants. "I'll take that with roasted potatoes and creamed spinach."

"Sir?" Joshua's girl prompts.

"Uh," Joshua stammers, but he can't speak. He is in the presence of beauty and it has stolen his reason. He feels himself flush hot all over. His hands tingle and he thinks for a moment he will have to steady himself by grabbing the counter.

Then a miracle occurs. The tall stranger glances at Joshua, his face brightens beyond its already angelic expression, and he winks. He shifts his weight from one foot to the other, reminding Joshua of a champion thoroughbred before it bursts from the gate.

Before he can catch himself, Joshua shudders. Then he wonders if the guy was actually winking at him, or if perhaps there is someone standing immediately behind Joshua and he's a big dope to think someone so remarkably beautiful would pay him the time of day. But they are too close for that to be the case; it would require a turn of the head. Impulsively, Joshua winks back at the man, and the stranger smiles. Now there's no mistaking the flirtation.

"Sir?" Joshua's cashier asks.

"Sorry!" he apologizes, flustered. "I'll have...whatever *he* ordered."

The counter girl seems surprised, but looks over at the register next to hers and rings the order.

"Is that for here or to go?" the stranger's cashier inquires.

"For here," the tall man says and gives Joshua an obvious look. "*Definitely* for here."

"And you? Here or to go?" Joshua's girl asks flatly. She either disapproves of the flirtation or is oblivious to it. To stay or to go...Joshua glances at his watch. He is supposed to meet a potential client in forty-five minutes and wants to get home and shower beforehand.

"For here?" he tries, as though by approaching the notion gently, he can indulge it without waking himself to its illogic.

In tandem, the cashiers ring the totals. Both men dig bills and coins from their pockets and move to the pickup window for their food. Joshua's chicken is ready first. He takes his tray and scans the tables of the restaurant for one with plenty of open seating nearby.

He finds a spot facing the back of the restaurant. Moments later, the stranger eases into a chair at the next table facing the opposite direction. Each man ignores the other, but Joshua is keenly aware of every movement, shift, and glance the stranger makes. He feels himself similarly scrutinized.

"I'm Timothy," the guy says after each of them has taken several self-conscious bites. His torso is so tall that his long forearms lie on the table and still seem to rest at his sides. "Timothy Lee."

Joshua melts. What a perfect name.

The sound of it resonates like a melody in Joshua's mind for the next day and a half. At Noble's on Saturday morning, he tells the story to Claire, Freddy, and Ritchie.

"Great," Claire deadpans. "Now you're both dating singers."

"I'm not dating him!" Joshua insists. "We've just met. I hardly know him."

"The lady doth protest too much," Claire observes, clearly pleased with her own cleverness.

"I do want to have his babies though," he concedes.

"Aha!" Claire capitalizes. "That's a sure sign."

"Of what?" Ritchie asks.

"Of wanting to be more than friends," Claire explains. "Unless he has astonishing genetics."

"That too," Joshua says, very nearly blushing.

"So when are you seeing him again?" Ritchie wants to know.

"Tomorrow night, if he's done at the studio. The record label has him on deadline to finish three tracks so they can listen and decide if they're going to commit to a whole album. It's a critical time for Timothy."

"You certainly got to know him well over one meal."

"One meal plus tea." Joshua recounts walking with Timothy down the street from Koo Koo Roo to a little Russian diner. They sat under the watchful scrutiny of the owner, a woman of indeterminate age...the body of a child's spinning top, hair as bleached and ruined and driftwood, and drawn-on eyebrows that gave her a look of constant surprise. Timothy and Joshua leaned across the table and sipped tea, shared their life stories, and played footsie under the table.

"How out is he?" Ritchie asks hypocritically.

"Not so out," Joshua allows. "But it's fine with me because I'm a publicist, after all, and I'm used to keeping people's business private."

"Nice try." Claire is skeptical. "Wait until the first time you want to hold his hand in public. Then we'll see how much you like having a closeted boyfriend."

"He's not closeted, he's just—not out."

"Same difference."

"Is he really worried about it because of work?" asks Ritchie. "Or is that an excuse for him not liking himself?"

"What I know is that *I* like him—"

"Clearly, based on your description," Claire remarks.

"Well?" Joshua asks, wondering what else she wants.

"Good for you." Claire says after a moment, seeming to speak for the group. "We look forward to meeting him—"

"Only maybe not right away." Joshua steels himself for Claire's comeback.

But Claire is done with the subject. She sighs, takes a sip of coffee, and turns to Freddy, who has been poking at sunny side up eggs, glum-faced, while the yolks slowly congeal.

"Why are you so quiet? And you look like hell, by the way." She is too harsh, as usual, but correct, and Joshua is glad she asked. It relieves him of having to broach the subject.

"Where's Justin?" Ritchie adds.

"Home," Freddy says unhappily. "He's been here for two

weeks now and the only thing he'll leave the house for is cigarettes or sometimes a walk late at night."

"Maybe he's a vampire," Claire speculates.

"Maybe you should shut up," he snaps, then covers his mouth and looks horrified. "I-I'm sorry."

Claire sniffs. "It's okay," she says aloofly. It's clear that with one sentence Freddy has put himself on probation with her and had better be nice for the rest of breakfast or he'll get a scolding.

Ritchie stands at his bathroom mirror and stares at his hair, turning his head from side to side. If he tugs on the tips of his bangs and straightens out the curl, it reaches his lips. It seems as though, just a few weeks ago, his hair was only to the tip of his nose.

"I have something very serious to tell you," he admonishes his reflection. "Your sister's injury was no accident. There was someone else on that roof. You have a twin, Jesse."

He sees himself on a big-time soap opera. The camera zooms in, music swells, and he looks his reflection in the eye, trying to come up with tears. He tries the line again:

"There was someone else on that roof." It has to be more menacing. "There was someone *else* on that roof!"

The third time through, Ritchie is satisfied with his line reading. He sprays some aromatherapy grease on his hair and fiddles with it so that it looks like he just rolled out of bed, but in a good way. The zipper on his purple trainer's jacket requires some experimenting—closed all the way looks dorky, but unzipped to his sternum, his chest bulges immodestly and it reminds him of how his uncle Sylvester used to wear his leisure shirts when he put on aftershave and went looking for girls.

Ritchie checks the bathroom clock. There is no time for further primping. He has a client in ten minutes at the gym. He grabs his keys to go, and just as he is about to pull the front door closed behind him, the phone rings. He stops and debates whether to answer it. Curiosity gets the better of him and he grabs for the cordless handset.

"Hello?" he says, slightly out of breath.

"Ritchie—it's J.W."

"Hey, man, how's it going?"

"Good. I want you to know I've been thinking about you a lot lately."

"Thanks! I was wondering if you were going to call. I mean, I didn't want to bug you at your office."

"No worries. Listen, I'm signing up for a series of training sessions with you at the gym. I gotta get rid of an inch or two around my waist before Oscars. I don't want to walk the red carpet looking like a whale."

"We can do that."

"And another thing. I'm really curious how you read. I want to bring you a script and have you learn a monologue. It'll give me a better sense of what to do with you."

"You can do anything with me you want," Ritchie blurts. Then he cringes, realizing the implication. J.W. acts as though he hasn't noticed.

"Great," he says. "I'll see you at the gym this week."

"Awesome," Ritchie exclaims, hanging up the phone and dashing out the door. In his glee, he very nearly tumbles down the front steps of the apartment building.

Once he's on the sidewalk, his footing recovered, he yelps for joy and jogs off in the direction of the gym.

"Remind me—how did we meet people for dating before the Internet?" Claire asks. She lies flat on her back on the sofa. Freddy is on his back too, though he's sprawled a little awkwardly on Claire's love seat, which doesn't quite support the length of his frame. She turns and looks at him and smiles privately at the awkwardness of his posture.

"There used to be this restaurant," Freddy recalls. "It was a few blocks down from Noble's. They called it Chit Chat and there were old desktop telephones on the tables. Each one had a number, and you could dial up other tables and hit on people."

"How was the food?" Claire asks. She can't remember the place.

"I have no recollection. I went there twice and got laid twice, which is all that mattered to me at the time. I was 24."

"A hundred years ago," Claire agrees. "You can't be expected to remember details."

"Thanks for that."

They are quiet for a moment. It's fairly late. They've watched a movie on video, eaten microwave popcorn, and consumed most of a two-liter bottle of Diet Coke, which Claire disallows her patients and will only drink in front of Freddy and a select few others whom she feels can keep a confidence.

Tonight is a break both she and Freddy needed. Justin, the crazy drug addict, has worn Freddy thin. He's not writing, he's not sleeping, and Claire is worried. Freddy doesn't look good. Her initial endorsement of Justin is long annulled. She knows not to press Freddy on the issue. A man possessed will inevitably follow the siren that has him hooked, words of reason will be rejected, and those who speak then will be cast aside in the process.

Claire doesn't want to be cast aside. Her mother has already left her wounded, and if Freddy were to reject her as well, it might be more than Claire could bear. Especially in light of the very strange greetings card sitting beside her on the coffee table.

"This is nice," she says, noticing the way the shifting glow of the fireplace makes shadows dance gently across the ceiling. "You needed to get out of the house."

"We both needed a break," he agrees. "Hey—can I see that card again? It's just so weird."

Claire retrieves the Hallmark and hands it to Freddy. It is addressed to Hugh, and has Claire's own address in the upper left hand corner. The writing is not hers, though, which makes sense because she never saw the card or its envelope before it arrived in her mailbox today with "return to sender" written across the front in red pen in Hugh's shaky hand.

Inside, he wrote, "I want you completely, love Claire." Claire surmises Hugh wrote the card, sent it to himself, then dropped it back in a mailbox with the rejection message.

"It's just so...psychotic," Freddy says, flipping the card over and examining all sides.

Claire's grim silence speaks her agreement. Freddy kisses her goodnight on the cheek and they both wish each other well.

The next day, while Claire is home from the office for a quick bite of lunch, the mailman brings another surprise. This time it is an envelope from Hugh, addressed normally, with a personal check for $100,000 inside along with a note that reads "This is a down payment on our life. I will be with you and Lisbeth and Dog forever."

Claire lets go of the paper and the check, which flutter to the floor of Claire's tiled foyer. She looks down at them as if they might attack her. She leans against the wall, her strength sapped. Dog approaches, huffing and tail wagging to see what is wrong with her mommy. Claire looks down at her and shakes her head no.

The sun is streaming through the blinds, traffic on the street zipping by. Claire imagines Hugh outside, peeping and peering. She goes to the front window and twists the rod so that the stripes of sunlight on the sofa grow thin and eventually disappear.

The telephone rings. Claire goes and gets it numbly.

"Hello?" she mumbles.

"Good afternoon," Hugh says crisply.

Claire cringes.

"Please," she whimpers before she hangs up on him, "leave me alone."

Freddy stands in front of the open refrigerator and tries to decide what to eat. He is almost out of cheese; there is not enough to make quesadillas. Tuna sandwiches would do, but he is out of mayonnaise. It's official: He must go shopping tomorrow.

There is a jar of marinara on the second shelf in the back. It is from three days ago and still mostly full, so he decides that dinner will be linguini with "used" sauce. Freddy takes out a large pan, runs water, and turns to the stove to set it to boil. But there is something wrong. There are no knobs on the stove, just holes where they should be attached.

"Justin," he calls without turning around.

There is no answer.

"Justin!" he hollers. With the continued silence, he sets the pot on the counter and goes to the bedroom, where he finds Justin crouched over a pad and paper making odd geometric patterns.

"Where are the stove knobs?"

Justin looks up at him as if Freddy's speaking gibberish.

"I know you know where they are," Freddy says testily.

"There's been nobody here but you and me. And I didn't take them."

Justin opens his mouth as if to speak, but seems baffled. He shrugs.

Freddy looks around. The knobs are nowhere in immediate sight.

"C'mon. We're eating out."

Warily, Justin shakes his head no.

"That wasn't a question," Freddy tells him. "It was a statement."

He calls Joshua, who agrees to meet them in fifteen minutes at Johnny Rocket's. It is a small chore getting Justin out of the apartment and into the car, but Freddy manages.

Joshua is waiting when they arrive, standing beneath a public address speaker playing Christmas tunes far too early in the season.

"You want to sit inside or out?" Joshua asks.

In reply, Justin pulls out a cigarette, waving it like a flag.

"So, out, then."

"I'm sorry," Freddy apologizes. Winter is coming. It is chilly tonight. And despite the large collection of sweaters that fill the shelves of Joshua's closet, he has come out in an oxford and jeans. It will be uncomfortably cool for him.

Justin makes a beeline for a table on the patio, lighting his cigarette on his way.

"Do you want to borrow my jacket?" Freddy asks Joshua, unzipping his Abercrombie hoodie. He'd rather suffer than subject Joshua to the pains of Justin's idiosyncrasy. But Joshua waves him off. To avoid a battle of politeness, Freddy shrugs and acquiesces.

They follow Justin and sit at the table where he's deposited himself. There are strings of Christmas lights hanging from poles the mall has erected. It reminds Freddy of a used car lot.

A waiter comes by with menus and water.

Justin seems fascinated by his own jacket, a pilfered bomber from Freddy's closet with the Paramount Studios logo embroidered on the back. He fusses with the sleeves, flailing as if the jacket is molesting him. Then he growls and lets out a stream of garbled obscenity.

"Justin!" Freddy cautions, glancing over to the next table where an overweight family sits eating hamburgers, "Watch your mouth. There are kids around."

Justin clucks sarcastically, fumbles with his lighter, and tries to rekindle his cigarette, which has gone out. Once he has succeeded and taken in another long draw of smoke, he seems calmer. Freddy watches queasily. He glances over at Joshua, who looks even more disturbed than he is.

"So, how are things at work?" Freddy asks, seizing on the first thing that enters his mind. It's an unnecessary question. He talked to Joshua this afternoon and knows perfectly well the proceedings of his day.

"Fine, thanks," Joshua plays along as if by rote. "The usual."

Justin yaps again. Freddy flinches.

"I'm going to the bathroom," Justin announces angrily. He is out of his chair and gone.

"He was talking to his jacket," Joshua says once Justin's out of earshot. "That's very, very weird."

Freddy's body feels extra heavy. He looks down at the table. He wants to say something to Joshua to justify Justin's behavior, but there is no good excuse. So he looks up at Joshua and nods slowly.

"It's gotten worse, huh?" Joshua asks.

"The other day," Freddy admits, "he took the dustpan and all my napkin rings and made this weird, meticulous sculpture out of them. It reminded me of a crop circle. I don't know whether to throw him out or get him a commission at MOMA."

They both smile at this, but they are interrupted by an unmistakable voice singing "Ave Maria" from nearby. Apparently, Justin did not go the bathroom after all. Freddy turns to look, fearing the worst. Justin is standing at the far edge of the patio, absurdly serenading the passing traffic:

> Mary, pray for us
> Pray for us sinners
> Now and in the hour of our death...
> *In ora mortis nostre.*

It is a slow, breathtaking telling of the song. Justin's voice is clear and mournful, his vibrato perfectly placed, his phrasing unhurried. When he is done, a bearded homeless man across the street bangs the wheels of his shopping cart in appreciation, then applauds broadly, flapping the sleeves of his dirty coat like a seal. Justin turns to Freddy, eyes aglow. His face is open and young, the creases gone.

"Holy fuck," Joshua says quietly, clearly astonished.

"Told you," Freddy tells him. "Now you understand."

Justin comes back to the table and sits down as if nothing unusual has happened. The waiter brings their food and Justin plows hungrily into the fries, upending a bottle of ketchup over them until they are drowned. He takes several enthusiastic bites then turns and gives Freddy a happy, ketchupy kiss on the cheek.

When the check comes, Freddy reaches for his wallet, but Joshua grabs the piece of paper out of his hand.

"Oh, no," Joshua says. "This one's on me."

Freddy and Justin drive back to the apartment.

"Look at those planes," Justin says, pointing at the dozen or so points of light hovering above the eastern horizon. Some blink on and off. "Where are they going?"

"LAX," Freddy answers. "They're landing."

"Guiding the wise men," Justin muses.

"Except," Freddy adds, "anyone who followed them would end up crushed on an airstrip next to the 405 Freeway."

They both laugh and Justin kisses him again, this time more sensually and minus the ketchup.

Passing through the dining room, Freddy discovers the knobs from the stove arranged on the floor along with several matchbooks and a handful of Brachs starlight mints in a meticulous, serpentine S extending from one corner.

"Did you do this?" he asks Justin, who has just hung his jacket over the back of a chair.

Justin looks at him brutishly, which Freddy takes as an admission of guilt.

"There's something we have to talk about," Freddy says, sitting down. He's reluctant to break the spell of pleasantness, aware that he may be dashing any hope of getting into Justin's pants tonight.

Justin turns, stoop shouldered, to leave the room.

"No," Freddy commands as Justin reaches the doorway. "Come here."

Reluctantly, Justin returns and takes a seat across the table.

"You're too isolated," Freddy begins.

"Maybe," Justin allows. "But you have it easier than me."

"How so?"

"You don't know how good you've got it! You have your friends. And you go see them every Saturday at that place on the corner of Third and Heaven and it all just flows. I've never had that, not in my entire life. You have no idea how much I'd give just to know what it feels like."

"There's a doctor I want you to see," Freddy says, thinking of the number he wrote on a pad next to the phone, a referral from Claire. "A shrink."

Justin freezes. "No."

"Yes."

Justin shakes his head sadly and looks as though he may cry. "No..."

Slowly, Freddy nods yes.

"Don't send me back there," Justin pleads in a voice that is barely audible, folding his hands on the table and leaning forward to lay his cheek on them.

Freddy is stunned. Nonetheless, he gets up, walks to the far side of the room, and drops to his knees in back of Justin, hugging him from behind. He stays there a long while before getting up to prepare for bed.

Two days later, they are in the lobby of the psychiatrist's office. Freddy is not happy about ponying up a hundred and fifty dollars an hour, but it seems worth it to find out if there's something wrong inside Justin's head.

The doctor, who turns out to be nattily dressed and probably gay, opens the door to his private office and ushers Justin in. At the doorway, Justin turns around and looks at Freddy, scared.

"You want me to come along?" Freddy asks, setting down the *National Geographic* he's been reading.

"Yeah," Justin says in a little voice. He looks relieved when Freddy gets up and follows him.

"Is it okay?" Freddy asks the doctor.

"You're the one who's paying for the session," the shrink reminds him.

Inside, Justin answers the doctor's questions directly and seems maddeningly sane for the first thirty minutes or so. Freddy begins to think he's wasted his money and resents Justin for not being crazier on cue.

But a shift occurs. Justin seems a little more relaxed, uncrossing his arms and sinking back into the doctor's plush sofa. He starts talking about his recently discovered awareness of patterns and hidden messages in the arrangement of flooring tile and automobile traffic.

"So you've been treated before?" the shrink asks.

"For crystal. I got dehydrated."

"But not for any mental conditions?"

"He tried to put me on Valium—the doctor."

"Did you take it?"

"Of course!"

"But never an antipsychotic?"

Freddy wonders where this is leading.

"I'm not psychotic—"

"Yes," the doctor says with a tactful smile, "you are."

"Am not—"

"I've been treating patients for ten years. Trust me, I know psychotic."

"How dare you call me crazy!" Justin is piqued.

"Not crazy, ill. There's nothing to be ashamed about."

Justin turns to Freddy for reinforcement. Freddy, relieved not to feel like the bad guy for the first time in a while, shrugs in reply.

"There are some very simple ways we can address this," the shrink says, reaching for a prescription pad from his desk. "You're both intelligent guys, so I'll be direct with this. We don't know if crystal meth caused the psychosis or if you're simply self-medicating to address the symptoms of underlying illness."

"I'm not psychotic," Justin says again, but he is losing steam.

"So we go after it from both ends. You stop using meth effective now, and I'm going to write a prescription for an antipsychotic that may make you drowsy for the first few days, but your body will catch up with it. At the end of the week, when I see you again, you should be fine."

"I don't want to take something that will mess with my brain."

"Trust me, it's mild compared to what you're doing to your brain now."

"Will I quit seeing things?"

"That's the point."

"I don't wanna."

The doctor weighs this, his brow knit. "You *like* your hallucinations?"

"I see patterns."

"And you consider this useful?"

"Vital," Justin replies.

"Try the meds," the doctors says, trying a different approach. "If you hate the way you feel, you can stop."

Justin is silent, thinking about it.

"Okay..." he says tentatively.

There is no conversation on the drive home from Beverly Hills, except for when Freddy phones the prescription in to the pharmacy. He drops Justin off at the apartment so he can go out and run errands.

"You sure you have your key?" Freddy asks before he pulls away.

Justin smiles and nods, waving Freddy goodbye. Freddy pulls out from the curb.

"Hey!" Justin calls after him.

Freddy stops short. "Yeah?"

"Thank you," Justin says meekly. "For today."

Freddy nods. They are both still, looking at each other in a moment of longing. Then Freddy steps on the gas. After a few moments he looks in the rear view mirror. Justin is still standing on the sidewalk, watching him disappear. Freddy considers looping around the block, surprising Justin with kisses and hugs. But he must not. He thinks of the blank computer screen at his desk, how he cannot write a single good sentence. Freddy is losing his life bit by bit, and he's got to stop.

Ritchie stands outside the Abbey with his back against the wrought iron fence that separates the sidewalk from the bar's patio. Droning beats thump from the speakers behind him and layer with the sounds of glasses tinkling and homosexuals laughing. The glow of gas heater lamps and the patio's red floodlights give the Abbey a hellish feel. There is a line of people waiting to get in that extends past the end of the building and into West Hollywood Park. Ritchie doesn't like coming to the Abbey nearly as much as he did when he first moved here. What was daring then has become obnoxious. Men pay too much attention to him—particularly to his butt, which gets pinched and patted as Ritchie navigates through the thick crowd.

He smooths his hair and tucks it behind his ears in a gesture that is quickly becoming habit. Satisfied, he licks his teeth to make sure there is nothing stuck there. He is here to meet J.W., who says he finally has the script he wants Ritchie to read. Ritchie doesn't understand why it can't wait until tomorrow, when their fourth training session is scheduled.

"Yo, papi," a clean-cut Mexican guy says, startling Ritchie. He ambles by with a smooth gait, turning his head as he passes and allowing his eyes to linger. Ritchie smiles, nods, and looks away. He doesn't date Mexicans, or Latins, or anyone with a skin tone from south of the Mason-Dixon Line. It reminds him too much of the boys from the block.

J.W. arrives wearing a sport jacket, turtleneck, and houndstooth slacks. In the gym he always has on a ball cap, but now his head is exposed and Ritchie notices that his hair is the color of soot and is transplanted in fairly obvious brush-like tufts across his pate. J.W. flashes a bleach-whitened smile and ushers Ritchie past the line and the doorman into the club. At the bar he orders a double martini.

"You want the same?" he asks Ritchie crisply.

"I'll take a flat water."

"Live a little."

"No, thanks." Ritchie smiles but feels a familiar warning click in his gut. *Please not now, not with this guy,* he offers in a fleeting prayer to Saint Genesius.

J.W. speaks to the shirtless bartender and flirts a little as he collects their drinks. He turns and hands Ritchie his glass of water along with a napkin.

"Cheers," J.W. says and upends his martini, swilling it in one galloping gulp. He follows this with a slight burp and a purse of the lips as the liquor settles. "I needed that."

"Looks like it," Ritchie says without trying to be smart.

J.W. points them toward a quieter area at the back of the club where there are small, canvas-draped cabanas and a fireplace. As they navigate the crowd, Ritchie scans the folds of J.W.'s jacket hoping to spot the bulge of a folded screenplay, but he doesn't see one.

As they pass the back bar, J.W. pauses, turning and sidling up to the hardwood and brass. "I think I could use another."

Ritchie stays where he is, biting the insides of his cheeks and rocking back and forth in his sneakers. J.W. is acting really uncool, and Ritchie is not sure what to do.

"Here we are," J.W. says, returning. He sips his drink theatrically, pointing Ritchie to an empty space along the back brick wall.

"So tell me about this script," Ritchie says, cutting to the chase.

"Pardon me?" J.W. cups his ear and leans in. Now he is standing too close.

"The script." Ritchie clearly enunciates his *p* and *t*.

"Oh! I'll give you that tomorrow. Tonight I thought we'd just celebrate." J.W.'s leer is so wide that it shows off a gold molar.

"Celebrate what?"

"A successful start to my training."

"Alcohol's fattening," Ritchie observes lividly, pointing to the drink.

"I'm sure you'll work it off me," J.W. gambols. He leans close enough for Ritchie to smell his aftershave. As if to punctuate his joke, he taps the tip of Ritchie's nose playfully with his index finger.

Instinctually, Ritchie jerks he head backward an inch, blinking a few times in rapid succession. He's been bitch slapped too many times to have someone make an abrupt move toward his face without the gesture giving him a start. He looks closely at J.W., whose cheeks have begun to redden and whose eyelids are slightly sleepy.

"C'mere," J.W. stage-whispers as he downs the last of his drink. He places a flat palm on Ritchie's stomach and aims down the front of his pants.

"No, thank you," Ritchie protests, squirming away. J.W. staggers after him, off balance, and both of them bump into the group of revelers next to them. J.W. tries to grope Ritchie again.

"Get the fuck off me!" Ritchie shouts. He shoves J.W. backward so hard that he hits his head on the edge of one of the cabanas. J.W. bawls a loud, drooling vowel of pain and there are suddenly two enormous bouncers grabbing Ritchie by the arms and dragging him toward the front of the club. The room swirls around Ritchie, flipping upside down. The music is above him, then below him. Someone is laughing.

"Let me go, motherfuckers!" Ritchie roars. They comply when they reach the velvet rope divider at the patio entrance. There, they dump Ritchie onto the sidewalk. He stumbles forward, grabbing the pole of a parking sign to keep from falling on his face. Enraged, Ritchie spins around to take on the bouncers. He is stopped by the shocked stares of dozens of gay men, cocktails in hand, jaws hanging.

Ritchie shudders hard several times and collects himself, raking the hair out of his eyes and wiping his mouth with the back of his hand. His palm is scraped and bleeding. He fixes his jacket and tucks in his shirt, trying not to get blood on the fabric, and looks around for a civilized escape from this great humiliation.

The park is close and it is dark. Ritchie hurries toward it, pigeon-toed like when he was little. He feels wheezy and doesn't care if he's running like a man or a girl.

Once he's safely in the dark and alone, Ritchie folds at the knees and drops to the dewy, muddy grass. He covers his face with his hands and lets out a slow, choked sob.

TWELVE

"Don't let me go," Joshua whispers.

Timothy is so tall that when he holds Joshua tightly in bed, Joshua feels completely encircled by warmth and safety. He isn't simply Joshua's type; he redefines the desire in Joshua's mind and groin. It is as if all the men Joshua's been with in the past were a prelude to this.

As much as Joshua looks askance at Freddy's illogical obsession with Justin Salvatore, Joshua now finds himself maddeningly subject to Timothy's whims.

"How are you?" he asks Timothy, struck by panic as they sit on Timothy's black leather sofa on Wednesday evening watching a repeat of *MTV Cribs.*

"Dude, you asked me that five minutes ago," Timothy laughs, reaching a lanky arm and tousling Joshua's hair. "Don't ask me again."

"I'm sorry," Joshua rues. He really is sorry, not just for asking the question twice, but for craving the answer. "I'll leave you alone."

But leaving Timothy alone is the last thing he wants to do. He'd rather crawl inside Timothy and become a part of him, live his silky skin and smell like he smells. He'd like to share Timothy's blood. He counts the minutes when they're apart. At the office, every time the phone rings, he has what feels like a palpitation, hoping Min will announce that it's Timothy on the phone.

They have spent the last four nights together. Joshua is getting used to it, which he knows is a dangerous thing. He decides to be bold and leave his toothbrush on the counter in Timothy's bathroom before he heads off to the office.

At 11 o'clock, Joshua calls Timothy's cell and it goes directly to voice mail. Timothy must be at the gym and have his phone turned off. Joshua calls again at 11:30 and a third time at noon. He leaves a message:

"Hey, honey, it's me. I've been trying you all morning." Joshua discovers himself knee deep in a pool of worry. "Are you okay? Call me."

He hangs up quickly and winces, wishing he hadn't been so clingy. Under his breath, Joshua repeats the message he just left, trying to imagine how it will sound to Timothy's ears.

Min puts through a call from Mamie Redbird, and Joshua is temporarily distracted by her fussing over several makeup items she's convinced her housekeeper has stolen.

"When's the last time you used the lip liner?" Joshua asks, glad for the distraction, but irritated at its source.

"That's not the point," Mamie growls.

"Did you maybe put it in your purse and leave it somewhere?"

"I never put makeup in my clutch. Too bulky."

"You carry a day planner from 1972 and a flask," he reminds her.

"A girl gets thirsty."

"And needs the phone numbers of dead people?"

"Joshua Moskovitz!" she exclaims, indignant.

"Sorry. I just don't believe Rosa stole your rouge."

At 2 Timothy calls the office. Joshua is in the front lobby. He grabs the phone out of Min's hand and perches on the edge of Min's desk.

"Where were you all day?" he asks. Then, realizing his excess of zeal, he punishes himself with an open-palm smack to the forehead.

"With my manager," Timothy says. There is a cutting quality to his voice that lets Joshua know he should not pursue the subject any further.

"So what's up for tonight?" Joshua asks.

"There's an album release party at the Palace for some new hip-hop group."

"Great!" Joshua blurts. "I love hip-hop. Should I wear a suit or a jean jacket?"

There is silence on the other end of the line.

"Hello?" Joshua asks gingerly.

"I'm going with a girl," Timothy says uncomfortably. "My manager said—"

"No, no!' That's fine," Joshua replies hurriedly. "I didn't mean to assume that—"

"Otherwise I'd totally take you."

"You've got to think of your image. I get it."

"Good, because—"

"Really. I'm fine with it."

There is silence again. Joshua swallows hard.

"Listen, I should go," Timothy mumbles. "I gotta pick out clothes for tonight."

"Right, absolutely. You go."

"Okay, then."

The line clicks and goes silent. Joshua fights the urge to smack himself again, this time with Min's handset.

"What did he say?" Min queries musically as he takes the handset from Joshua and places it back on the receiver with a raised pinky.

"Shut up," Joshua growls, sulking toward his office. "Type something."

In a few hours, Joshua is calmer. By the following afternoon, when he and Timothy meet at Joshua's apartment for daytime sex and a cup of cinnamon tea, he has forgiven Timothy.

Saturday, at the breakfast table at Noble's, he has his phone on vibrate but keeps it cupped in his palm, hoping Timothy will call.

"So I was watching this documentary on genetic expression in the Pacific Islands," Claire says, taking a conversational sojourn. "And I was noticing how certain gene markers express more in closed societies that breed close to the source as opposed to selectively like these nearsighted pinheaded children you see in Brentwood. Someone should tell their parents not to reproduce."

"We can take out a billboard," Freddy suggests.

Joshua's phone quakes.

"Excuse me," he says excitedly. He pushes back his chair with a loud scrape and turns toward the front door. "Hello?"

"Yo." It's Timothy, calling during a break at the recording studio. "Whassup?"

"Having breakfast with the gang. You?"

"Laying in backing vocals. These harmonies are crazy."

There is some loud conversation in the background.

"They're ready for me," Timothy tells him. "Gotta call you back."

The line goes dead. Joshua presses END and holds the phone tightly, remembering how it feels when Timothy curls around him, keeping him free from harm.

"And a lower rate of birth defects," Claire asserts, still on the same subject as when Joshua left. "Which shows, yet again, that nature was doing something right, and we had to go screw it up."

Charlie, the owner, comes by with a snapshot of himself with Angelina Jolie at some party. He's been showing it off to regulars all morning. In his eagerness, this is actually the second time he has passed it around to Ritchie, Freddy, Claire, and Joshua.

"She's so pretty," Ritchie exclaims, repeating what he said the first time.

"What happened to you?" Joshua asks Ritchie, noticing several scrapes on Ritchie's palm when he hands the picture back to Charlie.

"I fell."

"Really?" Joshua is skeptical.

"I tripped." He puts the injured hand in his lap and is suddenly very busy with the salt shaker and sugar bowl.

Joshua's cell vibrates again.

"Excuse me." He gets up and heads toward the front door for privacy.

Claire rolls her eyes.

"Hey, sweetness," Joshua says into the phone, seeing Timothy's number on the display.

"I need some ass," Timothy tells him, forgoing pleasantries. "Can you come by later?"

"That'd be a yes," Joshua giggles. "I have a conference call for my science fiction client at 7, so I could be at your place by about 8:30."

"Make it 7:30. I'm horny."

"I, uh—" Joshua scrambles, thinking swiftly. "Maybe I can move the conference call or have them handle it without me?"

He imagines himself on Timothy's bed with the comforter turned down. He lies on his back, naked. Timothy comes in from the bathroom, naked also, and climbs on top of Joshua, legs on legs, arms on arms, so that Joshua is covered by his warmth and smoothness.

"Yeah, you do that," Timothy instructs. "Out."

Back at the table, Claire gives him a chilly look.

"Don't let us interrupt your phone calls or anything."

"I'm sorry, it's just that—"

The phone vibrates again.

"Hello?" Joshua answers without getting up.

"Bring the lube," Timothy instructs.

"Thanks," he says as professionally as he can, "I'll take care of that right away."

"Are you for real?" Claire asks as he hangs up, not buying the act.

Joshua sighs. "You know what it's like when you want something really badly—"

"Like your business?" Freddy asks.

"He was never this nuts with the business," Claire observes coolly. "This is beyond—"

"Take it easy on him," Ritchie kindly interjects. "Both of you."

They are silent for a moment. Joshua feels his phone shake but he doesn't move. He hopes the noise of the restaurant will cover the buzzing, and it seems to, as none of others react to the hum. Joshua is dying to pick it up, or at least look down and see if it's Timothy, but he knows that to save face, he must not.

"You're anxious," Freddy notes, "and you don't look well—"

"Neither do you—" Joshua retorts.

"We're not talking about me."

Joshua huffs. Freddy should mind his own business.

"He's controlling you," Claire adds with a nod.

"And *you*," Joshua seizes a point, loudly, "are a fine one to offer advice."

"Sweetie," she insists, "this isn't advice. It's observation. Because we care."

Joshua exhales slowly. He has no comeback.

A cell phone rings a plucky split-octave summons. Claire moves quickly, grabbing the little fold-up device from her purse and flipping it open.

"Hello?" she asks with a smile.

She listens. Then her face falls. She takes the phone away from her ear and holds it out toward Freddy.

"I can't," she says.

Freddy looks confused. Claire shakes the phone at him. Reluctantly, he accepts it.

"Hello?" he says to the caller. The person on the other end speaks, and Freddy's own expression darkens.

"She's not available to speak with you right now," he says icily, "and she would appreciate it if you don't call her again."

Joshua realizes who's on the phone. He glances at Claire, who is pale.

"I don't think you heard me." Freddy is adamant. "She's not available."

Charlie hovers nearby, perhaps ready to show them his Angelina Jolie picture a third time. But he seems to know something is amiss.

"Yes," Freddy acknowledges to the caller, "this is Claire's friend Freddy...uh-huh? Well, I'm going to hang up the phone right now."

Charlie heads back toward the kitchen. Claire looks as though she is going to pass out. Ritchie reaches and puts his unblemished hand around her shoulder. It is a gesture that is unusual for each of them.

"I am hanging up," Freddy snarls and snaps the phone closed.

Nobody speaks.

With swift, apologetic gestures, the waiter refills their coffee and takes Ritchie's empty plate.

"That was creepy." Freddy says, breaking the silence. "He accused me of making homosexual overtures to him. And this is the first time I've even heard the guy's voice."

"Hugh?" Ritchie asks, not quite sure.

Claire and Freddy nod simultaneously.

"I'm sorry," Joshua offers, forgiving Claire's snappishness in light of how awful she looks right now.

Hugh is clearly cuckoo. The incident where he backwards-mailed Claire a greeting card made that plain enough. And the fact that he works with children gives Joshua the willies.

"Why don't you report him to the state board of psychiatry?" he asks.

Claire sighs and shakes her head no. "I worry it would only accelerate him. I was reading this article on the Internet—"

"There's a problem right there," Joshua interjects. Claire cuts him a harsh glance.

"Anyway," she goes on, "I'm scared that if I say something, I'll trigger him. And if I don't, it'll be worse."

Joshua's phone vibrates. With a pang of anxiety, he looks down at the display. It is not Timothy's number that appears there, but Claire's. Relieved but confused, he lets out a snort.

"What?" Claire demands.

"Do you have me on speed dial?" he asks.

Claire shrugs. "I guess so."

"Look at your phone," he tells her. She starts to object, but Joshua cuts her off.

"Just do it!"

Reluctantly she complies, then smiles slowly.

"You win."

It is early evening.

Freddy stares at the blinking cursor on his computer screen. There is no text in the top window. He keeps his word processor on "page view" so he can see how his words lay out. When he's being productive, it's inspiring. But at times like now, when he feels as though he cannot string together a worthwhile sentence, it is cruel—the empty electronic rectangle is heavy and monolithic.

Today is his two-month anniversary with Justin, counting from the first night they met in New York City. Things have been quiet around the house, with Justin taking the medication the shrink prescribed for him. At first for twenty hours at a stretch, then eighteen, and now twelve. When he's awake he seems less insane, if only because he's sedated. His conversation has begun to make sense and he's less prone to break into odd rhyming games when

Freddy asks him a serious question. Furthermore, no knobs have gone missing and, the last time Freddy checked, the dustpan was safe in the hall closet.

He hears Justin walking across the hardwood living room floor toward the kitchen. Apparently, the nap Justin's been taking since noon is done.

"It's our anniversary," Freddy informs him without turning around.

"Really? Time flies."

"When you're sleeping."

"Or tweaking," Justin concedes.

"You want to go out tonight and celebrate? At least consider it."

There is no reply.

Freddy turns around and looks at Justin, who is drinking a glass of milk. He is wearing one of Freddy's old T-shirts, a pair of wool socks, and nothing else. Freddy notices for the first time that he has well-developed calves, probably from dancing.

Justin shrugs once he has drained the glass. "Sure, I guess."

Freddy is pleasantly surprised, but knows not to question whether Justin's serious—better to seize the opportunity now before he changes his mind.

"Put on some pants," Freddy suggests. "Then let's go."

A few minutes later they are in the car.

"Shall we get dinner?" Freddy asks, apprehensive but wishful. He notices Justin has taken some of the bric-a-brac off his arms. Perhaps the antipsychotic pills really are working.

"How about a drink?" Justin suggests.

"Okay."

"Rage?"

Freddy sighs.

"Okay," he says, less enthusiastic about this proposition. But he will go along with it. After all, relationships are about compromise, even relationships with crazy drug addicts.

It is a warm evening, so they park a few blocks from the club and walk. Along the way they pass a Christmas tree lot that was a pumpkin patch a few weeks ago. There are still a few bales of hay shoved against the back fence. Freddy is amazed that it's not even

Thanksgiving and the holiday mania is already in full swing.

He looks at Justin, whose face is upturned to the string of glowing bulbs that ring the lot. His eyes sparkle, and he radiates one of his signature grins. It would be impossible, Freddy decides, for anyone looking at Justin right now not to fall in love with him.

They get to Boys Town and stroll blocks of Santa Monica Boulevard where the clubs are door-to-door with take-out restaurants and cheap clothing stores. Freddy hears '80s music echoing out of Rage and sees the street-side terrace full of smokers posing and chatting beneath the glow of the bar's neon sign. Madonna sings "Holiday," which seems appropriate. Through the archways across the front of the bar two go-go boys are visible, twisting and shaking in clingy shorts.

At the door, Freddy pulls out his drivers license and Justin produces a battered passport. The bouncer glances at both and ushers them in. Since Rage opened a smoking terrace a few years ago, the smell of the air inside the club is distinctly more pleasant, and Freddy is calm as Justin goes to the bar, shouts a drink order over the music, and pulls out a tight wadded ball of singles to pay. It's a sweaty-smelling money lump Freddy has fished out of the pocket of Justin's jeans more than once on laundry day. There are flecks of tobacco and lint stuck in its recesses. It gives Justin's pants a funny bulge that makes it look like he has a rubber ball in his pocket and oddly compliments the uneven bumpiness of his shirtsleeves.

Meeting Freddy at the empty side of the room, Justin hands over a grapefruit juice punctuated with a maraschino cherry and takes a pull of his own vodka and tonic through a skinny straw.

They stand watching the crowd.

Across the bar Freddy spots Sean, a furniture salesman he slept with once about four years ago then chatted with intermittently on the Internet. He wasn't a clever conversationalist, nor did he drop trousers in the specific way that interested Freddy, so he fell into the company of also-rans who are too handsome to delete from Freddy's buddy list but not compatible enough to warrant repeat punishment. Sean sees Freddy too and waves, making his way over. There are crow's-feet at the corners of his eyes, and his waist seems a little thicker than the last time Freddy saw him.

"Hey," Sean says broadly, sidling up to Freddy and Justin. He grabs Freddy by the arm, squeezes his biceps, and makes a face of mock surprise. Freddy would have been fine had Sean kept his hands to himself.

"So," Sean gushes above the drone of music and laughter, "is this the little lady?"

He helps himself to an eyeful of Justin, who does look smart in his Gap thermal and battered jeans.

"You've done well for yourself," Sean says cattily. "You always did like a little flavah."

Freddy wants to smack Sean across the mouth, especially for the way he swaggers on the word *flavah*.

Sean sniffs and touches his nose self-consciously.

Justin clears his throat.

Out of nowhere, Freddy has the sense there is an unspoken dialogue going on between the two of them. It's an energy they're both exuding, a swift avoidance of each other's eye contact.

"So," Justin asks Sean out of turn. "How ya doing?"

"I...am...excellent," Sean tells him. It's languorous and deliberate and he nods afterward for emphasis. "I need to hit the restroom. Talk to you guys later."

Sean turns and is gone.

"You've met him before, haven't you?" Freddy accuses Justin, who shakes his head no. Freddy stews, unconvinced, but isn't quite sure how to pursue this. He looks out at the crowd while taking nervous little sips of his grapefruit juice.

"Actually, I have to use the restroom," Justin says with an apologetic smile. "Be right back."

Something is genuinely amiss. Freddy keeps his eye on Justin as his tousled reddish-brown hair moves in a zigzag across the club and he disappears into the men's room. A man with a toupee bristles by Freddy and gives him a queasy, come-hither glare that Freddy acknowledges with the slightest of nods then tries to ignore.

Minutes pass—plenty of time for Justin to wait in line, pee, wash his hands, and fiddle with buttons of his shirt in the cracked washroom mirror. Freddy considers going after him, but dismisses the idea for multiple reasons. He might miss Justin in the thick of the crowd. Then again, he might run smack into Justin and find him doing something untoward that Freddy would just as well not have available to visual memory. The point is rendered moot when Justin appears in the crowd, bobbing to the music. He rushes to Freddy, grabbing him by both hands and giving him an enthusiastic kiss on the mouth.

"Come on," Justin begs breathlessly. "Let's get out of here."

Startled but not displeased, Freddy lets Justin drag him by the hand to the front door of the club and out onto the sidewalk. Justin runs ahead a few paces, jumping skyward with a jubilant whoop and tagging a low hanging tree branch with his fingertips.

Freddy watches the happy outburst, moving out of the way of the passing crowd and waiting next to a street vendor's table. After a moment, Justin heads to where Freddy is standing. He gives Freddy another kiss, then turns to the array of carved wooden crosses and fake ivory whatnots laid out on the vendor's black felt tablecloth.

"Let's get something," Justin spouts. His fingers seem itchy to touch the trifles.

The Rastafarian vendor holds up one trinket after the next, and Justin frets, considering his options. He picks out a little thread-wrapped doll, dismisses it in favor of a rosary, and in the end embraces Santeria over Catholicism by going back to the creepy doll.

"Only," he says apologetically, "I don't have any money."

Freddy looks at Justin's pocket where he money lump usually lies. Sure enough, the dirty denim is flat. Justin's fingers fidget and he is clenching and unclenching his jaw.

Beginning to piece things together, Freddy pulls out his wallet and hands the man in the knit cap and braids a five-dollar bill. He is owed some change, but Freddy refuses it. He picks up the figurine and holds it out to Justin, who thrusts it in his pocket, restoring the funny bulge.

They walk in silence for a moment.

"Okay," Freddy says, wheeling toward Joshua, "what did you buy in the bathroom?"

Justin's mouth opens in surprise. He tries a smile that doesn't quite work.

"I figured it was a special occasion, being our anniversary and all."

"So that makes it okay?"

Justin shrugs and his eyes dart around.

"You really don't get it," Freddy fumes, "do you?"

He pushes Justin aside, who is now in his way, and sets off toward the car.

"Freddy!" Justin calls after him, frantic.

Freddy ignores him and keeps walking with his head down. Justin trots alongside him, pleading, but his voice is swallowed up by the sound of the traffic.

Freddy does not break his pace.

THIRTEEN

It is a rainy afternoon, just before dusk. The sunset would be visible were it not for the murk of clouds that reaches down and presses against the Pacific, held in place by a fine foggy mist. For some reason, the phones in Joshua's office are even slower when it rains, a phenomenon he has yet to be able to explain. Do people not care about publicity when it is damp out?

Joshua has a small radio on his credenza that he listens to on afternoons such as this. He leaves it tuned to K-Mozart. Aside from being one of only three stations whose signal penetrates the steel frame of his office building, K-Mozart is a classical channel. Listening to orchestral pieces makes Joshua feel cultured and less like a show-business whore. Right now the station is playing a program of Gershwin tunes, which suits Joshua fine. He taps his feet, alternately in time to the downbeat and syncopation.

He needs to feel jazzy today. His powerlessness with Timothy is plaguing him, but his more immediate worry is the pile of bills he's examining. He sits at his desk, paying invoices from his checkbook. A large calculator sits in front of him. For each check he drafts, he subtracts a like amount from the account balance. The total on the glowing display gets dramatically smaller each time he enters a number and hits the "minus" key.

There are still several unpaid bills when the calculator readout says $432.53. This leaves Joshua with the choice of whether to write a check to the florist for the arrangements he's sent in the last month or get up to date with the limousine service he uses to pick up clients. As he weighs the liabilities of stiffing each of them, the phone rings.

Min answers and sends the call to Joshua's desk.

"Mamie on one."

"Hello dear," Joshua says cheerfully. "I was just speaking about you to someone."

"My career is dead," she wheezes.

"That's not the way to look at it."

"Shelly Winters works more than me."

"Not true," Joshua says, a little panicked.

"You've got a month to get me on TV."

"I'm not your agent."

"Thirty days."

"It's the holidays," he pleads. "Nobody's doing anything."

"New year, new publicist," she replies in a singsong voice.

"Calm down, would you?"

"If I were any calmer, I'd need life support."

Joshua has no comeback.

"Let me see what I can do," he says, worried, before hanging up.

The wisps of wet clouds stir outside his window and threaten to blot out the skyline entirely.

"Have you eaten?" Ritchie asks Joshua when Min puts through his call.

"I have no appetite," Joshua replies.

"What kind of talk is that?"

"Only pie," Joshua considers, "and still maybe."

"With a salad and some lean protein," Ritchie says like a mother.

"Pie!" Joshua stonewalls.

Ritchie sighs.

"Okay. Sweet Lady Jane's. Fifteen minutes."

Thinking of triple berry cake with whipped cream frosting, Joshua hangs up and grabs his jacket from the back of his chair.

"Forward my calls to my cell," he tells Min, passing through the lobby and walking into an open elevator stall.

He is on the streets quickly, and traffic is light on the narrow streets he takes as his shortcut from Century City to West Hollywood. Ritchie is waiting at the dessert shop when Joshua gets there, a mug of cocoa on a paper doily in front of him.

"Splenda, not sugar," Ritchie says right away, correcting any misapprehension that Joshua might have as to the source of his dessert carbohydrates.

"I'd expect nothing less," Joshua assures him, taking off his damp jacket. He flags the waitress for an espresso and a slice of berry cake, which he hopes has not all been portioned up and served for the day. He is in luck, the girl with the apron informs him.

"It's slow on account of the rain. We got almost a half a berry cake left. You can have two slices if you want."

Demurely, he assures her that only one will be necessary.

"So what's your beef?" Ritchie asks. It is incredible that someone so unsubtle can sense whenever there is the slightest fluctuation in Joshua's well-being.

"I have to get Mamie on TV in the next month or my gross goes down by a third. I won't be able to pay Min's salary."

"Or take me to Vegas."

"Since when was I taking you to Vegas?"

"Min doesn't need to be paid. He doesn't even really eat—"

"He likes rice," Joshua informs him, "and neapolitan popsicles."

"Which are from Italy, you know," Ritchie boasts. "And besides, you don't have anything to worry about with Mamie, because I have the solution."

"That quickly? You must be an imposter, and the real Ritchie is gagged and bound under the table. Set him free. He has asthma."

"You want to hear my idea or not?"

"I'm scared."

"Why would you be scared?" Ritchie asks. "But don't answer or I'll forget. The point is that my supervisor, Willie, said in the meeting this morning that CNN is going do a story on celebrity fitness. So it'd be the best thing ever if you had her come in and do a workout."

Joshua nods, thinking, amazed that Ritchie may have just had a "great idea" that is actually worthwhile.

"Yeah," he says. "That just might work."

Ritchie passes through the lobby of the gym, chewing gum and whistling. He knows this is dangerous because he might bite his tongue. The legs of his purple nylon jogging pants swish together. He's been eating better and pushing himself hard. He's gained three pounds and it seems to have gone directly to his thighs and butt. He is pleased with this, but it does make his pants fit even more awkwardly than before.

As he tromps up the carpeted stairs toward the workout floor, he hears the heaviness of his footfalls and is reminded of how his mother used to scold him.

"Always I know it is you," she would say, pinching her fingers together as if she was going to crumble some spice into a bowl, "because you walk like a truck."

Ritchie never figured out how, exactly, a truck would walk, but he knew that her admonishment wasn't kind. He tried to walk more flowingly for a while. Then his cousin made fun of him and pushed him into the upright piano for stepping across the rug like a ballerina. So Ritchie gave up and mostly stayed in his room.

"Catalano?" he hears Willie call when he reaches the workout level and passes the trainers office.

"Yeah?" He ducks his head in the door.

"You got a client?" Willie asks, looking at the clock, which reads 9:58.

"Yeah."

"Sit down."

Ritchie does as instructed, sure from Willie's tone that what he is about to hear is not cheery. Willie looks at Ritchie over his reading glasses as if he's making a spot assessment of his employee. Ritchie never likes to stare directly at Willie. He's the only black man Ritchie has ever noticed wearing a toupee, and Willie is slightly walleyed. Ritchie is unsure which side of the man's gaze to return.

"You have a client named J.W.?" Willie asks, looking at a poorly written message on a pink telephone pad.

So that is what this is about.

"Yes."

"You don't anymore. He cancelled his training package and sent a letter to ask for a full refund. When the district manager's secretary called to investigate, the guy complained that your training was sloppy and unprofessional—those were his words."

"It's not true—"

"Since I've been here, Catalano, this has become the highest volume club in Southern California, and we're up for the service award at the Christmas party week after next. I don't want to put too fine a point on this, but if I don't get the seven days and six nights in Maui that I'm gunning for, my wife is not putting out and I'll be holding you personally responsible."

Ritchie has no idea how to answer this.

"I can get Mamie Redbird in here to train next week for that TV thing," he blurts.

Willie glares at him with rheumy, misaligned eyes.

"And son, you need to cut your hair."

"Can I go now?" Ritchie asks.

On Saturday morning, Freddy stands beside the sofa where Justin lies watching television in an apathetic stupor. The air in the apartment is stale, and the blinds are drawn. Freddy holds Justin's pill and a glass of tap water.

"Now," he insists, "not later. I want to see you swallow it."

"Leave it on the table," Justin says distantly.

"I'm not playing around."

"And I'm not a child."

"Just take the goddamned pill," Freddy snaps, "for both our sakes."

Without taking his eyes off the cartoon playing on TV, Justin snatches the pill from Freddy's hand and pops it in his mouth. He swallows it without water.

"Will you leave me alone now?" he pouts.

It is a moment before Freddy realizes Justin's question was probably rhetorical. In the interim, he tries to come up with an answer, but he is at a loss for words. He wants to reach through the divide that separates them and embrace Justin, but their mutual anger will not allow it.

Freddy hates that anger.

He goes into the bathroom, shuts the door, and sits on the toilet with the lid down. He sees himself in the small mirror hanging in the shower stall. He looks tired and he doesn't want to go to breakfast at Noble's for fear of what the others will say. He shaved and put on fresh chinos but he's still a little haggard.

"Stop it!" he hears Justin shout at a villain of his own imagining. "Motherfucker! Get off me! This is my skin, my skin, my skin."

He lets out a long, tuneless wail that makes Freddy cringe.

By the time Freddy leaves for Noble's, Justin is snoring softly on the sofa, spit pooling at the corner of his lips. Freddy gently closes Justin's mouth, smooths his curly hair, and switches off the television with the remote.

He leaves the radio off during the drive to the restaurant, letting the silence speak to him. Claire waits outside the restaurant wearing an on old pair of jeans that hang saggy through the legs and are too short.

"You look crappy," he tells her once he's found a parking spot and walked up.

"You too."

"You look worse."

"I'm older, and I could beat you up."

"Which even if you could would not make you popular."

"Being popular is the last thing I—"

"And neither would those pants."

"Who didn't get their nap?" she teases, but looks down, displeased at her jeans.

"Try having a windup monkey in your house all week."

Charlie has seen them and come outside. His long apron strings are tied crisscross around his waist and seem to bisect his body.

"Hey," he interrupts jovially. "What you standing out here for? Scare away paying customers? I got your table ready."

They follow him in and the waiter has poured their coffee even before their jackets are off and hung on the backs of their chairs. Freddy misses Claire badly. He takes comfort in her sarcasm, the lines that map the corners of her eyes, and her Thierry Mugler perfume.

Joshua and Ritchie are a little late for breakfast. Joshua has a cold and Ritchie's excuse for tardiness is that he nicked himself shaving "down there." He couldn't get it to stop bleeding and didn't want to stain his white drawers. Now, as he sits down, Freddy watches to see if he shows any sign of discomfort.

"I was reading in a medical journal about the benefits of tomatoes," Claire lectures them once they've settled in their seats. "I was fascinated! They have more useful phytochemicals than we previously knew. Especially good for the prostate."

"You don't have a prostate," Ritchie reminds her.

"A fact," Claire replies dryly, "I never cease to regret."

"I'm sick," Joshua croaks, reinforming everyone.

"Eat some tomatoes," Claire suggests.

"I'm losing my mind with Justin," Freddy announces.

"Then the two of you will be in good company," Joshua decides, his voice wheezy because of his stuffed nose. Freddy tries not to find this funny. "And by the way, I was talking with this friend of Timothy's about crystal meth and he kept calling it 'powdered Satan.' Said it ate up his life and made him paranoid, and he did all kinds of crazy things. He ended up living out of a dumpster behind a supermarket and nearly got run over by a post office truck before wising up. The guy's boyfriend who put him out in the street was partying pretty consistently too, and he tore the plaster off the walls to get at the wiring that was supposedly radiating electricity through him."

"Al Gore would have backed that action," Claire says, "And Greenpeace would have lent him tools."

"Why don't you just break up with Justin?" Ritchie asks.

"And then what?" Freddy's mind reels, flooded with images. "He'd be on the street, and I'd feel horrible for whatever happened to him."

"What's the worst that could happen?" Claire asks.

Freddy shakes his head no. "It's bad..."

"You are not responsible for his well-being," Claire insists.

"Yes, I am," Freddy counters just as emphatically. "I took on the job."

"Well, then," she says, "you really are nuts."

The waiter comes to see if there's any deviation from their standard orders.

"Yes, actually," Claire tells him. "I'll have eggs Benedict with sliced tomato instead of Canadian bacon."

"Anything else?" the waiter asks.

Freddy is hit by a sudden urge.

"Pancakes!" he says quickly. "Bring me a full stack. And I'll take her Canadian bacon if it's going to waste."

The waiter acknowledges this and goes to the kitchen.

Claire raises her eyebrows at Freddy, but he refuses to accept the look.

Claire would pay plenty for the conversation she's about to have, but was informed, when she phoned, that the District Attorney's office doesn't take contributions.

"That'd be a bribe," the young man on the phone told her flatly.

Now she sits with a mug of espresso and steamed milk on the terrace at Urth Café in West Hollywood, at a table upwind of any smokers. A large, middle-aged black woman approaches from the street, seems to pick Claire out of the crowd, and waves and smiles politely.

"I'm Eileen from the D.A.'s office," she says, pulling out the chair across from Claire and taking a seat. Her thick woolen sweater covers her from her soft jaw to the ends of her wrists and makes her look even bulkier than she is. Claire wishes her something slimming, in cotton perhaps. Eileen digs in her large handbag and fumbles for a moment before finding a business card and extending it to Claire, who takes it and glances at the City of Los Angeles logo before setting the card on the wire mesh tabletop.

Eileen wrestles a manila folder from her handbag, and in order to read its contents produces a pair of ruby-encrusted reading glasses. As she slips them on, the temples disappear into her overgrown tousle of hair, which is so fiery red that if the color is not intentional, she's not to be trusted.

"I'm Claire, and thank you." Claire feels uncannily as though she is back in high school visiting the guidance counselor.

"I have your request here," Eileen says, "and the first thing I want to tell you is not to worry." This makes Claire worry.

"Stalking or excessive attention," Eileen notes, "is common after a breakup."

"We didn't break up," Claire corrects her. "We never really got started."

"Perhaps so, in your mind," Eileen says, giving a nod of thanks to the waiter who's just set down a glass of water for her. "But one of the keys to understanding what's going on in the world is comprehending how each of us lives in his or her own reality. Though yours may be in contrast to Hugh's, for him everything he thinks and feels is entirely real."

"He's a psychiatrist. So that's doubly scary."

"I can imagine." Eileen jots something in her folder. "And we'll work from the assumption that Hugh has the delusional belief you're in love with him—"

"At my own prompting," Claire ruminates, "according to my mother."

Eileen looks up.

"Whatever anyone thinks," she says, "that's their business. The law is on your side."

"I'm scared," Claire admits.

"So was I," Eileen tells her matter-of-factly, nodding. "Sweetie, I didn't get this job by accident. My ex-husband followed me around for six months. The whole time I was working downtown at Parker Center with cops around me, and it seemed like none of them gave a damn what I was going through. Then, one night, in my driveway, my ex stabbed me nine times and left me for dead."

"Oh, God." Claire covers her mouth. Suddenly, she understands the prim, bulky sweater, not wanting to imagine where on Eileen's body the scars must be. Claire looks down at her shoe. "Was there a lot of blood loss? Did you suffer functional impairment?"

"Relax. I'm better now."

There is a pause. When Eileen reaches out and touches her hand, Claire nearly jumps.

"Sorry," Claire says. She adjusts herself then picks up her spoon and pokes at the wetness of her coffee.

"The key is to act now before things go any further. You live alone, right? In a house?"

Claire nods.

"These guys will stop at nothing to insinuate themselves into your lives. They'll climb around in the crawl space under your house with a stethoscope listening to your life, tapping your phones and computer lines."

"How do you stop them?"

"A restraining order is the best thing we can do to prevent problems. I'll be honest with you, though, it only works maybe half the time. The reason the judge grants them in the first place is because somebody's out of control, so it's not shocking that they're often violated. How smart is Hugh?"

"Very. He's a child psychiatrist. Which is creepy if you think about it—someone that warped being around kids all day. I was considering reporting him to the state board. But I'm not sure if that would only make things worse. And he's also rich, so I don't know what tricks he's got up his sleeve."

"I agree with you on not reporting him—for now anyway. And a restraining order is going to look bad for him, regardless, if it becomes public record. There might be an intermediary step we could try."

"Such as?" Claire wonders.

"Getting him to sign a private agreement to leave you alone. Like a restraining order, but just between you and him, unless he violates it."

"Would it work?"

"There's no telling," Eileen responds with a shrug. "But with the reality schism you wrote about in your complaint, taking any other action right now might be playing with matches. I'm just being real with you. It's my job to file with the court if that's what you want to do..."

"No," Claire decides. "I'll wait."

"You should change your phone numbers, though. And your locks."

Claire thinks about this and is overcome with a swell of helplessness. She feels herself about to cry.

Eileen reaches out in another gesture of camaraderie, but Claire withdraws her hands from the table and drops them to her lap, gently clenching her fists. She bites her lip to forestall the tears.

"I'll take care of it right away," Eileen promises. She sits quietly for a moment before putting her belongings back in her back and standing up to leave.

"Let me know how things go," she tells Claire. "And my office can help you put that document together if you need."

Claire nods but looks at her coffee.

"Claire?"

Her eyes move cautiously to Eileen.

"Don't let him win," Eileen says gently.

FOURTEEN

This is the first time Joshua has been in the women's locker room at the gym on purpose. Once, two years ago, he accidentally pulled the door open after a yoga class and realized his error almost instantaneously. Several pairs of bras and panties galloping out of sight and a single girlie yelp of terror were enough both to permanently teach him the correct path to the men's locker room and to squelch any doubt in his mind that he's gay.

This afternoon, his presence in the women's restroom is expected. There are extra lights set up along the mirror above the sinks, and a makeup and hair stylist stand fussing over Mamie Redbird, who sits smartly. She is draped in a black vinyl cape, lest her shimmering purple leotard be smudged with mascara or Max Factor crème foundation. There is a cameraman in the corner, recorder rolling, his large lens trained on Mamie.

"We're ready upstairs," chirps the Fox producer, a cheery girl with a ponytail who reminds Joshua of his little sister, and not in a good way.

Regally, Mamie stands, slipping slightly as the heel of her shoe moves from the wooden rail of the director's chair onto the tile bathroom floor. Head high, she regains her footing and yanks away the stylist's cape with a tug at the Velcro neck.

The ponytailed producer leads a procession to the workout

floor. Mamie is close behind her, all pomp and decorum, bowing slightly to gym members whom she imagines as fans but are more likely simply gawkers. Joshua follows Mamie, and the cameraman brings up the rear.

Upstairs, Ritchie is waiting, leaning against a chest fly machine, trying to look casual. Joshua notices that Ritchie has put on a bit of makeup and, thankfully, he has gotten his hair out of his eyes with the help of some spray or gel. The producer puts a wireless microphone pack on Mamie and asks her to climb into a leg press machine, where her thighs are hoisted up as if for a medical exam.

"We're rolling," the cameraman barks.

"The point of this exercise," Ritchie informs them fluidly, kneeling beside Mamie, "is to engage both the quadriceps and the hamstring muscles—"

"Can you step out of frame, please?" the producer interrupts unceremoniously.

"Uh..." Ritchie is drop-jawed for a moment, then does as requested.

"Let's get some action shots of Mamie."

"Right," Ritchie seconds as if he has some say in the matter.

Mamie smiles, her head cocked to the side. With none of the machine's chromed plates engaged, she executes a few wobbly kneed repetitions.

"Excellent," the producer says. Either she is bluffing or Joshua has suddenly become a poor judge of what looks good on camera.

Ritchie lurks awkwardly a few feet away, clearly eager for an opportunity to inject himself into the action. But the producer is oblivious. Once she is satisfied with Mamie's leg strength, she moves everyone into the next room, where she positions Mamie on a bench and, with minimal assistance from Ritchie, has Mamie lift a featherweight dumbbell in a pantomime of an arm workout.

The only one who seems more pleased than the producer is Mamie herself, who gazes wistfully into the mirror as if she is exhibiting tremendous courage in the face of exhaustion. Ritchie does not get a word in, and looks pitiful, seeming to know he is a largely unwanted accessory to a carnival scene.

Through it all Joshua is silent, watching Mamie and the producer, waiting for any sign of distress he might need to quell. But none arises. There is a brief interview session during which the producer asks questions from her reporter's notebook.

"You've been working out for how long?"

"Thirty years," Mamie claims. The answer is both fictional and arbitrary. Joshua wishes she'd picked a shorter interval, lest he be called upon to in some way support her boast.

"Does it help you as an actress?"

"Im*meas*urably," she assures the producer with a strong rasp on the second syllable.

"Is there benefit in other aspects of your life, such as your recent public recovery from breast implant removal?"

"Why, yes." She glances down at herself with a slight twitch at the corner of the mouth.

They are finished and the sound and camera operators are coiling cables and putting their equipment away. Joshua, Mamie, and the producer tromp downstairs to their temporary post in the women's locker room.

"I'll be outside," Mamie informs Joshua as she gathers her things. Her face has returned to its more familiar glower.

"You want me to drive you home?"

She swats away the suggestion, fishing in her bag for a lighter.

"That was great!" Ritchie says, catching up with them.

Mamie nods at him painfully, a cigarette in the corner of her mouth.

"C'mon," she says to Joshua, dragging him toward the exit to the pool. Before she reaches the door, Mamie has lit up. Joshua knows there is no smoking allowed anywhere in the building or on the grounds, but he decides to stay quiet on the subject.

"Are you okay?" Joshua asks her.

"Are you shitting me?" she cackles under her already whispery voice. "I'm thrilled! And listen, kiddo—I'm sorry for ever doubting you. Which is a lot. You know I don't do 'sorry' and 'thank you' unless there's a paycheck involved."

"I know well."

"So..." Ritchie calls out awkwardly from behind them, "see ya later."

Joshua has forgotten his friend. He turns to see Ritchie standing alone, a little hunched, his face both guileless and defeated. Joshua is struck by a throe of remorse, but continues on his way.

The toe of Ritchie's sneaker is scuffed. He strongly dislikes this. It would be bad enough were he by himself, but he is at the mall with Joshua amid a crowd of holiday shoppers, and it feels as though everyone is looking at his feet. The scuff is a mar on his presentation, which today is tidy and carefully thought-out: a pair of Diesel jeans cut loosely enough that they don't stretch across the butt and thigh, a bluish vintage T-shirt with orange lettering, and blue Coach sneakers with orange accents. But then there is the scuff. It ruins everything. It is worse than if he had a giant pimple on his nose; that would be forgivable as an unkind act of nature, whereas a scuffed shoe comes off as straight-up slovenliness. He tries favoring the other foot, keeping the toe of the offending shoe tucked down and back a bit, but realizes from his reflection in a store window that this is making him look handicapped.

"What time are we supposed to meet Timothy?" he asks Joshua, who is walking beside him holding a shopping bag full of drinking glasses and fake flowers he's just bought at Pottery Barn.

"In fifteen minutes." Joshua is a little snappish. "I told you."

"Well, I forgot!" Ritchie says defensively.

They take the escalators down to the street level and pass the Macy's Men's Store, where a handsome, long-haired live model in the window is wearing nothing but a pair of jeans. This spectacle waylays them for a few moments, then they arrive at California Pizza Kitchen, the designated meeting spot for lunch with Timothy.

"Three, near the front if possible," Joshua tells the hostess, who shows them to a table and hands them menus.

They drink the water the busboy brings and look out the window, commenting cattily on passers-by. Ritchie keeps his shoe well-hidden beneath the table. Joshua fiddles with the paper wrapper from his straw which, dampened, is coming apart into little bits.

Several minutes pass.

"Where is he?" Joshua asks anxiously, looking at his watch.

Ritchie doesn't want to say the wrong thing, and he's not sure whether the question is rhetorical, so he merely grunts and nods.

"I wish he was about fifty percent more present," Joshua pines.

"And on time," Ritchie adds.

It is Joshua's turn not to reply. They both look at the menu. Joshua cannot sit still, taking out his phone and fiddling with it to mollify himself. Silently, Ritchie wipes the toe of his offending shoe on the opposite leg of his jeans, thinking that perhaps this will wear off the blemish the same way a dirty pencil eraser can be freshened against a clear sheet of paper.

At twenty minutes past the time Timothy was to have met them, the waiter comes by and asks, "Are you ready to order?" in a way that lets them know clearly that they ought to pick what to eat or clear out.

"I'll take a carbonara with extra bacon," Joshua says a little dismissively. "He'll have the veggie combo on wheat, no cheese."

When they're not at Noble's, Joshua usually orders for both of them. Though Ritchie is the more mannish of the two of them, he's glad to hand off husbandly duties to Joshua when it's just the two of them. It leaves him with less to get flustered about.

The waiter leaves and they make small talk for a while, though it's clear Joshua's heart is not in the conversation. Ritchie wonders if it's time to broach a subject he's been aching to attack but hasn't found the opportunity. Certainly Joshua is not at his best, but Ritchie isn't sure how much longer the topic can wait.

"Listen," he says. "I'm thinking maybe you should represent me."

Joshua's reply is a snort and he keeps playing with things on the table.

"I'm for real."

"I couldn't possibly—"

"Yes, you could!" Ritchie is emphatic. "You know people—agents, producers. Real ones, not the bullshit I've been dealing with. I just need a foot in the door, someone to vouch for me so the people I meet won't think I'm just another hack. You're my best friend—"

"And best friends are honest, Ritchie," Joshua says all in a rush. "You *are* just another hack. You're too big, you're too green, you're too...a lot of things. As an actor, you don't give me anything to work with. And for me, that's saying a lot."

"Stop!" Ritchie shakes his head in agony. "This is not what I need to hear."

"I try to sugarcoat it." Joshua is on a roll. "But I don't know if I'm really doing you a favor in the long run. And another thing—your time has come and gone. If you were 21 or 22, maybe you could get something going."

"Just *stop*," Ritchie begs, getting up. The restaurant is blurred by tears. "You're not my friend. You're an asshole and a fuckin' empty waste of space. You don't know me and I don't know you, okay? Goodbye!"

The room is closing in. Ritchie turns from the table and hurries toward the front door, pushing past the surprised waiter who is just arriving with their pizzas.

"I hate your hair," Joshua shouts after him. Ritchie keeps walking.

He is out the door and on the street, furious at all the shoppers around him with their bags, loathing the people waiting for the bus. Fuck Joshua! Fuck everyone. He has to get home. He has to get in his car. He has to get to away from Los Angeles as quickly as possible.

Saturday comes. Freddy, Claire, and Joshua meet at Noble's. The mood is somber. Thanksgiving passed uncelebrated except for the turkey dinner Claire ordered in from Koo Koo Roo. Along with Lisbeth and Justin they ate from plastic plates in her living room and left shortly thereafter, everyone going home to his or her own moping.

They've been on the phone with each other several times a day since Ritchie disappeared. Freddy hung out around the office at the gym, prying and eventually begging for information: "Please. It's for his own good."

"He called in day before yesterday," the manager told Freddy after a reasonable amount of hesitation and a dramatic sigh.

"Said he had the stomach flu. I haven't heard from him since. He's missed three clients. It would have been more except for the holiday."

Worrying that acute sickness—or worse—was the reason Ritchie wasn't answering his phone, Freddy went over to Ritchie's apartment. He knocked on the door repeatedly, louder each time, waiting in between knocks for an answer.

After many unsuccessful attempts, Freddy took a couple of steps back, rushed the door, and busted it in. The flimsy lock broke so easily that the door gave way, leaving Freddy to stumble forward into Ritchie's front hall.

"Ritchie?" he called out and was met with silence.

He walked gingerly to the bedroom, fearful of what he might find.

But the place was vacant. Drawers were pulled out, underwear tossed on the bed. It seemed like sloppiness Ritchie would not condone. The bathroom light was on, the exhaust fan whirring. The medicine cabinet was ajar. Moving to the kitchen, Freddy found apples and bananas in a bowl on the countertop rotting, turning spotty and hosting several fruit flies that flitted and danced about until Freddy took the bowl to the sink at arm's length, ran the tap on it, and squished the spoiled produce down the garbage disposal.

"You want some more coffee?" the waiter at Noble's asks, and Freddy startles.

"Sure," he mutters, moving aside when he realizes his arm is blocking his cup.

"I don't want to call the police again," Claire says. "They already think I'm a crank from the times I've gone after them about Hugh. And now this. They'll either assign me my own full-time detective or book me a padded cell at County Harbor."

"I'll call," Joshua insists. "It's my fault he's gone—"

"Stop it," Freddy admonishes. "You had a fight. It's human—"

"I said terrible things."

"That's okay," Claire says. "I thought them."

The busboy comes to clear their dishes. None of them had much of an appetite this morning, and the food is largely undisturbed. So too are the three slabs of bear claw pastry Charlie had the waiter bring over, compliments of the house, when he noticed how glum the trio of friends are this morning.

It's a shame to be so sad at Christmas time, Freddy decides, and after a few moments he realizes that this sacrilege is not self-correcting. The cheery music playing on the speakers overhead seems shrill and obtrusive.

"Christmas," Freddy grumbles.

"Christmas," Claire repeats as if it were a dirty word.

Joshua shrugs. "Hanukkah?"

They sit and stew.

"It's my fault," Joshua starts in again.

"Would you shut up about that?" Claire snaps.

"It is—"

"Isn't."

"Both of you!" Freddy shouts. "Please."

At that moment, the bell attached to the front door of the restaurant for Christmas cheer tinkles, signaling the arrival of a new customer. Freddy glances over, then sits up with a start. It's Ritchie who has just come through the door.

"Hey," Freddy says, standing up.

"Hey," Ritchie replies weakly, approaching their table.

He is a shadow of himself. A five-day scruff of beard darkens his face and a knit cap flattens his hair to the brow. He's wearing a soiled hoodie and a pair of pants that need to be ironed.

"You're alive," Claire observes cautiously as her face wrenches with emotion.

"Hi," Joshua says in a small voice.

Ritchie walks forward and envelopes him in a bear hug that makes Joshua say "Whoa!" He pats Ritchie on the back to beg for air. Over Ritchie's shoulder, Joshua gives Freddy a wide-eyed look of surprise at the embrace.

After he releases Joshua, Ritchie pulls out the vacant chair at the table and sits down.

"I went away," he tells them unnecessarily.

"But you're back," Freddy observes.

"I'm back. I went to the desert, past Victorville, past any

towns. There was this little motel. I didn't sleep much. I just had to sort things out."

Ritchie reaches for the plate of toast the busboy has not yet cleared and eats it hungrily. His three best friends watch him silently. Once he has finished and taken a long drink of Freddy's water, he continues.

"I thought of quitting all this and going back to Chicago, just packing my shit up and flying out on the next plane. But that would be like dying. I can't go back there. I have too much life in me to just give up."

Ritchie's eyes are a little sunken and the rims are red. But he seems more resolved than Freddy has ever seen him and gives off an air of strength despite his appearance.

"I'm so sorry. Can you forgive me?" Joshua asks.

Ritchie smiles and nods his head yes.

"You were right about everything you said," he tells Joshua. "Now I just have to figure out what to do about it. It's good that I went away."

"You could have called..." Freddy begins, then catches himself. He shakes his head. "We're glad you're safe."

"I'm not yet," Ritchie counters. "But I will be."

The darkness is returning. Joshua thought he had given it the slip, but it is insidious. Without realizing, he has crossed his bleak no-man's-land and is in trouble. The branches of the neighbor's old oak tree, now bare for winter, taunt him in the morning. Their presence is a cruelty.

Ritchie is back, but his return hasn't made things all better. The damage from the fight with Joshua seems to linger. There is a coolness between them now, an uncomfortable off-handed quality to their conversations.

"How are you doing today?" Joshua asks for lack of something else to say.

"Fine, thanks," Ritchie replies automatically.

It is awkward when they end a conversation. Each seems in a hurry to go, then waits for the other to hang up first. Never have things felt so strange between them.

A client has left Joshua's publicity roster. She published a coffee table book with pictures of flags following the 9/11 tragedy, and everyone's done buying her wares now, so there is no reason for her to continue her professional relationship with Joshua. At the same time a very minor sitcom actress he represents has gone off retainer. On the hope that she will find it in her heart to recompense him, he's decided to keep working for her even though he's not getting paid.

The rent at the office will be due for January first. Usually Joshua knows a month ahead where the funds to pay it will come from. This month, it will take an act of celestial kindness to cover his tab. Also, the phone company is about to disconnect his DSL service for lack of payment.

None of this is good. Any single item would be surmountable, but it is all coming at the same time. And now, when he should be the most available to his friend and his vocation, he would prefer to stay in bed and pull the blankets over his head.

Then, Timothy phones. Min puts the call through.

"Hello you," Joshua says hopefully.

"Hey." Timothy sounds far off, though he is just across the freeway at a studio in Westwood.

"What's going on?" Joshua asks gamely.

"Nothin', nothin'. Just working."

"Well, good for you," Joshua commends him. There is definitely something wrong.

"Gotta talk."

"Shoot," Joshua says, bracing himself.

"I can't keep seeing you," Timothy tells him matter-of-factly.

"What?"

"My manager thinks I need to focus on my career right now. I've got big things coming up, and I don't need distractions. And the gay thing...I don't know, Joshua."

"Yes, you do know. You know exactly. You're chicken."

"That's not fuckin' fair," Timothy defends himself. "I want to make it. I've been working for this since I was, like, 10 years old. I'm fuckin' Japanese, you know? It's stacked against me. So here comes my break. And I'm not going to screw it up."

"Being with me means screwing it up," Joshua says in disbelief.

"You're taking this the wrong way."

"I'm taking this the only way! Fine—do what your manager thinks is best. I can't believe you're letting him make decisions about our life together."

"Yo, man. Slow down. We don't have a life together. You're just a guy, okay?"

"You don't know how to stop when you're ahead," Joshua says, laughing bitterly.

"And you," Timothy replies, dead serious, "don't know how to stop when you're behind."

Joshua weighs this and wants to have a glib comeback, but none presents itself.

The phone line crackles.

"I should get going," Timothy says.

"I guess I will talk to you later," Joshua offers, though he knows he will not.

"Yeah. Later. Peace."

For a few moments, Joshua holds the phone handset, now an inert thing. Then he sets it down on the desk and kicks the waste basket. This feels good, so he kicks it again, and it is satisfying yet. After Joshua's third swift wallop of the metal can, Min shouts from the lobby in his most commanding lilt for Joshua to "Stop that right now!"

Joshua looks out at the lobby in disdain. Then, all of a sudden, he wants to go hug Min. But he doesn't. He sits still and looks out the window at the skyline of Century City, a cruel, soulless place with buildings that reach to drag their fingers through the clouds that swirl off the ocean. A red light blinks on the spire of one of the skyscrapers. It makes him think of Rudolph's nose. Christmas is coming, but not for the Jew boy from the land of Latter Days. For him there is no joy, no satisfaction.

Timothy has dumped him, and it is almost better to have the dull, throbbing ache of the last week replaced by a sharp new hurt. It gives Joshua somewhere to focus his ire, as opposed to creating an emotional valley in which his lack of fury may fester.

Joshua kicks the can one more time for good measure.

"Don't make me come in there," Min warns.

At this, Joshua smiles for the first time in days.

FIFTEEN

Claire is sitting on the patio looking out at her backyard when Freddy comes in. She told him to use the spare key he keeps in his glove box; Claire wouldn't leave the front door unlocked now, not with the Hugh situation. She is curled up in one of the Cape Cod chairs with her legs drawn under her. It is a still, dim afternoon and the air is cool. (Despite this, Claire is barefoot, and her toes are scratched from the chair.) The cordless phone from her bedroom is beside her, along with a mug of bitter green tea that has gotten cold. Dog runs on the lawn, rutting and nosing under the leaves that have fallen from the ash tree next to the garage.

Claire waits for Freddy patiently, hearing the sound of him shuffling through her house. When he appears in the doorway, she turns slightly and greets him with a glance.

"Thanks for coming," she says a little timidly. Claire is glad that he's here, but regrets how she made it sound like an emergency when she called. She is not usually one for histrionics.

"Of course." He has brought Claire's old chenille blanket from the sofa and lays it over her shoulders.

Claire accepts the kindness and pulls the warmth around her like a cape. She has been wavering for many minutes between tears and a dull, unpleasant loneliness.

Freddy slips into the chair opposite her and the zipper of his jacket knocks against the wood of the slatted back.

Claire feels her eye twitch slightly.

"You see that?" she asks Freddy, opening her eye theatrically wide for his inspection.

No, he doesn't see the twitch.

"That used to happen to me sometimes when I was little," she tells him. "And I thought it meant that I had a worm in my eye, just like we gave our dog pills for heartworm. It freaked me out and when I told my mom about it, she laughed."

Claire turns back toward the yard with a single, bitter chuckle. "I'm 42 years old. I don't need her approval."

Claire sees her mother standing on the back steps in Far Rockaway. She is wearing her long plaid winter coat with big buttons and her face is turned toward Claire, who skates on the rink her father made with water from the garden hose. Claire goes around in a circle with her arms stretched wide like Dorothy Hamill. Her mother applauds, but faintly, and hurries to the garage where she seems more interested in fighting with Claire's father than in Claire's prowess on the ice.

Claire skates harder, banking at the edge of the backyard rink.

"Mommy," she calls out, hoping to impress her mother, attempting an axle that spins out wrong and lands Claire on her shoulder on the ice. Her arm throbs.

"For God's sakes, Claire! Be more careful," her mother scolds.

Claire's cheek lies against the coldness. She lifts her head to look at her mother, who has already turned her attention back to the squabble with Claire's father. They are arguing about the car. Claire lets her face drop back against the ice, imagining what it would be like to disappear.

In Claire's grown-up backyard in West Hollywood, Dog has found a squirrel to bother. She chases it around and around and up the tree, which the squirrel can climb but Dog cannot.

"You need her," Freddy says.

Claire shakes her head no, but this is a lie. She needs her mother now more than any time since her accident on the way to senior prom. In recent years Claire and her mother only talk about once a week, but her mother's voice stays with her wherever she goes.

"Ah ah ah. Fattening," she warns when Claire picks up a package of macadamia chocolates at Trader Joe's and considers tossing it in her cart. Claire puts it back on the rack.

"That's my girl," her mother whispers in Claire's ear after Claire has solved the puzzle of a patient's malady that other doctors have been unable to treat successfully.

Claire sniffles slightly and realizes with a start that she has begun to cry. She looks over at Freddy, and now that the tears have started, they won't stop. They fall from her cheeks onto her lap. Freddy gets up and comes around behind her, holding her and stroking her hair.

Panicked, she tries to pry his arm from around her.

"Stop!" Her protest is soggy. "I'm a strong woman."

"Of course you are. I know, I know."

"I hate being seen like this," Claire wails, beside herself.

"Let it go," Freddy implores.

"No!" She struggles and gets away from him, scooting to the front edge of the chair and turning around. "I'm fine."

She wills her tears to stop, wiping at her face forcefully with both sleeves of her shirt.

"I think I just need to be alone. I'm sorry for calling you over here, then."

"I'm not going anywhere."

Claire pulls the blanket onto her lap and starts to fold it.

"Really. I think I just need to be alone for a while."

Freddy gets it. He straightens up, stands, and looks out at the yard.

"If that's what you need," he says sadly.

"Yeah."

Freddy nods, his lips pursed and his gaze distant.

"They bind us, don't they?" he says. "No matter how strong our friendships are, it's our families who define us."

He looks at Claire, who glances up at him for a moment before looking back out at Dog.

Freddy stands quiet for a moment. Claire doesn't move.

"I guess I'll be going then," he says in a small voice.

She nods and keeps watching Dog.

It is only after she hears the front door close that she relaxes back into the chair, her hair falling into her eyes.

Dusk is coming.

Ritchie prayed for two days and two nights, invoking every saint he could think of, kneeling before a bureau-top full of votive candles. He was there in the morning, closing his eyes and rubbing his palms together, whispering to the Lord for guidance as he saw his mother do, tearfully, after his great-uncle passed. There is a grocery on the corner run by a family of Mexicans—they carry rosary beads in red, ivory, and blue. Ritchie bought a string of them in each available color for good measure. He knelt on sore knees, face to heaven, until the wax from the candles dripped onto the carpet and into the top dresser drawer. Now Ritchie has no more wearable gym socks, but his heart has found its answer.

His savings account at the National Bank of California contains one thousand, four hundred twenty-eight dollars. He has decided he will spent most of the money before the year is out. There is a cluster of legit theaters on Santa Monica Boulevard a couple of miles east of Boys Town. They occupy several blocks of real estate that local boosters optimistically nicknamed "Theater Row" in hopes the idea will catch on. Yesterday, Ritchie rented a vacant space for two weeks and bought a dozen copies of *A Streetcar Named Desire* from the Samuel French store. He has cast two girls from his old acting class to play Stella and Blanche. He himself will take the role of Stanley Kowalski.

He doesn't see this as one of his notorious "brilliant ideas." He feels it's his last chance and, despite that, he believes he's approaching it smartly.

"Are you sure you want to do Tennessee Williams?" Freddy asks him skeptically when Ritchie calls to share the news.

"I'm absolutely sure. It fits me."

"Then why have you waited this long?"

"It wasn't time."

Ritchie sits in his apartment alone, running lines from the play:

> You remember the way it was? Them nights we had together? God, honey, it's gonna be sweet when we can make noise in the night the way we used to and get the colored lights going with nobody's sister behind the curtain to hear us!

He talks to the walls, trying to feel the character. He thinks of guys from back home. There weren't a lot of Polish in his neighborhood, but plenty of regular Italian dummies who worked the stockyards and docks. His pops played cards with them.

Ritchie closes the bathroom door and imagines Blanche DuBois behind it, unwilling to get out of the tub. He shouts at her: "Hey, canary bird! Toots! Get *out* of the *bathroom*!"

Ritchie goes to the corner store and buys a six-pack of beer. Back home, he turns up the heat until he sweats, then strips to an undershirt and wipes a bottle across his forehead to cool himself.

He talks like Stanley and walks like Stanley.

Once he finds the nerve, he calls Joshua.

"Hello?" Joshua is still aloof after their fight. Ritchie wants to shake him, but there are things more pressing.

"I need to talk to you about my show," he says.

"I'll e-mail an event release to the Hollywood News Calendar," Joshua offers, though he sounds distracted. "And if you need flyers—"

"Definitely I do—"

"I can have Min print some up."

Ritchie can't believe his ears.

"That would be very kind," he says.

"Suddenly you're so polite."

"Suddenly," Ritchie jokes, "I have something worth being polite about."

For the first time in a while, they laugh before they hang up.

Ritchie's next call is to Claire, who agrees unconditionally to pass around flyers for Ritchie's show at her medical building.

"You want me to wear a sandwich board? I can walk around in front of the elevators with a big picture of you on my stomach, which would get the message across."

"Not the right message."

"Any press is good press," she says, singsong.

"You sound like Joshua."

"Ptewy! For that I spit on you."

"Be nice. I love him," Ritchie blurts. "I mean—he's my friend."

"Mine too."

"But," Ritchie blushes furiously. "Yes. Of-of course he is."

He gets off the phone with Claire quickly, feeling a little panicky and odd. Maybe, he decides, he is getting sick. Ritchie looks in the bathroom mirror, sticks out his tongue, feels the glands in his throat.

"Joshua," he says to himself in wonderment.

The apartment is dark when Freddy gets back from the library.

He went intending to do research for a long-postponed article on the correlation between witchcraft and homosexuality. This isn't a very interesting topic to him, but he is supposed to get $500 from the magazine when he turns it in, and that amount of money would be useful right now, with just a few days left till Christmas and no presents bought. But instead of doing research, Freddy spent two hours people-watching. Deep down, he hadn't really expected to get work done. It was more of an excuse to get himself out of the house. Freddy has discovered that sitting home alone is bad enough; sitting home with a crazy boyfriend who's more crazy than friend is too much for Freddy to handle.

It has been raining for several days now, and Justin refuses to leave the confines of the now-familiar walls of Freddy's place. He won't go to the psychiatrist, despite heavy cajoling. He won't go to the movies; he won't even walk around the block despite Freddy's having brought him a fancy new umbrella and a pair of knock-off Gucci galoshes from Ross Dress for Less. Freddy himself has had few reasons to leave the house, other than runs to the supermarket and occasional forays to the gym.

He sets his keys down on the counter.

"Justin?" he calls, switching the kitchen light on.

The only reply is the gentle whir of the refrigerator compressor as the appliance kicks on. Freddy continues to the living room, fumbling for the light switch.

"Justin?" he says again, and again there is no answer.

The room is a mess: sofa pillows piled on the floor, magazines strewn, a bowl of melted ice cream slowly attaching itself with drippy vanilla glue to the glass top of the coffee table. Freddy wrinkles his nose in disgust and moves on to the bedroom, which he finds in similarly disheveled condition. Was it this messy when he left, and he is just seeing it with fresh eyes? Surely not! Freddy is reminded of his recent sleuthing through Ritchie's apartment and the wary trip he took from room to room, anticipating the worst.

Justin seems to be staging his own production of Ritchie's disappearing act.

He couldn't have gone out in the rain, Freddy reasons, or at least he wouldn't. He must be somewhere in the apartment building. If he's not in the hallway, and not on the roof—also out of the question because of the inclement weather—there is only one remaining possibility. Freddy fiddles with the lock on his front door so it will remain open, then makes his way to the basement stairs. It is creepy down there—bare bulbs illuminating the way, spiders and crumbled soil on the floor. There isn't a proper poured foundation for the building except in the section of the room set aside for chicken-wire storage lockers for the units upstairs. The rest is graded hillside. Now, Freddy discovers as he reaches the bottom of the stairwell and pulls the chain on a light fixture to turn it on, the floor is damp with moisture. It gives off the peculiar earthy smells of dust mixed with the sweetness of newly turned grave. Apparently the ground has soaked up all the rain it can, forcing trickles of water to meander across its surface.

"Justin," Freddy says hesitantly, and again there is no answer, but Freddy hears a scrape from the corner of the room. He pulls the chain of another light bulb and, in its illumination, walks around the corner of the building's rusting, disused washing machine. Justin is there, crouched in the shadow.

"What in God's name are you doing?" Freddy asks.

Justin stammers a brief reply that doesn't really sound much like English.

Freddy looks down. Sitting in the near dark, Justin has laid out an elaborate mosaic of pebbles, splinters of wood, and dead water bugs. It is macabre and makes Freddy shiver. Around this arrangement, as if to frame it, Justin has placed the coiled cord from Freddy's electric shaver, which has been missing for several days. The cord is cut in several places so that it gives the impression of a collection of pig tails or a handful of black fusilli pasta.

"Justin, no," Freddy says softly, but Justin doesn't move, instead staring at his work of art. "No, no, no."

They are both still for a moment.

"Can you hear me talking to you?" Freddy asks. Either Justin cannot or will not acknowledge Freddy, for he keeps staring down at the rough dirt floor, rocking back and forth like an autistic child.

Freddy drops to all fours, soiling his jeans and palms, and draws up alongside Justin.

"Please," Freddy begs in a whisper, "answer me."

The only acknowledgment he gives of Freddy's entreaty is a slight shift of his head in Freddy's direction.

Freddy reaches to pick up the severed bits of his shaver cord, but at this, Justin's far-off expression darkens, so Freddy leaves the cord alone and sits back against the washing machine next to Justin.

Several minutes pass in silence.

Freddy feels defeated, hopeless. Slowly, he rises, wipes damp dirt from his hands and heads upstairs.

"I'll be back," he tells Justin, who doesn't seem particularly in a state of mind to appreciate Freddy's departure.

Up in the apartment, Freddy goes to the computer and clicks on a discount travel Web site before phoning Joshua at the office.

"Can you come over?" Freddy asks once Joshua's said hello.

"I'm in the middle of a bunch of different—"

"Now would be good," Freddy interrupts. "If you can."

"Okay..." Joshua says. "Let me hand this stuff to Min. I'll be right there."

Freddy hangs up and turns his attention back to the computer, taking out his wallet to get his credit card number. He is operating in a dull, emotionless state, a place that resides beyond sorrow and remorse. Some call it resolve, but for Freddy it's far less sophisticated than that. It is more akin to pragmatism.

When Joshua arrives, Freddy has made his purchase and printed out a receipt.

"Have you got a couple of hours?" he asks Joshua, who nods yes and looks concerned.

"Let's pack," Freddy says.

He goes to the kitchen, gets a large black trash bag, and puts this in the middle of the bedroom floor along with Justin's surviving duffel. The dilapidated, duct-taped suitcases with which Justin arrived met the trash Dumpster many weeks ago. Slowly, Freddy sifts through the junk that he has accumulated around the apartment, putting into Justin's bag anything that looks to be of immediate practical use or emotional significance and throwing the rest in the garbage bag. A charm bracelet goes in the duffel. A zip-lock bag of cigarette butts goes in the trash. A stack of flyers on Scientology, which Justin picked up while he was out and about one day—trash, along with a large stick from the yard. A ratty pair of blue jeans—save.

Joshua helps, sorting through the mess in silence and holding out questionable items for a judgment call, which Freddy issues by pointing at one bag or the other. Again and again, they find crumpled dollar bills jammed in pants pockets, and occasionally they come across a five.

"At least he'll have cab fare," Joshua points out, smoothing a bill and adding it to a growing pile on the bed. Freddy nods a humorless acknowledgment.

The front door is unlocked and ajar. After about a half hour of their packing, Justin wanders upstairs, comes into the apartment, and stands watching them in silence. Once there is space cleared, he goes to a corner of the bedroom and sits, cross-legged, observing the scene in front of him as if it were a movie. Several times, Freddy looks up and wonders if Justin can comprehend what's happening.

"You're going back to New York," he tells him eventually. "On the red-eye."

Justin nods sadly. On some level, he understands.

Freddy shudders to imagine what will happen to Justin once he steps off the plane at LaGuardia, but he can't think about that now. It's not his worry. Justin must fend for himself. Freddy is done.

Justin begins to rock back and forth as he did down in the basement. Slowly, he begins to sing a little song. At first—predictably—it seems to have no tune. But after a few phrases, Freddy starts to recognize as one of the numbers from *The Jungle Book*. The melody is scrambled, and Justin keeps looping back and forth in the verse, but it is recognizable nonetheless.

In half an hour, the packing is complete. Justin's duffel bag is stuffed full, as are two large trash sacks. Freddy looks at the three containers waiting to be taken out the front door, marveling at how much space in his apartment had been filled by Justin's claptrap.

"Come on," Freddy urges Justin, who is still sitting in the corner of the bedroom on the floor.

"I'm not going," Justin says, suddenly lucid.

"Yes, you are."

Freddy glances over at Joshua and nods. They take Justin by the elbows and bring him to a standing position. Tears well in Justin's eyes and his bottom lip quivers.

"No," he protests almost silently.

"Yes," Freddy insists. "Here, put on socks and shoes. It's cold in New York."

Slowly, Justin complies. Then with the help of Joshua, Freddy walks him out into the hall, grabs a jacket from the front closet, and throws it over Justin's shoulders. With his free hand, he grabs the car keys and printed airline receipt and shoves both into his pocket. He pulls the front door closed behind him with a thump that sounds very final.

The drive to the airport is a blur for Freddy. It is the middle of the evening and pouring rain outside. The road signs and billboards are a series of snapshots dropping into a murky lake, one image growing dark as the next falls atop it. Nobody speaks in the car except for Joshua, who breaks the silence to point out that Freddy is about the pass the freeway exit for LAX.

They park and walk to the terminal. Justin has his duffel slung over his shoulder and carries his photo album and the picture program from *The Jungle Book*. Freddy and Joshua stand and watch as he goes through security. It is an elaborate procedure, slowed by the multitude of wristwatches and jewelry he wears strapped to his arms. The woman on duty with the wand is kind to him. She waits for the trinkets to be taken off, one by one, and passes them to her uniformed colleague at the metal detector, who places them in a basket. It takes Justin five attempts before he manages to make it through without setting off the apparatus.

"I bet they get a lot of crazy people going through security," Freddy muses.

"And drunks," Joshua adds with a nod.

Freddy leans against the wall, waiting for something in the security procedure to go awry and for Justin to come running back to him for comfort or guidance. But there is no glitch beyond the obvious slowness of the process, and Justin does not turn around until he has finished and is sent on his way to the gate, at which point he looks back and gives Freddy and Joshua a small wave goodbye.

At this point, a tsunami of sorrow washes through Freddy, stealing his footing and making him grab at the slick wall to keep himself upright. Joshua is quick with an arm of reassurance, but his efforts fall short of what Freddy needs. The grief is large and the shoring up would have to be also; it is more than Joshua can offer in the airport and probably more than Freddy can accept. So he falters, at loose ends, one hand against the wall to stabilize himself, the other clutching for Joshua.

Down the concourse, Justin walks away from them, his figure growing smaller and disappearing into the crowd.

Freddy turns and buries his face in the shoulder of Joshua's jacket.

"You did your best," Joshua says.

SIXTEEN

Other than his obsession with Claire, Hugh's job seems to be all he cares about.

The problem for poor Hugh is that if Claire is granted a formal restraining order, it may have a devastating effect on his livelihood. Even if Claire didn't make a direct report to the state board, a restraining order might give them a whiff of the dramatics and move them to censure Hugh in a way that would be publicly and professionally embarrassing.

Claire sees this as leverage. As much as the whole matter sickens her, she realizes that she is playing a tight game of chess with someone infirm and there is no way she can avoid it.

Just lately, she's been getting calls that come up "Richard Hoffman DDS" or "Dr. Evie Parks" on her caller ID. All of the numbers are in the 310 area code and have a prefix of 642. Claire suspects that now, unable to reach her from his own phone, Hugh has been calling from other lines in his office building. This would make him guilty not only of stalking, but of breaking and entering and, perhaps, some sort of identity theft.

In any case, Claire has successfully avoided Hugh for several days. She changed her house and cell numbers and seldom answers her own phone in the office. Kitty, her assistant, says there have been a number of hang-ups this week, especially on the answering service. Acting on a hunch, Kitty rerecords Claire's chipper outgoing message in her own voice. That evening, there is only one hang-up on the service. The following day, there are none.

On Wednesday, Claire is in the office alone all afternoon while Kitty goes to a soccer match to watch her boyfriend, a star on the UCLA team.

The main phone rings through to Claire's desk.

"Essential Osteopathy," she answers with a flash of a smile at the name of her medical practice. Freddy convinced her to use the name but it still sounds cumbersome when she says it at cocktail parties or on the phone.

"How are we this afternoon?" Hugh asks.

Claire's smile drops and her face goes numb.

"I'm hanging up now," she says quietly and succinctly.

"Wait! There's something I have to say."

"Really—goodbye, Hugh," she insists. "I can't do this—"

"I heard from the district attorney's office. You didn't have to do that, cupcake," he says with a treacly, preachy warmth. "So messy! Getting people involved in our private life. I had to call my lawyer."

"Call him some more if you like. Call anybody. Just don't call me."

"In all seriousness," he entreats, his tone changed, "I want to make you an offer."

She pauses.

"You have thirty seconds," she says warily.

"Don't file," he blurts. "For Christ's sakes. I'll have my guy draft something saying I'll leave you be. It's loathsome, but if it'll get you to back off—"

"Hugh, I'm not the one who can't back off."

"I'll get him to draft it and send it over. I'll stay away from you, fifty yards."

"A hundred. And never call me again, ever. And don't write."

"You're a very confused girl."

"I'm not a girl, and I'm hanging up now," Claire snarls, her finger ready to depress the button on the phone cradle.

"No-no, wait!" he begs hurriedly. "A hundred yards—you've got it. And I will leave you alone as long as you leave me alone too."

"If we don't talk again until the day I die, that's too soon."

"Do you believe in the afterlife?" Hugh asks, sounding sincere.

Claire scowls and hangs up the phone. She stares at it angrily. Then, with a sense of satisfaction, she reaches behind the base and unplugs the cord.

It is Christmas Day. Freddy joins Ritchie and Joshua at Claire's house for roast turkey and cranberry salad. It is the group's second off-tempo holiday in a row. Joshua, odd man out for a Christian celebration, is in a mood. Ritchie goes in and out of character as Stanley Kowalski, belching at odd times and shouting, "Stella-a-ah!" off the back porch at Dog, who whines and cries irritably in response.

Claire seems jumpy every time the phone rings, which today is mostly when Lisbeth calls to report on her progress through the holiday travel snarl. She and a girlfriend have decided to spend two weeks in a tree house somewhere in Belize.

As for Freddy, it has been a tough five days since he sent Justin away. As cluttered as the apartment was before, now—in a case of equal and opposite—it feels empty. Justin's absence screams from every tidy shelf and well-plumped throw pillow. The smell of cigarette smoke is gone; the last clothes Freddy wore in Justin's presence were what he had on in the car to the airport, and it has all been through the laundry. Justin has not called or e-mailed—though just today, Freddy has an uncanny sense that Justin's torment is gone and his poor soul is without worry. It is as if an angel has told Freddy this.

In consequence, he is quite touchy emotionally, subject to the whim of television commercials, such as the ones for cellular providers in which joyful calls between family members seem to make up for their absence in each others' lives.

Sitting on Claire's sofa, Freddy is absorbed in one of her books of journalistic photography. He almost bursts into tears at poignant images of soldiers in battle and stooped old women selling scrawny vegetables in Third World marketplaces.

The CD remote control is on the table. Freddy know that, were Justin here, Claire would have it well-hidden. She would have warned Lisbeth not to leave too many cigarettes available—especially the Gauloises, which Justin preferred to his domestic brand when he was putting on sophisticated airs.

The friends laugh as much as they can, which is not a whole lot right now. Claire has found a Puerto Rican recipe for turkey that calls for a heavy stuffing that's gloppy wet with spaghetti sauce. Freddy is vocally skeptical, but it turns out to everyone's liking. As a matter of fact, the turkey is the hit of the party. Freddy apologizes for having doubted Claire's culinary prowess and retires to the sofa to wait out his stuffedness.

His emotions will balance out, he decides, just as soon as Justin gets his shit together in New York and flies back a changed man to resume his destined position at Freddy's side. He will sing Freddy sweet songs in the morning and the afternoon and make sugary love to him at night.

As Freddy drives home from Claire's, rubber wipers flopping against the bottom of the windshield as if they cannot find a comfortable position in which to lie, he notices again how much his anxiety around Justin has lessened. You get someone out of your house, Freddy reasons, and a few days later, a bright white angel comes down and tells you not to worry, that everything is fine now. But it's not an entirely comfortable thing because the feeling is so strong and specific, and it involves an angel, a construct that Freddy rejects. And he doesn't want to think about what he fears. Yet the Christmas angel speaks louder:

"He is better now. His suffering has abated."

Freddy wonders whether he has eaten something bad at Claire's. After he crawls into bed and turns out the light, he falls into a shallow, feverish sleep. The angel, now clothed in a dark gray woolen coat over some kind of circus getup, is more like a bird of prey, though it has a head of human hair—blond ringlets that fall against its cheeks. It speaks the same basic message:

"He is at peace."

"You sound like a damned fortune cookie," Freddy retorts and wakes with a start, realizing he's actually spoken aloud. Wiping the drool from the corner of his mouth, he turns the other way in bed, thinking of the restless windshield wipers.

At about 2 in the morning, he is up wandering around the apartment in stocking feet and looks in the fridge, finding nothing there to tempt him. So he calls the Pink Dot delivery service.

"I'll take a pint of cookie dough ice cream," he says with hurried politeness when the lady answers, "a pint of strawberry, and a slice of chocolate blackout cake."

Twenty minutes later, he is drowned in sweet creaminess, regretting what he's doing and simultaneously not caring.

"You want some?" he asks, holding out a spoonful of ice cream to the angel, now invisible. When there is no reply, he shrugs and shoves it in his own mouth.

Freddy dozes again, and when he wakes it is pale morning. The power has gone off at some point during the night, so his alarm clock is flashing. He has to log onto the computer to find that it is 9:30. He doesn't feel well from the cake and ice cream during the night and the heavy meal before that.

The telephone rings a few minutes later. Freddy clears his throat to answer it, preparing a funny character for Claire or Joshua, whom he assumes will show up momentarily in the caller ID. But when the information flashes, it is neither of them. Instead, it is a Manhattan number.

"Hello?" Freddy says expectantly, waiting for the familiar sound of Justin's voice. Maybe he's gotten sober already—it *is* Christmas and all—and he's ready to make a fresh start.

"Is this Freddy Ruckert?" The man on the other end of the phone is a stranger, his tone bleak.

"Yes, who's calling?"

"I'm the day manager of the Chelsea Hotel. We have a guest registered by the name of Justin Salvatore. Do you know him?"

"I do," Freddy says as sick feeling descends on him. Instantly erased are the hopes for Justin's radical recovery. Instead Freddy wonders what fresh mess he's gotten into.

"He was a cash guest. We require a nonfamily reference when someone checks in without a credit card, and you were the contact he put down. We're all deeply sorry, sir—"

"What are you telling me?"

"Sir, Mr. Salvatore took his own life in one of our rooms yesterday."

"Oh, my God," Freddy gasps, doubling over.

"Housekeeping found him on rounds this morning. The police are here now. But I thought you might want to know."

"Yes, thank you for calling," Freddy chokes.

"Are you there?" the man on the phone asks eventually.

"I..." Freddy tries to compose himself enough to speak, but the task is difficult. When he talks it comes out in a weird squeak. "Yes, I'm here. May I ask how he—I mean, can you release that information."

"Do you really want to know?"

"Yes," Freddy tells him, probably more quickly than he ought to.

"He sliced his wrists, then hung himself with a belt from the shower rod. I guess he wanted to be sure it worked."

Freddy's body and face contort into a gargoyle of anguish. The picture in his head is horrible. He falls to the sofa and then to the rug and the phone slips from his hands. He can't breathe well. Somewhere, off in the distance, he hears himself moaning in little asthmatic huffs. This goes on for a length of time he cannot determine. There is no sense of tempo now, only tragedy, which is oceanic—elliptical and continuous.

Eventually he looks at the floor and sees the phone off its cradle.

"Hello?" he says, fumbling to pick up the handset.

"Yes, I'm here...we're all very sorry, sir. Some of the staff—they were fans of his."

"Did he leave a note?" Freddy asks in a hoarse whisper. "I mean, why did he do it?"

"There was no note, sir. The night manager says Mr. Salvatore called down to the desk on Christmas Eve for cigarettes and razors. After housekeeping dropped those off, that's the last anyone heard from him."

"Thank you for letting me know," Freddy manages to say. He hangs up with a minimum of formalities.

In the bedroom is a ratty teddy bear of Justin's that Freddy inadvertently forgot to pack when he was turning Justin out. Now he grabs it, stumbles around, and is back on the floor, overcome. Holding the teddy bear to his chest, he curls up in a ball near the foot of the bed and lies there, moaning in anguish, for what seems an absurdly long time.

He senses, at one point, the day slipping away from him, though the alarm clock is still flashing twelve o'clock.

The phone rings again. It is another New York call. For a moment, Freddy imagines it will be Justin calling, telling him everything was a wild hoax and isn't Freddy the sap for believing it!

Instead, it is a girl from the Walt Disney Company. Apparently, bad news travels quickly. She wants to know if Freddy can go to New York in two days for a memorial service put on by the producers of *The Jungle Book* who, along with Justin's mother, requested Freddy be there.

Freddy is unable to think clearly and is thick-tongued, but he agrees to come. He sits for some minutes, his mind looping and racing, before picking up the phone and calling Claire.

"Hey," he croaks when she answers.

"What's the matter?" she asks, concerned by Freddy's tone.

He pauses, looking up at the ceiling so he will not burst out crying again.

"You and I are going on a trip," he tells her with no ornamentation.

The plane lands at JFK fifteen minutes ahead of schedule. This is not necessarily good news, because it means Claire and Freddy will have a longer wait between their early morning arrival and the time they can check into their hotel room. But Freddy does not seem perturbed by this. He has kept to himself in a way Claire has never before experienced and seems driven to some purpose beyond the obvious.

She agreed to come, despite misgivings about her own schedule, because this is the sort of thing real friends do for one another. Freddy wants to rent a car, which seems odd to her, but she doesn't protest, as he is under duress and seems to have some elaborate plan worked out. She will go along with things, for once, and not question.

After they leave the car rental agency, carry-on luggage stowed in the trunk, Freddy steers them onto the drab, icy length of Rockaway Boulevard instead of Grand Central Parkway.

"You took the wrong turn," Claire instructs, pointing toward the on-ramp to the GCP in a way she hopes will not be invidious.

Freddy smiles faintly but doesn't respond. He makes several turns that bring them to Beach Channel Drive, not far from the spot where Claire had her accident. They pass the high school that was brand new when Claire went there. She is flooded with memories.

"Now you're really going the wrong way," she says a little more sternly.

"No," he counters, "I'm not."

It is at this moment she realizes that her presence on this trip is not happenstance, nor is it primarily for Freddy's comfort. He has an agenda. This puts Claire on edge.

"Tell me what's going on," she demands, adjusting her scarf, which is choking her a bit as a result of the over-aggressive seat belt. She notices, out the window, that there is now a Starbuck's in Rockaway.

"I have the memorial service this afternoon, but there's plenty of time for that." Freddy looks in the rearview mirror, puts on his turn signal, and makes a left onto the street where Claire used to play hopscotch.

"This is surreal," she says, a little panicked, "and a nice idea. I'll give you a tour sometime. But really—I'm not in the mood right now. So can we go to Manhattan?"

"Claire—"

"If the hotel won't let us check in," she hurries, "we can get breakfast somewhere and you can talk about your feelings, or whatever—just get me out of here."

Freddy reaches over and tries to take her hand. But the contact makes Claire shudder, and she pulls back before she can stop herself. Now she is a lousy friend, but so is Freddy for bringing her to Rockaway, especially with no warning. She feels like the victim of a large practical joke, and it angers her.

Freddy rounds the corner of her parents' block.

"I'm warning you," she declares, "this is so not appropriate. Don't even slow down."

But he pulls into the driveway of Claire's old house. She wants to open the car door and run down the block to get away. But there is nowhere to go. She is trapped. And she hates Freddy for meddling.

The house seems tiny. She looks up at the bay window and brick facade with a mix of longing and revulsion. Then she notices the front door is ajar. Why? It must be freezing! She can see, vaguely, into the living room through the screen door.

Then, someone appears in the doorway, lit from behind in silhouette. Squinting, she sees that it is her mother.

"She's waiting," Freddy says quietly.

"You called her?" Claire shouts, outraged. "Of all the ridiculous things you have done in your life, Freddy, this is the worst! I can't believe you had the nerve to—"

"Stop," he tells her with such force and calmness that she immediately complies. "Your mother is waiting."

And indeed, she seems to be, standing awkwardly looking out at the car. Claire's eyes are adjusting. Her mother looks old, resigned. Claire takes a deep breath and assesses the situation as best she can.

"Okay, look," she says, resolved to make the best of it. Then her resolve evaporates. Bitterly, she shakes her head no.

"Claire..."

"I can't," she says in anguish.

Freddy sits still. Claire's mother stands in the doorway. The next move is Claire's.

Slowly, cautiously, she undoes her seat belt and composes herself. The door lock gives her trouble, but with a little negotiation, she is able to open it. She gets out and stands, the wind whipping at her cheeks and hands, and walks very cautiously up the driveway. Frozen snow crunches under her shoes. She reaches the front steps, which are fractured where the cement has frozen and thawed a thousand times. Claire memorized the cracks when she was little because the ants ran in and out of them, which terrified her.

At the door, she stands and looks at her mother wordlessly. The two women are still, taking each other in. Then, ever so slowly, her mother pushes the screen door open. Now Claire can see the tears on her mother's cheeks.

Each of them steps forward a few inches. They get closer and closer. Claire feels herself shaking slightly.

Her mother's veiny hands rise, reach forward, and pull Claire into an embrace. It starts awkwardly and grows more and more tender until they are locked tight, mother and daughter, shivering and weeping with relief.

"C'mon," her mother says, urging Claire into the living room. Claire hesitates, turning around to look at Freddy, who waves her forward. She blows him a kiss and lays her hand over her heart for him to see, knowing that he will need all the courage in the world to get through what he is about to endure without coming apart.

In response, Freddy mimics the gesture and points at Claire, and raises the thumb and pinky of his free hand to his ear and mouth, indicating that he will call her. She nods, and as she turns around to head into the living room, she hears him put the car into reverse and back out of the driveway.

She offers up a fleeting prayer to God, in whom she does not believe, that her dearest friend be carried safe through this day and delivered from the sorrow that has plagued him so unjustly. If there really is a God, she decides, he may start to show himself by taking exceptional care of Freddy Ruckert.

SEVENTEEN

"It's normal to have an attack of nerves on opening night," Joshua assures Ritchie. "But try not to throw up again, would you? You'll be dehydrated and pass out on stage, which would really be out of character for Stanley."

They are backstage at the theater. It is the fifth of January, opening night for *A Streetcar Named Desire*. The show doesn't start for an hour and a half, but Ritchie made the actors' call time exceptionally early in order to allay his own anxiety. This strikes Joshua as justifiable, if unnecessary, as it's Ritchie's money backing the run and therefore his prerogative to decide who shows up when. He's been generous to the girls in the show, partitioning off a private dressing area for them and making certain there are snacks and their favorite sodas backstage.

"I think I'm going to throw up again," Ritchie warns.

"It'll be nothing but bile! Have you eaten, by the way?"

"Not in two days."

"Ritchie!"

"This is too important."

"It's going to be fine," Joshua insists. He has taken measures to insure the evening's success. The whole plan, however, hinges on Ritchie's giving a passable performance. It may seem shallow, but the thing Joshua is gladdest about is that Ritchie has finally given in and cut his hair. He is the opposite of Samson—empowered rather than disabled by the haircut. He looks five years younger now, leaner, less swarthy.

Freddy and Claire appear at the backstage entrance. They have returned from New York and are cleaned up nicely for the evening's event. Emotionally, Claire seems to be doing better than Freddy, but it only makes sense; he stands before a gaping loss, while Claire's wounds are largely repaired.

They wear New York black, as if schooled in advance on the proper attire for such an opening, and Freddy has brought the bottles of Perrier and Merlot Ritchie requested. It is great to be all together again, and especially for such a happy occasion. But Ritchie sends them away.

"I'm too nervous now," he apologizes. "I'll see you after the show."

Claire and Freddy hug him and tell him to break a leg—which, considering Ritchie's clumsiness and attack of nerves, Joshua hopes will not prove prophetic. Once they are gone, Joshua tells Ritchie to sit down in the café chair in front of them.

He steps behind Ritchie, who is already in his character's wife-beater shirt, and massages his shoulders. He kneads the thick muscles deeply and makes his way along Ritchie's neck to the base of his freshly shorn head, where he tickles Ritchie's scalp with his fingertips.

"That feels so good," Ritchie sighs.

"It's supposed to."

"No," Ritchie says, straightening up. "It feels *really* good. You better stop."

He turns around, and the two of them gaze into each others' eyes. This is entirely new territory for them, and the timing is lousy.

"Are you nauseous?" Joshua asks, willfully breaking the spell.

"Suddenly, yes," Ritchie replies gently. "But I feel some stranger things..."

"Thirty minutes, everyone," barks the stage director from the other side of the bed sheet Ritchie hung to separate his own dressing room from the others.

"You better get ready," Joshua says. Then he gives Ritchie a peck on the forehead. It is a quick gesture, but lasts long enough for Joshua to get a good, deep whiff of Ritchie's smell, which has always been tolerable but just lately has become delicious.

Joshua leaves the theater by the fire exit, walks around the side of the building and reenters through the tiny lobby—an exercise that is unfortunately necessary, given the limited space.

He sees that his friends from the *LA Weekly* and the *Los Angeles Times* Calendar section have come. The former—a tall, balding, bearded man with a turtleneck and a pot belly—gives Justin a toothy, yellow hello. The critic from the *Times*—a middle-aged biddy who manages to be mouthy and mousy at the same time—offers him a far less generous nod of acknowledgement. Joshua suspects she doesn't smile much because she has dentures and doesn't want people to know.

The only remaining guest with whom Joshua is concerned is Joel W. Cohen, a fast-talking megabudget action-film producer to whom Joshua said hello at dinner last week at the Four Seasons. In the conversation, Joshua happened to drop an invite to Ritchie's show. He knows Cohen's a fan of twentieth-century American theater, and thought this might be an in.

"Sounds like a plan," Cohen told him too swiftly to be believable. But when Joshua checked with Cohen's assistant yesterday, lo and behold it was in Mr. Cohen's calendar for this evening. His limousine will probably pull up at the last minute. If he catches ten minutes of the show, okay. The point will be that he's been here, and that gives Ritchie's production instant cachet around town. Subsequently, if the show is any good, Joshua will be able to invite whomever he likes, simply mentioning that Joel W. Cohen was there on opening night will make attendance almost compulsory.

The house seats forty-five people. At five minutes to 8, there are at least forty seated. Joshua is thrilled for Ritchie. He squeezes into an empty seat next to Claire and Freddy on the second row—the front row would be too obvious—with Min and Kitty from Claire's office directly behind them. Joshua fans himself with a copy of the program Min assembled according to his directives.

"This is so exciting," Claire whispers.

Freddy smiles his agreement. He doesn't seem to be in a celebratory mood just yet, but looks to be coming around more and more every day. It won't be long, Joshua predicts, before he's back to his old self.

The house lights go down for the performance. A recording of blues piano music starts low in the background and the stage lights come up on a brick-wall set to indicate twilight in New Orleans. Ritchie enters wearing battered overalls and a bowling jacket. He carries a blood-stained package from a butcher's shop.

"Hey, there! Stella, baby!" he bellows in a voice that is self-assured and wholly unlike his own.

The girl from his class steps around the brick wall from the opposite end. She is delicately dressed.

"Don't holler at me like that," she demurs in a dead-on Louisiana drawl. "Hi, Mitch."

She looks over to faintly acknowledge the actor who, dressed like Ritchie, has entered.

"Catch!" Ritchie-Stanley says.

"What?"

"Meat," he tells her in a tone that is both patronizing and sexy.

He heaves the package at her. She cries out in protest but manages to catch it. Then, she laughs almost breathlessly. Ritchie and his companion have already started back around the corner.

"Stanley!" she calls after him. "Where are you going?"

"Bowling," he bellows as if she's a moron.

"Can I come watch?"

He hesitates.

"Come on," he says, exiting stage right.

Ritchie has a way of speaking for Stanley Kowalski that is almost dangerous. But there is also an uncanny ease to the performance. Ritchie *is* Stanley Kowalski, which is something Joshua never expected.

Whatever nerves and misgivings Ritchie had backstage have evaporated in the heat of his performance. He is not simply good as Stanley Kowalski. He is luminous. Williams's intentions shine through like a candle in a crystal lantern.

The audience is enthusiastic at intermission. Joshua says little. It is time to observe rather than to effuse. He sees that Joel Cohen did indeed arrive, likely at the last moment. The fidgety, corpulent man is hunched in the corner with his cell phone. His pear-shaped, Armani-clad frame is turned away from the crowd and his scruffy beard hides any emotion.

The second half of the show is even better than the first. Ritchie savages the girl playing Stella about her sister's made-up past, finding layers of cruelty and machismo in Stanley that make Joshua want to drag Stanley out of the scene, lecture him on his manners, then rip his clothes off. Or maybe that's just what he wants to do to Ritchie. Joshua finds his own intentions unclear.

At the end of the play, the cast gets a standing ovation. They applaud the audience in return before turning and giving particular due to Ritchie. He accepts their accolade gamely.

"Thank you," he says, once everyone has quieted down. "This production is the culmination of over two years of doing everything completely wrong."

Everyone laughs.

"I hope you guys will dig the result and not give me too much crap about what I had to go through to get here."

At this the audience laughs and applauds again, pulling him genially from the stage for a round of attaboys.

In the lobby the superlatives flow, abetted by the bottles of wine disappearing into the patrons. Most of them are eager young fellow actors who are likely unfamiliar with Tennessee Williams's oeuvre.

Once most of the happy-go-luckies have left, Joshua marches his critic friends over to Ritchie, who is sipping some wine himself.

"Quite something," the bearded *Weekly* critic says. "You have pathos for the character few can bring. This is a real gem, and I intend to say so in print. Congratulations."

"I'm making this my 'pick of the week'," the grizzled, support-hose-wearing writer from the *Times* adds, perhaps trying to best her colleague. "I've seen the Brando version many times, and I have to say, you bring texture to this role that he never achieved. Bravo!"

She reaches up to Ritchie's neck and gives him a clumsy, old-lady hug, which Ritchie accepts. He looks over her shoulder at Joshua, who is giving him a wide-eyed thumbs up.

Freddy and Claire hang off to one side, waiting to close down the party.

Last to speak with Ritchie is Joel W. Cohen, who has handled three muttered cell conversations in the course of five minutes.

"I'm going to break all the rules here...but that's just my nature. I tend to run off at the mouth," he says, a little short of breath, when it is his turn to praise Ritchie. " So look—you know I make big movies where lots of things blow up. I'm about to go into production on what I hope will be the next big comic book franchise. The trouble is I haven't found a lead actor I like for the superhero role. I've gone through all the name actors, and none of them thrill me. We've done two rounds of casting for unknowns and there are several guys who could work, but nobody's been a dead ringer. But Ritchie, you *are* Thunderbolt. I mean, I see him and hear him talk, and it's exactly you. I've called my production manager three times just now. I've got to ask—who's your agent?"

"We've got meetings at ICM and William Morris next week," Joshua steps in, smoothly fabricating a story. "It's really a question of who has the stronger vision for Ritchie."

"You represent him for publicity?" Joel asks Joshua.

"Yes," Joshua says glibly.

"I've gotta be frank with you, Joshua," Joel says as he punches Ritchie on the shoulder affectionately. "This one is going to earn you a whole lot of money. We can hammer things out with whatever agent you choose, but as far as I'm concerned I've found my Thunderbolt. The rest is just paperwork until we start rehearsals in March."

Once Cohen has left, the four friends are alone. They look at each other.

"Am I having a hallucination?" Freddy asks. "Or did that really just happen?"

"I'm the one who should ask," Ritchie says, looking delightfully faint.

Claire and Freddy give him kisses and hugs.

"You want to go somewhere to celebrate?" Claire asks. "How about Canters on Fairfax? They're open all night."

"Great," Joshua says. "You two head over and Ritchie and I'll be there in fifteen."

After another round of hugs, Freddy and Claire take their coats and leave. At last it is just Ritchie and Joshua.

"So," Ritchie says.

"So," replies Joshua. He reaches behind the folding table set up for drinks and pulls out a paper bag containing a split of Dom Perignon.

Joshua uncorks the bubbly and the neck of the bottle is instantly covered in froth, which he slurps up, giggling. Ritchie does the same, tracing the curves of Joshua's fingers with his tongue. They pass the bottle between them, and each takes a few sips of the champagne.

"To Hollywood," Joshua toasts.

"To everything," Richie replies expansively.

Then they share a deep, unhurried kiss. Joshua reaches behind himself to set the champagne bottle on the table. It descends with an awful clank.

"Oops," Joshua says. They melt into each other's arms, making out like mad, moaning and messing up each others' hair.

"We should go meet Freddy and Claire," Ritchie gasps as he comes up for air.

"No...yes," Joshua replies, drunk not on champagne but on Ritchie.

They kiss again. It is sweet and satisfying.

"This is crazy," Joshua says, tittering with glee.

"No," Ritchie corrects him with yet another smooch. "Just long overdue. I love you."

Freddy is alone in his apartment.

The storms are finally over. It is a gentle, sunny afternoon. He opens the windows and draws back the drapes so that a mild breeze moves through the rooms.

He opens a new page in his word processor and hesitates, watching the blinking cursor for a moment before beginning to type:

> If Paris is the city of lights, and New York never sleeps, then I live in the city of dreams. Despite its mild reputation, Los Angeles is one of the coldest cities on earth. We certainly sleep here; we sleepwalk, contented in our Spanish apartments

with warm furniture, warm-colored walls, and warm weather outside. Meanwhile, Los Angeles dupes the suggestible, which is almost all of us. She is cunning, promising salvation and delivering sorrow. There is little reality here, and the artifice that stands in its stead is exalted and celebrated instead of foresworn, as it ought to be.

Freddy pauses and reads what he has written. Then he plunges ahead:

I have lost my youth here—and my youthfulness to boot—while I have gained things far more valuable. I have come to understand that the one thing real in this town is love. Here, money trumps determination, drugs trump decency, bling trumps taste. But unwilling to play their game is love, which really does conquer all. It is the through-line of all things living, even in an environment as unfriendly to love as this.

I realize today that I am wealthy, not in cars and movie deals, but in love, however much I feel beggared by it. I've endured a most peculiar year. My heart is bruised and the man I love is dead and buried. One of my closest friends was haunted by love gone awry, and my two others are suddenly a joyful couple. There is no predicting to this. One can only love, laugh at the absurdity of living, and love some more.

At this point, Freddy saves the file and takes a break to go make himself a sandwich. When he returns, he drafts an e-mail:

To:LiteraryAgentDeluxe
From:FreddyWrites
Subject: Book pitch
1 Attachment: love_book.doc

Dear Annette,

I am sorry for being so badly out of touch. This should in no way be interpreted as a lack of gratitude on my part for your representing me as a writer. As you know, I've been blocked for some time. But that is over now.

I have an idea for a book. I'm not sure exactly what shape it will take, but it has to do with the pervasive power of love. I will

> tell you more as it reveals itself to me, but I'm attaching a few paragraphs I've just drafted. I believe this is the beginning of something large.

Freddy looks over what he's typed and, satisfied, clicks SEND. He sits back and takes a bite of his lunch.

Then Freddy realizes he is not alone in the room. The angel whose presence he felt on the night of Justin's death is nearby. Freddy closes his eyes and allows himself a slow, contented smile that grows, finding its own momentum, until he is beaming and cannot stop.

"Thank you," he whispers gratefully.

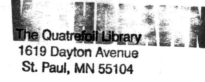